Thomas Slaughter

THE COLONIAL PERIOD OF
AMERICAN HISTORY

THE SETTLEMENTS
II

THE COLONIAL PERIOD

OF

AMERICAN HISTORY

BY

CHARLES M. ANDREWS

With a New Foreword by Leonard W. Labaree

THE SETTLEMENTS

II

NEW HAVEN AND LONDON · YALE UNIVERSITY PRESS

Published in Great Britain, Europe, Africa, and Asia
(except Japan) by Yale University Press, Ltd.,
London. Distributed in Latin America by Kaiman &
Polon, Inc., New York City; in Australia and New
Zealand by Book & Film Services, Artarmon, N.S.W.,
Australia; and in Japan by Harper & Row, Publishers,
Tokyo Office.

ISBN: 0-300-00271-8

CONTENTS

CONTENTS

FOREWORD

THE four volumes of *The Colonial Period of American History* which Charles McLean Andrews published between 1934 and 1938 were the culmination of a lifetime of thought and study by the man who was generally recognized as the outstanding American colonial historian of his generation. He had produced his first work in the field in 1889, and as his books and articles continued to appear during the years that followed, the special features of his approach and interpretation became increasingly evident. They found their fullest expression in these four volumes, his last major contributions to our understanding of the Colonial Period.

A combination of three characteristics sets this work apart from all other general histories of the American colonies which had gone before or have appeared since Andrews wrote: First, the volumes give strong emphasis to the English background. He viewed the colonies as what they were at the time—parts of the expanding English world—and not as what some of them later became—units of a transatlantic republic. They were the products of a great movement in the British Isles for the occupation and settlement of fruitful areas across the ocean. The men, the circumstances, and the institutions in England responsible for that movement and later the policies developed in Great Britain for the exploitation and development of these "plantations" all receive major attention. Second, Andrews wrote not only of the colonies which declared their independence in 1776, but also of those which did not: Bermuda, the West Indies, Nova Scotia, and Newfoundland. In the seventeenth century and most of the eighteenth the English colonial world was a single indivisible whole; to understand that world as it actually was, it became necessary in Andrews' judgment to understand all its interrelated parts. No other work on a comparable scale has treated all these seventeenth-century settlements as equally significant parts of the general history of English colonization in the New World. Third, in common with many scholars of his generation, Andrews adopted a largely institutional approach. While earlier writers usually followed a narrative "political" thread for the most part, and many more recent scholars have been chiefly interested in social, economic, or intellectual developments, Andrews believed that a people's institutions—chiefly though by no means exclusively their political institutions—offered the best clues to that people's character and development.

The first three volumes, subtitled *The Settlements,* deal with the English background of the colonizing movement and with the establishment of communities of Englishmen along the Atlantic coast of North America and on nearby islands. Each such community is treated separately. The first two volumes are concerned with those projected before 1650, the third with those settled in the second half of the seventeenth century. In each instance the author carries the narrative down to the date (which differs from one colony to another) at which it can be said to be firmly established, when its institutions are well rooted and the direction of its further development can be clearly discerned. The fourth volume, called *England's Commercial and Colonial Policy,* describes the gradual development in the mother country of a program through which these overseas possessions could be brought into an effective and profitable relationship to Britain herself. As the subtitle suggests, this program and the laws and regulations adopted to carry it out were largely economic in emphasis. In the minds of Englishmen of the seventeenth and eighteenth centuries colonies were worth having and worth protecting against foreign enemies only if their trade and commerce could be so channeled and controlled and their economic life so developed that they would benefit the homeland as well as themselves. This volume is still the most thorough and complete treatment in print of the evolution of British colonial policy and of the means adopted to carry out that policy, its successes, and its failures, in the years before 1763.

One day early in December 1937, Andrews said to the writer of this foreword: "This morning I took the finished manuscript of my fourth volume to the Press. I have now done the job I promised the Press and myself that I would do. If I live and am able to complete the other volumes I planned, well and good. But if not, I am satisfied. These four volumes are the ones I just *had* to write." He had indeed planned three more parts of this work, but serious illness intervened while the fourth volume was in page proofs (he had just celebrated his seventy-fifth birthday), and though he lived until September 1943, he never regained sufficient physical strength to resume the heavy burden that writing on this extensive scale required.

The fact that he never completed the other volumes called for by his original plan has led some critics to accuse him of having only a limited and partial approach to the general subject of his *magnum opus*. Recognizing that this might be so, he wrote an extended paper, probably sometime in 1938 or 1939, in which he explained his scheme for the whole work, which he said had been "clearly in mind from the beginning," and his specific intent for the volumes which he never wrote. In accordance with his wishes, this paper remained unpublished until after his death.[1]

Upon the broad base of the first three volumes on colonial settlement, he explained, stood the fourth volume representing the British side of the developing Anglo-American structure. The fifth projected volume was to present the other side; in it "we would take our stand on colonial soil and see what was happening there during the first sixty years of the eighteenth century." Instead of dealing with institutional aspects of colonial history, it would be concerned with the "social, economic, educational, domestic, and religious, and in some respects political," evolution of American life and would reveal "trends and divergencies [from British patterns] indicating a progressive movement and indicative of what may be called an Americanizing process." These developments, as Andrews saw them, fostered change and growth in the political and institutional aspects of colonial society. Volume 6 would therefore be a political, and especially a constitutional, history of eighteenth-century America, which would give particular emphasis to the evolution of the colonial assembly and its slow winning "of a place in each colony analagous to that of the House of Commons in England at the same time." The seventh and last volume would deal with the years after 1763, when the colonies, with "practical self-government" achieved, came into conflict with the British government, which still adhered to its policy of holding the colonies in strict subjection and was even introducing new forms of enforcement. "Thus the colonial situation which was hardly American at all in the seventeenth century, takes on an Anglo-American coloring during the first sixty years of the eighteenth, owing to the formulation for the first time by the mother country of a clear-cut colonial policy, and becomes discordantly Anglo-American during the years 1763-1776, when the issue takes

1. "On the Writing of Colonial History," *William and Mary Quarterly*, 3d Series, I (1944), 27–48.

the form of an open conflict between self-government on one side and centralization on the other."

This was the plan on which Andrews would have carried through his project had he been able. We must regret that the final three volumes had to be left unwritten. Yet we can only be grateful for the four he did write during the five years after his retirement from more than four decades as a college and university professor. In this reissue of *The Colonial Period of American History* a new generation of readers will still find not only a great narrative of American beginnings, skillfully told, but a broad view of the characteristics and attitudes of the men and women on both sides of the Atlantic whose faith and optimism made those beginnings possible.

New Haven, Connecticut
February 1964   LEONARD W. LABAREE

THE COLONIAL PERIOD OF
AMERICAN HISTORY

CHAPTER I

ROGER WILLIAMS AND THE FOUNDING
OF RHODE ISLAND

THE rapid flow of immigrants into the Massachusetts Bay colony during the decade from 1630 to 1640 affected in many ways the lives and activities of those who occupied the region and was in no small degree responsible for many of the difficulties that arose during the period. Settlers came in faster than the colony could absorb them and they filled the land with a people who found it none too easy to adapt themselves to a frontier environment or to the principles of government and the social order that the Puritans laid down for the guidance of all. Though in the main the frontier Puritan was sincere, law abiding, and in sympathy with the aims of the great migration, he was not docile or always ready to conform to the rigid rules imposed upon him. From the beginning there was controversy and disagreement as to questions of strictness and leniency, and even the leaders did not always agree among themselves. Likewise their adversaries held opinions widely at variance with theirs and even at variance with the opinions of each other. Winthrop thought the views of Wheelwright more dangerous than those of Williams and the insurgency of Child and the Remonstrants more subversive than either. Vane and Winthrop differed vitally in their ideas of a commonwealth, and Winthrop, Dudley and Haynes, commanding men in the colony, were never in entire accord as to how the government should be carried on. Humfry, Vassall, and Pynchon had been among the signers of the Cambridge agreement of 1629, yet Humfry had nothing to say that was good of the colony and soon left it; Vassall became a veritable thorn in the flesh to the authorities of both Massachusetts Bay and Plymouth and eventually made his way elsewhere; while Pynchon, who went off to Springfield in 1636, got so out of tune with Puritan orthodoxy that he wrote a book about some aspects of it, which in 1650 the

Massachusetts general court ordered to be burned on the common at Boston, because it contained many errors condemned by the Bay theologians.[1] Stoughton, the younger Saltonstall, Bellingham, and Bradstreet were always opponents of the oligarchical rule of the magistrates.

The inflow likewise brought an unusual number of ministers—sixty-five of the cloth between 1630 and 1641[2]—whose interpretations of scripture and of the purpose of God in his relations with men, often expressed with considerable vehemence, represented many shades of opinion, ranging from the stiff fundamentalism of Wilson and Norton to the more fluid ideas of Cotton and Eliot. The very reverence in which the clergy were held and the deference paid to their judgments—divinely inspired, as most men believed—together with their natural preëminence as leaders of their respective flocks, tended to make them opinionated and resentful of opposition. Thus the colony was gradually filled with an overplus of strong minds and wills, influential out of all proportion to their numbers. Probably at least two-thirds of the colonists were loyal in their allegiance to the commonwealth, while among the remaining third were the servants, from whom concurrence could hardly be expected, forming from one-sixth to one-fifth of the population.[3] Some of the latter had come over bound for a term of years to the masters who paid for their passage, while others were sent at the beginning by the company or by such private individuals as Cradock and Saltonstall. They were not a desirable element and while many were undoubtedly religiously minded, there were more who were out of accord with the purposes of the settlement. They were often quarrelsome and coarse in their habits and demeanor, and their chief offenses were crimes against morals, such as fornication, profanity, drunkenness, and theft.

The rapid increase in population had a further effect. Land was plentiful but composed of marsh and heavily wooded areas was not easily brought under profitable cultivation, and at first the settlers showed no desire to move back into the interior beyond the reach of communication by water. To the newcomers used to the towns and manors of old England, contact with the frontier and the Indian must have been a novel and often terrifying experi-

1. *Massachusetts Colonial Records,* III, 215, 216; IV (1), 29.

2. *New England Historical and Genealogical Register,* V, 289.

3. Parkes, "Morals in Colonial New England," *New England Quarterly,* July, 1932, p. 435.

ence and nearness to the coast seemed to them their only guaranty of safety. They pushed south as far as Mount Wollaston and Weymouth and north as far as Newbury near the Merrimac, a plantation which had been cut off from its parent town, Ipswich, in 1635, and though in the wilderness was nevertheless a river town. Dedham and Concord, the farthest west, had access to running streams, the one to the Charles, the other to the Concord River. At the same time the pressure of population and the migratory habits of the explorer and trapper had been forcing men for many years to penetrate the forests, to associate with the Indians, and to learn what they could of the unoccupied spaces beyond the line of settlements. Many made their way by water along the shores to the south and southwest, reversing the routes taken by such Dutch seamen as Rasier and others on their visits to Plymouth; while a few hardier souls, such as Winslow, Oldham, Stone, Norton, Baker, Hall, and their companions, allured perhaps by the tales of the Indians who visited Boston in 1631, penetrated the back country by way of the Indian paths and brought home reports of their impressions to their fellows of the coast. Whereas three or four such venturesome spirits find mention in contemporary literature, there must have been others of whose exploits no trace remains. Whether anyone had been overland to Narragansett before Roger Williams went there or whether there had been any English visitors to the Connecticut valley before Winslow and Oldham we shall probably never know.[1]

The founding of new colonies in New England was largely the result of an overflow of population from Massachusetts. In a few instances settlements had begun before the coming of the Puritans, as at Plymouth, Weymouth, Salem, Strawberry Bank (Portsmouth), and Dover, or were afterward founded by pioneers coming directly from England, as at Milford and Guilford, but the greater number

1. There was a more or less frequent intercourse among all the New England colonies during these early years, kept alive by the Indians, who used the paths, summer and winter. Hooker, Allyn, and Lieutenant Holmes of Connecticut visited Williams at Providence in 1636, and Hooker seems to have been there again in August, 1637. Travel between Providence and Boston, by messengers—Indian and other—and by white men, was a very frequent matter. Roger Williams mentions one William Baker of Plymouth, who may have been with Holmes when he set up his trading post at Windsor in 1633, as one who had gone native, that is, turned Indian, worn no clothes, used the Indian language, and cut (shaved?) his hair. Williams had heard him ill spoken of at Plymouth, when he himself was living there, as having had sexual relations with an Indian squaw. Williams' Letters, Facsimiles, January 10, 1638.

of the new plantations were founded by men and women who, willingly or unwillingly, left Massachusetts to find homes elsewhere. Some of these people were deliberately driven out of the Massachusetts Bay colony—a procedure that finds no exact counterpart elsewhere among the English colonies in America, except it be in the exodus of Roman Catholics and Puritans from Virginia, where the Church of England was established by law and toleration no more prevailed than in Massachusetts. Others left voluntarily for divers reasons, comparable in part with the motives that in later times induced men, both as individuals and as groups, to move once, twice, or even three or more times in search of permanent abiding places. Of the unwilling wanderers the first was Roger Williams.

After the decree of banishment had been issued on October 9, 1635, the authorities at Boston, who planned to send Williams back to England by a boat about to sail, dispatched Captain John Underhill to Salem to apprehend him. But warned in time, perhaps by Winthrop himself, who always had a tender spot in his heart for the great tolerationist, Williams made his escape and when Underhill arrived was already three days on his way southward toward Narragansett. There, Winthrop had advised him, was a region free of any English patents or claims.[1] Thus parted from wife and children, from trading house and prosperity, Williams started from Salem on or before January 15, 1636, and with a young man, Thomas Angell a member of his family,[2] journeyed by land,[3] during an inclement winter season and through forests largely unknown to the white man, until he found a refuge among the Indians, with whom he had come into contact during his residence at Plymouth three years before. In all probability he stayed at Massasoit's village at Sowams (near the present town of Warren, Rhode Island) and, engaging in friendly efforts to secure peace among the warring tribes, he remained there nearly fourteen weeks in the "filthy smoke holes," as he called their wigwams. In the spring he moved on again, setting

1. Winthrop, *Journal*, I, 168.

2. Thomas Angell had come over with either Endecott in 1629 or with Williams himself in 1631. His descendants hold an honored place in Rhode Island history. He is the ancestor of former President Angell of Michigan and of his son, President Angell of Yale.

3. The land route was probably the same as that taken by Mrs. Hutchinson and her family in 1638 and by "Brother Hibben" in 1640—to Mount Wollaston and then across country to Narragansett, going over or along the rivers in canoes. Chapin, *Documentary History*, II, 32, 87–88.

himself down on land purchased of Massasoit near the Seacunk or
Seekonk River and adjoining a cove formed by an inflowing stream.
It was with bitterness that he recalled this experience when afterward he wrote with emotion of the "winter snows which I feel yet,"
exposed as he had been to the "miseries, poverties, necessities, wants,
debts [and] hardships of sea and land" among the barbarians.[1]

At Seekonk Williams was joined by three others, wanderers like
himself, William Harris, Francis Wicks, and John Smith, the last
named of whom, a miller of Dorchester, had been banished from
his own town much as Williams had been from Salem. Later two
more joined the group, Joshua Verin and William Arnold, the latter
the ancestor of Benedict. But no sooner were they beginning to build
and plant on a small plot near a spring, when they were warned by
Governor Winslow of Plymouth, who was familiar with his colony's
boundaries as stated in the Bradford patent of 1630, that they were
trespassing on Plymouth territory. Therefore, once more Williams
and Angell moved on to find a new site for a home, the others following later. Paddling down the Seekonk they rounded the point,
Fox Hill, into the Great Salt River, a broad estuary from Narragansett Bay, and there on the eastern bank, at the junction of two small
and sluggish streams—the Moshassuc and the Wanasquatucket—
they established their settlement. Whether Williams, when he left
Massachusetts, had in mind the erection of a plantation is uncertain;
he may have wanted to do no more than install a mission to the
Indians,[2] in whom he had already become greatly interested and
whose language he had begun to acquire. He may even have had
in mind a trading house, similar to the one that he had left behind
in the Bay, for in leaving Salem he had cut himself off from his
resources, and to his own serious embarrassment[3] had left behind

1. Letter to Mason (1670), *Narragansett Club Publications*, VI, 333; *Mr. Cottons
Letter Lately Printed*, preface and p. 33.

2. Winthrop, *Journal*, I, 168, says that the reason why the magistrates decided to
send Williams back to England was that he designed, with his twenty converts at
Salem, to erect a plantation somewhere along Narragansett Bay. The "Town Evidence"
seems to record the purchase by Williams of the Providence lands as early as 1634
and 1635, "upon the two fresh rivers called Mashasick and Wanasquatuckett."
Chapin, *Documentary History*, I, 1–2.

3. In 1637 Williams joined with Governor Winthrop in purchasing—for two coats
and forty fathoms of wampum—Prudence Island, twenty miles away, where he kept
his goats and swine safe from wolves, and where at times he thought of building a
little house, that he might live a more simple life (*Narragansett Club Publications*,
VI, 70–71, 75, 85; *Collections*, Rhode Island Historical Society, III, 29). He frequently

property that he was never able afterward to recover. He may even have had in mind a refuge, isolated and remote, like that of Blaxton who lived about ten miles up the river, where he might dwell and meditate in peace. It is quite possible that he had some or all of these objects in mind.

But Williams was not fitted to be a recluse. His controversial spirit demanded contact with his fellow men and his vigorous idealism called for a field of experimentation within which to apply his religious and political doctrines. He welcomed the coming of the humble and unwanted folk who had been unable to find peace at either Plymouth or Massachusetts Bay and who like himself were at war with the orthodox and conventional in life. There on the lower slope of the ground, rising gently upward from the Great Salt River, near a spring of fresh water that probably determined their choice, he and his fellow pioneers began the erection of a row of simple houses, for themselves and the members of their families who soon joined them.[1] Their settlement, which extended in a straggling manner for nearly two miles along the shore, with a road between the houses and the water, differed as strikingly in appearance from the lay-out of a Massachusetts town as the shapelessness of the Rhode Island religious organization differed from the orderliness of the Massachusetts system. Every settler was given a frontage on the street and river, a five-acre home lot and a six-acre farm or cornfield, and enjoyed equal advantages in whatever else the locality afforded.[2] Williams himself purchased the land of the Indians, apparently mortgaging his house and land in Salem for the means wherewith to transact the sale, and then distributed the tract among the others of the community, admitting them "with fellowship of any purchase" and receiving eventually £30 to pay for his outlay.[3] The vagueness

went back and forth in his canoe, his only means of travel by water, and on one of these trips nearly lost his life (*Narragansett Club Publications*, VI, 178, 277). He afterward sold his half to Governor Winthrop, in order to obtain (so it is said) enough money to pay his expenses to England in 1643. He had a trading house or houses also in Narragansett (*Calendar State Papers, Colonial*, 1677–1680, p. 589), which netted him one hundred pounds a year, and these too he sold in 1650 for money with which to go to England in that year.

1. Mary Williams with her two children did not join her husband until the summer, making her way, on foot and by canoe, through the wilderness and along the rivers, probably following much the same route as that taken by Williams himself.

2. Orr, "The Planting and Growth of Providence," Rider, *Tracts*, no. 15 (1879), *passim*.

3. Chapin, *Documentary History*, I, ch. IV.

and inaccuracy of these early grants and divisions led later to bitter and persistent controversy.

The quality of the settlement improved as the years wore on, but Providence—a name selected in appreciation of God's mercy—never equalled the grandeur of Newport which, though founded only three years later, very soon gave indications of more prosperity than her less progressive neighbor, whose chief assets were not commercial but agricultural—the raising of corn, tobacco, swine, goats, cattle by 1641, and sheep and wool by 1666. In fact sheep and tobacco became such outstanding Rhode Island staples that they were known to the colonists both in Massachusetts and New Haven, and before the middle of the century tobacco was sent to Boston for export. The Providence settlement was built up without capital or any outside assistance and its people, possessing only arms, tools, and very simple house furnishings—no silver, only wood and pewter—and with no ploughs, only hoes, it remained a poor town as long as the agricultural period lasted. There was no grist mill until 1646, and no bridge across the Moshassuc until 1662, when one was built at Weybosset Point, though probably there had been a number of lesser bridges constructed before that time.[1] The increase in population was very slow and the amount of accumulated wealth was for a long time inconsiderable.

In organizing the government of the little community Williams proceeded according to the simplest possible plan, one fitted only for the needs of a very small plantation. The heads of the families met once a fortnight to consult about the common good and later, as numbers increased, young single men were admitted to an equality with the others. Williams drew up an agreement, in the form of a social compact, according to which the signers promised each other, with free and joint consent, to subject themselves in active or passive obedience to such orders and understandings as should be the will of the greater number of the householders present—until they should hear further of the king's royal pleasure. This compact, when later signed by the young men and by certain newly admitted inhabitants, bore the added phrase "Only in civill things," a qualification that did not appear in the first draft.[2] Thus Williams gave early expression

1. *Providence Records*, II, 130; Kimball, *Providence in Colonial Times*, pp. 118–121.

2. *Collections*, Massachusetts Historical Society, 4th ser., VI, 186; Deane, *Roger Williams and the Massachusetts Charter*, p. 15, note (Williams' letter of 1636);

to his convictions that the state should not interfere in matters of religious concern, and this same principle of religious liberty he further enforced when, in distributing the lands which he had purchased of the Indian chiefs he laid down two main rules—equality of shares and recognition of the fact that the place was "for those who were destitute especially for conscience's sake," a rule that became fixed in the life of the plantation.[1]

While thus Williams and his associates were founding the town of Providence, another band of exiles, led by William Coddington and organized, before leaving Boston, as a body politic incorporated in the presence of the great Jehovah, started in April, 1638, in search of a place where they could be free to perform the duties of their religious life. Coddington, at first an Antinomian and afterward a Quaker, had been a friend of Williams at Boston and was one of those who were implicated in the Hutchinson controversy, though he was never formally banished. He was accompanied by Dr. John Clarke, John Coggeshall, William Aspinwall, William Dyer, Randall Holden, and others, all of whom made their way by boat around Cape Cod and up Narragansett Bay to Providence. Mrs. Hutchinson and her family had preceded them in March, going overland to the same place. While there, Coddington, with the aid of Williams, purchased of the Indians the island of Aquidneck, and in the spring of 1639, he and the Hutchinsons laid out a settlement, at the northeastern end of the island, called Pocasset, which a year later the settlers named Portsmouth. In Biblical fashion Coddington was

---

Providence Records, I, 1; *Rhode Island Colonial Records,* I, 14. The form of the agreement as customarily printed is manifestly a second state, designed for the young men and certain newcomers. The "Only in civill things" may have been added at their request; it was evidently not in the first draft. In the first record-book four pages were left blank for additional names, but these pages were never filled in. The date of the agreement cannot be accurately determined, but it was before 1638. In his letter to Winthrop, Williams raised the question whether, under the circumstances, he was not justified in asking that his neighbors admit no one without his consent, but there is nothing to show that he ever acted on the suggestion, which hardly shows a "democratic" spirit. A facsimile of the document is given in Chapin, *Documentary History,* I, facing p. 96.

1. For the well known Verin case, in which liberty of conscience was upheld, see *Providence Records,* I, 4; *Rhode Island Colonial Records,* I, 16–17; Winthrop, *Journal,* I, 286–287. Verin was disfranchised, left the settlement two years later, went back to Salem, and from there sailed to Barbados (for the Verin family in Barbados, Moriarty in *The New England Genealogical and Historical Register,* LXVII, 369). With the aid of William Harris he attempted and successfully to recover his land rights in Providence (*Providence Records,* III, 40) and until the time of his death retained his purchase share.

chosen judge of the little community, where none was to be accounted a delinquent for doctrine and where a land-owning "democracy," in the sense understood in the early seventeenth century, was the accepted form of political organization. In this settlement, strange as it may seem, William Coddington, rich in this world's goods, worldly wise, and politically sagacious, and Anne Hutchinson, spiritually minded and dominating, managed to get on together in harmony for a considerable period of time.[1]

But this state of affairs at Portsmouth could not last. The minority party, headed by the Hutchinsons and strengthened by one Samuel Gorton, of whom more later, found itself out of accord with Coddington, who disapproved strongly of Gorton's coming, disliked his religious eccentricities, and disagreed with his views regarding government. Only nine months after the settlement the minority party hatched a revolt against Coddington, while he was absent from the settlement, and on April 28, 1639, put him out of his judgeship and elected William Hutchinson in his place. At their first meeting the leaders of the reorganized party made a new declaration to the effect that "We whose names are under[written do acknowledge] ourselves to be Loyal subje[cts of] King Charles and in his na[me] erect our[selves] into a Civill body politicke a[nd submit ourselves] unto his lawes according [to] matters of Justice." This document, signed by William Hutchinson, Samuel Gorton, and others, bears unmistakable signs of Gorton's high regard for English law and the recognition due his royal sovereign, wholly unlike the original Coddington compact made in the presence only of the "great Jehovah."[2]

Ousted from Portsmouth, Coddington and his followers, who were soon joined by others, moved by boat to the southern end of

1. The documents in the case are in Chapin, *Documentary History*, II, chs. III–V. In Portsmouth there was no clear idea of the separation of church and state and even in Providence the rule was laid down that it was not proper to sail or to drive cows to the pound on the Sabbath, for "civil actions must be done in civil not sacred time."

2. *Portsmouth Records, 1639–1697*, p. 1. The same regard for English law and authority appears in the "engagement" that had to be taken by all "admitted or received inhabitants," who were approved at any town meeting "of the free inhabitants." Each person so admitted had to give "engagement to the state of England and the government of this place," before he could take a part in the transaction of such business "as shall be presented them." All decisions made in town meeting were "to stand as firmly as if all were present they all having lawful warning." *Ibid.*, pp. 19, 23, 29, 32, 35, 669.

the island and there on the eastern side fronting the bay established a plantation on May 1, 1639, which they called Newport. Coddington, still the head or judge of the settlement, lived up to the implications of his office, interpreting Scripture and, with the advice and consent of three "elders," determining without appeal the relations of temporal and spiritual affairs. There was still discord in both Portsmouth and Newport and many difficulties confronted the settlers of these places in their attempts to control the distribution of lands and to form and organize the churches. In the main, however, with the exception of a system of landholding for all comers[1] and the separation of church and state, the fundamental ideas, particularly of religious liberty prevailing at Providence prevailed on an equally broad basis at Newport also.[2]

Coddington was not satisfied, however, with the existence of two separate and independent communities and set about making a single colony of the whole island of Aquidneck, of which he already possessed the title in his own name and of which he wished to be the head. He was beginning to consider the possibility of having a colony of his own distinct from that of Williams at Providence, which should include Aquidneck and adjoining islands and be free to pass its own laws and to manage its own affairs, or, as Dr. John Clarke put it, "through the help of Christ to get clear of all and be of ourselves." To this end, finding that many at Portsmouth were willing to join him and that Gorton and Mrs. Hutchinson were not getting on well together, Coddington obtained the appointment of commissioners, in the autumn of 1639, to consider the matter. As the result of a winter's negotiation Newport and Portsmouth were united in March, 1640, but the organization was less a union than a consolidation of two towns under a common administration, of which Coddington was the governor, William Brenton, formerly of Portsmouth but at this time of Newport, the deputy governor, and two men from each town as assistants. This was the most complete and orderly form of civil organization thus far created in the Narragansett region, and it continued for seven years, each town sharing

1. At a town meeting, December 23, 1644, at which "the major pt of fremen were psent" it was "mutually Agreed that the Right and priviledges of the land undisspossed of Remaines in the bodye of freemen as it was mutually agreed at a publike meeting 14 Novermber last past that the freemen which are the purchassers have the onlye power to dissposs of the land that is to be disposed off." *Portsmouth Records,* 1639–1697, pp. 30–32.

2. Chapin, *Documentary History,* II, chs. VI–X.

in the offices. In 1641 the leaders drafted an instrument of agreement which declared that the new state was "a democracie or popular government, that is to say, it is in the Powre of the Body of freemen orderly assembled or the Major part of them to make or constitute just Laws by wch they will be regulated and to depute from among themselves such ministers as shall see them faithfully executed between man and man." It was "further ordered by the authority of this Present Court" that none be accounted a Delinquent for Doctrine: Provided it be not directly repugnant to the Government or Lawes established." The next year this affirmation was confirmed in these words, "It is ordered that that Law of the Last Court made concerning Libtie of Conscience in point of Doctrine is perpetuated." The court planned a seal which should bear "a sheafe of Arrows bound," with the motto "Love conquers all" (*Amor vincet omnia*), a somewhat ironical device under the circumstances as fraudulent in life as in love.[1] In the same year Coddington tried to secure from England a patent for Aquidneck, which should crown and legalize his efforts, but in this he was unsuccessful. Because of this failure and of the insecurity of the union from a legal point of view the experiment lasted only seven years. In 1648 Portsmouth, influenced undoubtedly by Williams' success in obtaining for the colony the patent of 1644, to be discussed later, passed the following vote: "It was voated and by the Voate concluded unanimously by the townsemen of Portsmouth that they would act apart by themselfes and not jointly with Newport and be as fre in their transactions as anie of the other townse in the Colinie."[2] Thus Coddington's first venture into the sphere of state building came to a disastrous end.

Among those who supported Anne Hutchinson in her revolt against Coddington at Portsmouth was Samuel Gorton, a man of strong opinions and marked originality, whose early career is not

1. *Ibid.*, II, 108, 110, 114. As a "democracy," this arrangement would hardly commend itself to the modern mind. A large majority of the Portsmouth freemen were not included among the "freemen" of the union, who may have constituted something less than half the adult males of the two towns put together and formed the "democracy" referred to.

2. *Portsmouth Records, 1639–1697*, p. 37, January 27, 1647(8). August 26, 1647, 'At a town meetinge it was voated that the grounds presented were not suffissient for a General Assembly to be Called and therefor voated to have none." "It is concluded by this present meetinge that theare shalbe a demurr of an answer to the letter sent from Newport to voate the opinion of the legallitie of the Corte and orders thereof held at Pro[vidence]" (*ibid.*, pp. 35, 37).

even yet fully understood.¹ He arrived at Boston in 1637, aged forty-four, at the height of the Antinomian controversy, and sought liberty of conscience first at Boston, then at Plymouth, and finally at Portsmouth, where he remained for three years. Having joined in the *coup d'état* against Coddington, he was unalterably opposed to the consolidation of the two towns, on the ground that the act, representing the minority only, was irregular and illegal. His instinct for justice, his demand for the enforcement of the common law of England, and his vociferous and unparliamentary protests, at both Plymouth and Portsmouth, against verdicts rendered by self-appointed authorities brought him into conflict with the courts, the legal constitution and jurisdiction of which he denied. If we are to believe Winslow, he was presented by the grand jury at Portsmouth for refusing to acknowledge the authority of the government there, for contemptuously reproaching the magistrates, calling them "great asses" and the judges "corrupt judges," for dubbing a freeman who, he thought, swore falsely in the court "a saucy boy" and a "jackanapes," and for generally defying the men in office until they ordered

---

1. Too much dependence in the past has been placed upon the warped and partisan statements regarding Gorton to be found in Winslow, *Hypocrisie Unmasked;* Winthrop, *Journal;* Morton, *New England Memorial;* Lechford, *Plain Dealing;* and Johnson, *Wonder-Working Providence,* and too little upon his later career and his own writings, especially his letter to Morton (1669, Hutchinson, *History,* Mayo ed., I, 455-459; Force, *Tracts,* nos. 6, 7, and his letters to Winthrop, *Collections,* Massachusetts Historical Society, 4th ser., VII). Massachusetts historians find it difficult to give Gorton a square deal. Some of the older writers took a more impartial attitude, as in Hutchinson, *History,* I, 102-107; Charles Deane ("Notice of Samuel Gorton," *New England Genealogical and Historical Register,* IV, 201-220), who calls the treatment of Gorton by Massachusetts "atrocious" and "cruel"; and William Aspinwall (*Proceedings,* Massachusetts Historical Society, June, 1862, p. 47), who says, "Unwarrantable attempts were made to destroy him because, unconsecrated by ordination and not privileged by a university education, he presumed to exercise the functions of a scriptural teacher, and because he was as steadfast as he was extravagant and heterodox in his religious opinions, insolent under provocation and too ready to return railing for railing, yet the whole tenor of his life shows that he was conscientious, sincere, and, in matters of fact, honest and truthful." The Rhode Island historians, writing in his defense, though as a rule inclined to minimize his early eccentricities, are more just and historically reliable: Staples, ed. *Simplicities Defence against Seven Headed Policy,* with an introduction, notes, and nineteen appendices; Brayton, "Defense of Gorton," Rider's *Tracts,* no. 17 (1883); *New England Magazine,* May, 1898; Rider's *Book Notes,* V, no. 11, p. 71; VI, no. 16, pp. 164-167; Janes, *Samuell Gorton* (1896), with a list of Gorton's writings and in the text an illuminating analysis of an unpublished Gorton manuscript, "A Running Commentary on the Lord's Prayer"; A. Gorton, *The Life and Times of Samuel Gorton,* chiefly historical, with but a brief commentary on Gorton's character and opinions, largely made up of quotations from Brayton and Janes. There are references to Gorton in Stiles, *Diary* and *Itineraries.*

him to prison. Comment on these incidents, in one of which Gorton was condemned for his conduct in his own trial and in the other for his conduct in the trial of a maid servant of his, will depend somewhat on our understanding of his own defense. He opposed the courts in each case because he denied their validity. In neither instance were these courts held by charter authority from England nor were they conducted according to the rules of the common law; while in the second trial, the one before Coddington at Portsmouth, Gorton believed that the court was arbitrarily imposed upon the Portsmouth people without their consent, and had "no legal authority to deal with me," as he expressed it.[1]

Banished from Portsmouth, Gorton and his followers moved to Providence, where according to a letter supposedly written by Williams but the authenticity of which has been questioned,[2] he made trouble "bewitching and bemadding" the community "both with his uncleane and foule censures of all the ministers of this country . . . and denying all visible and externall ordinances in the depth of Familisme, against which I have a little disputed and written." He and the others applied for admission as freemen but were denied "as not fit persons to be received in and made members of such a body," partly because Gorton's reputation at Portsmouth and Plymouth had preceded him and partly because of their "despising and scorning the civil state" by their conduct.[3]

1. At Plymouth, Gorton was charged in the official records with "misdemeanors in the open court toward the elders, the bench, and with stirring up the people to mutynie in the face of the court," was fined twenty pounds, and ordered to leave the colony in fourteen days (*Plymouth Records,* I, 101, 105). This was in connection with the case of the widow Aldredge, a servant of Gorton's wife, Mary, during the administration of Prence (1638). It is strange that Bradford makes no mention of Gorton's stay in Plymouth. A convenient account of the matter, with extracts from Winslow and Morton, is given in Ford's edition of Bradford, II, 391–394. *Simplicities Defence* omits the incident entirely. After the departure of Coddington from Portsmouth Gorton seems to have got on peaceably enough, "disturbing no man, conducting himself civilly to all men and courteously," until Coddington attempted to assume authority over the town, apparently without the consent of the freemen there. This assumption of authority Gorton opposed and, in a case involving the arrest and trial of a maid servant of his, charged with alleged trespass and assault, he vehemently denied the jurisdiction of the court of trial held by Coddington at Portsmouth and declared the proceedings unfair and without warrant of law.

2. "There are strong reasons for questioning the authenticity of this letter" (Janes, *Samuell Gorton,* p. 35, note). The language is certainly very unusual for Williams and of an offensive kind unknown elsewhere in his correspondence. It is dated March 8, 1641, and is printed in Chapin, *Documentary History,* I, 128.

3. *Ibid.,* pp. 129–133. Williams' name is not signed to this letter of November 17,

Driven from Providence, Gorton and his people went to Pawtuxet, about three miles to the southward on the other side of the
bay, where they came in touch with John Greene, a young man
about twenty years old, who had been imprisoned and fined at Boston for saying that the magistrates had usurped the powers of Christ
in his church. Greene now became one of Gorton's chief followers
and the leader of his company, after it finally ended its wanderings
and settled peacefully in a permanent home. When Pawtuxet under
the Arnolds declared for union with Massachusetts in 1642,[1] Gorton
knowing what would be his fate if he came within the jurisdiction
of that colony—imprisonment or shipment to England—purchased
of the head sachem, Miantonomo, through the agency of John
Greene, land lying south of Pawtuxet and in November of that year
occupied Shawomet, which was afterward named Warwick.

But the Arnolds and Massachusetts would not let Gorton rest in
peace. On the pretence of a title to the territory obtained from two
under-sachems, Pomham and Socconocco, who claimed local jurisdiction, Massachusetts summoned Gorton and his companions to
Boston to answer the complaints of the Indians that they were being
kept out of their legitimate hunting grounds. Socconocco had originally joined Miantonomo, the head sachem, in signing the deed to
Greene, but in 1643 he was persuaded by Gorton's enemies, particularly Benedict Arnold who acted as interpreter, to repudiate his signature and with Pomham to submit to the authority of Massachusetts, asking for protection and promising "to be willing from time
to time to be instructed in the knowledge and worship of God."
Gorton, denying any right of Massachusetts to act in the matter and
fully aware of the Arnolds' influence with the Massachusetts authorities, refused to obey the summons, declaring that he and his company were out of the jurisdiction of that colony and were subject
only to "the state and government of old England," an answer that
Massachusetts said was "disdainful and contemptuous." Immediately
commissioners were despatched, accompanied by an armed body
under Captain George Cooke and Captain Edward Johnson, who

164–, sent to Massachusetts by the minority party in Providence (*ibid.*, 134–137),
giving "true intelligence of the insolent and riotous carriage of Samuell Gorton and
his company." The signatures of the Arnolds, William Harris, and others show that
had we all the facts we should probably find that there were two sides to the controversy.

1. *Massachusetts Colonial Records*, II, 26, 40–41; *Simplicities Defence*, p. 95.

may have seen in the adventure a manifestation of a wonder-working providence. Followed by many Indians the cortège moved southward into the Shawomet territory and despite protests from the Gortonists, expressed in a letter signed by the "Owners and Inhabitants," and a stiff defense put up from a block house fortified against the "army," seized Gorton and ten others and carried them away to Boston. There after an examination they were condemned for holding erroneous religious opinions, twenty-six in number,[1] and sentenced to confinement in irons. But the harshness of the magistrates and elders found little response among the people at large and the Massachusetts authorities were finally shamed into releasing them. Gorton went to England, got an order from the Warwick commissioners granting him a safe-conduct through Massachusetts territory, and instructing the magistrates there to cease their molestations of Shawomet.[2] Though many troubled years were to pass before that settlement was to be made secure in the permanent and peaceable possession of its lands, yet for the time being the struggle was over and Gorton returned to his home, where he lived as an honored member of his community and a popular and influential participant in the affairs of the colony until his death in December, 1677, in the eighty-sixth year of his age.

No person in early New England history has been the subject of so much adverse comment on one side or of eulogy on the other as has been this strange and much maligned man. In the intricacies of his theology he was no more obscure than were some of the Puritan

1. There was actually no religious question involved, even though Gorton was convicted in Boston because of his erroneous views on certain doctrinal points. Massachusetts and the Arnolds wanted Gorton's lands as additional territory and as furnishing an outlet to Narragansett Bay. The Arnolds were in frequent correspondence with the authorities at Boston, William Arnold "humbly desiring that my name may be concealed" (Hazard, *State Papers*, I, 556).

2. *Simplicities Defence*, pp. 91–105, 114–150. The presence of Major Humphrey Atherton as one of the commissioners discloses the fact that while Massachusetts' action was ostensibly in the interest of the Indians it was actually in the interest of an expansion of Massachusetts territory and commerce. In 1659 Atherton became the leading member of a company, formed two years before, that endeavored, in the face of protests from the colony, to obtain grants from the Indians in the Narragansett country. This intrusion upon the lands of Rhode Island, in which men both of Massachusetts and of Connecticut were implicated, had begun with the attack upon Shawomet in 1643 and was not brought to an end until the royal commissioners in 1665 took over the territory, as the King's Province, and placed it in the hands of the crown (*Rhode Island Colonial Records*, II, 93–95; *Calendar State Papers, Colonial, 1661–1668*, §§965, 1000.

divines. He formulated his own theological ideas, which were personal and not those of a sect, and he stood for liberty of conscience and denied the right of the civil government to interfere with spiritual things. He was vehemently opposed to the formalities and perfunctory worship of the churches, and would have nothing to do with conventionalities in universities and schools, preferring "the universitie of humane reason and the reading of the great volume of visible creation." He had in his theology much that was in accord with the teachings of Mrs. Hutchinson, particularly as regards the doctrine of grace before works, but he disagreed with her in his conception of Christ and with the Quakers in their doctrine of the "inner light," because he believed less in emotionalism than in a rational interpretation and understanding of "revelation" based on sound learning and a thorough acquaintance with the Scriptures in their original tongues. He was not a Trinitarian, viewing the Trinity as but three manifestations of spiritual distinctions in the nature of Christ. He followed no man's thinking, but developed a theology that was peculiar to himself.[1]

In his devotion to English law and its enforcement in the colonies he was not unreasonable, except in his defiant attitude toward the colonial authorities, construing the law of England as binding in New England despite the importance of the law of God. He would not accept the authority of the civil magistracy there, because he could not recognize the legality of any judicial system that did not find its rooting in English common and statute law, or of any administration of justice that departed from the familiar forms of the English courts. He did not deny the right of the people to self-government, but he demanded that this right be in accord with the rights of Englishmen and with the principles which governed their relations with their fellows in local and central affairs. He was profoundly convinced of the necessity and efficacy of charters and tenaciously adhered to claims based on deeds and patents. Liberal as he was in all that pertained to theology and ecclesiastical policy, he was a strict constructionist in his belief that English law and practice

---

1. Janes, *Samuell Gorton*, ch. VIII. Perhaps it is not surprising that the Massachusetts and Plymouth men used the harsh language they did to characterize Gorton. They spoke of him as an "arch-heretic," a "beast," a "miscreant," a "proud and pestilent sinner," a "subtle deceiver," a purveyor of "cursed principles and opinions," and a "most prodigious minter of exorbitant novelties." He questioned their infallibility, their judicial authority, their ecclesiastical caste, and their theology, and for their own preservation they were bound to resist what they deemed his heresies.

should be followed in all that pertained to legislation and the exercise of justice and administration.

Thus Rhode Island at the beginning was formed of four separate communities—or even five, if we count Pawtuxet, which for a time was a distinct community. Each of these was in embryo a petty state, and each possessed a marked political and religious atmosphere of its own. No one of these communities had at first any other than an Indian title for its lands and an agreement or social compact as the basis and legal warrant for its government. Each recognized the king of England as its sovereign and acknowledged its subordination to the authority of the king's officials at home. The people of Portsmouth in 1640 proclaimed themselves "the loyal subjects of King Charles" and Providence and Warwick[1] both subscribed officially during the Interregnum to a true and faithful allegiance to the commonwealth and after the Restoration, repudiating their former declarations, entered upon their records similar expressions of loyalty to their lawful king. These four communities, thus settled by people of deep-seated and often antagonistic religious and political opinions, found coöperation and union, for any length of time, difficult and seemingly impossible. Each was a unit by itself and its separatistic tendencies were made more intense by differences of a local nature and by the strong dislikes which sprang up among them, leading to personal and neighborhood quarrels that sometimes took the form of charges and counter-charges, acrimonious and lasting. As private persons contended with each other, so the towns were rivals and antagonists, due in part to the fact that two of them, Newport and Warwick, were formed by separation from the others, Providence and Portsmouth. The latter generally lined up against Newport, opposing the efforts of Coddington to erect a separate government with Aquidneck and Conanicut as his domain.

But as events turned out it was not William Coddington the Quaker, with his wealth and superior qualities as a man of affairs, but Roger Williams, the Seeker, idealist, and man of God, who was destined to become the dominant figure in Rhode Island history during the forty years of his life in the colony.

The opinions which Williams held, at the time of the founding

---

1. "Warwickmen offered up to Richard Cromwell a great fire aboute a tree and a pitch barell in the top thereof they being mistically minded most like intended a light to aw: and a fire to consume Richards and theyr enemies." *Harris Papers*, p. 235. Compare p. 269.

of Providence in 1636, can be learned only from the documents which record his controversy with Massachusetts in the years from 1633 to 1635. These documents reveal his eager and often impetuous attempts to defend his ideas regarding oaths, land titles, separation from the Church of England, and the authority of the magistrates over the first table of the law.[1] During the next six years these ideas matured rapidly, doubtless taking shape and definiteness in his mind as he meditated upon them, while wandering on foot among the Indians (for he never owned a horse), bending over his hoe in the cultivation of his fields, or laboriously plying the paddle as he passed up and down the rivers or made his way back and forth between Prudence Island and the mainland.

Williams never really systematized his ideas and after 1640 directed his attention in considerable part to problems of government as well as religion. His first great work, *The Bloudy Tenent*,[2] as also his later writings stript of their verbiage, are treatises on political science as well as on theology. They deal with government in church and state, with the principles that should control life and conduct, and with problems of peace, arbitration, education, and the general welfare of the individual and the community. His fundamental theses may be very briefly presented. He viewed the church not as an integral part of the state, with the ends identical and the individual its servant—as did Massachusetts, Connecticut, New Haven, and the Puritans generally—but as one of the many civil corporations that the state was bound to protect. Hence he naturally arrived at the idea of liberty of conscience and the separation of church and state. He willingly conceded that the magistrate was superior to all others in place, honors, dignities, and earthly powers, but he demanded that the church, being the superior ecclesiastically, should be entirely independent of magisterial interference and free to regulate its own affairs. He insisted that the magistrates had no power to set up any form of church organization, to elect church officers, or to punish with church censures; that their authority was temporal not spiritual, just as the authority of the church was spiritual not temporal. These ideas regarding the separation of church and state he ex-

1. See Volume I, 471–474.

2. "O let not this be told in *Gath*, nor heard in Ashkalon! and O! how dimme must needs eye be, which is *blood shot* with that *bloody* and cruell Tenent of Persecution for cause of *Conscience?*" *Narragansett Club Publications*, III, 385.

pressed in a great variety of ways and supported with a great variety of arguments.

In matters ecclesiastical Williams went far beyond mere toleration. Massachusetts took the ground that no other church, practicing another form of church discipline, could be approved as having a right to exist in the colony, though an individual church conducting its affairs in the presbyterial way was the least of such evils. Richard Mather put the situation well when he said in 1643 that if "the discipline which we here practice be (as we are persuaded of it) the same which Christ hath appointed and therefore unalterable, we see not how another can be lawful, and therefore if a company of people shall come hither and here set up and practice another we pray you think not much, if we cannot promise to approve of them in so doing."[1] Roger Williams believed, on the contrary, that the world was full of admirable people—men and women—who not only thought differently from himself in matters of church polity and discipline, but who might not be Christians at all,[2] and in his famous allegory of the ship going to sea, contained in his letter to the town of Providence, in 1655, he includes in his "true picture of a commonwealth" Papists, Protestants, Jews, and Turks, all of whom, in his estimation had a right not only to be tolerated but to live and worship in their own way and not to be "forced to come to the ship's prayers or worship nor compelled from their own particular prayers if they practice any."[3] Thus he stood for absolute equality, as far as liberty of conscience was concerned. At the same time he was always

1. *Church Government and Church-Covenant Discussed* (London, 1643), p. 83.

2. He would grant liberty even to "seducing teachers" who, whether pagan, Jewish, or anti-Christian, might still be obedient subjects of the civil laws, and if the civil laws were not broken then the peace would be kept. *Narragansett Club Publications*, III, 171.

Williams' letters are to be found in *Narragansett Club Publications*, VI; Letters and Papers of Roger Williams, 1629–1682, in facsimile, Massachusetts Historical Society, 1924; two in the *New England Historical and Genealogical Register*, LIII, 314–320; three in *Proceedings*, Rhode Island Historical Society, 1877–1878, pp. 62–73; and eleven in *Collections*, the same, VIII, XXVII. A short letter is printed in *Providence Records*, XV, 209, and a statement in Williams' handwriting, pp. 219–220, both concerning rates. There are letters in the Facsimiles that are not in the *Narragansett Club Publications*. The editor of the *Publications* has modernized the language and has omitted certain parts of the addresses. In a few instances there are discrepancies as to dates.

3. January, 1655, *ibid.*, VI, 278–279; *Collections*, Rhode Island Historical Society, VIII, 51. Williams was fond of this metaphor of the ship as applied to both church and state. *Narragansett Club Publications*, III, 376, 394.

ready to enter into arguments on theological questions, as he did for three days with the Quakers at Newport and Providence in 1672, a debate that led to the issue of the pamphlet *George Fox digg'd out of his Burrowes,* which is a narrative of this disputation,[1] and to which Fox replied in *A New England Firebrand Quenched,* presenting the Quaker version.

Thus to Williams the state was purely a civil not a divine institution, external in its administration, internal in the minds of men, and wholly unconcerned with spiritual affairs. He accepted the idea of the social compact but interpreted it in the light of a community-consciousness of a common purpose. To him the state was a commonwealth of families, agreeing to live together for the good of all— a body of people who had fundamentally in themselves the source of power to select what governors and government they pleased. He rejected totally the divine origin of government and the divine character of the magistracy, upon which Massachusetts laid so much stress. He was profoundly convinced that kings and magistrates were invested with no more power than the people entrusted them with, a conviction he voices over and over again in his writings. "The sovereign, original, and foundation of civil power lies in the people . . . and such a people may erect a form of government as seems to them most mete for their civil conditions"; he says again: "such governments have no more power nor for a longer time than the civil power or people consulting and agreeing shall betrust them with"; and "the sovereign power of all civil authority is founded in the consent of the people." He distinguished carefully between "civil power," which lay in the people of the community, and "civil government," which was the exercise of authority by those whom the people elected for that purpose.

Williams's idea of individualism was not that of an isolated personality, but rather one that found its highest expression through the enforcement of law and the limitation of individual activities. To him freedom was not the ability to do as one pleased, but a privilege acquired by him who was one of a social group, in which the individual had duties as well as rights. This linking of rights and duties,

1. Fox characterized this work as "a very wicked and envious book, which Roger Williams, a priest of New England (or some colony thereabouts) had written against truth and friends," and Fox, William Penn, and John Burnyeat spent three weeks at Penn's home in Sussex, concocting the reply. See Fox's *Journal* (Penney ed.), II, 217–218.

which oddly enough is not to be found in our own federal constitution and which appears for the first time in the French constitution of 1792, was very much in Williams's mind and appears often in his writings. It was given a kind of statutory form in the Rhode Island acts and orders of 1647. Williams opposed the arch-individualist, William Harris of Providence, not only because of the latter's land claims, but even more because Harris held views quite unlike those of Williams on the duties of citizenship. Harris made a public avowal of anarchy and adhered to the Generalist doctrine of unrestrained individualism, echoing the cry, uttered by others of his ilk, "No lords, no masters." He believed that "he who can say 'it is his conscience' ought not to yield subject to any human order among men," a belief that approached dangerously near a complete negation of government and order.[1] This refusal to distinguish between liberty and license—a difference it must be confessed that was never very clearly comprehended by a large number of the early settlers of Rhode Island—underlay many of the troubles with which Williams was confronted in his efforts to create of Providence a model community.[2]

Williams's troubles were not confined to the men of his own race. He labored long and earnestly to preserve the peace among the Indians and between the Indians and the white men and he heaped coals of fire upon the heads of his uncharitable neighbors by his services to all the New England colonies in times both of peace and of war. In the early years of his residence in Rhode Island scarcely a week passed that he did not advance the interests of the English among the Indians of southern New England, hazarding his life,

1. In his letter to the town of Providence, where there were others than William Harris who believed that it was against the rule of the Gospel and therefore "blood-guiltless" to execute judgment upon those who transgressed against the public and private weal, Williams drew a sharp line between liberty and license, endeavoring to show that liberty of conscience did not mean liberty to indulge in tyranny and licentiousness or to refuse to obey orders in civil things. "Oh that I should ever speak or write a title that tends to such an infinite liberty of conscience is a mistake and which I have ever disclaimed and abhorred."

2. Ernst, *The Political Thought of Roger Williams* (1929). This study of Williams' political philosophy is stimulating and provocative, but it is over-systematized, repetitious, and written too much in the manner of a modern treatise on political science. Some of the author's statements seem unduly eulogistic and extravagant. A more convincing contribution is his "Roger Williams and the English Revolution" (Rhode Island Historical Society, *Collections*, XXIV, 1–58, 118–128). He has also written *Roger Williams, a New England Firebrand* (1932), a learned work but loosely constructed, hastily put together, and marred by many typographical errors.

traveling from one Indian chief to another, and in the end preventing a league between the Pequots and the Narragansetts that more than any other single effort averted a prolonged Indian war at a critical time. He was frequently a visitor at the Indian wigwams and often entertained the Indians at his house, to the inevitable discomfort of his long suffering wife, Mary. He knew their language, that "barbarous rockie speech," as he once called it, and was familiar with the gossip that went among them. The natives trusted and respected him and dubbed him "their right hand, their candle and langthorne, the quencher of their fires." Nevertheless Williams must have found contact with them often repellent, for he spoke of some of them as the "miserable drones of Adam's degenerate seed" and of others as "a few inconsiderable pagans and beasts wallowing in idleness, stealing, lying, whoring, treacherous [and given to] witchcrafts, blasphemies and idolatries." However, despite the swinish conduct of a few Indians, Williams stood in close and intimate relations with the leading sachems and urged Massachusetts and John Eliot, who at the time was gathering his Indian flock of converts at Natick, not to be discouraged but to pursue the work of conversion to the end.[1]

Williams's most serious troubles in Rhode Island came not from the Indians but from those of his fellow colonists in whom the spirit of separation and insubordination was active, from the persistent quarrels that arose over land titles and claims, and from the disputes that were frequent and prolonged with the adjoining colonies of Massachusetts, Plymouth, and Connecticut. We have already found in each of the various Rhode Island settlements men strongly opinionated, individualistic, and independent. There was Providence with Roger Williams, William Harris, Richard Scott, and Gregory Dexter; Portsmouth with the Hutchinsons (until 1642 or 1643), and the Dyers; Newport with William Coddington, John Coggeshall, Nicholas Easton, and Dr. John Clarke; Warwick with Samuel Gorton, John Greene, and Randall Holden; and Pawtuxet with the Arnolds.[2]

1. *Narragansett Club Publications,* VI, 271; Letters and Papers in Facsimile, July 6, 1637. When Williams heard of the murders by the Pequots in Connecticut he wrote that the event "cries for vengeance to Heaven," *ibid.,* June, 1638.

2. In 1657 Williams wrote that the inhabitants of Pawtuxet had "all along renounced subjection unto us and solemnly and absolutely subjected themselves to Massachusetts, who have a long time protected from them us in all their complaints against us" (*Proceedings,* Rhode Island Historical Society, 1883–1884, pp. 80–81). But

These men and women were strong-minded and stubborn, with definite opinions and the will to express them and to attempt their enforcement. In the absence of any centralizing and controlling governmental authority, such as was present in both Massachusetts and Connecticut, each group exhibited a marked tendency toward local independence and a religious cult of its own. Though there was agreement on many points of organization and doctrine, the disagreements were conspicuous and prevented mutual understanding and accord.

The ambitions of Coddington at Aquidneck for a long time divided the colony and checked the march toward union and this threatened separation of islands from mainland was for fifteen years a very serious menace to the integrity of the colony. Coddington was two years older than Williams and his wealth, political experience, and education gave to Newport, because of its favorable location for trade and sea-going enterprise, an early superiority over the other settlements. In coöperation with Coggeshall, a former silk merchant in England, and Clarke, a physician of shrewdness and skill, he had brought about, as we have already seen, the union of Portsmouth and Newport under a common administration, which had lasted from 1640 to 1647. He had in mind a separate colony in which he should be the leader and master mind, a colony in which commerce should be a controlling factor and closer relations with Massachusetts and Plymouth and with the Dutch at New Amsterdam a definite feature of its external policy. Whether he aspired to the headship of a larger union of all the towns of the colony is doubtful, and is attested by no evidence at our command.

The first great movement toward federation of the four towns was not, however, the work of Coddington with his personal ambitions, but of Roger Williams, who wanted nothing for himself but who realized that if Rhode Island were to remain intact there must be mutual coöperation and support. The situation in 1643 was a serious one. Massachusetts and Plymouth were pressing their claims to parts of the Rhode Island territory, and the formation of the New England Confederation in that year, of which Rhode Island was not

the situation was altered the next year when the inhabitants of Pawtuxet petitioned Massachusetts for a release from her jurisdiction and accepted the overtures of Williams for a reconciliation (*Simplicities Defence*, Staples ed., pp. 206–207). In so doing William Arnold lost financially in his transactions regarding the cattle taken from the Gortonites in 1643 (*ibid.*, pp. 207–212).

asked to be a member,[1] seemed designed in part to support these claims and to bring Aquidneck and Providence under its control. Also both Coddington and the Arnolds were playing into the hands of Rhode Island's enemies and threatening to disrupt the colony. Again the danger of Indian attack was always present and the isolation of the towns rendered them defenseless; while so uncertain was the title to the land based solely on Indian deeds that the need of more legal protection was imperative. Consequently in that year, his scruples against an English patent overcome, it may be, by the insistence of Gorton, Williams determined to go to England for the purpose of obtaining a charter from the Long Parliament. Forbidden by the Massachusetts magistrates to sail from Boston, he made his way, in March, 1643, to the Dutch settlement at New Amsterdam and about four weeks later reached England, which he found in the throes of civil war.[2] Having secured the patent through the influence of the committee for foreign plantations, of which Warwick was the head and among the members of which were Saye and Sele, Haselrig, Vane,[3] Pym, and Cromwell, he threw himself into the fray, fighting not with arms but with the pen. Before returning to Rhode Island he wrote *The Bloudy Tenent,* composed in haste and published anonymously, thus contributing to the controversy then raging between the Presbyterians and the Independents, and exercising a powerful influence upon the insurgent thought of the time that was greatly concerned with such questions as liberty of

1. Rhode Island was not included in the original membership of the Confederation in 1643, and was refused when she asked to be admitted in 1644, 1648, and 1655, on the ground that there was no stable government in the colony and that the anarchistic principles underlying Williams's idea of a state were shocking to the other members.

2. Four months before, Thomas Weld, through his own unauthorized efforts, obtained the so-called Narragansett Patent, an engrossed instrument on parchment still preserved, which purports to be a grant to Massachusetts, dated December 10, 1643, of the territory which substantially constitutes at present the state of Rhode Island. This document is commonly thought to have had no validity, even if it is not an outright forgery. It never passed the commission at any regular meeting, was signed by an insufficient number of names, and was never enrolled or registered. The date is Sunday, a day on which the commission never sat. Aspinwall, "Remarks on the Narragansett Patent," *Proceedings,* Massachusetts Historical Society, June, 1862, pp. 41–47, in reply to Deane's defense, February, 1862, p. 404. See also New York Historical Society, *Collections,* 1869, p. 147.

3. In his letter of August 28, 1658 (*Narragansett Club Publications,* VI, 306), Williams specifically refers to the assistance he received from Vane in obtaining the charter. For his intercourse with Vane in England see Ernst, *Roger Williams,* pp. 280, 314–315, 323.

conscience, the separation of the church and state, and right of the people to elect their governors. This famous work became one of the handbooks of the sectaries and levellers and in some measure at least sowed the seed for the revolution of 1648 and the victory of the Independent party.[1]

Williams returned in September, 1644, bearing a safe-conduct from Warwick for passage through the Massachusetts Bay territory, which the authorities there did not dare disregard, and was received with enthusiasm by his friends and neighbors of Providence. The patent which he had obtained with so much diplomacy and adroitness authorized the union of Providence, Portsmouth, and Newport, under the name of The Incorporation of Providence Plantations.[2] It was not a charter properly so called, but it granted these towns full power and authority in civil concerns to rule themselves and such others as should thereafter inhabit within any part of the region bounded on the north and northwest by Massachusetts, on the east and southeast by Plymouth, on the south by the ocean, and on the west and northwest by the Narragansett Indians, for a distance of about twenty-five miles. The patent was later construed to include Warwick also, which in 1643 had hardly reached the stage of a settled community. It checkmated for the moment Coddington's move for a separate patent for Aquidneck and for the first time gave a kind of legal recognition to the Rhode Island settlements.

Williams, who had so vigorously inveighed against the Massachusetts charter ten years before, may have squared his conscience by looking on the new document as only a confirmation of his Indian purchases and not as a grant of land from a higher authority in England. Certainly the text lends itself to such an interpretation, for nowhere does it specifically mention what Williams so strongly objected to, the prior right of the crown to the soil. It is a commission to govern rather than a detailed instruction as to how the colony was to conduct its government. Nowhere does it attempt to determine the principles according to which affairs were to be carried on, leaving such matters to be decided afterward by the colony itself.

1. *The Bloudy Tenent* was issued July 15, 1644, and on August 9 was ordered burned by the common hangman (*Collections*, Rhode Island Historical Society, XXIV, 9–12). On the influence of Williams's writings in bringing on the English revolution of 1648 see Ernst, *ibid.*, 1–58, 118–129.

2. *Rhode Island Colonial Records*, I, 143–146. The patent is dated March 14, 1644, and is signed by Warwick, Pembroke, Saye and Sele, Wharton, Haselrig, Holland, Vane, S. Vassall, Rolle, Corbet, and Spurstowe.

The patent was not put into force at once, partly because of the existing agreement between Portsmouth and Newport, which the former did not repudiate until 1647, and partly because of the uncertainty which prevailed as to the outcome of the civil war in England. Charles I was still king, and should he win the war, any patent from parliament might easily be construed as worthless. But the battle of Naseby in 1645 decided that issue and a general assembly was called at Portsmouth in May, 1647, composed of freemen from the four towns,[1] with John Coggeshall as moderator, to organize a government and to draw up a body of laws. Under the patent a federal system was created, in which the individual towns became parts of a larger community. They retained corporate rights but had neither legal nor political supremacy. The state thus formed was a step toward a centralized control and away from the powerful forces making for decentralization, and it represented a noteworthy advance from loosely organized groups of men to a fairly systematized federal commonwealth.[2]

The acts and orders of 1647 constitute one of the earliest programmes for a government and one of the earliest codes of law made by any body of men in America and the first to embody in all its parts the precedents set by the laws and statutes of England. They were adopted at the sessions of an assembly which sat at Portsmouth on the 19th, 20th, and 21st of May of that year. A government was set up which was to cover executive, legislative, and judicial business and to maintain a careful line of demarcation between the powers of the central authorities and those of the towns. At its head was to be a president, four assistants, a recorder, a treasurer, and a sergeant, with functions well defined. All of these officials were to be nomi-

---

1. See the instructions, drawn up by Williams, from the town of Providence to its committee of ten men, who were elected in town meeting on May 16, to represent the town in the general court. *Rhode Island Colonial Records,* I, 42–44.

2. Providence and Warwick had only a town meeting government, with town orders but no executive head until 1648, when they began to exercise the privileges conferred in formal town charters issued by the general court (*ibid.,* I, 148, 214–216; *Warwick Records,* pp. 36, 252–254); Portsmouth had a judge and elders, 1639; Newport and Portsmouth, a governor and deputy governor, and assistants, 1640–1647. All were separate sovereignties till 1647. Under the patent of 1644 the whole colony had a president, assistants, and general court, 1647–1651, when Portsmouth and Newport withdrew, and two distinct commonwealths existed until 1654. After the reunion in the latter year the system of president, assistants, and general court was continued for the whole colony to 1663.

nated by the towns and chosen at the court of election held in May. For the first year the assembly was a primary gathering of as many of the people as could be brought together, with a quorum of ten men from each town to act with full authority in case a majority of the freemen could not be obtained, but after 1650 it became solely representative, six from each town.[1] Thus in practice as well as in principle the government was to be "democratical," that is, it was to be conducted by the free and voluntary consent of all or a greater part of the inhabitants who were landowners.[2] By the adoption of certain specified contrivances it was prevented from becoming unduly centralized and officious. These contrivances were frequent elections, the right of the towns to initiate legislation, the recall by popular vote of an undesirable law, and the referring of measures, before enactment as law, to the people for their approval. For example, at a town meeting held in Portsmouth, November 12, 1650, it "was agreed by voate that two men shall be chosen out of this present meeting to speak with the rest of the inhabitants of the towne who are not present and receive their voates concerning the laws presented to the towne in case they dislike any and the sayd two shall return the sayed voates into the office forth with."[3] But this procedure proved in practice overcomplicated and was remodeled

1. It is assumed by both Richman (*Rhode Island: its Making and Meaning*, p. 245) and Ernst (*Roger Williams*, p. 273) that the general court of 1649, as well as that of 1648 was a primary gathering of freemen. It is hard to reconcile this assumption with the entries in the *Warwick Records* of February 26, 1648–1649, "That we agree to send [certain ones] from the towne of Warwick" (p. 41), or with that in the *Providence Records*, April 27, 1649, "Ordered that the six men formerly chosen" (II, 40). Furthermore the order of May 23, 1650, "It is ordered that in case the committee shall fall shorte of six out of each towne," etc., does not read as if the practice of representation were introduced for the first time in 1650 (*Rhode Island Colonial Records*, I, 221). Apparently we have in 1648 and 1649 a combination of freemen and delegates. The court of 1650 was representative only (*ibid.*, 228), the delegates being known first as commissioners and later as deputies. The court sat as one house, though as early as 1654 Warwick petitioned for a separation into two houses (*Warwick Records*, p. 145).

2. For a resident to become a freeman did not require the taking of an oath of allegiance until after the receipt of the charter, owing probably to Williams's known hostility to the taking of such an oath. But it did require the possession of land in the town where the voters registered their decisions. The voting upon all matters that concerned the central government was not at large but by towns. Such a practice increased the tendency toward town independence. Richman, *Rhode Island: its Making and Meaning*, pp. 314–315.

3. *Portsmouth Records*, p. 47.

in 1650, 1658, and 1660,[1] though in revised form it continued to be retained, as a kind of referendum, until 1663.[2]

At first this general court or assembly—which was a perambulatory body meeting in rotation in each of the four towns, because it was easier for the assembly to go to the people than for the people to go to the assembly—was a judicial court as well as a law-making body. Having spent a number of days in passing laws and completing its work in that direction it sat the next day as a general court of trials for the colony, superseding the former quarter courts, which had been introduced for Aquidneck after the union of Portsmouth and Newport in 1640 and had met quarterly, alternating between the two towns. Later, in 1655, a separate court of trials was established, meeting three times a year, in each town in succession, constituting a circuit court of oyer and terminer with grand and petit jury and dealing with actions for trespass, wages, debt, damages, breaches of the peace, and offensive conduct and speech against the colony or any of its officials.[3] In operation it proved dilatory and slow, because jurymen disliked to attend and preferred to pay the fine imposed and stay at home. To meet this situation the fine was increased in amount and if not paid rendered the juryman liable to distraint of his property.[4] But at best the jury system was never very efficient.

Below this court were the town courts of trials, meeting four times a year and exercising the jurisdiction provided for in the town charters for the preservation of the local peace.[5] Both the general court and the town courts were common law courts, their juries being chosen by the landowning inhabitants of the towns. Williams, who was president of the general court of commissioners and the general court of trials from 1655 to 1657, resorted as often as he could

1. *Warwick Records*, pp. 80–81. The laws were publicly read in each town before being acted on. This right of appeal or "libertie to disanull any law to them presented from the courts of Commissioners" was accorded by an act of 1647 (*Rhode Island Colonial Records*, I, 148–149) and repealed by act of October 26, 1650, when a new law was established (*ibid.*, 229). This act was modified November 2, 1658, and again modified May 22, 1660 (*ibid.*, 401, 429), extending the period of consideration by the towns from ten days to three months.

2. Reports of most of the sessions are printed in Chapin, *Documentary History*, II ch. XV.

3. *Rhode Island Court Records: Records of the Court of Trials for the Colony of Providence Plantations*, I, 1647–1662, II, 1662–1670; *Rhode Island Colonial Records* I, 305, 395.

4. *Ibid.*, I, 502.   5. *Warwick Records*, pp. 253–254.

to arbitration, which through his influence got well established as a method of settling disputes, and at times he was able to bring about mutual agreements, particularly in cases of partnerships, by having auditors go over the accounts.

Even more significant than the organization of the government and the creation of a judicial system for the whole colony was the passage of a series of laws which were adopted by the general court at its first meeting and at other meetings in the years that immediately followed. These acts and orders were not completed all at once, nor were they intended to be final. They were fundamental but not organic, for they were changeable at the will of the assembly— though the changes were rather formal than basic—according to Williams's doctrine that any system of law should be a matter of continuous growth. Williams was not a lawyer and had no knowledge of English law and probably not much of the English constitution, and while there is no doubt that he supplied many of the leading ideas and principles, it is equally clear that he was not qualified either as a lawyer or a law maker to give the laws their proper legal form or to furnish the necessary English precedents. These laws, notably those of 1647, were modeled after the law of England and, unlike those of the Puritan colonies, were founded not on the word of God but on the statutes of parliament. Nearly every one of them, as well as many adopted in the years that followed, is accompanied by a reference to the English statute book.[1] Beginning with the four general provisions which make up a bill of rights—the first of which is the restatement of a clause in Magna Carta—the code runs through a series of capital crimes[2] and minor offenses, such as concerned artificers, the poor, alehouses, licenses, marriage, the probate of wills, and in later measures, prisons, procedure at trials, the appointment

1. For example, *Rhode Island Colonial Records*, II, 513.
2. The only annotated edition of the acts and orders of 1647 is that of Staples issued in 1847. The remaining acts and orders may be found in *Rhode Island Colonial Records*, I, 208–214. Staples contrasts at length the crimes capitally punished in Rhode Island with those of Plymouth and Massachusetts (pp. 32–37, notes). In Rhode Island the death penalty was imposed for high and petty treason, murder, manslaughter, robbery, burglary, arson, witchcraft, and unnatural sexual practices. During Williams's time there were only two executions, 1670, 1671 (*Rhode Island Colonial Records*, II, 342, 344, 351, 363, 393, cf. 356–357) and two trials for treason, neither of which resulted in condemnation, Hugh Bewitt (*ibid.*, I, 254–255) and William Harris (*ibid.*, 361, 364; *Rhode Island Court Records*, I, 25). There were no trials for witchcraft in the colony.

of an attorney and solicitor general for the colony,[1] banishment, strangers, divorce,[2] payment of members, slavery, freedom of trade, sale of land to the Indians, and the like—all "in the name and powre of the free people of this state." That Gorton had a hand in the making of this code we may not doubt, for he was a firm and obstinate believer in the necessity of basing legislation and judicial procedure on the English common and statute law and of giving to every individual the benefit and protection which that law afforded. He is supposed to have been the author of the well-known act against negro slavery, passed in 1652 during the Coddington secession, when only representatives of Providence and Warwick made up the assembly. As Williams was in England at the time of its passage it is exceedingly likely that Gorton, the moderator for that year, was the one chiefly responsible for its adoption.[3] The act was no more than an expression of good intentions, for it was never enforced and was a mere irony in the eighteenth century, when Rhode Island had no less than four thousand negroes, largely in the towns along Narragansett Bay, with Newport the center of the slave trade. But it was never repealed and therefore stands as the first legislative act of emancipation in the history of the colonies.

Though the men who drew up these acts and orders laid exceptional stress upon the preservation of the peace and the punishment of wrong doing, they had nothing of importance to say regarding philanthropy and education. The care of the poor was left entirely to the towns, as was the case under the famous Elizabethan act of 1601 which Rhode Island carefully followed, and all measures looking to the elevation of the standards of living and the providing of schools for the improvement of the youth of the colony were conspicuously lacking, such matters being considered the concern of town and family and not of the state. Gorton was an educated man

---

1. *Rhode Island Colonial Records*, I, 225–226.

2. Though the colony was, not unnaturally, opposed to banishment, there is at least one case in which an offender named Welton was ordered out of the jurisdiction (*ibid.*, I, 280, 314, 319; Chapin, *Documentary History*, II, 152; *Newport Historical Magazine*, II, 120–121, 186). The "Stranger" law (*Rhode Island Colonial Records*, 230, 307) should be compared with that of Massachusetts (*Massachusetts Colonial Records*, I, 196) for liberality. Rhode Island welcomed strangers, Massachusetts did not. There were no prisons in the colony until 1656–1658, only stocks and whipping posts. The prison at Newport does not appear to have been finished until the latter date (*Warwick Records*, p. 110; *Rhode Island Colonial Records*, I, 212, 213, 335, 391).

3. *Ibid.*, I, 243.

and Williams had some knowledge of Hebrew, Greek, Latin, French, and Dutch. He had a Dutch testament and could read it, and had himself in England "taught two young gentlemen, a parliament man's sons, as we teach our children English, by words, phrases and constant talk," but there is nothing anywhere to show that either he or Gorton believed such matters to be a part of the public business. During these early years the towns were occupied in defending themselves against attacks of the Indians and of rival colonies and in expending their energies on the gaining of a bare subsistence, and had little time or money for education. Even at Newport, where the conditions were more favorable than elsewhere,[1] an early effort to establish a school was premature, for the minister, the Rev. Mr. Lenthal, who in 1640 was "by vote called to keep a public school for the learning of the youth" and for his encouragement was granted a homelot and a hundred acres of land, remained only a year and a half and the school went by default. During the first thirty years neither the colony nor the towns made any attempt to promote manners, education, the arts, or even morals in any marked degree such as one is accustomed to find in a more settled order of society. There was no public education in the colony until after 1670.[2]

How far Coddington had a part in the activities of the general court it is difficult to say. He was one of the assistants from Newport in 1647 and the president of the court in 1648, his election to the latter office being manifestly an attempt to conciliate the Aquidneck party and to bring it into line with the others in order to strengthen the whole movement toward consolidation. But the attempt did not succeed. Coddington was not friendly to the patent of 1644 and was still determined to keep Aquidneck intact as a separate colony free to act as it pleased. He was already in secret communication with Massachusetts in regard to the annexation of Warwick and Providence, and in 1648 petitioned the New England Confederation for the admission of Aquidneck as an independent member, but the commissioners rejected the petition unless the island would come in

1. The wealth of Newport in 1661, compared with that of the other towns, can be measured by the amounts appropriated in that year for the expense of obtaining the charter: Newport, £85; Providence, £40; Portsmouth, £40; Warwick, £35. These amounts were increased later, but the proportions remained the same (*ibid.*, I, 444, 448, 481). Under the charter Newport had six representatives in the assembly, the other towns four each.

2. Higginson, *A History of the Public School System of Rhode Island* (1876), pp. 1–11.

as a part of Plymouth or Massachusetts. Both at this time and afterward he was suspected of being in correspondence with the Dutch,
who were always covert if not open enemies of Rhode Island, and
in general he seemed to be working underhandedly for the overthrow of the government under the patent and the supremacy of
his own island propriety.[1]

Williams, always a peacemaker and an upholder of the union
under the patent, endeavored to persuade Coddington to arbitrate
their differences, hoping that they might settle the difficulties themselves, without resort to England, which would be "unreasonable
and most chargeable," or to the neighboring colonies, which would
be neither "safe nor honorable."[2] But Coddington refused to agree
and Williams wrote pessimistically to John Winthrop, Jr., "This
land and poor colony is in civil dissensions. Their last meetings [of
the general court] at which I have not been [present] have fallen
into factions. Mr. Coddington [the president] and Capt [John] Par-
tridge at the head of the one and Capt [Jeremy] Clarke and Mr.
[Nicholas] Easton the heads of the other factions. I received letters
from both inviting me, etc, but I resolve, if the Lord please, not to
engage unless with great hopes of peace-making. The peace-makers
are the sons of God."[3] The court brought charges against Coddington and William Baulston of his faction, laying down the general
rule that if at any time the president left the colony to go to another
colony or to England, as Coddington was threatening to do, then
the chief assistant of the town where the president was to be chosen
should act in his stead. Coddington refused to attend the general
court after the charges were made and Clarke took his place. In
October, 1649, he sailed for England with the intention of presenting
his case to the Council of State and soon after his arrival petitioned
the council for a grant of the two islands of Aquidneck and Conanicut. Despite the efforts of Edward Winslow who claimed Conanicut
for Plymouth, the committee of the admiralty reported his case
favorably and a draft commission was made out in March, 1651.
This draft was passed upon formally in April appointing Codding-

1. Turner, *William Coddington* (Rider, *Tracts*, no. 4), is antagonistic to Coddington, while Adlom, *Origin of the Institutions of Rhode Island* (1871), p. 8, is distinctly friendly. Coddington's letters to Governor Winthrop are in *Collections*, Massachusetts Historical Society, 4th ser., VI, VII, and his commission from the council of
state is in Rider, *Book Notes*, XXIV, no. 24, pp. 185–189.

2. Williams's letter to Providence, August 3, 1648.

3. Williams to John Winthrop, Jr., *Narragansett Club Publications*, VI, 166.

ton governor for life of the two islands, with power to administer the law in the name of the keepers of the liberties of England, to raise forces for defence, and to appoint councillors to be nominated by the freeholders of Newport and Portsmouth. This was an extraordinary commission for the Council of State to issue, for it abrogated and superseded the patent of 1644, which probably the council had no right to do. As Coddington claimed the ownership of the islands, his commission made him to all intents and purposes a feudal proprietor, a status well suited to one of his extraction, education, and wealth, who looked with aversion upon the poverty and individualism of Warwick and Providence.

Although Coddington claimed that he had the support of most of the people of the island, the fact turned out to be otherwise. A powerful group opposed him on his return and selected Dr. John Clarke to go to England to obtain a rescinding of the commission. Providence and Warwick lent their aid and at a meeting of the general court in October, 1651, urged Williams to go over as their agent to coöperate with Clarke in the task and to obtain, if possible, a renewal of the patent of 1644, which many thought might have been impaired by the Coddington commission. Williams was very loth to go, for it meant leaving wife and children and enduring the discomforts and dangers of two long trips at sea, but he finally accepted, and to meet his expenses, for ready money was necessary, sold his trading house at Narragansett. He and Clarke sailed from Boston in November. With the help of Sir Harry Vane, who befriended him in all his efforts and whom Williams calls "the sheet anchor of our ship," and with the good will of Cromwell, with whom he had several conversations, he was able to aid Clarke in carrying out his mission and to execute successfully his own particular task. In reply to a petition sent in on April 7, 1652, the Council of State the October following annulled the Coddington commission, largely because of Coddington's intrigues with the Dutch at New Amsterdam, and confirmed the patent of 1644, thus effectively frustrating the *coup d'état* of 1651.[1]

1. *Calendar State Papers, Colonial,* 1574–1660, pp. 337, 338, 353, 354. The story is told in Rider's *Tracts,* no. 4. One would like to know more of how these documents—the patent to Williams and the commission to Coddington—were obtained. Evidently the usual processes of the seals were dispensed with and the instruments issued, in the case of the patent, by the committee for foreign plantations, and in the case of the commission by the Council of State. There is nothing to show that the first received the king's sign manual or that either bore the great seal. When the

But the collapse of the Coddington plot did not bring peace to the troubled colony. The forces making for disruption were too strong to be easily overcome, and the one man who had the interest of the entire colony at heart was away in England, not to return until 1654. Despite the efforts of 1647, there was widespread distrust of a central government, a dread of executive authority, and a deep-seated dislike of any power superior to that of the towns themselves. Everywhere was there a lack of cohesion, a want of mutual confidence, an excess of desire for soul liberty, individualism, and democracy that inevitably led to divisions and disorders. The Arnolds of Pawtuxet were looking to Massachusetts for support and were co-operating with her in the effort she was making to annex the Warwick territory. The Coddington faction, still contumacious and defiant of the orders of the general court, was refusing to unite with the mainland even though Coddington's own peculiar schemes had been brought to naught. In Providence the inhabitants were broken into discordant groups, with liberty running into license and individuals openly contemptuous of all government and opposers of all authority. Beyond the borders, the encroachments of the neighboring colonies were finding support from the commissioners of the New England Confederation, a union just ten years old, who would have been happy to get rid of Rhode Island altogether as a center of corrupting influence and a plague spot of erroneous ideas. From 1651 to 1654 the colony was divided into two antagonistic parts—the

question of the boundary between Connecticut and Rhode Island came before the Privy Council for adjudication, the council's committee reported that the patent of 1644 "cannot be reputed valid in law" (*Acts Privy Council, Colonial*, V, §12). Harris said the same when he wrote that the patent "not having the s^d Royall assent is void" (*Harris Papers*, pp. 108, 113–114). Yet later when a charter was wanted from the king, the colony tried to strengthen its case by assuming that the patent of 1644 was regularly granted by Charles I. This statement is true only by implication and is probably not true in fact, for the only reference to the king in the patent is in the sentence "most conducing to the General Good of the said plantation, the Honour of his Majesty and the service of the state" and in the royal style at the end, where it is stated that the patent was issued in the king's name. Evidently in 1662 the colony wished to make the best impression possible by leading Charles II to think that the patent was actually issued by his father—"given and granted by the most potent and royall power aforesayd" and "the encouragement which they received from the late king, who in 1644 granted this charter" (*Rhode Island Colonial Records*, I, 434; *Calendar State Papers, Colonial*, 1661–1668, §10). A more accurate statement appears in the colony's petition and letter of 1665 in regard to the Narragansett territory, "by virtue of a charter granted in his late Royal Maties Name by the Lords and Commons in 1643[4]" (*Collections*, New York Historical Society, 1869, pp. 140, 147).

islands and the mainland—each forming in fact a distinct community, the general court continuing to sit with delegates from only two towns, Providence and Warwick. Despite the patent and the act and orders of 1647 Newport and Portsmouth retained, to all intents and purposes, their complete independence, and resisted, until compelled to give way by sheer force of necessity and of pressure from without, all attempts made to bring them into line with the mainland in loyalty to a common cause.[1]

On the return of Williams in 1654 plans were immediately set on foot to counteract these divergent tendencies. He was determined to restore the government as it was under the patent of 1644, to reunite the four towns once more in a bond of allegiance to the colony as a whole, and to put into effect, as he quaintly expressed it, "some course concerning our dissenting friends." Commissioners were summoned from each of the towns who drew up articles of agreement and in September of that year Williams was elected president of the court and thereby obtained the opportunity to take up the task in earnest. He faced a difficult situation with which he was physically not fit to cope. He was tired and broken in health, worn by his labors in England and the torments of the ocean voyages. "I am like a man in a great fog," he wrote, "I know not how to steer. I fear to run upon the rocks at home, having had trials abroad. I fear to run quite backward, as men in a mist do and undo all that I have been a long time undoing myself to do, viz: to keep the name of a people, not enslaved to the bondages and iron yokes of the great, both body and soul, oppressions of the English and barbarians about us, nor to the divisions and disorders within ourselves." Thus he poured out his thoughts to the people of Providence.[2]

But he had no intention of withdrawing from the leadership to which occasion had called him, and once more in control proceeded step by step to restore the colony to the position it had occupied before 1651. His confidence was greatly increased by a letter from Cromwell, now Lord Protector of the Commonwealth of England,

1. A detailed account of this confusing period, 1647–1660, is manifestly impossible here. Excellent chapters on the subject may be found in Richman, *Rhode Island: its Making and Meaning*, chs. IX, X, and in Ernst, *Roger Williams*, pp. 297–397, the latter containing the only adequate narration of Williams's activities in England.

2. *Narragansett Club Publications*, VI, 263. Williams mentions several times his physical infirmities—"much lamed and broken with such travels" (*ibid.*, 206–207), "my old pains and lameness" (*Collections*, Rhode Island Historical Society, VIII, 147).

Scotland, and Ireland, written March 29, 1655, which bade the colony go on in the government "according to the tenor of your charter formally granted on that behalfe, takinge care of the peace and safetie of those plantations; that neither through any intestine commotions or forraigne invasions, there do arise any detriment or dishonour to the Commonwealth [of England] or yourselves, as farr as you by your care and diligence can prevent."[1] Drastic measures were taken: ringleaders of cliques and contentious groups were threatened with transfer to England for trial, lesser offenders were told they would be fined or whipped, if they continued in their course of opposition, and so far was the spirit of contrariness subdued that in March, 1656, Coddington himself freely submitted "to the authoritie of his Highness in the Colonie as it is now united and that with all my heart."[2]

The worst of the danger was over. The central government had won its victory over the recalcitrant towns and the law of the colony once more became the law of the entire land.[3] Factional disorders were ended, old-time enmities were harmonized, even William Harris for the moment became less turbulent, and the Pawtuxet men, led by William Arnold and William Carpenter, deserted Massachusetts and allied themselves once more with Providence, submitting to the jurisdiction of the colony government. Williams never rose to greater heights as a loyal public servant than he did during these two critical years. Retiring from the presidency in the summer of 1657, he continued, as one of the commissioners from Providence, to control the course of affairs through the coöperation of the new president, Benedict Arnold, who since Williams' return from England in 1644 had become one of his most efficient supporters.

1. *Rhode Island Colonial Records,* I, 316–317; *New England Historical and Genealogical Register,* XXXVIII, 383–384.
2. *Rhode Island Colonial Records,* I, 327.
3. "It is ordered that noe law or order apoynted and ordayned by the general and publicke authoritie of this colonie shall be any wayes obstructed or neglected under pretence of any authoritie of any of the towne charters; but that the general authoritie shall have it done and placed according to law in all wayes." *Ibid.,* I, 333.

CHAPTER II

THE RHODE ISLAND COLONY FIRMLY
ESTABLISHED

IT seemed as if the men of Rhode Island were never to experience the joys of peace or stability, for no sooner had they begun to see some sort of unity and order emerging from the conditions that had threatened to disrupt their colony from within than they were compelled to cope with circumstances arising beyond their borders that were endangering not only the integrity of their landed possessions but even the very existence of the government itself. The first menace came from the Atherton Company, to meet which they had no certain defense as long as their right of occupation remained without legal confirmation from the crown and as long as their boundaries remained undefined.

In 1659 the Atherton Company, composed of Major Atherton, John Winthrop, Jr., of Connecticut, and others, some of Rhode Island and some of Massachusetts, traders and speculators, purchased of the Indians a tract in the northern part of the Narragansett territory.[1] In a letter to Massachusetts, Williams with some bitterness characterized this purchase as "an unneighborly and unchristian intrusion upon us, as being weaker, contrary to your laws as well as ours, concerning purchasing lands without the consent of the General Court." Appeals to Atherton proved of no avail and protests to the commissioners of the New England Confederation brought no response whatever. The general assembly of the colony complained grievously of the efforts of these same commissioners to retard Rhode Island's progress and injure its economic prosperity, by cutting off its trade, controlling the price of its commodities, and refusing to deal with its people except on their own terms, "Whereby [the assembly said] (though they gaine extraordinary from us), yett

1. *New England Historical and Genealogical Register,* I, 464–465; *Records of the Proprietors of the Narragansett, otherwise called the Fones Record* (1894), I, containing the deeds and the names of those concerned. Also *Calendar State Papers, Colonial,* 1661–1668, §§493, 494, 967.

for the safeguard of their own religion may seem to neglect themselves in that respect; for what will men doe for their God."[1]

In the autumn of 1660, when the struggle with the Atherton Company was at its height and appeals from its agents were bringing the issue to the attention of the authorities in England, a second and even greater disaster threatened Rhode Island. News came of the restoration of Charles II to the throne, with its import of uncertainty and confusion. To ward off the danger the general court acted immediately. Before anything was done by the other New England colonies it ordered proclamation of the king to be made (October 18, 1660), in the presence of the delegates and of the train bands called out to add solemnity to the occasion.[2] Later the court prostrated itself "at his Majesties feet to beseech his Majesties favorable continuation of his goodness to us, his most faythful, tho poore and unworthy subjects in these remote parts of the world."[3] The situation was a difficult one and the leaders of the colony had to walk warily, because the restoration of the king rendered doubtful the legal validity of the patent of 1644. It is to be remembered that parliament, though acting in the king's name, had issued the document without following, as far as we know, the regular process required for a letters patent, and also that the patent had served in Rhode Island to enforce principles of government that were, in many important particulars, analogous to those of the Commonwealth and Protectorate which England had just discarded. Whoever was to overcome the royal scruples and obtain from the king a confirmation of the patent had to be a man of honor, shrewdness, and tact, and possessed of unswerving concern for the public weal. That man was Dr. John Clarke.[4]

1. *Rhode Island Colonial Records*, I, 397–398. Brenton, Baulston, and Clarke speak of "those incredible oppressions wee endured, of scorne and contempt, slander and reproach, threatening and molestations, captiving and imprisoning, fining and plundering the people of this colonie" and of "a combination of all the colonies to roote us up and expose [us] to ruine." *Collections*, New York Historical Society, 1869, p. 145. The date is June 16, 1665.

2. *Rhode Island Colonial Records*, I, 432.   3. *Ibid.*, 443.

4. No satisfactory life of Clarke has ever been written, that of T. W. Bicknell, *Story of Dr. John Clarke* (1915), being of little value. There is an essay on Clarke by F. G. McKeever, in *Early Religious Leaders of Newport*, but it is not conspicuous. A good account, though brief, is in the *Dictionary of American Biography*, and some additional information can be obtained from Backus, *History of New England*, I, 348, note. A certain amount of biographical data is to be found in *Ill Newes from New England* (1652), reprinted in *Collections*, Massachusetts Historical Society, 4th ser., II; from Chapin, *Documentary History;* and from the *Rhode Island Colonial*

Clarke was born in Westhorpe, Sussex, in 1609 and was therefore six years younger than Roger Williams. Without educational advantages but with natural gifts and powers of application, he was a man of force, intelligence, and unimpeachable honesty. He came to Boston at the end of 1637 and though in sympathy with Antinomianism and the doctrine of grace before works took no part in the controversy and removed soon to Exeter and later to Providence. Accompanying Coddington to Portsmouth and then to Newport, he was conspicuous as one of the founders of the latter town, of which for many years he was the preacher and physician, forming what Cotton Mather called "the Angelic Conjunction," combining the cure of the body with the cure of the soul. The church of which he was the pastor, according to the scheme and principles of the Baptists, was organized before 1648, the first Baptist church in New England. He was one of those responsible for the union of Portsmouth and Newport in 1640 and continued an influential member of his own community for many years. He was commissioner of the general court of 1647 and twice general treasurer, and his eulogists have seen traces of his handiwork in the framing of the laws already passed. It must be said, however, that the share of the four leading men of the colony—Williams, Gorton, Coddington, and Clarke—in shaping the legislation of those four years from 1647 to 1651 can never be satisfactorily determined. All we certainly know is that the laws were drafted "wth excessive travell and charge."

In 1651, with Obediah Holmes and John Crandall, fellow Baptists, he went to Lynn, Massachusetts, and held a service there in the house of one William Winter, an elderly blind man who had formerly been a member of the Newport church and had asked them to come. When the news of their preaching reached the ears of a local magistrate, one Bridges, he sent two constables with a warrant, who arrested the three men and despatched them to Boston for trial. There Governor Endecott treated them contemptuously, declaring that all deserved death and that he would not have such trash in his jurisdiction. The Rev. John Wilson added his word of greeting when, as Clarke avers in his report of the event, "he strook me before the judgment seat, and cursed me saying The curse of God or Jesus goe with thee." Holmes was cruelly treated, but Clarke

Records, I, II. Clarke retired from active public service in May, 1672, and died in October of that year.

got off with a fine of £20, which tender-hearted friends paid for him. The incident aroused bitter resentment in Rhode Island, where Clarke made it known through his pamphlet, *Ill Newes from New England,* issued in 1652.[1]

In November, 1651, Clarke and his wife accompanied Williams on the voyage to England for the purpose of obtaining the annulment of the Coddington commission, and there he was destined to remain for thirteen years. Of his life overseas we know very little. He resided in Westminster and London, acting as agent and attorney of the colony, and for a livelihood probably practiced his dual vocation as preacher and physician, though doubtless with only moderate success. Despite "patience, content, and self-denial" he was barely able to eke out a living. He .was frequently called upon by the colony to undertake important duties that required tact and discretion, such as winning the favor of Cromwell, to whom the colony presented its humble submission in 1655 and from whom it received a comforting letter in the same year. For this favor it expressed its profound thankfulness. Through the aid of English friends Clarke was able to negotiate a supply of powder, shot, and bullets for distribution among the towns, but whether these friends were ever recompensed by the towns, who were supposed to pay for what they received, is doubtful, for as a rule the towns were very slow in paying their debts.[2] A more difficult assignment was the management in England of the charge of high treason against William Harris, which the colony deemed beyond its knowledge and competency to decide. But nothing ever came of that effort. Again when the colony,

1. The story is told in *Ill Newes from New England,* pp. 27–62. Modern versions are by H. M. King, *A Summer Visit of Three Rhode Islanders in the Massachusetts Bay in 1651* (1896), and Richman, *Rhode Island: its Making and Meaning,* pp. 325–332. For Williams's comments, *Narragansett Club Publications,* VI, 213, 224–225. The narratives of Gorton, Clarke, Fox, and Maverick brought to the attention of Englishmen the worst side—the inhuman side—of the Massachusetts Puritan character and cannot have done the Bay colony any good at home. Even an apologist cannot condone—however well he may understand—the treatment by Massachusetts of Gorton, Clarke, and the Quakers.

2. Fifty pounds were voted Clarke in 1659, in addition to fifty pounds previously sent, but so slow were the towns to respond to the court's demands that the latter threatened to distrain on the estates of individuals who resisted the payment of their share of the rates. The difficulties met in paying the cost of obtaining the charter will be noticed later in the proper place. After Clarke's return the court voted not to continue the agency in England on account of the heavy expense. There can be no doubt, however, that Clarke was eventually paid in full for all his actual cash disbursements in England.

troubled because it had entertained the Quakers, became fearful lest the New England Confederation cut off its trade Clarke was notified in a letter of some length to intervene with the Protector in its behalf. "The last year," the court added, "we have laden you with much imployment," and it expressed its gratitude for the ability, diligence, and loving care which Clarke had displayed for the welfare and prosperity of his own people. "In all straits and incumbrances," the court wrote with appreciation, "we are imbouldened to repayre to you for your further and continued councell and helpe, finding that your sollid and Christian demeanure hath gotten no small interest in the hartes of our superiours, those worthy and noble Senators with whome you have had to do on our behalfe, as it hath constantly appeared in your addresses made unto them, which we have by good and comfortable proof found haveing plentiful experiance thereof."[1]

The greatest test of Clarke's ability and skill was yet to come. With the restoration of the monarchy it became imperative that the colony secure a confirmation of its patent in the form of a royal charter guaranteeing its privileges and protecting it against the encroachments of its aggressive neighbors. To that end it drew up in October, 1660, a formal commission authorizing Clarke to act as its agent and attorney. It appropriated two hundred pounds for expenses, to be raised by "the free contributions of the well affected members of the Collony" instead of by a rate, "which might have eclipsed and anticipated their most joyfull presentation of this resolutior." Evidently the response of the "well affected" to this appeal was unsatisfactory, for the money was not forthcoming and the next year had to be raised by rate.[2]

The expense of the agency was a heavy burden upon the colony. Many urgings of the general court were required before the money was raised even in part, and in the meantime Clarke was obliged to mortgage his house and lands in Newport for £140 in ready cash to go on with. In 1666, the entire amount not having been collected (it had not all been collected in 1680), Williams wrote to the town of

1. *Rhode Island Colonial Records*, I, 396–399. In its letter to Clarke of 1663, the court announced its vote, "That in consideration of Mr. John Clarke's great paynes, labour and travill with much faythfulness exercised for above twelve years on behalfe of this Collony in England, the thanks of the Collony be sent unto him" and a gratuity of £100 in current pay of the country be awarded. *Ibid.*, 510.

2. *Ibid.*, I, 440–444, 448, 480–481, 496, 506, 507, 510; *Portsmouth Records*, March 16, 1663, rate levied to meet Clarke's expenses.

Warwick, which was more backward than the others in gathering its quota, a caustic and incisive letter, upbraiding the inhabitants for their want of loyalty and appealing to their sense of fairness, equity, and common honesty. He recounted their blessings and advantages and declared that they should be willing to pay something for the liberties their colony enjoyed above all other colonies. He warned them of storms and tempests to come, of the dangers that threatened the integrity of Rhode Island, of the hazards run in not discharging debts, of their ingratitude to Clarke, and of the damage to the reputation of the community as a whole, the credit of which ought to be precious in their eyes, should they fail to meet their obligations.[1]

The commission from the colony was drafted in October, 1660, but it was not until January, 1662, that Clarke's first petition was received in the office of the secretary of state. It was sent on behalf of the purchasers and free inhabitants of Rhode Island and, after recapitulating the circumstances of the settlement, begged the king that these same free inhabitants might "find such grace in yor sight, whereby, und^r the wing of yor royall Protection, we may not onely be shelter'd, but caus'd to flourish in o^r civill and religious concern-m^{ts} in these remote p^{ts} of the world, so shall yor servants take th^m-selves greatly oblig'd, while they are quietly permited, wth freedome of conscience to worship the Lord th^r God, as they are p^{r}suaded, to pray for the life of the King, even th^t he may live for ev^r and ev^r, and make it th^r studie, wch way they best approve th^{m}selves." In the second petition, received February 5, Clarke repeated the former representation regarding the circumstances of the settlement and asked for "a more absolute, ample and free charter of civill Incorporation," because "y^r petitioners have it much in their hearts (if they may be permitted) to hold forth a lively experiment, that a flourishing civill State may stand, yea, and best be maintain'd and that among English spirits, with a full liberty in religious concern-m^{ts}."[2] The petitions were ordered to be brought before the Privy

1. *Collections,* Rhode Island Historical Society, VIII, 147–153; Facsimiles, January 1, 1666: The Facsimiles are not paged.

2. Colonial Office Papers, 1:15, nos. 4, 34. The date of the first petition offers something of a puzzle. It bears the endorsement "Rhode Island Address, unto his Majesty Rec^d 29th Jan^{ry} 1661," which should mean January 29, 1662. But the duplicate (no. 34) is endorsed "Rec. from Mr. Sec^y Nicholas the 28 of March 1661, with direction from his Matie that he read it at the next sitting in Councill," which means what it says, March 28, 1661. Clarke did not date this petition, and there is nothing in the text to throw light on the problem. There is reason to think that the com-

Council at its first meeting after March 28, but there is nothing to show that this order was carried out.

The reason for the delay in Clarke's case may be found in the fact that Governor Winthrop of Connecticut had already arrived in England on a similar mission, and had set the wheels in motion for obtaining a charter for his colony at this time. Winthrop was a university graduate, widely traveled, and familiar with the traditions, ways, and men in the higher walks of official and social life. He came fairly well provided with funds and soon after his arrival was made a member of the Royal Society, and read at its meetings a number of papers on a great variety of subjects. How soon Clarke learned of Winthrop's coming and purpose there is no way of finding out, nor do we know that the two men met at all outside the field of their respective missions. Winthrop lived in Coleman Street, Lothbury, and Clarke in Westminster, two miles apart, and they probably had little in common either socially, theologically, or scientifically. Yet there may well have been a bond between them for one was a physician and the other medically minded, and both Williams and Gorton knew of Winthrop's medical skill and were to turn to him later for medical treatment.[1] Besides, Winthrop was a valued friend of Williams. But in view of Winthrop's influence at court it is not surprising that his petition was given precedence and his wishes priority of consideration. He had handed in his petition on February 6, 1662, asking for a renewal of the Warwick patent and in his request mentioned the territory desired as bounded on the "east with the Narragansett Bay."[2] Naturally, therefore, in the first draft of the Connecticut charter and in the charter itself as finally

mission and letter of credence of October 18, 1660, was either not sent to Clarke at that time or, because improperly signed and sealed, was written over again August 27, 1661. In the latter case Clarke would not have petitioned until the end of 1661 or the beginning of 1662. Furthermore, he may have been hampered for lack of funds. The evidence clearly favors the winter of 1661-1662 as the time when the petitions were sent in. These documents are printed, not quite accurately, in *Rhode Island Colonial Records*, I, 485–491. The petitions, though containing frequent references to liberty of conscience as the end and aim of the colony's existence, lay especial stress upon the fact that the code of 1647 was founded upon the laws of England, as near "as the nature and constitution of the place, with the premised cause and state of their conscience would permit."

1. W. R. Steiner, "Governor John Winthrop, Jr. as a Physician," *Bulletin*, Johns Hopkins University, XIV, 298; see *Collections*, Massachusetts Historical Society, 4th ser., VII, 601–631, especially, pp. 604, 605.

2. Bates, *The Charter of Connecticut* (1932), p. 15. These points will be discussed more fully in the chapter on Connecticut.

sealed on May 10, the same boundary line appears. Of this disheart-
ening fact Clarke must have heard at once, for on May 16, he addressed to the king a letter, which came into the hands of the Earl
of Clarendon, begging that the business of the Rhode Island charter
might receive speedy despatch and that "the charter lately granted
unto my neighb^r Mr. Winthrop may again be review^d by yor Majesty, for as much as thereby he hath injuriously swallowed up the
one half of o^r Colonie."[1] Clarendon, who had all these petitions in
hand and was the arbiter in the dispute, temporarily held up the
Connecticut charter,[2] called the petitioners before him and listened
to their respective pleas. We are told, by a none too partial or dependable authority,[3] that "my Lord Chancello^r in his heering and in
publick audience asked M^r. Clarke if hee were not ashamed so
Impudently to Vilify and accuse M^r. Winthrop (and M^r. Winthrop
being present) and my Lord Chancello^r should say he wondered
how M^r. Winthrop Could have the patience to bare itt."[4] That Winthrop had been instructed both by the Connecticut colony and by the
Atherton Company, of which he was a member, to obtain Narragansett Bay as an eastern boundary we know, and there can be little

1. *Collections*, New York Historical Society, 1869, pp. 44–45; Clarendon Manuscripts, 76, f. 272.

2. This is certainly implied in Williams's letter to Mason (1670), "Upon Mr.
Clarke's complaint your grant was called in again, and it had never been returned,
but upon a report that the agents, Mr. Winthrop and Mr. Clarke, were agreed by
mediation." *Narragansett Club Publications*, VI, 341–342. Compare also the letter of
Greene and Holden to Blathwayt, August 20, 1680, *Calendar State Papers, Colonial,
1677–1680*, §1487.

3. The man who said this was Colonel John Scott, a good deal of a rascal and a
thorn in the flesh to the authorities of both Connecticut and Rhode Island and to
many other people besides. He was an agent of the Atherton Company, of which he
was a member and for which he was endeavoring, by backstairs methods, to obtain a
patent that might become the legal warrant for a new Narragansett colony. In all his
activities, here as elsewhere, Scott was working for his own real estate interests all
the time. He is a strange personage to find in the group with Winthrop and Clarke,
two honest men who were to checkmate the designs of a dishonest one. What Scott
was doing in company with Winthrop, Robert Thompson, and Nathaniel Whitfield
at William Hooke's house in 1663 is not easy to surmise (below, p. 141). His story
is told, but not fully told, by Abbot, *Colonel John Scott of Long Island* (1918).
There is also an account of him in *Proceedings*, Massachusetts Historical Society,
June, 1863, pp. 65–74, notes, and letters from and about him in Arnold, *History of
Rhode Island*, I, 383, and *Hoadly Memorial*, pp. 10–11. Scott was still alive and at
his old tricks at the end of 1696, when over sixty years of age (letters of Edward
Wright to Pepys, dated November 10, 12, 1696). The date of his death is not known.
His activities will be referred to in subsequent chapters.

4. *Collections*, New York Historical Society, 1869, p. 47.

doubt that as an honorable man he felt it would be a betrayal of his duty to depart from his official instructions in any particular whatever.[1] However, despite this fact, he consented to submit the issue to arbitration, a concession which was afterward repudiated at home on the ground that Winthrop's authority to bind Connecticut ended with the granting of the Connecticut charter. The arbiters selected, jointly and mutually by each contestant, were William Brereton, Major Robert Thompson (the brother of Maurice and the owner of Whitfield's house in Guilford),[2] Dr. Benjamin Worsley, Captain Richard Deane, who had taken the mortgage on Clarke's property,[3] and Captain John Brookhaven, a fair-minded group of men, unlikely to be influenced by the machinations of the Atherton Company or the lobbying of its agents. After much debate they rendered their decision on April 7, 1663, in favor of Rhode Island, naming the Pawcatuck River as the boundary between the two colonies, but they advised—in order to reconcile their findings with the language of the Connecticut charter—that the river be known as the "Narrogansett River."[4] Thus the stage was set for a quarrel with Connecticut over boundaries which lasted for sixty years.

The advice of the arbiters having been offered and accepted by both Winthrop and Clarke, the business of passing the Rhode Island charter went forward rapidly.[5] The only further obstacle that lay in the way of its issue was the admission into its text of a clause guaranteeing religious freedom for the colony, which Clarke, acting undoubtedly on instructions from Roger Williams, had made a conspicuous part of his petitions. He had asked for "freedom of conscience to worship the Lord their God" in their own way. Winthrop may not have known of the existence of this clause in the draft presented by Clarke, but in any case, having obtained a satisfactory charter for Connecticut, he was ready to aid a neighboring colony, and went out of his way to solicit the despatch of the Rhode

1. *Connecticut Colonial Records,* I, 581; Arnold, *History of Rhode Island,* I, 379.

2. *Hoadly Memorial* (Connecticut Historical Society, XXIX), pp. 2, 4.

3. *Warwick Records,* pp. 169, 171–172. Is Captain Richard the "Deane" mentioned in the *Harris Papers* (p. 342) as aiding in the redemption of Harris? The index enters him as "Thomas," but he is not so named in the text. He may have been "Richard" or, if "Thomas," a relative.

4. *Rhode Island Colonial Records,* I, 518–519; *Calendar State Papers, Colonial,* 1661–1668, §443.

5. The decision to issue a charter to Rhode Island was reached by the Privy Council as early as September 2, 1662. The charter says that the western boundary, the Pawcatuck River, "was yielded [by Connecticut] after much debate."

Island document. As the king, Clarendon, and Secretary Bennett thought well of Winthrop, the charter passed the seals "rather upon the good opinions and confidence we had in the said Mr. Winthrop" than because of any belief that the trouble about the boundaries had been settled or that the wording of the document was just what it should be.[1] To Winthrop, therefore, more even than to Williams or Clarke who wrote the preliminary draft, is due the fact that in the charter appears the following memorable phrase, embodying the fundamental principle upon which Rhode Island was founded: "that noe person within the colonie, at any time hereafter shall be in any wise molested, punished, disquieted or called in question for any differences in opinions in matters of religion . . . but may from time to time, and at all times here after, freelye and fullye have and engage in his and their own judgments and consciences, in matters of religious concernments . . . not useing this libertie to licentious-nesse and profanenesse, nor to the civil injurye or outward disturb-ance of others." It may have seemed an extraordinary clause to receive the royal imprimatur only three years after the fall of the Protectorate, only a year after the passage of the Act of Uniformity of 1662, and at a time when the Cavalier Parliament was performing its dual rôle of persecuting the Nonconformists in England and of reëstablishing the Anglican Church there. But it must be remem-bered that the idea of liberty of conscience was very much in the air at the time and that, despite the Act of Uniformity, men interested in the colonies were realizing the necessity of offering exceptionably favorable conditions of settlement if they were to persuade colonists to migrate overseas. If Jamaica and the new proprietary colonies were to enjoy freedom of worship why should not Rhode Island enjoy it also?

The Rhode Island charter was sealed at Whitehall, July 8, 1663, and at the earliest possible moment was sent over to the colony in charge of Captain George Baxter, a Boston sea-captain, to whom Clarke entrusted the precious document for safe carriage to Boston and thence to Rhode Island. For this service Baxter was afterward allowed twenty-five pounds. At "a very great meeting and assembly of the freemen," held at Newport on November 24, Baxter "with much becoming gravity" held the charter, bearing "his Majesty's Royal Stampe and the broad Seale," up on high in "the perfect view

1. *New York Colonial Documents*, III, 55.

of the people" and then read it aloud to the gathered multitude. Without a dissenting voice the meeting, which had been legally called and brought together in an orderly manner, voted the thanks of the colony to the king for his "high and inestimable, yea, incomparable grace and favour," and to Clarke its gratitude and its binding obligation to save him harmless in his estate and to meet all his expenses in going to England and all his expenses and engagements "there already laid out," an obligation it afterward met with difficulty.[1]

Well might the colony express its relief and thankfulness. Whatever troubles were ahead and they were many and serious, it was at last assured of its legal right to exist under the royal protection and to pursue its career free from that danger of molestation which had hung over it like a threatening cloud for nearly thirty years. In giving confirmation to what Rhode Island had thus far accomplished the charter did far more than set the seal of the king's approval upon the right of these people to occupy a portion of the royal domain in America. It guaranteed, and for the first time permanently, the legal status of this outcast among the New England settlements and placed it, as a lawfully chartered political organization, upon the same footing as its proud neighbors, Massachusetts and Connecticut, who hitherto had claimed preëminence and superiority. Rhode Island had won a great victory over the New England Confederation, the members of which cannot have viewed with equanimity this royal recognition of a colony which formerly they had refused to admit to their councils. However much they may have disliked the king's recognition of this plague spot of erroneous political notions, they must have been far more disquieted by the king's confirmation of the colony's highly prized religious ideas, to conserve which Rhode Island was settled. Henceforth there could be no interference from without to alter whatever religious policy the colony saw fit to adopt.[2]

1. *Rhode Island Colonial Records*, I, 509–511. The George Baxter here mentioned may be the same as the George Baxter who played an important part in the later history of New Netherland, though the identification is not certain.

2. The Massachusetts and Connecticut Puritans were not the only ones who condemned the religious situation in Rhode Island. Dominies Megapolensis and Drisius, the intolerant Dutch Reformed (Calvanist) ministers at Manhattan, spoke of Rhode Island as a place of fanatics, errorists, and enthusiasts, called by the English themselves "the sink of New England" (*New Netherland*, Original Narratives, p. 400). The report of the royal commissioners of 1664–1665 is also interesting, in this con-

Thus the colony was assured of the integrity of its political jurisdiction. Among the grantees mentioned in the charter were representatives of all the towns—Williams, Coddington, Gorton, Greene,
Coggeshall, Dexter, Holden, and Dyer, men who had in the past
taken part as participators in the disorders and divisions which for
years had wracked the settlements and had intensified the forces
making for separation and town independency. All were now committed to the support of a common cause and to the continuance of
the colony as a single corporate unit with a strong central executive,
legislative, and judicial system. As defined in the charter, this system was essentially the same as that which had been in existence
since 1647, with a governor instead of a president, a deputy governor
—an office hitherto known only in the union of Newport and Portsmouth after 1640—ten assistants instead of four, and an assembly of
eighteen, six from Newport and four from each of the other towns.
It possessed full power to make such laws as were not contrary to
those of England, "considering the nature and constitution of the
place and people there," a phrase borrowed with a slight change of
wording from the patent of 1644. Neither in this charter nor in any
of the colonial charters of so early a date was the requirement imposed that the laws be sent to England for confirmation or disallowance.

The general assembly, consisting of the governor or deputy governor, the assistants, and the deputies—all of whom were to give
their solemn engagement to the new government by oath or by
affirmation if their conscience were against taking oaths—was to sit
twice a year, in May and October, or oftener if necessary. It was to
have extensive authority over the affairs of islands and mainland,
to set up such courts of common law as it should think fit, to create
towns and cities, and to inflict penalties, pecuniary and corporal,
upon delinquents and offenders according to the course of other
corporations "within this our kingdom of England." The inhabitants of the colony were granted free power and liberty of fishing
upon the coast of New England, the right to go a-whaling, and all
privileges of trade and the transportation of settlers "not prohibited
by any laws or statute of this our realme." They could without molestation pass and repass into and through any other English colony

nection. It is too long to be quoted here. *Calendar State Papers, Colonial*, 1661–1668,
pp. 341–343.

upon their lawful and civil occasions, an allowance which Williams must have welcomed with especial thankfulness as he thought of the day twenty years before when Massachusetts would not permit him to sail from any of her ports.

But supremely comforting to the colony was the preservation of its invaluable "liberty in religious concernments," a phrase that runs through both of Clarke's petitions, is found in the charter, and appears not infrequently as one of Williams's favorite expressions. True piety rightly grounded upon gospel principles was, in his mind, the best and greatest security to sovereignty. To him it must have seemed a wonderful demonstration of God's goodness that the king, while allowing the colony the free exercise and enjoyment of its civil rights, could of his "especial grace, certain knowledge and mere motion" (familiar words in all royal charters) grant the people there that liberty in the true Christian faith and worship of God which they had sought to establish with so much travail but always with peaceable minds and in loyal subjection to the king's progenitors and to himself. To him it must have seemed still more wonderful for the king to say that he hoped it would be no breach of the unity and uniformity established in England to declare that no persons in Rhode Island should be molested for any differences in the field of religion but should enjoy their own judgments and consciences "in matters of religious concernments, any law, statute or clause, usage or custom of realm to the contrary thereof not withstanding." Nevertheless such a statement is remarkable chiefly as the official utterance of a government the executive and legislative members of which were to continue for twenty-five years longer in England a policy of religious persecution.[1] Probably Roger Williams did not realize the widespread desire among the people of that country for measures of forbearance and toleration or the willingness of men of influence to allow in the colonies what they would not concede at home.

The charter also defined the boundaries of the colony and seemingly settled for all time the troubles which Rhode Island had been having to keep her territory intact.[2] The northern boundary was

1. Governor John Archdale of South Carolina had the idea when he wrote of the proprietors of that colony as having "an Over-plus Power to grant Liberty of Conscience, altho' at Home was a hot Persecuting Time" (*Early Carolina*, Original Narratives, p. 294).

2. For a detailed account of the tangled story of the Narragansett land claims, which cannot be given here, see Richman, *Rhode Island: its Making and Meaning*, ch. XV.

easily and simply described as the southern line of Massachusetts, which though wrongly surveyed by Woodward and Saffery in 1642, was finally and without great difficulty determined with a slight loss to Massachusetts in 1751.[1] But the eastern and western lines, as defined in the text, involved Rhode Island in prolonged controversies with Plymouth and Connecticut, largely because the words of the charter were interpreted by men who were filled with that passionate desire for land which characterized this early period and who were determined to defend their positions with an almost total disregard of any other point of view than their own. How could such men agree on the drawing of a line, which in the words of the charter extended "toward the east, or eastwardly, three English miles to the east and northeastern parts of Naragansett Bay, as the said bay lyeth or extendeth itself from the ocean on the south, or southwardly, unto the mouth of the river which runneth toward the town of Providence, and from thence along the eastwardly side or banke of the said river (higher called by the same of the Seacunk river), up to the falls called Patuckett falls, being the most westwardly lyne of Plymouth colony, and soe from the said falls, in a straight line, due north untill it meete with the aforesayd line of the Massachusetts Collony"?

This obscure and almost unintelligible description was bad enough at best, but its meaning was rendered much more difficult by the Plymouth claim under the Bradford patent, which Rhode Island refused to recognize on the ground that her charter was a letters patent direct from the crown while the Plymouth document was only a land grant from the Council for New England, itself an inferior corporation.[2] Twenty years before, in 1642, Plymouth, aroused by the want of orderly government in Providence and the "riots and disorders" occurring there, proposed to annex the whole territory,[3] but it was not until she had become a member of the New England

---

1. *Rhode Island Colonial Records*, V, 322–325.

2. The Privy Council committee, to which the appeals from Rhode Island and Massachusetts were referred, said, in its final report recommending the dismissal of the appeals, that "the recital of said letters patent in the deed from the Council of Plymouth [the Council for New England] to Bradford is not sufficient evidence against the King's charter—that the Council of Plymouth being a corporation could not create a corporation." Plymouth colony was never a corporation and its legal status was never equal to that of Rhode Island. When, however, Massachusetts acquired the Plymouth territory in 1691 the situation changed; after that date the contest was between two corporations of equal legal standing.

3. *Plymouth Colony Records*, II, 37.

Confederation and had the backing of the three Puritan colonies that she decided to take definite action and annex Aquidneck.[1] The charter brought that effort to an end and threw Plymouth back within the bounds of the Bradford patent. But even so, what did the words of the charter mean? In December, 1665, the royal commissioners in order to effect a temporary settlement for the sake of peace, ignored Rhode Island's assertion that the charter gave her "a thread of land three miles broad all the length of the mayne land lying next to Narragansett Bay" and drew the line at the water's edge to a point opposite Mount Hope, thence to the Seekonk and up the Seekonk and Pawtucket rivers to the south line of Massachusetts.[2] As there was nothing in the commissioners' report binding on the colony, Rhode Island paid no attention to it and, later, boldly pushing her boundary line further to the east and claiming that the headwaters of the Taunton River were the starting point, drew the line thence southward to the ocean. Massachusetts, who had acquired Plymouth by the charter of 1691, indignantly refused to consider any such encroachment and took her stand upon the commissioners' report. A deadlock ensued which sent Rhode Island to England in an appeal to the king (1734). Nothing was done until 1738, when the Privy Council took the matter in hand and during the next three years obtained reports from the Board of Trade and two commissions of review, one after another. To the findings of the second of these commissions Massachusetts objected so strongly and demanded with so much insistence a rehearing of the case as to arouse the resentment of the council. The latter, declaring that the Massachusetts demand was both "frivolous and vexatious," dismissed the appeals of the two colonies and on May 28, 1746, confirmed without further discussion the recommendation of the second commission, that of 1741. This ended the matter. The line was run in 1747, pretty much as it is today. Five towns—Tiverton, Little Compton, Bristol, Warren, and Cumberland—were taken from Massachusetts and given to Rhode Island.[3]

1. *Ibid.*, IX, 23, 110.

2. *Rhode Island Colonial Records*, II, 128. The Privy Council committee said that the action of the royal commissioners in 1665 "appears to have been only a temporary order for preserving the peace on the borders of both colonies, without determining the rights and titles of either." *Acts Privy Council, Colonial*, III, §445.

3. *Ibid.*, §323 (pp. 436–449), appendix v; *Rhode Island Colonial Records*, V, 199–201; *Report on the Boundary Line between Rhode Island and Massachusetts, 1664–1836* (1840). The representation of the Board of Trade of June 17, 1740, recom-

The western boundary, between Rhode Island and Connecticut, would seem to have offered fewer opportunities for differences of opinion, inasmuch as the agreement between Winthrop and Clarke had paved the way for the line as described in the Rhode Island charter. The colony was to be "bounded on the west, or westerly, to the middle or channel of a river there, commonly called and knowne by the name of Pawcatuck, alias Pawcawtuck river, and soe along the sayd river, as the greater or middle streams thereof reaches or lyes upp into the north country, northward into the head thereof, and from thence by a streight line drawn due north, untill it meets with the south lyne of the Massachusetts Collonie." This would seem to be clear enough and to show that in 1663 the crown intended Pawcatuck River to mark the western border of Rhode Island. This intention was confirmed two years later when the royal commissioners erected the Narragansett country into the King's Province, with full right of control vested in the king and powers of administration in the hands of five commissioners appointed by Rhode Island. Bona fide settlers were allowed to remain but traders and land speculators were excluded. In this way the English authorities hoped to place the situation beyond dispute. But they had not reckoned with the ingenious reasoning of the New England Puritan. Connecticut not only repudiated the agreement between Winthrop and Clarke on the ground that with the sealing of the Connecticut charter Winthrop had ceased to be the colony's agent and so was without authority to act for the colony, but she also repudiated the doings of the commissioners because their most important member, Colonel Nicolls, had not been present when the decision was reached to set apart the King's Province.

The story of the long-drawn-out negotiations between the two colonies would easily fill a volume. At first neither side would yield a hair's breadth, Rhode Island standing on her charter, claimed to the Pawcatuck River; Connecticut, insisting that her charter was the older, claimed to Narragansett Bay. "By Narragansett River," said Connecticut, "we mean that which was granted to us and which was known by that name thirty years ago." To which Rhode Island

mending a commission of review, and giving the "heads and clauses" of such commission, is in Colonial Office 5:917, pp. 306–307, 308–314. These "heads and clauses" are also in *Acts Privy Council, Colonial*, III, §§440–443. The part which the Board of Trade played as referee can be traced in the *Board of Trade Journal*, 1735–1741, and 1742–1749, indices.

replied that her charter and the king's commissioners made it perfectly plain what that river was and that it was not Narragansett
Bay. Said Connecticut, "To reiterate the same thing is tedious and
unprofitable." Rhode Island retorted, "We cannot but admire [won-
der] you should complain of reiteration." Connecticut came back
with, "We cannot but admire with you that when we speak playne
English it should be so difficult for you to understand." This sort of
repartee went on for years, rejoinder and counter-rejoinder making
up the bulk of the argument. Men living along the border and
claimed by both colonies were wholly at a loss to know in whose
jurisdiction their lands lay and to whom they should pay their
taxes. Quarrels ensued, reprisals occurred, individuals were arrested
and jailed or compelled to give bonds of obedience, and the whole
region was in an uproar.[1]

The dispute was carried to England several times, commissions of
review were appointed, and what seemed like an agreement was
reached in 1703. Connecticut receded from Narragansett Bay to a
line drawn north and south through Worden's Pond, thus yielding
about half of the territory, but Rhode Island would not accept this
and the line was finally drawn at Pawcatuck. An attempt to run
this line was made in 1714 but Connecticut suspended operations
and the dispute was taken up again. Connecticut first went back to
Narragansett Bay, then offered to compromise on the Worden's
Pond line, and at last apparently frightened at her own temerity,
wrote the king to do as he pleased "notwithstanding the priority of
our charter." Wearied with the prolonged wrangling she declared
that she was willing to leave the settlement to the Privy Council,
hoping thereby to put "a perpetual end to the controversy and confirm that peace between us and them which your lordships have
been pleased to express such a regard for."[2] The final line was agreed

1. *Connecticut Colonial Records*, II, appendix x.
2. *Acts Privy Council, Colonial*, III, §4. The documents in the case are very voluminous and may be consulted in the printed volumes of the Connecticut and Rhode
Island colonial records (especially *Connecticut Colonial Records*, II, appendix vi)
and in the manuscript volumes in the State Archives, Boundaries, three volumes
(especially I, no. 28), and Foreign Correspondence, two volumes. The representations
of the Board of Trade on the subject are dated March 22, 1723, and January 25,
1726, and are to be found in Colonial Office 5:1293, pp. 280–286, 346–351. The
first of these became the basis of the committee's report to the council and the second
is the answer to the Privy Council's request of January 17, 1726, that the board ascertain whether the two colonies were "willing to submit themselves to His Majesty's

to in 1727 and surveyed in 1738, both sides holding out in small details to the end.[1]

The experience had been very bitter and very expensive for both colonies. There can be no doubt that both Rhode Island and Connecticut, against whom charges for alleged misdemeanors had long been on file in the plantation office at Whitehall, were brought to terms not by any conviction reached on either side as to the merits of the case, but by the fear of losing their charters. The Board of Trade recommended in 1721 and again in 1723 and 1726 that they be requested to surrender these precious documents voluntarily and accept annexation to New Hampshire. So tangled a web had the colonies woven in their many years of mutual recrimination that the board said that if the royal authorities did not intervene the dispute was likely to become perpetual, "to the great disturbance of the peace of these colonies and the utter discouragement of those wishing to plant and settle there." The New England character was enduring in more ways than one, and the executive authorities in England performed many a real service in cutting Gordian knots that the colonies could not undo for themselves.

The confusion caused by these inter-colonial disputes was to the Rhode Island leaders the more embarrassing because of the willingness of some of the colony's own people to listen to the siren voices from without suggesting that they aid in disintegrating the territory by bringing their lands under the jurisdiction of their neighbors. We have already noticed the efforts of Coddington and the Arnolds, who at one time or another intrigued to detach large and small portions of the colony's area. Even Williams himself, in a moment of discouragement at the seeming hopelessness of his task, had thought of putting the colony under the government of Massachusetts and might possibly have done so had not Cromwell ordered it to continue as a separate community and bring to an end its domestic quarreling.[2] But the overt act within the colony that had kept it in a state of disturbance for some forty years was the attempt of William

immediate government." The course of the inquiry in England may be followed in the *Board of Trade Journal*, 1723–1728, pp. 8–12, 209–210, 213, 329.

1. *Connecticut Colonial Records*, VII, 178–179. Bad feeling continued to exist between the two colonies, each claiming that the monuments erected along the line were unfairly placed, so that the line was not finally accepted by each until 1742. In 1840 the line was resurveyed, but no material changes were made, the boundary remaining approximately as agreed upon in 1703.

2. *Narragansett Club Publications*, VI, 295.

Harris and his associates to obtain control of large tracts of territory in the central and western parts comprising, it has been estimated, 300,000 acres or a little less, covering perhaps a third of the whole.

William Harris, the so-called anarchist, malcontent, and litigant, was the one man that Roger Williams distinctly did not like. He was a turbulent soul, with a considerable knowledge of English law and procedure and possessed of unquestioned business shrewdness, sometimes of a dubious sort. He was amazingly active in mind and body, frequently changing his opinions, both political and religious —a habit that bore witness to the discontent that raged within him. He was given to controversy and was persistent in his efforts to obtain what he considered were his honest rights, particularly in matters of land. He spoke of himself as a "long and great sufferer" and "a weary traveller for the space of almost forty years in the wilderness of New England"; and though he was against the government in denying the right of the state to limit the sovereignty of man, he was hardly the "damnable villain and impudent morris dancer" that his enemies called him in language that was often violent and inflammatory. He had many redeeming qualities, won the confidence of men both in Rhode Island and in England, and was successful in nearly all his suits at law. He was Williams's chief opponent at Providence and the leading insurgent there, and so outspoken was he that in 1657 Williams brought a charge of treason against him "for his open defiance against our charter, all our laws and courts, the parliament of our Lord Protector Cromwell and all governments, and for saying that it was against his conscience to yield obedience to any human order amongst men."[1] Sidney Rider, one of Rhode Island's most learned antiquarians, writing in 1890, said that the history of Harris's land suits had never been told, that no one in Rhode Island understood them, and that nobody outside had ever tried to do so. But this statement will hardly hold true at the present time.[2]

The starting point in this protracted series of land litigations, in which Harris played the part of libelant, was the vagueness of the early memoranda recording the purchases from the Indians. These

1. *Rhode Island Court Records*, I, 25.
2. An excellent outline of the controversy, though brief, is given by I. B. Richman in his introduction to the *Harris Papers* (1902), but it is deficient in all that relates to the English end of the story. On Harris, as Connecticut's agent, see *Connecticut Colonial Records*, II, appendix xx; III, index.

memoranda, at first probably oral but later written down, were drawn with a looseness of phrase which though characteristic of many Indian deeds of the time were in this case exceptionally brief and ambiguous. Williams was not well versed in the language of conveyancing and the friendly sachems, Miantonomo and Canonicus, were unconcerned regarding the exact detail of boundaries and distances. The result was a series of law suits and attempted execution of judgments that kept the colony in something of a turmoil for twenty years. The clash of strong minds and the bitterness of feeling which accompanied this litigation created a state of discord and political ill will that for the time being destroyed the peace of the community. Providence in particular presented anything but a happy family group during this period and the good effects of the coming of the charter, which had promised to bring harmony and mutual coöperation in its train, and eventually did so, were, for the moment at least and as far as Providence was concerned, already spent. Williams might well speak of his "worne and withered brain" and call the greed for land in Rhode Island "one of the Gods of our New England which the eternal will destroy," as causing men to strive "vehemently about Lands! Lands! in this day of the Lords great judgments."[1] Nevertheless, despite the provocation, Williams's attitude toward Harris forms one of the least pleasant of the episodes in his career, for Harris with all his defects of character was not without friends. Though naturally Warwick was against him, Newport and Portsmouth were sympathetic and he had a loyal following even in Providence. He was influential in the affairs of the colony, was elected one of the assistants in 1668 the year after the events narrated above and continued to be so elected four times in the ten years that followed, after the Quakers came into control of the government in 1670 and before he himself went to England in May, 1679. But his whole life, as his son said later, was one of "journeys and charges, impoverishment and grievous toil and labour." We may not be surprised that the same son could speak of his "aged crasie mother,"[2] for the wives of many of these early settlers were

---

1. *Ibid.*, 1877–1878, Williams to Winthrop, August 24, 1669, pp. 64–67. The "bill containing several matters Composed in fowre particulars," mentioned in *Providence Records*, p. 105, is printed in *Harris Papers*, pp. 77–82, under the title "The ffirebrand discovered," a favorite term of Williams's as applied to Harris. In his *George Fox digg'd out of his Burrowes*, p. 205, he speaks of "W. Harris (a Fire-brand of Town and Colony and Country)."

2. *Publications*, Rhode Island Historical Society, IV, 198.

martyrs to their husbands' idiosyncrasies. In the main Harris commanded the confidence of all but the Providence and Warwick contingents, whose interest it was to oppose him, and he had the good will even of men of the type of Richard Wharton, a merchant of Boston, who befriended him and wrote of the "great respect" he had for him. Though self-willed and obstinate in his convictions, whether they touched his conscience or his land claims, he must have had some compensating characteristics or his fellows, many of them, would not have spoken so well of him or stood by him in emergencies. It is unfortunate that some of the leading founders of Rhode Island, such as Gorton and Harris, are known and judged only by the fervors and indiscretions of their youth or early man hood.

The tale of the Harris litigation is a long one,[1] but it is most illuminating as disclosing the domestic difficulties of Rhode Island, the relations existing among the New England colonies after the Restoration, and the dependence of all on the mother country in whatever concerned their boundary disputes. Then too the troubles in Providence throw light on the tendency to disorder which prevailed in the towns, in none of which was there any efficient local judicial system or regular method of watch and ward for the sake of keeping the peace. The early introduction of stocks, pillories, and whipping and the appointment of sergeants and constables helped somewhat to cope with the prevailing habit of fault finding and defamation, but the Rhode Island communities unlike those of Massachusetts and Connecticut never exercised a minute and disciplinary care over their members, and the entire absence of any single church organization and control made for an abundance of backbiting, slander, and scurrility. There were no Sunday laws or regulations that compelled attendance at church and the magistrates exercised very little authority except to punish breaches of the Sabbath as offenses against the civil law. There were the customary cases of drunkenness, theft, fornication, profanity, and assault and battery, but the number was not unusual, and there were the familiar modes of punishment, though they were not exceptionally severe. One rarely meets with mutilation, such as clipping the ears. A few offenders—men and women—were whipped, degraded, fined, or imprisoned, but again the number was not large.

1. See NOTE at the end of the chapter.

Many disputes were settled by arbitration, agreements were reached without trial, and individual differences seem rarely to have reached the point of personal encounters. As might well be expected in a colony of so many diverse claims and jarring jurisdictions, there were frequent verbal expressions of discontent, which took the form of "giving contemptuous speeches against the government," "speaking disrespectfully of the governor," "defaming the order of the colony," "and casting out defiant remarks against those in authority."[1] But such defiance of constitutional rule was not an unusual thing in New England, though perhaps more common in Rhode Island than elsewhere because of the separatistic sentiments of towns and people and the local dislike of magisterial interference.

As long as Rhode Island, island and mainland, remained isolated from commercial contact with such centers of trade as Boston and New Amsterdam, each of which was extending its activities and reaping the benefits of overseas intercourse, her people were veritably dwellers in the wilderness far removed from the world. Newport early felt the prick of commercial ambition and in time took the lead not only in Rhode Island but in some respects also of all other colonial seaport towns, except Boston and Philadelphia. It has been well said that "Rhode Island in the early days, and for nearly a hundred years, was synonymous with Newport, which like Venice depended on her ships for a place in the sun. She ploughed the sea. The back country was neglected, save as it furnished surplus products for her ships."[2] In all the towns at first wampum and peage, at so many shells a penny, passed current for payments and became legal tender for the discharge of rates and other public obligations. Soon such commodities as were raised by the labor of the colonists' own hands—corn, sheep, cattle, tobacco especially—supplemented the shell coinage and became the most important medium both within and without the colony. Little if any hard money was in circulation until after the coming of the charter, for the efforts of the commissioners of the New England Confederation to boycott trade

1. *Rhode Island Court Records, passim.* Robert West, the wife of Richard Scott, Ann Williams, and Rebecca Throckmorton were charged with being "comon aposers of all authority" (p. 26); others as "Ringleaders in new divisions in the colony" (pp. 27, 34). In Warwick a number of men were disfranchised, one of them for calling the officers of the towns "rouges and thieves," the whole town "rouges and thieves" also, and threatening to kill both mares and men.

2. Preston, *Rhode Island and the Sea* (Providence, 1932, p. 2; "Newport in the Eighteenth Century," *Publications,* American Antiquarian Society, October, 1906.

and to deal with Rhode Island only on their own terms,[1] checked for a time the circulation of the new silver coins of Massachusetts or "New England silver," as these coins were called. After the capture of Jamaica and the arrival of the charter both New England silver and Spanish silver from the West Indies began to trickle in, standing at a ratio with country commodities of twenty-five per cent appreciation. This meant that sterling, New England silver, country commodities, and peage at four a penny,[2] stood in a proportion of three, four, five, and sixty—nine pence sterling equaling one shilling New England silver, one shilling New England silver equaling one shilling three pence in kind, and one shilling three pence in kind equaling sixty shells of wampum or peage, a quarter of a fathom.

Of the commerce of Rhode Island in the seventeenth century we know very little. That it early began to flourish is more than probable, though in 1656 the statement is made that the colony was "not in a capacity to send out shipping" because of the oppressive attitude of the New England Confederation. One William Withington, presumably of Newport, hired in 1649 a half part in the ship *Beginning* of Boston, which he planned to send on a voyage to Barbados and Guinea and back to Barbados, Antigua, and Boston. Boston merchants sent to Rhode Island for tobacco, which in largest part they reshipped to London and elsewhere, and the frequent money transactions that are recorded seem to show that despite the attitude of the New England Confederation financial relations were maintained between the two colonies.[3] Coddington was sending horses to the West Indies in 1656 and it is evident that the traffic had been going on for some time, not only with Barbados but with Boston and New Amsterdam as well. Horses were shipped to South Carolina before 1682.

Our fullest information comes from the letter book of Peleg San-

1. *Rhode Island Colonial Records*, I, 397–398.
2. Before 1647 three shells went for a penny, later the rate fell to eight for a penny white, until finally (1662) peage was discarded altogether as a legal medium. For wampum as money in the colonies, see Weeden, "Indian Money as a Factor in New England Civilization," Johns Hopkins University *Studies*, II, viii–ix; *Rhode Island Colonial Records*, I, 217, 400, 474; Philhower, "Wampum, its Use and Value," *Proceedings*, New Jersey Historical Society, 4th ser., XV, 216–223; and in general, Beauchamp, *Wampum and Shell Articles Used by the New York Indians* (1901), pp. 351–356.
3. *Aspinwall Notarial Records*, pp. 220, 234, 321–322, 411, 412; *Rhode Island Colonial Records*, I, 337–338. The trade with the Dutch is mentioned as early as 1658, *ibid.*, 389.

ford (1666–1668), a native of the colony, who lived in Barbados until 1665. In that year he returned to Rhode Island where he played an important part in its affairs, as governor, lieutenant colonel, member of Andros's council, and finally judge of vice-admiralty. While in Barbados he and his brothers, whom he left behind him when he came back to Newport, served as agents or factors for their correspondents in Newport and Boston, the chief imports being cotton, rum, molasses, and sugar, which were exchanged for mares and horses, ewes and wethers, wool, pork, venison, beef, dried peas, bread, butter, pipe-staves, and anything else that Rhode Island furnished. There was communication elsewhere also, by land as well as by water, for sheep and probably hogs also were driven across country to Boston, as there were many flocks of sheep and many hog farms in the colony.

Of shipbuilding there is little trace. Anthony Low had a sloop built at Warwick in 1668 and in the same year a vessel of a hundred and twenty tons was on the ways at Newport, but the statement that the "phantom ship" of New Haven was built at Rhode Island in 1645 cannot be true.[1] Local shipbuilding developed slowly and for a long time the colony continued to employ vessels that were bought or hired from the shipwrights and merchants of both Boston and New Amsterdam. English goods in considerable variety came to Newport from Boston and Barbados—cloth, silks, haberdashery, iron work, and household furnishings—and the people of that town more than the others reaped the benefit. Sanford was a shrewd business man, as was Coddington, and was always ready to complain if the goods received were not satisfactory or the prices too high.[2] Thus early began that interchange of amenities between the colonists and their factors abroad, concerning inferior quality, exorbitant prices, misfits on one side and trash, refuse, underweights, and slow payments on the other—bickerings which were characteristic of all the colonies in the eighteenth century.

It is a remarkable fact in the history of New England that such a colony as Rhode Island should have emerged from its unpromising beginnings and developed in later times into a well compacted and united state. Roger Williams, its leader and inspiration, was a visionary with a profound belief in the efficacy of human liberty, but he

1. Atwater, *History of the Colony of New Haven*, p. 219. See below, p. 176, note 3.
2. *The Letter Book of Peleg Sanford*, 1666–1668, pp. 46, 57, 69–70, and *passim*.

cannot properly be called a statesman, for he knew little about practical government or the business of setting up a strong central organization. He never realized his ideals, for the traditions, habits, and limitations of his time were against him. The right of all men to have a part in government, which seems inherent in his understanding of the "consent of the people," was abrogated from the beginning by the definition of a freeman as a landowner and not an individual as such, and the property qualification thus imposed was retained in one form or another well on into the nineteenth century, long after all the states except Connecticut had rid themselves of the incubus. Soul liberty, though never seriously impaired, was in a measure repudiated by the disfranchising of the Roman Catholics in 1729, when Williams's doctrine that no one should be excluded from civil rights for his religious opinions was cast aside and a qualification was imposed based on what a man believed in matters of faith. His conviction that all forms of government should rest upon popular consent was ignored by the selfishness of a landowning minority that eventually brought upon the state the Dorr Rebellion of 1842. Though he worked for harmony, cultivated the spirit of humility, and made many personal sacrifices in the interest of peace and safety—accommodating and pacifying "their sad differences," as he wrote the town of Providence—he was constantly thwarted by those elements in the colony which were antagonistic to authority and which expressed themselves later in many acts of non-coöperation with other colonies and after 1787 with the federal union. The license which followed the attempts to apply the ideals of liberty of action and liberty of conscience as well as the vagueness of the early deeds and the looseness of the early organization made for thirty years of dissension which destroyed the harmony of the settlements and delayed union and peace. There is much justification for the remark that in the beginning Massachusetts had law but not liberty and Rhode Island liberty but not law. Few states have suffered more from the conflict between ideals and actualities or have labored more earnestly to establish their independence and to maintain their principles of government and conduct than has Rhode Island. It happened there, as it has happened elsewhere, that the new political, religious, and social experiment, noble though it might be, was able to succeed but slowly, as long as the people in whose interest it was undertaken showed themselves unable by habit or unwilling by temperament and convictions, to aid in its advancement.

NOTE: The original grant to Williams from the Sachems was for lands on the western side of the Seekonk, extending from the Pawtucket to the Pawtuxet rivers and on westward to certain landmarks familiar to the Indians. Of this area Williams conveyed the southern portion, October 8, 1638, to William Harris and twelve others, a grant containing some of the best meadow and grass land in the colony.[1] The original deed, or "Town Evidence" as it is usually called, gave to Williams "the lands and meaddowes upon the 2 fresh rivers, moushausuck and Wanasquatucket . . . from the River and Fields at Pautuckett, the great hill of Nestaconkitt on the norwest and the Indian towne of Mashapauge on the west," but sometime later, perhaps in 1658, there was a postscript, generally believed to be a forgery, which reads "m[emoran]d[um] 3 mo[nth] 9 die. This was all again confirmed by Miantunnomu he acknowledged this his act and hand, up the streams of Patuckett and Patuqutt without limetts we might have for our use of cattle."[2] This memorandum apparently is signed by Benedict Arnold and witnessed by Williams, but the latter in 1677 disclaimed his signature, when he wrote of "this hasty unadvised memorandum which one amongst us (not I) recorded," while Benedict Arnold is reputed to have denied on oath that he ever signed the document.[3]

A reason for the alleged forgery may be found in the following circumstance. On May 17, 1659, the general assembly authorized the town of Providence to buy out and clear off the Indians within its bounds and to add not more than three thousand acres to the territory it already possessed.[4] Immediately Harris took it upon himself, without the knowledge and consent of the others, as far as is known, to obtain from certain of the Indian sachems, brothers of Miantonomo and grandsons of Canonicus, three confirmatory deeds—confirmatory, that is, of the memorandum—of land for the use of the men of Providence and Pawtuxet, which extended twenty miles west from Providence and included not three thousand but three hundred thousand acres. The confirmatory deeds contain such large and loose phrases as "up the streams without limit or as far as they shall think fit" and "as far as the men aforesaid of providence and of Pawtuxet shall judge convenient for their use of cattle, as feeding, plowing, planting and all manner of plantation whatsoever."[5] In its possible implications such language opened up the whole western and northwestern region to the occupations of the white man, and though it favored the proprietors of Pawtuxet more than it did those of Providence the Providence town meeting indirectly approved of the purchase by "owning" the extension of the line, which had already

1. The Pawtuxet portion conveyed to Harris constituted the southern part of what may be called the township of Providence. In 1640 a division line was drawn for a short distance westward, separating Providence and Pawtuxet, about half way between the Wanasquatucket and the Pawtucket rivers. Maps may be found in Chapin, *Documentary History*, I, facing p. 216; *Harris Papers* (Rhode Island Historical Society, *Collections*, X), facing p. 376; and especially Richman, *Rhode Island: its Making and Meaning*, facing p. 461.

2. A facsimile of the "Town Evidence" is given in Chapin, *Documentary History*, I, facing p. 64, and various versions are in *Providence Records*, IV, 70–71; V, 296. On the forgery see Rider, "The Forgeries connected with the Deed given by the sachems Canonicus and Miantonomo to Roger Williams of the land on which the Town of Providence was planted," *Tracts*, no. 4; *Proceedings*, Rhode Island Historical Society, new series, I, pp. 185–213, 214–229; IV, 194–198, 231–234; Rider, *Book Notes*, VII, 157–162; X, 159; XI, 109–110, 277–279; XII, 148, 241–244, 280; XXII, 137; *Harris Papers*, p. 151. Mr. George T. Paine who had made a careful study of the Harris controversies, denies the fact of the forgery, Rider strenuously upholds it.

3. *Narragansett Club Publications*, VI, 398; *Harris Papers*, p. 34.

4. *Rhode Island Colonial Records*, I, 418.   5. *Providence Records*, V, 300–306.

been drawn in 1640 between Pawtuxet and Providence, for seventy miles or "as far as the men of Providence and the men of Pawtuxet see fitt." This recognition of the new territory as legitimately acquired rendered unnecessary any further reference of the matter to the general assembly of the colony, where it might have been more strictly scrutinized.[1]

As the Town Evidence fixed the western boundary at a hill and an Indian town, only three miles or so from Providence it is evident that the phrase in the memorandum "up the streams . . . without limetts . . . for our use of cattle" authorized the settlers to go no farther than three miles westward and that deeds confirmatory of the genuine Town Evidence could add nothing more. But Harris interpreted the confirmatory deeds differently. Insisting that the hill and the town were not proper boundaries he construed the range of the grant as extending to the headwaters of the Pawtuxet and Wanasquatucket rivers and by virtue of the confirmatory deeds he claimed all the land bounded on the south by the Pawtuxet. Acting on this claim he began his long and contentious career as a litigant by bringing suit against certain of the Gortonites at Warwick for trespass and damages. These individuals denied the charge on the ground that the territory in question, though north of the Pawtuxet, was within the Warwick bounds and consequently there had been no trespass. Harris in reply flouted the Warwick land claim as based on a purchase from inferior and "underling" sachems, while his own, based on the confirmatory deeds, was from those of a "most superior" sort. He brought the case before the court of trials and was awarded damages. Another suit against one Harrud went the same way, but in this case Harris though successful in his suit could not get execution, as Harrud threatened to kill anyone who attempted to enter upon his land. Even an appeal to the general assembly brought no better results.[2]

Harris next took up the matter with the town of Providence and demanded that the two towns, Providence and Pawtuxet, come to an agreement regarding the extension westward of the dividing line between them, which, as we have already seen, had been run for a short distance in 1640. This request brought the issue into the open, for if Williams and his friends should do as Harris wanted it would mean that they would have to come out publicly in favor of what Harris was doing. Now Williams viewed Harris's efforts with repugnance, for he considered the whole scheme a fraud upon the colony and Harris himself a pirate who had broken the laws of God and man. The proposal to extend the dividing line split the town into factions, one led by Harris, the Olneys father and son, and Thomas Field, the other by Williams, Arthur Fenner, Gregory Dexter, and John Throckmorton. Each faction held a town meeting, the Harris group making a violent attempt to break up that of its opponent, and each elected its own town officers and its own deputies to the general assembly. The Fenner meeting drew up a remonstrance to be sent to the other three towns, begging them to take notice of the "illegal and unjust proceedings of several persons at this meeting Endeavoring to prevent the Legall choyse of the officers for this Towne and also to declare [in general assembly] as in theyre wisdom they shall see cause." The assembly called the next month, July 2, 1667, did so de-

---

1. *Ibid.*, II, 125.

2. The constable reported that he and his assistant went to apprehend "the persons aforesaide but they resisted him and would not obey his word or warrant; the saide persons went all into the howse . . . and stood with axes in theire hands againste the doore it being open and holding them up redy to strike, and saide to the Constable and his ayde stand off at yoᵣ peril, but the Constable drew neere to the doore but could not enter with out danger of his life by reason of John Harrud and his Company which stood in a desperate posture, holding their Axes up at the Constable and his ayde and the said John Harrud did vow and proteste as he was a living man that if the Constable did sett foote within the doore he would knock him downe." *Harris Papers*, pp. 69–70, 154–157, 348–349. See also Nicolls's letter to Winthrop, July 24, 1667, *New York Colonial Documents*, III, 158–159.

clare and decided in favor of the Fenner meeting and admitted the Fenner delegates.[1] The Harris faction, angered by this decision, charged its adversaries with riotous conduct—the counter-charge bearing witness to the hysterical state of affairs in Providence—and again was turned down by the assembly.

The remainder of the Harris story can be quickly told. Inasmuch as Harrud and others of Warwick refused to give up their lands, against which execution had been ordered by the court of trials,[2] and threatened to resist whomsoever might be sent to compel them to do so, and inasmuch as Massachusetts and Plymouth as well as Connecticut were preparing to revive their claims to the Narragansett territory, Harris determined to appeal to the king, asking for the appointment of a commission—consisting of the governors of Massachusetts, Plymouth, Connecticut, and Rhode Island, sitting as a court with a jury—to act as a board of review and to render a report.[3] On receipt of this appeal the Privy Council referred the matter to its committee, the Lords of Trade, which recommended that such a commission be issued.[4] The Privy Council approved of the recommendation and caused commissions to be sent to each of the governors, August 4, 1675.[5] Action in New England was delayed by King Philip's war, but the court finally convened and the jury rendered its verdict, October 5, 1678, in Harris's favor.[6]

The town of Warwick, objecting to the unfair composition of the court, made up as it was of men unfriendly to both Providence and Warwick—"their mortal enemies," as Warwick's agents, Holden and Greene, called Massachusetts and Connecticut[7]—applied to the commissioners for permission to appeal to the king, but they refused saying that "it would be of il consequents to alow of any appeal to his Majesty." The town then sent John Greene and Randall Holden on the long and expensive journey to England to pray that a stop might be put to the execution of the verdict.[8] The petition was referred as before to the council's committee, which after a careful consideration of the case reported, on January 2, 1679 (approved by the Privy Council on the 31st), that Warwick should not be disturbed in the quiet and peaceable possession of its lands and that all other matters should remain as they were before the commission sat, until Harris and his partners had had an opportunity "in a lawfull defence of their rights before his Majesty in Councill" to make out a sufficient title to support their claims.[9]

In the meantime, before this order of council could reach Rhode Island, the "men of Providence" (Williams and Fenner), to whom the court of governors had entrusted the drawing of the dividing line between Providence and Pawtuxet, entered upon their task. With considerable ingenuity they succeeded in evading successfully the intent of the court order, which was to run a western boundary or "thwart" line from the upper reaches of the Wanasquatucket "directly" to the Pawtuxet, that is, at right angles to the river and by the shortest route. What they did was to locate the "head" not at the upper reaches, but considerably lower down, where several tributaries joined to make the main stream, and from there they carried the line at an

---

1. *Providence Records*, III, 102-106; *Harris Papers*, pp. 74-77; *Rhode Island Colonial Records*, II, 200-202 (for the general assembly's letter to Providence, *ibid.*, 202-204); *Warwick Records*, p. 178; *Proceedings*, Rhode Island Historical Society, new series, I, 223-224; *Rhode Island Court Records*, II, 80.

2. *Harris Papers*, pp. 154-155.   3. *Ibid.*, pp. 129-142.

4. *Acts Privy Council, Colonial*, I, §1025; *Calendar State Papers, Colonial*, 1675-1676, §§766-768, 1044; Colonial Office 5:903, pp. 319-329, 346-350 (not printed in the *Harris Papers*); *Harris Papers*, pp. 119-179, 214-220, 220-222.

5. *Connecticut Colonial Records*, II, appendix xx.

6. *Acts Privy Council, Colonial*, I, §810.

7. *Calendar State Papers, Colonial*, 1677-1680, §1026; *Harris Papers*, p. 269.

8. *Calendar State Papers, Colonial*, 1677-1680, §§766-768, 858.

9. *Acts Privy Council, Colonial*, I, §1244; *Harris Papers*, pp. 312-334; Colonial Office 5:903, pp. 319-329; *Calendar State Papers, Colonial*, 1677-1680, §672.

acute angle to a point on the Pawtuxet only three and a half miles from the mouth where it flowed into Narragansett Bay, thus shutting off entirely Harris's western claims. The line was not accepted by the commissioners and another was run which starting as did the former ended at the mouth of the Pachaset River, only six miles farther up the Pawtuxet. This was not satisfactory to Harris, who demanded that the line end some ten or twelve miles farther on. When he asked the commissioners just where they meant the line to go the latter asked the jury what it meant by its verdict. Nine of the jurymen replied[1] that they had in mind "a square line . . . W.S.W. . . . to the Pawtuxet River." This said the commissioners was the line that ought to be run, but as there seemed to be some doubt as to the legality of the procedure, it was agreed to leave the final determination to the king.[2]

Consequently Harris in May, 1679, set sail for England, arriving there just as Holden and Greene were returning to Rhode Island, and he spent the first weeks of June in obtaining a re-opening of the case. As Holden and Greene had complained of the unfairness of Massachusetts and Connecticut and as Harris was convinced that Rhode Island was partial to the other side, furthermore as the Privy Council and the king were exasperated with Massachusetts because of her recent purchase of New Hampshire from the Gorges descendants, the decision was reached by the Lords of Trade, June 19, 1679, and by the Privy Council, July 2, to re-try the case, with the governor and magistrates of Plymouth sitting as the court.[3] The court met at Providence, October 28, 1679, heard the evidence and decided, as the court of governors had done, in Harris's favor.[4]

Harris, who had returned from England in September of the same year, now applied for the execution of the verdict, the last of many which he had received since the first trial in the colony's court in 1660, nearly twenty years before. In answer, the governor and council of Plymouth named John Smith, town sergeant of Newport, to carry out the royal order and to put Harris in possession of his property. Smith was a Warwick partisan and one whom Walter Clarke, the deputy governor, and Thomas Ward, an assistant, both of Newport, objected to as "not a meete man to be employed in this service."[5] And so it proved. Smith accompanied by John Greene and calling for Harris to join them and point out his properties, failed to go anywhere near Masantatuck, where Harrud and others held possession by force, but, apparently on the ground that Harris could not show a deed to the property, contented himself with entering on property several miles away.[6] Harris, disgusted with Smith's chicanery and dissatisfied with the drawing of the "thwart" line, refused to have anything more to do with Smith and hastily, almost secretly, prepared to go to England for the third time (1664, 1679, 1680), in order to obtain an order from the king regarding the execution and the western boundary.

He sailed, December 25, 1679, in the *Unity* of Boston, but on January 24, 1680, the vessel was taken by the Algerines[7] and he was sold as a slave in the market-place of Algiers to a "pateroone," who confined him awaiting the payment of a ransom. His release was finally effected through the activities of William Blathwayt, a "Mr. Deane," and the colony of Connecticut, whose agent Harris was,[8] on the

1. The other three, the Rhode Island members of the jury, declined to answer, on the ground that the case was closed and could not legally be opened.
2. *Harris Papers*, pp. 264–265, October 5, 1678.
3. *Calendar State Papers, Colonial*, 1677–1680, §§1026 (inadequately calendared), 1044, 1056; *Acts Privy Council, Colonial*, I, §1291; *Harris Papers*, p. 271; Colonial Office 5:903, pp. 346–350.
4. *Harris Papers*, pp. 314–317; *Calendar State Papers, Colonial*, 1677–1680, §1173.
5. *Harris Papers*, pp. 319, 347–350, 355.   6. *Ibid.*, pp. 286–297.
7. *Ibid.*, p. 332, *Calendar State Papers, Colonial*, 1677–1680, p. 589; Hull, *Diary*, p. 246 (*Transactions*, American Antiquarian Society, III).
8. *Connecticut Colonial Records*, III, 51, 72, notes; appendices, xxi, xxiii–xxxvi. That

payment of £300, the total amount with additional charges coming to £439. He reached London probably late in 1681, worn out with worry, travel, and hard usage, and died there three days after his arrival, at the house of his friend, John Stokes, a baker, who kept an inn "at the sign of the pub," in Wentworth Shrub, near Spital-fields.[1] With his death the chief litigant in the case was removed, and though his associates and their heirs made several attempts to obtain an execution of the king's decree and petitioned first Governor Sir Edmund Andros and later Queen Anne nothing came of the effort, and on June 12, 1707, the appeal was finally dismissed and the case ended.[2] The final dividing line between Providence and Pawtuxet was amicably agreed on and run in 1711–1712.

Connecticut should have selected Harris as her agent in England to defend her boundary claims against Rhode Island is suggestive as showing the attitude toward that colony of each party to the arrangement.

1. *Harris Papers*, pp. 322-331, 343, 350-351.
2. *Ibid.*, pp. 345-347, 351-353, 354-355, 360-362, 364-367; *Acts Privy Council, Colonial*, II, §980.

CHAPTER III

THE BEGINNINGS OF CONNECTICUT

THUS far in our narrative we have seen that those who left Massachusetts Bay, either as the result of an edict of banishment or because of a dislike of the Puritan system, had made their way to the southward, toward that great body of water which forms so large a part of the present state of Rhode Island. But already there were indications of migration in another direction. Not until 1632, as far as we know, had any white man attempted to penetrate that vast wilderness stretching as a dense and forbidding barrier between Massachusetts and the Hudson River. Except for a few trading posts and rudimentary villages that the Dutch had established, the whole region was almost unknown and entirely unoccupied save by the Indian tribes, amongst which the Pequots, driven eastwardly by invading Mohawks, were a disturbing and menacing factor. At the beginning the Massachusetts settlers had pushed almost but a few miles back from the bay, and as long as land was available, had clung to the rivers as convenient lines of communication with the more thickly inhabited area along the coast. No white men, except occasionally a trapper, hunter, or explorer, had as yet made his way into this wilderness of forest, which covered more than nine-tenths of New England,[1] and no group of men had as yet faced the difficult task of clearing the land and establishing a settlement under such unpropitious conditions. Implements of husbandry brought from England were not well adapted to fell the huge trees, clear the matted undergrowth, and subdue the stubborn soil that made the region what it was, and for the moment there was no inexorable necessity of widening the area of occupation. The Dutch from Manhattan had sailed easterly along the southern coast in their search for favorable trading sites, and men of the Oldham type had

1. There appears to have been few if any open "barrens" or rocky "barrens" in New England as there were in the South. Maryland, for example, had many open spaces, often miles in extent, dry land without timber (*Maryland Magazine*, XXX, 121–122). Still there must have been in New England much marshland along the rivers and rocky upland with little timber back from the coast, and along the Connecticut were many "pine barrens interspersed with unimprovable swamps."

doubtless trodden the Indian paths and visited the Indian clearings and villages in pursuit of bargains in furs, but no permanent results had come of their effort beyond the gains acquired from barter and trade.

The Dutch, early in their search for trade, had brought to the colonists at Plymouth and the Bay a knowledge of the existence of a great river flowing southward from the interior into Long Island Sound, and local Connecticut Indians, seeking protection from the warlike Pequots, had added further information regarding the fertility and wholesomeness of the upper river meadows and their accessibility, either by water or by way of the numerous paths that the Indians were accustomed to use in their journeyings from one part of the country to another.[1] But the first man, of whom we have record, to seek the inner waters of the Connecticut River for the purpose of exploration and the discovery of opportunities for trade was Edward Winslow of Plymouth, who, having returned from an agency in England in the summer of 1632, set out soon after to investigate the possibilities of profit in the Connecticut valley. Among the Plymouth people he was the most energetic of all in contriving ways and means whereby his fellow "undertakers" might increase the wealth of the colony in order to pay off the debt to the London merchants in England. Some years before, after the break with the merchants, he had gone to the Kennebec in the interest of fishing and since that time had been indefatigable in his efforts to enlarge the scope of the colony's activities. He had familiarized himself already with the back country of Plymouth, having gone into the interior as far as Sowams and Narragansett Bay, and except for Roger Williams he probably knew the Indians, though not their language, better than anyone else of his time in New England.[2] The remarkably exact boundaries of the Bradford patent of 1630 were undoubtedly due to him. That two years later he should have ex-

1. There were ten or more small Indian tribes occupying the region afterward settled by the people from Massachusetts. They were all peacefully inclined toward the English and in the main continued friendly during the years that followed. The most important were the Podunks, Scanticooks, Saukiogs, Massacoes, Wangunks, Poquonacks, Metianucks, and Tunxis. The sachem Waginacut of the Podunks and Natawanut of the Metianucks were the ones who in 1631 visited Plymouth and Boston, hoping to persuade the English to come into the Connecticut valley, by describing the advantages of the region. Winthrop refused, but the information may have led to the trip which Winslow made the next year.

2. See his "Account of the Natives of New England" in 1624. Morton, *New England Memorial* (1855), pp. 486–494.

tended his quest to the Connecticut River is not only reasonable in itself but is proved by recorded evidence also. In his letter to John Winthrop, the elder, in 1644, he speaks of his "experimental knowledge of the first beginnings" there and of his selection "of a place (and the place after possessed) the year before the Dutch began in the River . . . which was not a *vacuum domicilium* but inhabited the year before."[1] The implication of these words is that Winslow was at the site of the present Windsor in 1632 and did something more there than merely view the land. He evidently picked out and occupied temporarily the spot that Lieutenant Holmes purchased the next year.

Officially Massachusetts would have nothing to do with the proposal made to her in July, 1633,[2] by Winslow and Bradford, who journeyed to the Bay for the purpose of persuading the Puritan leaders to join with Plymouth in a trading expedition to Connecticut; but others of the colony were not so backward. They may have been, as Hubbard says, directed by a special providence to make the venture, but their main inducement was to take advantage of an opportunity for trade which the new information furnished. Among those who were ready at once to try out the wilderness was John Oldham, a pioneer of many experiences with both white men and Indians in early New England. He with Samuel (probably not John) Hall and two others, went overland in September, 1633, and "taking a view of the country discovered many very desirable places upon the same river, fit to receive many hundred inhabitants."[3]

1. *New England Genealogical and Historical Register*, XXIX, 238–239. The same letter is in Davis' edition (1826) of the *New England Memorial*, pp. 394–396. A similar statement is to be found in the proceedings of the New England Confederation, 1644 (Hazard, *State Papers*, II, 215). For Plymouth in Connecticut see Bradford, *History*, II, 164–171.

2. Information regarding this proposal must have been sent to England by Winthrop or some one else in Massachusetts, for Emmanuel Downing knew of the existence of the Connecticut River in 1633. Historical Manuscripts Commission, *Twelfth Report*, II, 39.

3. Winthrop, *Journal*, I, 108; Hubbard, *History of New England*, pp. 169–170. Roger Williams, in his preface to *The Bloudy Tenent*, mentions a John Hall as one who at this time went to Connecticut, and Winthrop may be referring to the same when he says that in August, 1633, "a bark was set forth to Connecticut and those parts to trade" (107). The two Halls are quite different persons. Samuel Hall (possibly the one who was at Ipswich in 1635–1636) died at Malden, Essex, in 1680; John Hall is said to have arrived at Boston in 1633, was admitted a freeman, May 14, 1634, and died at Wallingford, Connecticut, May 3, 1676. Possibly Hubbard knew Samuel Hall personally and may have got his information directly from him. Williams may be referring to a later journey, that of January 20, 1634 (Winthrop,

Returning with specimens of beaver, hemp, and black lead, Oldham persuaded a number of others from Watertown, where he was living as a freeman of the colony, to join with him the next year in a second expedition. Consequently in the autumn of 1634, with eight or nine companions, the names of whom have been identified,[1] he went again to the Connecticut, probably this time by water,[2] and passed the winter in hastily erected houses at Pyquag, the Indian name of Wethersfield, which he made his headquarters for trade among the Indians. He was a man of a roving disposition, moving from place to place in quest of corn and furs, and going back and forth between the colonies as occasion demanded. He was probably frequently away from his Pyquag cabin, leaving others to look after his interests there. Mrs. Winthrop writes of sending a letter by him to her son at Saybrook in 1636, which he could easily have delivered as he went in his pinnace to the mouth of the river on his way to Long Island or to one of the lesser islands at the eastern end of the Sound in pursuit of Indian trade. We know that he was at Saybrook in April, 1636,[3] and was undoubtedly well known to the residents of the fort there. The fact that he was murdered by the Indians at Block Island shows that he went far afield in pursuit of his bargains and it is not at all unlikely that he delivered Mrs. Winthrop's letter on this very expedition. Also Roger Williams must have known him, for Oldham had a claim to an island in Narragansett Bay, and Williams may well have entertained him at his house in Providence.

The Dutch, aroused to activity by the appearance of the Englishmen on the river, had already sent a small vessel thither in June, 1633, and had erected on the southern side of the little river flowing into the Connecticut, which today bisects the city of Hartford,[4] a

Journal, I, 108), in which John took part. On the identity of these Halls, Stiles, *Ancient Wethersfield*, II, appendix ii; James Shepard, *John Hall of Wallingford* (1902). Winslow's report may well have induced a number of Watertown people to undertake the journey. Such activity would not be surprising as Watertown at this time faced the frontier.

1. For the list, with brief sketches, see Stiles, *Ancient Wethersfield*, I, 24–29.
2. If Oldham made his way overland where did he get the pinnace in which he navigated the river and Sound? He could hardly have built one at Pyquag (Wethersfield) large enough to sail to Block Island.
3. *Collections, Massachusetts Historical Society*, 4th series, VII, 66.
4. The Dutch claim to a settlement on the Connecticut River in 1623 rests on their belief that the first colonists came to Manhattan in that year and immediately "sent two families and six men to Hartford River," as Catherine Trico puts it in her deposition of 1683 (*Documentary History of New York*, III, 50). In all later accounts of their own beginnings they insisted on such early settlement (*New York Colonial*

"slight-forte," upon which they mounted two guns. Three months later Lieutenant William Holmes, who had been commissioned by Winslow, then governor of the Plymouth colony, to occupy the place picked out the preceding year, sailed up the river and past the Dutch fort, bearing the ready-made materials for a trading house.[1] He set up this frame structure about nine miles farther on, within a short distance of, but below, the "rivulet," as the Tunxis or Farmington River was then called, surrounded it with a palisade, and purchased of the Indians land on both sides of the great river. Thus, before Oldham reached Pyquag, there were two trading posts at well selected points to the northward, one of the Dutch and the other of the Plymouth people, the latter the better located because lying nearer the main source of the fur supply up the stream. Oldham in his traffic did not compete with these others because his field of action was down the river into the Sound.

The restlessness of the Bay reached a climax in 1635, when a desire to migrate seized upon many of the people of Dorchester, Newtown, and Watertown, later spreading to Roxbury. Reports of the attractiveness of the Connecticut region were partly responsible for this desire, stimulating the urge for more and better land, always an incitement in frontier movements everywhere. The fear of the

Documents, I, 286; II, 133) and apparently believed the place had been continuously occupied since that time. Such an early occupation is not impossible, in view of the plan of the Dutch West India Company to erect four forts at advantageous localities for trade, one of which was to be on the Connecticut, but the date 1623 must in any case be rejected because "there were no settlements of families in New Netherland before 1624" (Paltsits, "Founding of New Netherland in 1626," *Proceedings,* American Antiquarian Society, April, 1924, p. 53). Continued occupation is, however, wholly unlikely, for there is every reason to think that the place, if ever actually taken over, was early abandoned. Samuel Blommaert was granted a patroonship there in 1629 (Vol. III, index), but he never took up the grant, a fact which would seem to indicate that the place was still an empty wilderness. There are no references anywhere to activities on the Connecticut until 1633. We know a great deal of what was happening at Manhattan, Fort Orange, and the South River, but of anything taking place on the Connecticut the records are silent.

1. What a Pilgrim post looked like can be seen from the illustrations in Lombard's article on the restoration of Aptucxet, at the western end of Manomet portage, Cape Cod (*Old Time New England,* XXIII, 159–174; also Bradford's *History,* II, 215, to which oddly enough, Lombard does not refer). There is a mention of Aptucxet in *New Netherland* (Original Narratives), pp. 109–110. The Windsor post was probably a much smaller building than that at Aptucxet, as its beams and clapboards had to be carried in Holmes's vessel. Bradford tells us that it was surrounded by a palisade. The "old palisade" in Windsor was built later by the inhabitants at the time of the Pequot War as a place of safety. Most of the townspeople seem to have removed within its walls.

Indians, which had been a deterrent in the past, having diminished somewhat through the news that a plague of smallpox had
greatly reduced their numbers, a pioneer group from Dorchester,
with perhaps a few from Newtown and Watertown, ventured, in
the summer, probably toward the end of June, to make the journey,
either through the woods or by shallops around Cape Cod, under
the lead, it is supposed, of Roger Ludlow.[1] This company was followed later by others, who as reported by Jonathan Brewster—son
of Elder Brewster and agent in charge of the trading house at
Windsor[2]—were arriving almost daily. From one quarter or another,
by land and by water they came, "hankering," as Brewster puts it,
for the lands of the valley. Though not a little embarrassed by the
unexpected invasion, Brewster received the newcomers kindly, fed
and housed some of them, provided others with guides and canoes,
and became their intermediary in an unsuccessful negotiation with
the Dutch for a part of the latter's territory.

For these friendly offices he was ill-requited. The Dorchester
people ignored the Plymouth title to the meadows north of the
rivulet and proceeded to lay out their home lots and build their
houses along the high ground above and west of the great river.
They even seized upon part of the territory which the Plymouth
people had purchased of the Indians, just as Holmes had occupied,
under Winslow's prior claim, lands which the Dutch had acquired
not of the local Indians but of the Pequots. They called it "the
Lord's Waste" and therefore open to all, under the conviction then
prevailing among many of the Puritans that they had "a common
right to [all new land] with the rest of the sons of Noah." Only

1. There is reason to think that those who founded the Dorchester plantation in
1635 went by water. In the deed of purchase half the price is recorded as paid down
and the remainder to be paid "at the coming up of our next pinnace." Matthew
Grant also used the phrase "up here," that is, up the river, in speaking of the Dorchester men who came from Massachusetts. Windsor Land Records, I, 196.

If Ludlow was with this first party, as is stated by Sir Richard Saltonstall in his
letter to Winthrop, then he must have returned to Dorchester with those that went
back in the early winter of 1635–1636, as his presence there is attested by the Dorchester records. We know that he took part in the negotiations that winter between
John Winthrop, Jr., and the Hooker-Haynes group.

2. Was Brewster on the vessel with Holmes in 1633? He was in charge of the
trading post in 1635, and remained in Windsor until 1650 when he became a freeman of the colony. Later he removed to the Mohegan country, where at the junction
of the Quinebaug and Shetucket rivers (Norwich) he set up a trading house. He was
made an assistant to the magistrate at New London in 1657. *Connecticut Colonial
Records*, 1636–1665, p. 209.

after two years of wrangling, during which their "unkindness" was not soon forgotten, were they persuaded to pay for what they had appropriated.[1] Finally, on May 15, 1637, for £37 10s., Plymouth sold about fifteen-sixteenths of the whole, reserving only the trading house with forty-three and three-quarters acres of meadow and forty acres more of upland near the Hartford bounds, together with a proportion of all lands within the area afterward to be divided. Eventually all, people and lands, were absorbed in the town of Windsor.

Soon other settlers appeared, coming in such numbers during the last part of the year 1635 as to mark that time as the effective beginning of the Connecticut settlement. Among them was a special group whose arrival was in this wise. Sir Richard Saltonstall, a member of the Massachusetts Bay Company and one of the lords and gentlemen to whom the Earl of Warwick in 1632 had deeded the lands he expected to receive from the Council for New England, wished to start a private plantation of his own for the purpose of occupying the territory. In his own vessel and at his own expense, he sent over Francis Stiles, a master carpenter of London, Stiles's two brothers, also carpenters, and eighteen indentured servants, who landing in Boston about the middle of June sailed ten days later for Connecticut. They were coldly received by the Puritans in possession at Windsor and were forced to take up lands on the northern fringe of the settlement, where, as was soon proved, there was insufficient pasture, meadows, and arable to meet the needs of the newcomers.[2] For these and other reasons it is more than likely that the lords and gentlemen, with at least three places of refuge to select from— Piscataqua, Windsor, and Saybrook—would have rejected Windsor in any case. Saltonstall was angry at the result. "Had I but imagined [he wrote] they would thus greedily snatch up all the best ground on the river, my pinnace should rather have sought a pilot at Plymouth than to have stayed ten days as she did at the Bay and given

1. The bargain was made by Thomas Prence, governor of New Plymouth, 1633–1634, who came to Connecticut for the purpose. The land sold included a portion on the east side of the river, which the Plymouth people had purchased but not occupied. Windsor Land Records, I, 227.

2. Bartholomew Greene to Saltonstall, December 30, 1635 (Collections, Massachusetts Historical Society, 5th series, I, 216–217). Henry Stiles was the eldest of four brothers. He and four of the servants are mentioned in the Connecticut Colonial Records, 1636–1665, pp. 1, 6, 8.

them such warning thus to prevent me."[1] This comment shows that the Dorchester people under Ludlow's guidance, on hearing of the arrival of the Stiles party, had hastened their departure and in so doing had anticipated Saltonstall in the occupation of the valley lands. It was a piece of sharp practice, and Saltonstall's treatment at the hands of his fellow Puritans may have had something to do with his refusal to return to Massachusetts from England, after his brief sojourn of only one year in the colony.

Thus far the people of Newtown have hardly come into the picture. In 1634 six Newtowners had gone in the *Blessing of the Bay* on its trip to New Amsterdam, to take a look at the Connecticut River with the intention of preparing the way for a general exodus of their fellow townsmen, and there is some reason to think that a few Newtown people had accompanied the Dorchester group under Ludlow in the summer of 1635. But as yet no great number had taken part in the westward movement. It required time to dispose of houses and lands and to settle personal affairs in anticipation of removal. Though many of those desiring to go were recent arrivals at the Bay, others were residents of some years' standing who were loth to leave their properties until purchasers could be found to take them over. The Newtowners were reputed wealthy and as their substance consisted of lands and cattle as well as houses it was difficult to depart at a moment's notice, however much they may have wanted to do so. Nevertheless a beginning had to be made. Sometime in October, 1635, a company of fifty persons—men, women, and children—along some one of the Indian paths westward, reached their destination toward the end of the month. As the Windsor lands were already taken up, they moved southward in the direction of

1. Stiles, *Ancient Windsor*, I, 48, 737–740. Sir Richard's experience in New England cannot have given him much satisfaction, for to add to his ill luck the pinnace which brought the Stiles party was wrecked off Cape Sable (Winthrop, *Journal*, I, 163). New England had no place for a private plantation, either that of Cradock at Medford or of Saltonstall at Windsor, and it was probably fortunate for Simonds d'Ewes that he finally refused Winthrop's proposal to start a "colony" somewhere in Massachusetts (*Publications*, Colonial Society of Massachusetts, VII, 70–71, 75). Even after Stiles and Robert Saltonstall received "Saltonstall Park" near Warehouse Point, Massachusetts protested on the ground that the land was north of the Woodward-Saffery line and consequently within her jurisdiction (*Massachusetts Colonial Records*, I, 324). None of the Saltonstalls ever cultivated the park or improved it, though the name continued in use well on into the eighteenth century, but with the fort at Saybrook it serves to perpetuate the memory of the Puritan lords and gentlemen in England, who proposed to find a refuge in America should circumstances go against them at home.

the Dutch fort and began to lay out their homesteads and build their houses upon the ridge above the meadow and back from the river. Thus they became the "northsiders" of the later town of Hartford, the Suckiaug of the first comers. Twelve of the men had accompanied the party to assist its members in preparing winter quarters and building a palisade and when that work was accomplished they returned to their homes in Massachusetts. On the way back during ten days at the end of November, they lost one of their number by a fall through the ice and would have starved, all of them, had they not been able to find refuge in the wigwams of the Indians.[1] Others, some seventy in number, part of the Windsor community, half-starved and thoroughly discouraged, struggled through deep snows to the mouth of the Connecticut, where they found the *Rebecca,* a vessel built at Medford in 1634, attempting to make its way up the river for the relief of the settlements. Caught in the ice, the boat went no farther and after a brief delay returned with the fugitives to Boston. The Connecticut pioneers with difficulty escaped the experience of some of the settlers elsewhere, a fate that might well have befallen her first inhabitants had they been separated by three thousand miles from their source of supply, as were those of Virginia and Sagadahoc. Evidently the winter was an early and a cold one and those that remained must have experienced their bitter meed of suffering. Such were the perils of frontier life in the early New England days.

The greater and more famous migration took place under conditions quite different from those that attended the coming of the first pioneers. In a sense the latter were squatters, in that save for their rights as the sons of Noah, they had no other title to the lands upon which they settled than such as had been acquired by purchase from the Indians. Now a new aspect was given to the situation by the attempt of the lords and gentlemen to enforce their pretensions to the Connecticut territory based on the deed from the Earl of Warwick. To be sure Saltonstall had sent his Stiles party to occupy a portion of the river lands, but there is nothing to show that he was acting in any official capacity or had been instructed by his fellow grantees to do so. In 1635 the latter made an important decision. On July 7 Saye and Sele, Fenwick, Saltonstall, Haslerig, Lawrence, and Darley, in the name of the entire body, authorized John Winthrop,

---

1. Winthrop, *Journal,* I, 165; Love, *Colonial History of Hartford,* pp. 14–15.

Jr., to go to New England and there at the mouth of the Connecticut River to lay out lands, build a fort, and erect houses suitable for himself and such other men of quality as might desire to take refuge there. They supplied him with men, ammunition, and £2000 for the purpose.[1] Thus the Puritan refuge, to which Cromwell, Lord Saye and Sele, Sir Matthew Boynton,[2] and possibly others might have come, was located on the Sound instead of at Piscataqua or Windsor, probably in part at least with the idea of anticipating a possible Dutch occupation there and of taking advantage of both the river trade and the coast trade with Boston.

Winthrop came over in the *Abigail,* arriving early in October, with young Henry Vane and the Rev. Hugh Peter as co-agents, and soon after reaching Massachusetts instituted an inquiry into the whys and wherefores of the settlements already made within the territory of the Warwick deed. Possibly he was induced thereto by the recent departure of the Dorchester group and by the news which must have come to him soon after his arrival of the experiences of the Stiles party.[3] He wished to know by what right or pretence these people were entering and laying claim to the lands of the grantees and he demanded that all going to Connecticut or who were already there should acknowledge the legal rights of the same

1. Trumbull, *History of Connecticut,* I, 527–528. The date 1635 is an interesting and suggestive one. The deed had been in the hands of the grantees for three years and yet nothing had been done. Now in the midst of the efforts that Gorges was making to recover the lands granted him by the Council for New England and in the same year as that in which the quo warranto was issued Winthrop was sent over. Were the patentees afraid of losing their territory?

In his pamphlet on the Warwick Patent, Mr. Hoadly has given us the names of nineteen of the patentees, the eleven named in the deed and eight others, with William Jessop as secretary. Jessop was also at the time secretary of the Providence Company, a little later secretary of the Warwick parliamentary commission, and after 1650 one of Cromwell's clerks and advisers, acting in somewhat the same capacity as was John Milton whom he knew well. He was closely identified with all these Puritan enterprises. See below, p. 133, note 3.

2. Neal, *History of the Puritans* (1848), I, 340–341; *The Boynton Family,* p. xviii. I owe the reference to Boynton to the Rev. Melville Knox Bailey of Old Saybrook, who tells me that the present Lord Saye, in his *Hearsay,* believes firmly that his ancestor meant to come to America, having plotted with Cromwell and Hampden to that end at Broughton Castle. There is ample evidence elsewhere to show that Boynton and a number of others planned in 1635 to come to the settlement at Saybrook, *Collections,* Massachusetts Colonial Society, 4th ser., VI, 459; VII, 162 n., 164.

3. One wonders whether Stiles, who must have been in Saltonstall's confidence, raised the question of the title to the soil on his arrival at Windsor. It is not impossible that Winthrop, when he reached Boston, heard of the treatment of Stiles and was influenced thereby.

grantees and submit to the counsel and direction of himself as their governor, or else leave the territory. He and his fellow agents stated very emphatically that Connecticut lay beyond the jurisdiction of Massachusetts and that settlement there could be made only with the consent of those to whom the grant had been made.[1] Here was a troublesome but perhaps not an unexpected obstacle in the path of migration, confronting not only those who had gone before but also those who were preparing to go, for the Massachusetts general court had already given permission to the inhabitants of Dorchester, Watertown, and Newtown to remove to Connecticut. The court had appointed a single constable for their protection and out of the colony's store had given them three pieces of ordnance.[2] It was undoubtedly well known that the Rev. Thomas Hooker and his church at Newtown were ready to move as soon as their business affairs could be satisfactorily arranged.

Conferences on the subject of removal, in which the agents, representatives of the Massachusetts general court, and Hooker, Haynes, Ludlow (back from Windsor), and Stone, and perhaps others of the Connecticut group must have taken part, lasted from October, 1635, to March, 1636. Efforts were made to arrive at an understanding such as was fitting among men who were friends and fellow Puritans,[3] but the problems were not easy to solve and the discussions were conducted with the greatest secrecy. The grantees wanted settlers and the emigrants wanted security and a legal title. Final decisions were reached sometime before March, 1636. Hooker and his colleagues recognized the claims as laid down by Winthrop and accepted him as governor of the whole territory; the agents agreed to the proposed settlement within the bounds of the Warwick deed. But as the latter had no authority from the grantees to permit the establishment of an independent government within the borders of their grant—for nothing of the kind is to be found in Winthrop's

1. Winthrop, *Journal* (Savage ed.), I, 477–478.

2. *Massachusetts Colonial Records,* I, 119, 148, 159; Winthrop, *Journal,* I, 161.

3. Hooker, or some one else, must have tried at this juncture to get into touch with Lord Saye and Sele, in order to find out what the grantees wanted, but no answer had been received up to the date when the commission of March, 1636, was drafted. This is clear from the sentence "and neither the minds of the said personages (they being writ unto) are yet unknown or any manner of government [by them] is yet agreed on" (*Massachusetts Colonial Records,* I, 170–171). The same is implied in Connecticut's letter to Lord Saye and Sele, June 7, 1661 (Trumbull, *History of Connecticut,* I, 544–549).

instructions—some way of meeting the difficulty had to be devised. The contrivance was ingenious. The Massachusetts general court was accepted by both parties as qualified to give proper constitutional character to the proposed plantation and was invited to serve, not officially or as a principal, but as a go-between or friendly broker, in the task of putting into authoritative form the agreement arrived at. On March 3, 1636, the court issued a commission, on its own behalf and that of John Winthrop, Jr., and in the interest of "divers friends, neighbors, freemen and members of Newtown, Watertown, Dorchester and other places, who [were] resolved to transplant themselves and their estates into the river Connecticut, there to reside and inhabit." This document contains some of the essentials of a plan of government and was probably drawn up by Ludlow with the coöperation of Hooker and others, for in no way did it represent the Massachusetts idea of how a government should be carried on. It may therefore be looked upon as containing the first expression of the political principles which were later embodied in the Fundamental Orders of 1639.

"Where there are a people to sit down and inhabite," so runs the commission, "there will follow upon occasion some cause of difference"; therefore eight men, Ludlow, Pynchon, Steel, Swaine, Smith, Phelps, Westwood, and Ward—all of whom were either in Connecticut or preparing to go there—were given full authority to exercise judicial powers to inflict punishment, to make decrees and orders as best might conduce to "the peaceable and quiett ordering of the affairs of the said plantation," to exercise military discipline, and to make war if necessary. They were also empowered "under the greater part of their hands, at a day or dayes by them appointed, upon convenient notice, to convene the said *inhabitants* of the towns [not church members only as in Massachusetts] to any convenient place that they shall think meete, in a legal and open manner, by way of court, to procede in executing the power and authority aforesaid." Here we have a clear cut statement of government by consent of the "inhabitants," though no attempt is made to determine just what the word "inhabitants" meant, and we have also, in the use of the same word, an early indication of why these men wished to leave Massachusetts. Half of them, at least, were members of the general court which drew up the Fundamental Orders two years later and as some of the terms used anticipate the language of the preamble to that document,[1] we have a right to believe that the two instruments of government are clearly related and that all those named in the commission were in sympathy with Hooker and Ludlow in their desire to place authority in the hands of a wider popular constituency than was the case with Massachusetts. The commission was to last only for a year or until the lords and gentlemen should have made up their minds as to the form of permanent government they wished to establish for their territory.[2]

This important matter having been settled to the satisfaction of all—for both Winthrop and the emigrant leaders had got what they wanted—the westward movement was resumed. John Warham, at the head of the Dorchester church, guided his people, among whom was Ludlow himself and many who had struggled back to Massachusetts the previous winter, to the spot where their fellow townsmen were living at Windsor. William Pynchon, who had inspected the land the September before, sailed with a few others in two shallops to Agawam (Springfield), where he built a trading house, locating it first on the west side of the river and then on the east, because of difficulties which he experienced with the western Indians, whose cornfields were trampled on by his cattle and rooted up by his swine. Men and women from Watertown, in groups and organized parties, continued to cross the country or to sail around by water, until some fifty or more had arrived at Pyquag (Wethersfield) in sufficient numbers to constitute a sizable plantation. And lastly John White, Samuel Wakeman, and possibly Samuel Stone, Hooker's assistant at Newtown—the forerunners of the larger migration to come—conducted a number of people to join the group already located "at the New Towne upon Quinatucquet River." They carried the commission drawn up in Massachusetts and under

1. A comparison of the commission with the Fundamental Orders will show certain similarities between the two, in the words and phrases employed and in the principles of government later given statutory form. This would not be surprising if, as we suppose was the case, Ludlow wrote both documents.

2. *Massachusetts Colonial Records*, I, 170–171; Love, *Colonial History of Hartford*, pp. 65–68. For a commentary on what the Massachusetts general court understood the commission to mean, see *Massachusetts Colonial Records*, I, 320–321, where it is distinctly stated that the commission was "propounded and drawn out by some of the magistrates of each party, without any order or alowance of this court." Haynes was governor of Massachusetts at the time and did not go to Connecticut until May, 1637; Pynchon was one of the assistants; Ward and Swaine were already in Connecticut; Ludlow, who had been an assistant and also deputy governor, was once more in Massachusetts, having returned from Connecticut the autumn before.

its guidance set up the first court in the history of the colony. On April 26, 1636, five of the eight commissioners—Ludlow, Steel, Phelps, Westwood, and Ward (Pynchon and Smith were up the river at Agawam)—came together at Hartford and passed a few simple orders, swore in constables for the three plantations, and ratified the dismissal of six Watertown men from their church in Massachusetts, on their promise to renew their covenant and to erect a church of their own in Wethersfield. This (with one other) the six did, seven being of the number deemed sufficient for a church by the "ancient ministers" of the Bay.[1] Thus organized government began in Connecticut nearly two months before Thomas Hooker and his company entered the valley and all the essentials of self-government, based on the settlers' own ideas of the form such government should take—ideas embodied in the March commission—nearly three years before the Fundamental Orders were adopted.

In October, 1635, there came from England in the *Defence,* at the same time with the arrival of John Winthrop, Jr., in the *Abigail,* the Rev. Thomas Shepard, B.A. of Emmanuel College.[2] He and his company soon made their way to Newtown, where he was welcomed as Hooker's successor and where he and his people either began to occupy houses already vacated by those who had gone to Connecticut or proceeded to bargain for the purchase of others that belonged to men who were soon expecting to go. The opportune appearance of the Shepard company relieved in part the business uncertainty, for though some of those going to Connecticut were sufficiently well off to retain property in Newtown after their departure, there were many others who had to sell their landed possessions as a necessary step preliminary to removal. As we have already seen, some had departed in 1635 and others in the spring of 1636, but Hooker and the members of his church still lingered. It was difficult even for individuals to depart quickly, but it was even more so for a covenanted church group which had been established for three years, to break from its moorings and remove a hundred and more miles into the wilderness. Shepard, as soon as possible, set about the raising of a new church organization, and on February 1,

---

1. Winthrop, *Journal,* I, 173. Eight men constituted the church at Springfield.

2. Shepard's autobiography, Young, *Chronicles of Massachusetts;* also Mather's *Magnalia,* bk. III, pt. II, ch. V. The article on Shepard in Sprague, *Annals of the American Pulpit,* I, 59–68, is based entirely on these two sources. Mather calls Shepard the "Pastor Evangelicus."

1636, asked for the attendance of the neighboring ministers that he might be properly instructed in the New England way of ecclesiastical polity and the proper forms of ecclesiastical procedure. Instruction having been given to the contentment of all, the new members entered into a covenant whereby they became a church, which John Cotton, in the name of the rest, accepted in the bonds of fellowship. The ordination of Shepard as pastor was deferred until another day, "wherein there [should be] more time to go through the other solemnities proper to such a great occasion."[1]

Thus providentially, the way was prepared for the withdrawal of Hooker and the members of his church, just as soon as business arrangements could be completed and word had been received from Connecticut that all was ready. February was not a propitious month for a journey through the wilderness by the large number of men, women, and children, and livestock that were expected to go, so that the actual departure was postponed until May. How the two churches got on together during these four months and how the housing problem was solved history has not revealed. It was an eventful day when on Tuesday, May 31, this company of thirty-five men, with wives, children, and servants, started on their pilgrimage, under summer skies, along one of the Indian paths westward.[2] Presumably their household goods were sent around by water. Mrs. Hooker and her son Samuel travelled in a horse litter, while the band of colonists drove one hundred and sixty cattle, feeding on the milk of the cows by the way. Hooker carried letters to the younger Winthrop from his father, the governor, who took advantage of the opportunity to send along in charge of Lieutenant Thomas Bull of the company, assisted by one of Winthrop's servants, six cows, four steers, and a bull, to be delivered to his son at Saybrook.[3] As the travellers went on foot and could make but ten miles a day the journey lasted nearly a fortnight, and all slept in the open, "having no pillows to use to take their nightly rest but upon such as their father Jacob found in the way to Padan-Aram." Crossing the Con-

1. Winthrop, *Journal*, I, 173–174; Mather, *Magnalia*, bk. III, pt. II, p. 87.

2. For the controversy over the Hooker route, see Crofut, *Guide to the History and Historic Sites of Connecticut*, I, ch. I, where the Agawam route is defended. Mr. H. A. Wright, *The Genesis of Springfield*, however, definitely states that there is no evidence that the Bay Path, connecting Boston and Springfield, "was known or used by the English at this time."

3. Winthrop, *Journal*, I, 180–181; *ibid*. (Savage ed.), I, 468. Winthrop writes, "I sent such as might be fittest both for travel and for your use."

necticut, probably in canoes at Windsor, they took up their location mainly on the south side of the little river adjoining the Dutch fort, and became the "southsiders" of the Hartford settlement. Hooker and others of the leaders, however, remained north of the river.

In the founding of Connecticut no question of religious freedom was involved and there was no intention of establishing a religious colony in any way different from that of Massachusetts. In matters of ecclesiastical polity, creed, and discipline the Connecticut churches adhered in all particulars to the New England way already defined, to which two of the churches had conformed in Massachusetts and which all of them continued to practice unchanged in Connecticut. Hooker had no sympathy with the religious agitation associated at this time with the names of Roger Williams and Anne Hutchinson, and what influenced a majority of those who went to Connecticut at this time was not a desire to alter their religious creed and practice, but the allurement of a fertile valley fed by a navigable stream, where land could be obtained of the Indians and where relief could be felt from the pressure of a rapidly increasing population and there was freedom to grow and expand. This is the one and only reason assigned by the colonists themselves when later they had occasion to state the causes of their going. "In that part of the country, neer the port of their first arrival [Boston] they setled for a time, till upon experience they found that place would be too streight for so great a number if they should continue all there long together."[1]

There can be no doubt that available and desirable land was becoming scarce at the Bay and that pasture and meadow, so necessary to a people whose interests at that time were entirely rural and whose lives depended on their stocks of cattle, goats, and swine, was insufficient for their needs. A little later Southampton on Long Island was settled from Lynn,[2] because there the arable and pasture had become limited and the opportunities for success fewer, and there must have been other towns that felt similar restrictions upon their growth. Newtown, which lay between Charlestown and Water-

---

1. *Connecticut Colonial Records*, 1636–1665, p. 582. In a petition sent to the Privy Council, probably in 1643, by John Whiting, Thomas Marshall (Marshfield), Edward Hopkins, and John Alcock, appears the following statement, "The new plantaĉon of Conecticot in the South of New England, distant from the old plantaĉon about 120 myles, who by reason of the hardshipps and wants wch they formerly underwent in the old plantaĉon removed to Conecticot in hopes of better accomodaĉons." Colonial Office Papers, 1:9, no. 130.
2. *Southampton Records*, p. 5.

town, "being in form like a list cut off from the broadcloth of the two fore-mentioned towns,"[1] also had complained of the dryness and sandiness of its soil and the insufficiency of its grazing ground; and its people, tired of tillage, expressed a desire to turn to the raising of cattle as a more profitable and less wearisome pursuit. Massachusetts was well aware of the state of affairs at Newtown, for the town of Ipswich reproached the men of that community for seeking "the good of their cattle more than [that] of the commonwealth,"[2] and the general court tried to meet the emergency by offering the Newtowners land in other parts of the colony, notably along the Merrimac. But neither reproaches nor offers had any effect. Loyalty to the Massachusetts commonwealth was not conspicuous among those men who went to Connecticut, as later events were to show, and lands elsewhere in Massachusetts presented no compensating advantages in comparison with the unrestricted stretches of low, rich meadow that lay along the Connecticut, reports of which had been sent or brought back by those who had ventured thither. To the mass of the people land was still, as it always had been, the object of their desires and its possession a necessity in a pastoral and agricultural age.

The leaders of the movement may have had other reasons for their discontent. The years 1635 and 1636 were uneasy ones at the Bay. Not only was there prevalent a fear that the colony might lose its charter and a governor general be appointed, but there was also dissatisfaction in some quarters with Winthrop's management. Among the discontented was John Haynes, "a gentleman of great estate" in England, highly honored in the colony and the leading lay member of Hooker's church; and also Thomas Hooker himself and Roger Ludlow, both of whom were nursing certain ideas of their own as to how a colony should be governed and regarding certain foundation principles upon which such government should rest. These three men were conspicuous among their fellows— Haynes and Hooker the Moses and Aaron of the new wandering of the Israelites and Ludlow, trained in the law, a man of a somewhat masterful disposition and possessed of a desire for leadership,[3] and the directing agent who translated into legal forms the common

1. Johnson, *Wonder-Working Providence* (Original Narratives), p. 90.
2. *Collections,* Massachusetts Historical Society, 4th series, VII, 25.
3. Ludlow moved from England to Massachusetts Bay, from Massachusetts Bay to Windsor, and from Windsor to Fairfield, where he remained for fourteen years, the

ideas regarding government and administration. Others of lesser prominence, in accord with these three, willingly embraced the opportunity to escape from Massachusetts and find a new field for the exercise of that authority which was difficult to obtain at home. Pynchon, Wolcott, Steel, Phelps, Westwood, and Ward were afterward important men in Connecticut. They had found Massachusetts an uncomfortable place to live in, because of the differences of opinion that prevailed there and because of the overshadowing importance of the magistrates and clergy with their rigid, inelastic methods of oligarchic control. Many a man of the day in New England, orthodox or heterodox, who possessed the instincts of one having authority—Williams, Coddington, Gorton, Pynchon, Davenport, Hooker, Ludlow, and the younger Winthrop—wished to have each his own little world, where he might set up his own system of theology or government or pursue his own independent way of making a living and a profit apart from, though not out of touch with, others of his ilk in other localities.

Hooker had his own personal reasons for discontent. They are suggested in a letter from one of Winthrop's English correspondents, who wrote that "Mr. Hoker before he went away preached against the strictness of the Massachusetts rule regarding admission to the churches" and was "moved to remove" because of the "great division of Judgement in matters of religion amongst your ministers and people."[1] This remark refers of course to the Antinomian controversy, but it refers also to Hooker's disputation with John Cotton, the influential teacher of the Boston church, which took the form of an exchange of views, during the years 1635 and 1636, in the customary manner of opinions, objections, and answers, before Antinomianism became a matter of state concern. Cotton held that faith was built upon Christ, not upon sanctification obtained from

chief leader of the settlement. Later he returned to England and Ireland, where he died. Whatever the cause, his was an uneasy life.

1. The writer states that in England the opinion was wide-spread "that you are so strict in admission of members of your church that more than one-halfe are out of your church in all your congregations, that Mr. Hoker before he went away preached against it (as one reports who heard him). Now although I know all must not be admytted, yet this may do much hurt, yf one came amongst you of another minde and they should joyne with him. . . . There is a great division of Judgement in matters of religion amongst your ministers and people, which moved Mr. Hoker to remove. . . . I am sorry much for your divisions, we heare greate speeche of them and I am sure that they da[u]nt many wise faythful Christians and men of ability from coming, fearing least a kingdome divided and canot stande." *Ibid.*, pp. 10–12.

preaching, teaching, and good works, and that man first attained assurance of faith of his justification by the witness of the spirit of Christ in a free promise of grace. He declared that faith went before works; that in receiving "the Guift of ffaith wee are merely passive, that in receiving Christ or the spirit of Christ we are passive also— an empty vessel fit to receive Christ and his righteousness"; and that sanctification was but a "created Guift" and a secondary witness. He took the position that sanctification could not be the first evidence or "evident cause" or ground of justification and that to believe otherwise was "flatt Popery," an implication that Hooker may well have resented. Cotton declared further that a "faith made by a word [preaching and teaching] and a work [some outward act] without the witness of the spirit and *before it* was not a faith wrought by God's Almighty Power," and that "the word without the Almighty power of the spirit was *a dead letter*." He insisted that the controversy with Hooker ("if it be indeed a Controversie and not some mistake, as I would gladly hope it is") was not the opposition "between Grace and Works" but "between Grace and the meritt of Works," or as he elsewhere puts it, "between Grace and the debt to Works," a subtle distinction. All of this Hooker denied and it is quite possible that some of the imputations contained in the objections and answers may have aroused considerable bitterness of feeling between the two men, even though Winthrop in his kindly way thought the contrary. In his writings Winthrop always minimized the differences of opinion among the elect.[1]

Just when the controversy began and ended we do not know, but it must have lasted quite a long time. Cotton's first polemic was followed by a reply from Hooker, to which Cotton in turn made answer. Hooker replied again and Cotton counter-replied, evidently in the hope that Hooker would continue the argument, but Hooker refrained. It is not unlikely that at this stage of the debate Hooker was planning to go to Connecticut and did not wish to carry the

1. Winthrop, who always minimized the effects of controversy in the colony, denied that Hooker left Massachusetts because of "any difference between Mr. Cotton and him, for they doe hould a most sweet and brotherly communion together (though their judgᵗˢ doe somewhat differ about the lawfullnease of the Crosse in the Ensigne), but that the people and cattle are so increased as the place will not saftice them." *Publications,* Colonial Society of Massachusetts, VII, 73. This difference of opinion between Cotton and Hooker regarding the cross in the ensign is a phase of the controversy of which Hooker wrote something in a letter, printed a few years ago in the *Proceedings* of the Massachusetts Historical Society, Vol. 42, pp. 272–280.

discussion further. We learn of the encounter from Cotton's last reply, which was sent to England for the inspection of Archbishop Laud, probably in 1637, on nine small sheets of paper in a writing so fine as to be almost undecipherable.[1] The subject matter shows that in origin this exchange of opinion dates back to the days when Cotton was a Hutchinsonian sympathizer and Hooker on the other side. These differences between the two men in doctrinal and other matters (such as the cross in the ensign, which is mentioned in Cotton's reply but of which we know little more), in which Cotton was the more liberal thinker, may well have been accentuated by the fact that Hooker held more progressive views than did Cotton regarding the share of the people in affairs of government—ideas that were not capable of application in a colony where church membership was a qualification for freemanship and where the magistrates were deemed the oracles of God. Each of these men was something of a prophet in his own community and, as the historian Hubbard says, nature did not allow two suns to shine at the same time in the same firmament. Cotton Mather adds the equally wise remark that two such men were likely to be more serviceable apart than together.[2]

But Hooker's discontent was not confined to matters of doctrine or limited in its expression to Cotton only. Other causes of uneasiness arose which became manifest as early as 1634, only six months after Hooker's arrival in the Massachusetts Bay colony. What these causes were can be inferred from his letter to Winthrop, written from Connecticut in the year 1638, protesting in vehement and almost passionate terms against the efforts which Massachusetts was making, not only in New England but in Old England also, to discredit Connecticut in the eyes of the English world—the "common trade that is driven amongst multitudes with you" is his way of putting it.[3] It is not easy to believe that so sharp an arraignment of the Puritan habit of criticism could have found utterance within

1. Colonial Office Papers, 1:9, no. 71. In Cotton's final reply the "Objections" are stated and the "Answers" follow, very much as in his controversy with Williams. The course of the disputation can be traced in such phrases as "I say noe more of the text, because you have it further cleered in the answer to your Reply"; "my long answer to your Reply"; "I come now to the 3rd and last controversy"; "I will not proceed to further needless disputačon until I hear further [from you]."

2. *Magnalia*, bk. III, pp. 63, 117.

3. *Collections*, Connecticut Historical Society, I, 1–18; *Life and Letters of John Winthrop*, II, 421.

two years of Hooker's arrival in Connecticut had there not been behind it unpleasant experiences of longer standing. In 1635, a year before Hooker's departure, Ipswich had complained of "too many unjust detractions in the bay to serve their own ends," and we know that censoriousness and criticism were characteristic Puritan failings.[1] "The strong bent of their spirits to remove thither," as Winthrop sums up the situation, is a phrase which may well cover many symptoms of unrest. "Sir," wrote Hooker, "he wants a nostril that feels not and scents not a schismatical spirit in such a framer of falsifying relations to gratify some persons and to satisfy their amends. . . . Do these things argue brotherly love?" One cannot avoid the conclusion that in this letter are to be found some of the emotions that drove Hooker and the Newtown church to undertake their western pilgrimage. Between the placid lines of Winthrop's journal may be read many things of which Winthrop makes no mention—discontent, vexation of soul, and even animosity.[2]

Later remarks also demonstrate the Connecticut state of mind. When in 1648 a dispute arose among the commissioners of the New England Confederation regarding the jurisdiction of the two colonies and Massachusetts insisted that the emigrants from Watertown, Newtown, Dorchester, and Roxbury had taken possession of Connecticut in her name and right, the Connecticut delegates indignantly replied that on the contrary the commission of 1636 originated with the emigrants themselves and "not from any claymes of the Massachusetts jurisdiction over them."[3] From this it is clear that the Connecticut people, twelve years after Hooker's arrival, held firmly to the belief that the commission was the work of the emigrants themselves and had its origin in the determination of these

1. *Collections*, Connecticut Historical Society, III, 332; *Collections*, Massachusetts Historical Society, 4th series, VII, 24.

2. Bradford's *History* and Winthrop's *Journal* must at times be used with caution. Winthrop frequently presents the side of the case most favorable to his own cause. He seems always to be smoothing down the account of the antagonisms among his people and giving an appearance of harmony and brotherly love that was manifestly not present. In the few instances where we get glimpses of the other side of the story we are quite certain that matters were not running as "lovingly" and as "cheerfully" as Winthrop would have us believe.

3. Hazard, *State Papers*, II, 119. The assertion by the Massachusetts commissioners at this time is in direct contradiction of the statement made by the general court in 1635 (*Massachusetts Colonial Records*, I, 134–135), when Massachusetts did not consider the Connecticut valley as within her jurisdiction.

emigrants not to remain longer in a colony with the spirit and government of which they had no sympathy.[1]

Hooker did not like the Massachusetts system and expressly said so. He told Winthrop in 1638, in the letter already referred to, that he objected to the Massachusetts practice of leaving so much to the discretion of the magistrates and of using the clergy as counselors in purely secular affairs. In dealing with civil things he preferred "a general counsel chosen by all," which was to concern itself with issues that were of importance to all. Answering Winthrop's statement that it was unsafe and unwarrantable to refer matters of counsel or judicature to the body of the people and that the best part was always the least and of that best part the wiser part was always the lesser, he declared that he "chose neither to live or to have his posterity live under such a government." Unlike many of the deputies and two or three of the magistrates in Massachusetts, who, as we have seen in the previous volume were working to liberalize the government from within, Hooker, Haynes, and Ludlow preferred to depart from the colony and set up a government of their own outside the Massachusetts boundaries. They wanted to start afresh with a system based on a broader foundation of political principles, the most conspicuous of which was the idea that authority should be vested in such part of the people as was deemed competent to exercise it.

Whether they arrived at this fundamentally important idea by a natural process of reaction against the Massachusetts system of government by divine immanence or by some subjective reasoning of their own it is impossible to say. Roger Ludlow has left no writings of any kind from which to form an opinion as to what his political views were. Hooker in his printed works says nothing about political things, but in his conception of the covenant we may find a possible clue. In *A Survey of Church Discipline* he wrote, "Mutual covenanting and confoederation of the Saints in the fellowship of the faith according to the order of the Gospel is that which gives constitution and being to a visible Church."[2] Starting with the fact,

1. The usual authorities on the withdrawal to Connecticut are Winthrop and Hubbard. The latter follows Winthrop very closely. He, Cotton Mather, and Trumbull all refer to the rivalry between Cotton and Hooker, of which Winthrop says nothing. Brief statements are in George Leon Walker, *Thomas Hooker*, pp. 86–90, and *First Church in Hartford*, pp. 79–82, though strangely enough Dr. Walker says very little about the doctrinal differences between the two men.

2. Part I, p. 46.

accepted by all in the New England way of the churches, that members covenanting in a church way had a share in the government of the church, he could easily arrive at a similar idea as to the meaning of the social compact in its application to the state. In determining who these members should be, Massachusetts limited their number to the "regenerate" only, a policy Hooker refused to follow, perhaps because he knew the difficulties accompanying any attempt to find out who were truly regenerate in spirit as well as in outward conformity. He may well have believed that Massachusetts rejected many who were better Christians than some who were admitted, and he was therefore willing to admit all who professed Christianity, provided they were freeholders, as were the voters in England, to a share in government, whether they were church members or not.

At the same time the general principle inherent in the Congregational system that the members of a church had a right to elect their officers and if the latter did not live up to the terms of their election, to remove them and place others in their stead fell far short of a democracy, a form of government repellent to the Puritans. The latter believed that the people might choose but that those chosen—elders in the church and magistrates in the state—were to rule. When the elders proposed anything the people of the church gave their assent, when the magistrates reached a decision the people were to do as they were told. This was as true of Connecticut as it was of Massachusetts. The point has been well expressed by Mr. Perry Miller who says, "The component elements of [Puritan] society did not draw up the fundamental law or delegate to the government any sovereignty they originally held. . . . The congregation retained no 'residuary powers.' "[1] This remark applies very aptly to the political situation in Connecticut, and Hooker may well have had a commonwealth in mind when he wrote of the church, "The elders are superior in regard to Office, Rule, Act and Exercise; the people are superior in point of censure. Each have their full scope in their own sphere and compass."[2] In Connecticut this was exactly what happened in governmental practice: the people, that is, the freemen, elected and set bounds, but the magistrates took the lead and laid down the principles according to which the people made their decisions. Another similarity is to be noted. Just as no one was pro-

1. Miller, *Orthodoxy in Massachusetts,* pp. 172, 179, 180–183.
2. Part I, pp. 99–100.

pounded for admission to the church without the consent of the elders, so none were admitted as members of the commonwealth without the consent of the general court. No man could exercise the franchise in Connecticut simply because he had been born and had been able to live to a certain voting age.

It is quite possible that Hooker was influenced by the example of Plymouth, where for fifteen years the Pilgrims had been applying a not dissimilar principle of political government. Some conception of a form of popular coöperation was clearly in the minds of Hooker, Haynes, and Ludlow when they drew up the commission of 1636, providing that the "inhabitants" of the Connecticut plantations should convene in a court for the execution of the powers entrusted to them, and this idea grew and found concrete expression during the years 1636, 1637, and 1638. But not until Hooker delivered his famous sermon or address on May 31, 1638, was it stated in so many words. Certain phrases in that sermon are so reminiscent of the language used by Roger Williams in *The Bloudy Tenent* and elsewhere that one is tempted to believe that Williams had some influence upon Hooker in the working out of this political doctrine. "The foundation of authority is laid in the free consent of the people" is even better expressed by Williams in "The sovereign power of all authority is founded in the consent of the people." Hooker and Williams had known each other in England, for they had lived for some time in the same neighborhood,[1] and on one occasion that we know of he and Cotton and Williams had ridden to and from Sempringham arguing about common prayer and possibly other

---

1. Chelmsford, the shire town of Essex, where the assizes were held, was only twenty-nine miles from London and the center of a powerful Puritan group. In its near neighborhood were the Riches of Leighs Priory, the Barringtons at Barrington Hall, and Sir William Masham at Otes, all Puritans and interrelated by marriage. Roger Williams was with the Mashams, and Thomas Hooker for ten years was an influential preacher and lecturer at Chelmsford and teacher at Little Baddow, where John Eliot was his usher. Ezekial Rogers was with the Barringtons for a time; William Pynchon was born at Springfield near by; and Haselrig, Saltonstall, and others were from that locality. Essex was notorious for the scandalous conduct of the established clergy there, was seething in superstition, and, as we have seen (Vol. I, 384, note), was the leading center of the witch-hunting mania (Ewen, *Witchcraft and Demonianism*). Robert Lord Rich, the father of the Earl of Warwick, was the most powerful landlord in Essex, possessing seventy-five manors, a majority of the advowsons, and three hundreds with all their rights and liberties. When these facts are considered it is easy to understand Warwick's interest in the Puritans, and to realize that frequent and friendly meetings between Hooker and Williams in England were quite possible.

things. Hooker visited Williams at Providence at least once, in 1637, and there are extant three letters from Hooker to Williams, written between January and May, 1638. From whatever source these ideas came—whether Hooker was influenced by Williams or Williams by Plymouth, or both by Plymouth—the fact remains that Plymouth, Connecticut, and Rhode Island not only conducted their governments in a manner quite unlike that of Massachusetts, but that in their respective colonies they also accepted the political cooperation of at least a part of the people unrestricted by membership in any ecclesiastical organization.[1]

Thus was Connecticut settled and thus there came into existence at the very beginning a form of self-government in which the admitted inhabitants and the freemen of the colony had a definite and important share.

The commission of March 3, 1636, contained, though in very rudimentary form, the first definition of government for the colony. The eight men named in it were to have full power and authority to exercise judicial functions, to make such orders and decrees as were for the peaceable and quiet ordering of affairs, to regulate matters that concerned trade, planting, building, and distributing lots, and to enforce military discipline. They were empowered to call together the "inhabitants" of the plantations at any convenient place they deemed suitable, for the purpose of carrying out their instructions, thus placing the government on a bottom broader than in Massachusetts of a considerable measure of popular coöperation. For the first year, however, the commissioners, acting on the discretion allowed them, apparently did not call either a popular assembly or a general court but conducted the administration themselves, sitting as a "cort" from April 26, 1636, to March 28, 1637.

The commission government lasted but a year. It was not imposed on the settlers from without but was the product of their own minds and the expression of their own wishes. No attempt was made to choose a governor, for John Winthrop, Jr., was recognized as the head of the territory and the right of the lords and gentlemen to appoint a successor if they wished was undoubtedly agreed to

---

1. The contrast in governmental organization is well brought out by the language used a few years later, when the acceptance of the articles of the New England Confederation was under consideration. The plan of union was to be referred to the supreme authority in each colony—to the "state" in Massachusetts and to the "magistrates and people" in Connecticut.

at the time the commission was drafted. Not until the framing of the Fundamental Orders, when the lords and gentlemen had manifestly withdrawn from their enterprise, was provision made for the election of a governor. In all other respects the commission enabled the Connecticut people to look after their own affairs until a more complete system could be established. When it expired in 1637 the colony went on as before, with one important distinction. A general court was called, apparently for the first time, an action made necessary by the impending war against the Pequots. So serious and dangerous an undertaking demanded that what so intimately concerned all should be approved by all and that the people who were to carry on the war should be responsible for the means and methods employed. To this end the inhabitants were instructed to come together in their respective towns for the election of representatives or "committees," as they were called, to join with the magistrates in a general court at Hartford, in order that the necessary preparations for such a war should be made. With one exception the magistrates were the same as the old commissioners, but that exception shows that some arrangement was entered into whereby the personnel of the magistrates might be changed. What this arrangement was we do not know certainly, but Hooker says in his letter of a few months later that local elections took place in the towns and that the committees thus elected came to the general court and there chose their magistrates. This selection of magistrates may have been made either independently or from those nominated by the towns.[1]

The first and only important business of this general court was to declare "that there shalbe an offensive war agt the Pequoitt" and to distribute the burden of that war proportionately among the three plantations. The Pequots after invading the river valley had passed southward and southeastward until they came to rest in the region between the Thames River and the present boundary of Rhode Island. They had defeated or pushed aside the peaceful river tribes and in opening a new hunting ground for themselves—covering both the eastern part of Long Island, the mainland, and the islands off the coast—had made enemies not only of the English but also

---

1. Hooker speaks definitely of "our election" (*Collections*, Connecticut Historical Society, I, 13). The words of the commission would seem to show that the men who drafted it had in mind a general court in the form of a primary assembly made up of all or a part of the inhabitants instead of one composed of their representatives only. Evidently at the time such a plan was found to be impracticable, though later in 1638 such gatherings were held, but just for what purpose we do not know.

of the Niantics, the Mohegans, and the powerful Narragansetts under Miantonomo, each of whom took a part, though not a very active part, on the side of the English in the war that followed. The immediate cause was a series of three murders: that of Captain Stone[1] and a few companions, itinerant traders from outside the colony;[2] that of John Oldham, who had located himself for purposes of trade at Wethersfield; and lastly, that of three women and six men of the same plantation in April, 1637. The war, which was an undertaking of exceptional boldness for an infant colony, lasted three weeks and was brought to a successful issue under the leadership of Captain John Mason, Captain John Underhill (formerly of Massachusetts), and Lieutenant Robert Seely, with Samuel Stone as chaplain. The soldiers attacked and burned the Pequot fort two miles from Mystic and, two months later, others pursued the survivors to their retreat near the present village of Southport. There in a swamp fight they completed the destruction or dispersal of the tribe.[3] From this time forward, for nearly forty years, relations with the Indians were peaceful enough, though the settlers suffered from occasional alarums and engaged in a few punitive expeditions. The local Indians were a good deal of a nuisance as well as a danger, and strict orders had to be issued against trading with them or selling them liquor, guns, powder, and shot. There were occasional difficulties in determining Indian land claims and purchases, and Connecticut's share in the quarrel between the Mohegans and the Narragansetts, that is, between Uncas and Miantonomo, is not to her credit. The New England Confederation took the side of the Mohegans, as was not unnatural, the Mohegans being Connecticut

1. For Captain John Stone, see *New Netherland* (Original Narratives), pp. 191–192, 203; Bradford, *History*, II, 190–192, 233–234, 243 note; Winthrop, *Journal*, index. Winthrop says that the war was begun to avenge the murder of Stone (I, 214), though he was of Virginia and "none of ours" (140, 214).

2. Rasier, writing in 1628(?), says that the Pequots had conquered and made tributary to themselves the Shinnecocks at the east end of Long Island (*New Netherland*, Original Narratives, p. 103).

3. The four accounts of the Pequot war—those of Vincent, Underhill, Gardiner, and Mason—have been reprinted (that of Mason only in part) in Orr, *History of the Pequot War* (1897). Mason's full account is in *Collections*, Massachusetts Historical Society, 2d series, VIII, 120. A recent narrative is by Bradstreet, *The Story of the Pequot War, Retold* (1933). Also *Connecticut Colonial Records*, 1636–1665, pp. 74, 95, 197, 295, 324, and *Particular Court Records*, pp. 128–129, 175 for the later relations of the colony with the Indians. There is a singular metrical, highly dramatic, and fanciful version of the Pequot War in Wolcott, *Poetical Meditation* (1725), pp. 19 and following.

Indians, but the cold-blooded murder of Miantonomo by the treacherous Uncas was a deed for which the colony must always bear the blame.

For two years, 1637 and 1638, the three plantations continued under the simple forms of self-government thus far employed. The householders in the towns were engaged in apportioning land and building houses and in looking after such matters of daily routine as were essential to their existence as traders and planters. The three settlements were still in the plantation stage and can have had no other organization than the meeting of their inhabitants to take common action in the choice of committees to the general court and the management of their agricultural, military, and prudential obligations.[1] Their relations with the general court were probably much the same as those which prevailed after the Fundamental Orders were adopted. They sent their committees to act for them whenever the general court was to be held and at the first meeting which, following the Massachusetts practice, was even then construed as a court of election, the committees named the magistrates nominated by each town and the whole body gave its approval in a formal election. The general court, thus made up of magistrates and committees, sat eight times and probably more during these two years, and there is reason to believe that particular courts, composed of the magistrates only, met for the transaction of judicial, financial, and probate business.[2] The powers of the general court were much the

1. Roger Welles, in an article printed in the *Connecticut Magazine*, 1899, pp. 86–93, 159–162, takes the position that the commissioners of 1636–1637 were authorized by the terms of their instructions to extend to the plantations in Connecticut the Massachusetts law of March 3, 1636, defining in great detail the powers of the Massachusetts towns, and that therefore the three plantations, from April, 1636, to 1639, were in possession of all necessary town privileges and exercised them as completely as the Massachusetts towns were doing. This is a purely gratuitous assumption and is contradicted by every evidence at our disposal. The plantations of Connecticut were organized as towns for the first time in 1639 (*Connecticut Colonial Records*, 1635–1636, pp. 36–39; *Collections*, Connecticut Historical Society, VI, prefatory note).

2. The meeting of February 9, 1637, was undoubtedly a general court, if we are to judge from the language used and the powers exercised, though only Captain Mason of the committees is recorded as present. Among the entries mention is made of a particular court to meet in May, but as the records of the proceedings are missing for nine months it is impossible to say whether or not the court met. Hooker tells us that another court (either particular or general) was held in the autumn of 1638. Dr. J. Hammond Trumbull thinks that Hooker's sermon was delivered at an adjourned session, May 31, 1638, of the April court. Of this session no record exists. In September, 1639, a committee was appointed to complete certain unfinished busi-

same before 1639 as they were afterward, and the nature of the government carried on between 1636 and 1639 does not appear to have differed either in principle or form from that of the more systematized and orderly arrangement which followed the Orders and the formal setting up of the Commonwealth.

One phase of the situation, significant because of its relation to important subsequent events, demands a brief consideration here. At the beginning Springfield was included among the river towns and Pynchon and his son-in-law Henry Smith had been named as among the eight men selected to govern the settlements under the March commission. Pynchon sat only once with that body and neither he nor anyone else from Springfield attended the general courts the next year, probably because of the distance and the threatening dangers from the Indians at the time of the Pequot War. All the plantations during the war were left in a measure unprotected, and Springfield, a small community situated in a dangerous quarter, was peculiarly defenseless. The people there were not required to furnish any men for the expedition, but Pynchon's shallop was called into requisition, probably without his consent, and later the plantation was assessed £86 15s, a sum that Pynchon said was equal to his entire estate.[1]

Though Springfield was represented in the general courts of March and April, 1638, and possibly the Springfield representatives attended other courts held during the latter year, trouble soon arose between Pynchon and the men of the river towns. The cause was Pynchon's failure (so Connecticut alleged) to carry out his part of a contract for the supply of Indian corn, which he was to furnish in return for a monopoly of the Indian trade up the river in furs and corn—a monopoly he had not asked for and to which he was

---

ness, but what that business was is nowhere mentioned. For these reasons I am unable to accept the opinion of the editor of the *Connecticut Colonial Records*, 1636–1665, that the blank pages which appear in the original record book were designed for the entering of the Fundamental Orders. It is more than likely that they were left blank for the recording of the proceedings of these nine months. The late Governor Baldwin, who inclines to this view of the case, thinks that the failure to enter the minutes was due to a change of secretaries, Edward Hopkins replacing John Steel. If Dr. Trumbull's opinion be accepted then we are confronted with the almost incredible fact that for nine critical months in the history of the colony no meetings of the general court were held. This is not only difficult to believe, but is disproved by the evidence given above.

1. *Proceedings*, Massachusetts Historical Society, 58, p. 388; *Connecticut Colonial Records*, 1636–1665, p. 12.

strongly opposed. Connecticut charged that "he was not soe care-full to promote the publique good in trade of Corne as hee was bounde to doe,"[1] and at a general court held on April 5, in his own presence as a magistrate, fined him forty bushels of corn "for the publique and the said Corne to be delivered to the Treasurer to be disposed of as shalbe thought meete." Pynchon was deeply offended at this ill-advised action of his fellow colonists, and taking advantage of the fact that there was considerable uncertainty as to whether Springfield was or was not within the Massachusetts jurisdiction, he decided to have no further connection with the lower plantations.

The importance of this decision was enhanced at this juncture by the plans under way in 1637–1638 for a union of the Puritan colonies in a loose confederation for mutual support. Should Springfield come in as a part of Massachusetts or of Connecticut? Debate on this question gave rise to considerable ill will between Connecticut and Massachusetts, and served in part to postpone the final agreement. The situation was further complicated by the necessity which the Connecticut leaders felt of giving to their own political system a more centralized and uniform governmental organization in order to prepare their colony for entrance into the new combination. Before working out a plan they had to decide whether or not to invite Springfield to become a member of the commonwealth they proposed to set up. Pynchon settled that question by opposing the plan and electing to throw in his lot with Massachusetts. In consequence the Connecticut leaders in drawing up their frame of government left Springfield entirely out of the new combination.

Also there were other reasons than the anger which Pynchon felt at the injustice of the fine imposed by the general court to explain the separation of Springfield from the river towns. Hooker and Pynchon did not get on any better together than did Hooker and Cotton, and the differences between them, as was so often the case with the Puritan elect, were apparently irreconcilable.[2] Hooker re-

1. For Pynchon's defense, *Proceedings,* Massachusetts Historical Society, 48, pp. 35–56. Pynchon was granted the monopoly in furs, with a tax of 5s on each skin, a privilege that he did not ask for and did not want. He was quite satisfied with an open competition, in which he was likely to come out ahead. He was also placed under contract to supply 500 bushels of corn to the river towns in return for a monopoly of trade in corn with the Indians, to meet a great scarcity which had occurred in the summer of 1637. This was the contract that Connecticut charged him with failure to carry out, fining him for his "infaithfulness."

2. *Proceedings,* Massachusetts Historical Society, 64, pp. 70, 85–87.

sented the Massachusetts claim of jurisdiction over Springfield, a claim that for some reason had not been made at the time of the migration. He was deeply indignant that Pynchon, who had been one of the chief participants in the westward movement, had shared as a magistrate in Connecticut's beginnings, had taken the oath of fidelity to the common cause, and was a member of the general court, a committee of which was engaged in drawing up the Fundamental Orders, should have been willing on so slight a pretext to break away from his former allies. It is quite possible, too, that Pynchon's Calvinism did not suit Hooker, who was one of the most orthodox of the Puritan clergy, just as later it did not suit the Massachusetts general court, when it ordered a Pynchon book, *The Meritorious Price of our Redemption,* to be burned on the Boston Common.[1]

These reasons, together with the distance and the difficulties of navigation up the river and the fur-trading interests of the northern plantation as contrasted with the agricultural activities of the plantations down the river, are sufficient to explain why Springfield entered the New England Confederation in 1643 as part of Massachusetts and not of Connecticut, and thus had no place in the commonwealth which was erected under the Fundamental Orders in 1639. Because Massachusetts did not for ten years admit into her general court deputies from Springfield, it was necessary for that small plantation, occupying land on the east side of the Connecticut River and independent of outside help, to set itself up, under Pynchon as its dominant head and under his direct control as long as he remained in New England. In 1641 Massachusetts appointed him to execute the office of chief judge and magistrate, with a right of appeal from his decisions to the court of assistants at Boston. In 1642 he was chosen one of the assistants and in 1649 deputies from Springfield appeared in the general court at the Bay.[2] He returned

1. *Massachusetts Colonial Records,* IV (I), 29: Burt, *First Century,* I, 86–125.

2. The chief authorities are the article by the late Governor Baldwin, "The Secession of Springfield from Connecticut," *Publications,* Colonial Society of Massachusetts, XII, 55–82, and Morison, "William Pynchon, Founder of Massachusetts," *Proceedings,* Massachusetts Historical Society, 64, pp. 67–107. See also, *ibid.,* 48, pp. 35–36, 47–48, and *ibid.,* 58, pp. 386–388. There is a brief biography of Pynchon by John Eliot in *Report,* Boston Record Commissioners, 6, p. 73. For Pynchon's will, *New England Historical and Genealogical Register,* April, 1894, pp. 2–6. Local Springfield histories are Burt, *First Century of the History of Springfield,* two volumes, largely documentary but with a long "Historical Review," and Green, *History of Springfield, 1636–1886,*

to England in 1652, partly because of his difficulties with Massachusetts, and partly also because of the necessity which he felt of looking after his extensive properties there. He left the settlement in
charge of his son John, under whom the town prospered as a self-
governing republic, extending widely its fur trading interests, establishing frontier trading posts at Westfield, Hadley, and Northampton, and doing business even as far west as Albany. John Pynchon died in 1703.

The controversy which ended in the secession of Springfield from
Connecticut is thus closely bound up with two events of major importance in the early history of Connecticut and of New England.
The first of these was the proposal which came from Connecticut in
1637 that a confederation be formed of the Puritan colonies for
mutual protection against the Indians and the Dutch, for the disposal of the Pequot country and the extension of the fur trade, and
for the maintenance of the common faith and the common good.
Agreement was not easily reached and the discussion was prolonged
for six years. The claims of Massachusetts to the Pequot country,
her support of Pynchon in his determination to withdraw from
Connecticut, misunderstandings regarding the boundary line between Springfield and Connecticut, and, later, disputes regarding
Connecticut's right to levy tolls at the mouth of the river, all these
matters delayed the ratification of the articles of the confederation
and endangered the continuance of the union even after an understanding had been reached in 1643. The antipathies thus created
continued to vex the members of the confederation until its usefulness, though not its existence, came to an end with the absorption
of New Haven by Connecticut in 1665.

The second important issue sprang from the necessity that the
Connecticut men felt of giving to their plantation system a compact and authoritative constitutional form and of consolidating the
experience of the preceding three years in a written document that
would represent the principles and policies already tried out in
practice. Connecticut as yet had no formal instrument of government. Massachusetts had her charter, and Plymouth her Mayflower
Compact and Bradford patent of 1630. New Haven, though as yet
hardly founded, was soon, in June, 1639, to settle "a Civill Govern-

a readable but unreliable narrative. The best account of early Springfield is by H. A.
Wright, *The Genesis of Springfield* (1936), a valuable and dependable contribution.

ment according to God." We do not know that the Connecticut towns had even plantation covenants as had New Haven, Milford, and Guilford, holding their members together in a common obedience to such constituted authority as these members might elect. Undoubtedly the Connecticut towns came very early to some understanding regarding local affairs and entered into definite agreements regarding the distribution of their lands, but there is nothing to show that either Hartford, Wethersfield, Windsor, or Springfield had drawn up any formal civil agreement before or after they entered the valley.[1] Hooker, confronted with the withdrawal of Pynchon and believing that it was every man's right to choose his jurisdiction as he pleased,[2] probably felt that the time had come to bind the inhabitants of the river towns firmly together in a common loyalty to a central government. The assurance that the lords and gentlemen had deserted their settlement and would never erect any government of their own, and the imperative need of creating a jurisdiction that was sufficiently defined for Connecticut to enter the confederation on equal terms with the others were added reasons why in the year 1638 the general court of Connecticut faced the important task of framing the Fundamental Orders of the colony.

1. The document printed in Burt (I, 156–158) is not a plantation covenant. It is rather a formal agreement regarding things to be done at the beginning of settlement, such as might well have been entered into by each of the river towns before 1639.

2. "Yes, taking it for granted that it is each inhabitant's liberty . . . to choose his jurisdiction (which is to me beyond question)," *Collections,* Connecticut Historical Society, I, 14. In Pynchon's case, however, Hooker evidently deemed the oath of fidelity more binding than the "liberty" mentioned in this quotation. Just how Hooker squared his leaving Massachusetts with the oath of a freeman which he had taken there we are not told. Pynchon would seem to have had as much right to secede from Connecticut as Hooker had to secede from Massachusetts.

CHAPTER IV

FROM FUNDAMENTAL ORDERS TO CHARTER
IN CONNECTICUT

THUS by the spring of 1638 circumstances were forcing the Connecticut leaders to take action in two important directions—first, to prepare as hitherto they had not done a body of fundamental law, which should define their procedure as a government and their status as a properly constituted civil jurisdiction, in order that they might enter the projected confederation on equal terms with the others; and, secondly, to combine and unite with the colonies of Plymouth and Massachusetts so far as to walk and live peaceably and lovingly together to maintain the common cause and to defend the "priviledges and freedomes wee now enjoy against all opposers." To this end there was gathered, sometime in May, 1638, what Ludlow calls in his letter of May 29 to the Massachusetts Bay authorities, "a generall assembly of these plantacons in this River," at which were considered "divers particulars that might or may concern the general good of these parts."[1] Matters of so important a character might well have been brought to the attention of the free planters of the colony, and though Ludlow makes it quite clear that what he is writing about is the plan for a confederation with Massachusetts and nothing else, nevertheless the idea of drafting fundamentals for the colony might well have been among the subjects presented for the assembly's approval. This assembly, whatever it was—and we do not know anything more about it— probably met, transacted its business, and departed. That it lasted for any such length of time as to be still in existence when Ludlow wrote his letter on May 29 and Hooker delivered his sermon on the 31st is clearly impossible. Were it still sitting on the 29th Ludlow would have used some other expression than "There being of late a generall assembly," which, if words mean anything, distinctly refers to an event that has come and gone. The connection of this

1. Ludlow to the Governor and Brethren of the Massachusetts Bay, May 29, 1638, *Collections,* Massachusetts Historical Society, 5th ser., I, 260–261. In a second letter, this time to Winthrop, July 3, 1638, he says that they have been too busy "to draw one people together" but will do so as soon as they conveniently can (264).

"assembly" with the Fundamental Orders is therefore wholly a matter of conjecture. The assembly may have given the general court some kind of a warrant to go ahead with the drafting of the Orders, or it may not have done anything of the kind. As the colony had already been governing itself for two years, it could hardly have seemed to the leaders necessary to call the planters together before putting into written form what already had been tried out and been shown by experience to be workable; whereas the proposal to combine with Massachusetts was so novel that the leaders might well have hesitated to act without the wider consent.

However that may be, Hooker on May 31, 1638, delivered a famous sermon. Before whom he delivered it we do not know, but unless the free planters were called together again, as is most unlikely, he probably spoke to the members of the general court. As to whether what he said was solely his own or represented the opinions of others than himself, we are also in doubt. The probabilities are that he was simply putting into an expository form certain principles already agreed on, according to which a civil government should be erected. There was nothing specially new about these principles, for they had been in process of test in Connecticut for the preceding two years, and in others of the New England colonies, notably in Plymouth and Rhode Island, they had found and were to find application in one form or another. The chief difference in the civil practices of these colonies, including Massachusetts and New Haven, lies in what was understood by the "people," a word which has always been easy to misinterpret in the history of mankind. Hooker's statement on this point is idealistic, broad, and far from precise, if we are to judge from the brief synopsis of his sermon that has come down to us. He said that the foundations of authority were laid in the free consent of the "people" and that therefore the choice of public magistrates belonged unto the "people" by God's own allowance; that the privilege of election was to be exercised according to the blessed will and law of God, because by a free choice the hearts of the "people" would be more inclined to the love of the persons chosen and the more ready to yield obedience; and, lastly, that they who had the power to appoint officers and magistrates had also the power to set the bounds and limitations of that power and place unto which they called them.[1] What

1. *Collections,* Connecticut Historical Society, I, 20.

Hooker meant by his sermon was just what Roger Williams meant in *The Bloudy Tenent,* that authority ought to come from *below* and not from *above.* Everything in the working out of this idea would, therefore, depend on what was understood by "below," a term, which as we shall see later, Connecticut defined in her own peculiar way.

Under the stimulus of Hooker's powerful words the general court set about its business of framing a government. We are left without any information as to how the work was done. The preliminary task was undoubtedly placed in the hands of a committee, consisting certainly of Ludlow and Haynes and probably of Wells, Steel, and Hopkins also. That Ludlow shaped the instrument in its final form can hardly be questioned. Its brevity, clarity, and compactness are the earmarks of an exceptionally good legal mind, wholly unlike the verboseness of the average Puritan writer. When finished the draft was put to the vote and adopted January 14, 1639, either unanimously or by a majority of the members present. We have no details.

The contents of the document, new chiefly in the form in which they are cast, consist of a preamble and eleven orders or laws. The preamble is a civil covenant binding the inhabitants of the three towns or plantations to be guided and governed in all civil things by the orders that followed. These orders are the fundamentals of the "public state" thus erected, the "laws or orders of general concernment," as they were later called by the court itself,[1] which gave body to what Hooker calls the "combination." This "combination" was brought into being, not as something struck off for the first time but as a confirmation of an already established system by a government which had been functioning since 1636 and performing important political, financial, religious, and judicial duties.[2] From the beginning this government had contained within itself all the essentials of self-rule, free from the regulating influence of any outside authority other than God himself.

The preamble was the counterpart of the church covenant, the outward and visible sign of a civil as contrasted with a religious compact. By the latter a group of people entered into an agreement with God and each other to form a church; by the former they entered into a mutual agreement and common accord to form a state

1. *Connecticut Colonial Records,* 1636–1665, p. 39
2. Even the particular court dates back to a time earlier than the adoption of the Fundamental Orders.

or commonwealth. The Connecticut preamble differed from the usual plantation covenant in that it was the work of three plantations, not one plantation,[1] but it did not differ in principle from the covenants that had gone before and were to come after. The covenant idea lay at the bottom of the Puritan organization in both church and state.

The eleven orders that follow the preamble are in the form of a series of statute laws and differ from similar laws adopted or to be adopted in Plymouth, Rhode Island, and New Haven only so far as they are combined together in a concise, well systematized scheme or frame of government and embody, in unadorned, well chosen language, the essentials of popular rule such as the Connecticut leaders had conceived and Ludlow had competently drawn up. In its main features this government followed the Massachusetts model, based on a trading company's charter, with which these men were familiar. There were the same two general courts—one a court of election and legislation meeting in April (later changed to May),[2] the other a court of legislation meeting only in September and doing in addition much administrative and judicial business. Also, and for the first time, a governor was provided for—Winthrop's commission having expired in the summer of 1636 and no successor having been named—and special rules were laid down concerning his election. He was to be a member of some approved congregation, was to be taken from among the magistrates, and was to hold office for only one year, though after another year had elapsed he could be re-elected. This rule, which was in striking contrast with the rules of the other New England colonies, was retained only until 1660 when the restriction was removed and the choice thrown open. In order that neither governor nor magistrates should be hastily chosen, there were put into practice a series of checks, whereby names of such magistrates as were "fitte to put to election" should be tendered at a previous general court by the deputies from the towns, and then, after presentation by the secretary, be formally accepted at the court of election in April (or May). Thus the governor and magistrates were to be elected "by the vote of the country."[3] Just what this

1. At the founding of Exeter, New Hampshire, thirty-five men signed an agreement to establish "such government as should be to their best discerning agreeable to the Will of God." Belknap, *History of New Hampshire* (Farmer ed.), pp. 20, note, 432–433.

2. *Connecticut Colonial Records*, 1636–1665, p. 39.   3. *Ibid.*, p. 140.

phrase actually meant will be considered later. The court if it wished could add to the names brought in by the deputies as many more as it judged requisite. Provision was made also for the orderly election of deputies from the towns, though no details are anywhere given as to how the local elections were to be conducted, except that those who exercised the local franchise were to be "admitted inhabitants" of the towns in which they resided.

This matter of the franchise at the beginnings of Connecticut's history has been greatly misunderstood. Apparently it has been assumed that every male adult in the colony was given a right to a share in government and that in the exercise of that right the majority ruled. Nothing could be farther from the truth. The Fundamental Orders, as well as later laws, make a sharp distinction between one who voted in the town and one who voted for colony officers, that is, between an "admitted inhabitant" and a "freeman," though they are none too clear as to the precise qualifications of each. An "admitted inhabitant" was any householder of "honest conversation," whatever that may mean, who had taken a carefully phrased oath of fidelity to the commonwealth, which by the words used, "Soe helpe me God in o^r Lord Jesus Christe," testifies to the fact that it could be taken only by a Trinitarian.[1] When admitted by majority vote of those properly qualified in town meeting, he could take part in local affairs, join in the election of local officials, and vote for deputies to the general court. But being an "admitted inhabitant" did not make a man a "freeman." The latter was any "admitted inhabitant" who had been selected for freemanship either by the general court itself or by some one or more of the magistrates who was authorized by the court to make "freemen."[2] Only when thus admitted to freemanship could the adult male householder offer himself for election as a deputy, vote for the higher officials of the colony and himself fill the post of magistrate. Only a "freeman" could attend the court of election, either in person, or by proxy

1. For a commentary on the oaths of fidelity and allegiance in New England, with special reference to Massachusetts but with a section devoted to Connecticut and New Haven, see Evans, "Oaths of Allegiance," *Proceedings,* American Antiquarian Society, October, 1921. The Connecticut oath is in *Connecticut Colonial Records,* 1636–1665, pp. 62–63.

2. *Ibid.,* pp. 62–63, 139, 290, 351, 389. In 1639 Haynes and Wells went to Stratford to give the planters there the "oath of fidelity and make such free as they see fit." They were to order the planters to send one or two deputies to the two general courts in April and September (p. 36).

in case he lived in a distant town.[1] Thus the "admitted inhabitants" were the householders in the towns, including also the adult males, married or unmarried, in their families, who as landowners and Trinitarians, were the substantial and godly men in their respective communities; the "freemen" were only such of the "admitted inhabitants" as were deemed by the general court fit to take part in the affairs of the commonwealth itself. As neither women, servants, apprentices,[2] nor anyone convicted of a scandalous offense[3] were allowed to exercise the franchise or to have any part in the government of town or colony, it happened from the beginning that in the actual working out of the system the words "people" and "inhabitants" acquired a meaning much more restricted than that commonly given to them today.[4]

1. The Connecticut practice, both before and after the receipt of the charter, conformed closely to that of the corporate boroughs of England, where the parishioners governed through their vestries, but where only freemen of the wards could vote for aldermen and common councillors. In some boroughs the right to vote was limited even more narrowly, but of course nowhere in England was it dependent on a religious requirement as it was in Massachusetts, Connecticut, and New Haven. In civil procedure the Connecticut, Massachusetts, Rhode Island, and New Haven systems followed very closely the London ward practice of sending two councillors to the common council. Only men free of the City could vote for City officials, just as only "freemen" in the Puritan colonies could vote for the higher officials of government. Local administration was in the hands of the vestries and the ward moots, which were equivalent to the town meeting; general business was in the hands of the mayor, aldermen, and common councillors. It is curious how little in the way of forms and methods of government, either in the towns or the colonies, the Puritans invented or contrived for themselves. The practices which they adopted trace their origin to the gilds, corporate boroughs, and trading companies of the mother country, just as their laws are often the reproduction of the common law dispensed in the English local courts, with which they were frequently in contact as they were not with the higher common law courts at Westminster. In England only freeholders could vote for the knights of the shire who represented them in parliament, and this was the rule generally in all the English colonies in America.

2. Many servants and apprentices were in the colony from the beginning, large numbers coming in with the first settlers, particularly with the Hooker company. By 1644 they were reported to be numerous—"stubborn, refractory and discontented"—a class that had to be controlled by special laws (*Connecticut Colonial Records*, 1636–1665, p. 105, also pp. 8, 84, 127, 173, 174, 316; *Particular Court Records* (*Collections*, Connecticut Historical Society, XXII), *passim*. Mention is made of "negar servants" and of Indian servants (*Connecticut Colonial Records*, 1636–1665, p. 349; 1665–1678, pp. 308–309). The Code of 1650 has a section devoted to "Masters, Servants, Sojourners," including also apprentices (*ibid.*, pp. 538–539).

3. Two cases of disenfranchisement are recorded: one for "scandalous, lascivious and pernicious carriage, thereby interrupting the peace and tending to corrupt the manners of his Maties Subjects" (*Particular Court Records*, p. 267); and the other for a similar offense (*ibid.*, p. 268).

4. In 1663, the Connecticut colony, in its controversy with New Haven, defined

In the towns the "admitted inhabitants" had to be religious and godly men with a competency of estate, though not necessarily members of a congregation, and they were the ones who ran local affairs and voted for deputies; but in the colony the control of government lay in the hands of the "freemen" only, constituting probably less than one third of the "admitted inhabitants," the specially chosen of the godly men, the last sifting in the winnowing of the grain, according to the Connecticut standard, who as the "freemen" constituted what Dr. Bronson calls "a kind of popular aristocracy—the trusted pillars of the commonwealth."[1]

Thus the practice of the colony defined the ideas of the founders as to what they conceived "consent of the people" to mean. To them it meant no more than that the source of authority was below and within and not above and without. Their notion of the "consent of the people" was not the consent of all the inhabitants but rather the consent of those only who, according to the Puritan idea, were of a "religious carriage," and therefore by God's will most qualified to give such consent. Numbers and majorities, though recognized as necessary to an ultimate decision, had very little to do with the running of the government. The founders of Connecticut differed from their Puritan brethren in Massachusetts Bay and New Haven only so far as they wanted popular self-rule to rest on a broader religious base than was the case in the other two colonies, and they defined

its franchise qualifications as follows. "We are ready to grant that they [the "freemen"] shalbe men of a religious carriage visibly soe, haveing and possessing Some competency of estate, and shal bring a Certificate affirmative that they are thus Quallified from the Deacons of the Church and Two of the Selecmen of the Towne where they live, And if there be noe deacons, then some other knowne and approved persons w'th the Select men as before . . . That the ffreemen of these Plantat⁸ shall have power to chuse all Publ country officers except Assistants to weet: Commission'ʳs, Deputies and Constables. As for Select men who are to ordʳ the civil prudentiall affaires of the Respective Townes they are to be yearly chosen by a maior Vote of the approved Inhabitants wᵗʰ other necessary Towne officers in thʳ respect. Pl. in this country." Connecticut Archives, Miscellaneous, I, no. 72; New Haven Colonial Records, II, 493, 494.

1. "Early Government in Connecticut," Papers, New Haven Colony Historical Society, III, 313. Dr. Bronson says, "Evidently the freemen were not numerous . . . I cannot find that more than twenty-three were admitted in the first ten years after 1639. From 1639 to 1662 two hundred and twenty-nine admissions are on record, while the increase in population may have been three thousand [it was three thousand in 1643], one quarter of them males of legal age." There is nothing to show that in Connecticut any more than in Massachusetts a man could be compelled to become a freeman, or could become one merely because he wanted to. In Plymouth, however, it was customary "to persuade, sometimes compel them, to be free."

their religious requirement in the oath of fidelity which every man
had to take before admittance. They were willing to concede a share
in government to anyone who was godly, in their sense of the word,
and was responsible, trustworthy, and law-abiding, for to have done
otherwise would have been to belie their Puritan heritage and convictions. To the Puritan what we call democracy was looked upon
as an aberration of the human mind, disapproved of God and his
faithful elect; and only those who were Christians, of honest and
peaceable conversation, substantial, respectable, and reliable fathers
in Israel were considered worthy to build up a community the
design of which was religious.

The Fundamental Orders, as far as defining the functions of a
government is concerned, are very imperfect and incomplete and
scarcely go beyond a statement of what the framework of such a
system should be. They are much less elaborate than is the outline
drawn up by John Cotton in 1636, representing the government of
Massachusetts, or than the New Haven "fundamentals" of 1639 and
1643. Except in the portions relating to the powers of the general
court they make no attempt to determine where lay executive, administrative, and judicial authority, probably because the compilers
of the instrument considered these responsibilities as vested in the
general court itself, by which, if desired, they could be delegated to
specially appointed officials. The governor was given the right to
summon the general court, which could be prorogued and dissolved
only by vote of its own members; and the magistrates, who in these
early years were largely concerned with judicial matters, constituted,
with the governor and deputy governor, a particular court "to administer justice according to the Lawes here established and for
want thereof according to the rule of the Word of God." The supreme authority in the commonwealth was the general court. It
was given power "to make lawes or repeale them, to grant Levyes,
to admitt of Freemen, dispose of lands undisposed of to severall
townes or persons, to call either court or magistrate or any other
person whatsoever into question for any misdemeanor, and for just
cause displace or deal otherwise according to the nature of the of-
fence, and also to deale in any other matter that concerns the good
of this commonwealth except election of magistrates which shall be
done by the whole body of Freemen." No provision was made for
a speaker (*eo nomine*) or for any rules of parliamentary procedure,

except so far as to allow liberty of speech, which was not to be exercised in an unreasonable and disorderly manner. Any one so offending was liable to a reprimand from the presiding officer—governor, deputy governor, or moderator. Later, secrecy was enjoined upon all. The presiding officer was to put all things to vote and in case of a tie was to have the deciding voice. The general court sat as a single body in the meetinghouse at Hartford.

There are certain provisions among the Fundamental Orders that represent the fears these men felt regarding the danger of a powerful magistracy and their desire to give ultimate control into the hands of the "freemen"—not of the people at large, for as we have already seen there was a wide gulf fixed between the "freemen" and the "inhabitants and residents" named in the preamble. Such fears may have arisen from their experience with Massachusetts, where the power of the magistrates was one of the reasons for their dissatisfaction with the government there. Therefore the orders decreed that should the governor or the major part of the magistrates neglect or refuse to summon the general court, in regular or special session according to the method prescribed, then the "freemen" or the major part of them could petition the magistrates to do so, and if the latter continued to refuse then the "freemen" could take it upon themselves to order the town constables to bring together the "admitted inhabitants" for the election of deputies. These deputies could meet, choose a moderator, and proceed "to doe any act of power wch any other court may." Furthermore, the deputies at any time when attending the general court might meet beforehand to prepare an agenda "of all things as may concerne the good of the publike as also to examine their own elections whether according to order," and if they found that any election had been illegally conducted they could exclude the deputy in question, temporarily, until the matter had been passed on by the general court in regular session. At this preliminary meeting the deputies could impose fines upon any that were late or that were disorderly after the meeting had come together. As it happened, however, no court composed of the freemen-deputies only was ever convened; though occasionally at this early period a court was held without a governor or deputy governor;[1] and rarely was an election ever called in question by the general court.

1. *Connecticut Colonial Records*, 1636–1665, pp. 250, 252, 288, 348.

The men who were responsible for this noteworthy document had no intention of creating an organic law that was to be sacrosanct against the general court's complete control over legislation. They omitted, either intentionally or unintentionally, all reference to their royal sovereign across the seas and seem to have wished to cut themselves off from all connection with English authority and English law,[1] but they fully expected future courts to elaborate, alter, and add to the general rules already laid down. There are many other fundamental laws to be found among the early records of the colony that are so called although not contained in the eleven original fundamentals,[2] for the word "fundamental" was in frequent use among the Puritan lawgivers and had no more subtle meaning than a general law—one of the foundation stones upon which the governmental structure rested.[3]

The Fundamental Orders were frequently added to and eight times altered in the ensuing twenty-two years. A study of these alterations throws some light on the way the original orders were

1. Yet in 1662, before the receipt of the charter, a charge was brought against a woman for "Treason agaynst his Matie" (*Particular Court Records*, p. 248). In 1662 the situation was quite different from what it had been in 1639 or even in 1650.

2. Sergeant Walter Fyler of Windsor "charged upon Mr. Stone the Breach of A Fundamental Law" (*ibid.*, p. 140). The law referred to cannot be any one of the eleven Fundamentals, thus showing, as other evidence also shows, that there were other laws of the colony than the eleven Fundamentals which were deemed "fundamental." It is an interesting fact that the term "fundamental" was not only frequently used elsewhere in New England, as stated in the text, but was in common use wherever the Puritans settled. It was applied by the town of Oyster Bay on the north shore of Long Island even to the Duke's Laws, adopted at Hempstead in 1665, though these laws were not of the town's own making (*Oyster Bay Town Records*, I, 34). Newark in New Jersey, settled from Milford, Branford, and New Haven in 1666, had its "fundamental agreement." The "Common Law or Fundamental Rights and Privileges" or "the great Charter of Fundamentals" of the Quaker province of West New Jersey were called "the Foundations of Government" and could not be altered by legislative enactment. The general assembly there was constituted "according to these Fundamentals to make such laws as agree with and maintain the said Fundamentals and to make no laws that in the least contradict, differ or vary from the said Fundamentals, under what Pretence or Alligation soever." Any one who did this was to be proceeded against "as traitors to the said Government" (*New Jersey Archives*, I, 252). The same was true of the Fundamental Constitutions of Carolina issued in 1669, which in the final article were declared to be "the Sacred and Unalterable Form and Rule of Government of Carolina for ever." The Connecticut Fundamental Orders contain no such binding clauses as these, and in practice the Connecticut general court did not hesitate to pass laws modifying or adding to the fundamental law of the colony. The Connecticut Orders were "fundamental" but they were not "immutable" as were those of West New Jersey and Carolina.

3. See NOTE at the end of the chapter.

probably adopted, for in five cases out of the eight the change was brought about by act of the general court itself and in only three— one relating to the summoning of the general court, another to the tenure of the governor, and the third to the number of deputies from the towns—were the "freemen" called upon for their approval.

In 1644, five years after the orders were voted, the general court "ordered and adjudged" that the number of magistrates present, sufficient to constitute a lawful court, should be three instead of four as stated in the tenth fundamental,[1] and this change in a "fundamental" was effected by the simple fiat of the court itself. In 1647 the court "ordered, sentenced and decreed" (the very words used in the orders themselves) that the governor or deputy governor with two magistrates should have power to hold a particular court according to the laws established, and in case the governor or deputy governor were absent, then three magistrates could choose a moderator and proceed to business. This was really equivalent to a twelfth fundamental and it too was issued by fiat of the general court as a law like the other fundamentals.[2] Three times, in the years 1646, 1657, and 1659, as will be noted later on, were the law and practice of the franchise materially changed and in each case the general court acted entirely on its own responsibility. In 1661 a further remarkable provision was made, that in an emergency a general court "with full power and authority" might consist of only the deputies from the towns "on the river," with "so many magistrates as the law requires."[3] These instances seem sufficient to show that in certain important matters the court could alter the fundamentals with entire confidence in its power and right to do so.

Only three times before the coming of the charter were the "freemen" called on for their approval. In 1654 "the 'freemen' voted and ordered to be added to the Fundamentals" that in the absence of the governor and deputy governor the magistrates, by majority vote, could call a regular assembly, choose a moderator, and pass laws in the usual manner.[4] As the number of "freemen" was increasing, thirty-six having been admitted at this very court, their influence was increasing also, and the matter at issue concerned them very closely. A second revision brings out this point still more clearly. In 1660 the decision was reached by the general court to alter the

---

1. *Connecticut Colonial Records,* 1636–1665, p. 119 and note.
2. *Ibid.,* p. 150.   3. *Ibid.,* pp. 138, 290, 293, 331.
4. *Ibid.,* p. 256.

law regarding the tenure of the governor—the most important change thus far suggested. In putting this decision into effect the procedure adopted was as follows. The general court drafted the recommendation and ordered the secretary to insert in the warrants for the choice of deputies the proposal that the choice of governor should be thrown open and not restricted as in the Fundamental Orders. This proposal was made of course only to the "freemen," who elected the governor and magistrates, and they were instructed to vote on the question at the next court of election.[1] Again in 1661 a third proposal was made that the number of deputies from each town in the colony be reduced one half. This proposal was referred to the "freemen" but was not acted on, probably because of the opportunity offered by the charter to bring about the same result. Had the recommendation been adopted it would have altered the eighth fundamental, which allowed the three original towns to send four deputies each.[2] The procedure in each of these cases is much the same, proving that in matters of great moment the "freemen" were the final seat of authority, as far as the administration of the colony, apart from that of the towns, was concerned, and that in certain important situations, though by no means necessarily in all, their approval was deemed advisable. In most cases, however, the action of magistrates and deputies in general court assembled was undoubtedly considered sufficient in matters of legislation.

But even when the approval of the "freemen" was sought a striking manifestation of Puritan political philosophy is revealed. As the general court itself decided who were worthy to be made "freemen" and made only such as it saw fit—not under any mandatory law defining freemanship but by God's own allowance—it becomes evident that the court was referring these questions to a limited number of the members of the colony, who had been selected as "freemen" by act of the court itself. If the general court could make a "freeman" at will and, for scandalous offense, unmake him, then it approached very near the possession of more than supreme power, inasmuch as it could determine who should exercise what the "freemen" were supposed to possess, and that is ultimate consent. Only in the choice of deputies did the "admitted inhabitants" have any determining influence and even then their choice was restricted to "freemen" only. This is a curious situation to exist in a colony that

1. *Ibid.*, pp. 346–347.   2. *Ibid.*, pp. 372–373.

by popular repute is thought to have started as a "commonwealth-democracy."[1]

The truth is that the ideas of the Connecticut Puritans regarding the political and religious organization of society was far removed from the democratic ideas of later times. They sought the welfare not of the individual but of the community and in town and colony relegated the individual as an individual to a subordinate place in the social order. No one can study the history of the Connecticut towns during the seventeenth century without realizing how at every point the freedom of the individual was under restraint whenever the needs of the community at large were involved. During the century the towns were covenanted groups quite as much as were the churches. In the distribution and settling of lands; the selling and accumulation of lots; the reversion of land to the town in case the individual moved away; the control of the meadows after the haying season was over; the obligation of the individual to join in labor for the common welfare as in making roads, clearing brush, and killing blackbirds; the access to the commons, woods, and waste; the use of timber and other natural resources; the attitude toward strangers and aliens and the making of grants to artisans, millers, fullers, tanners, and the like, where the title was not absolute but only usufructuary—in all these cases the interests of the community came first and those of the individual were of secondary importance. Town liberty was conserved but not individual liberty. "Saving the good of the community," though not often expressed, was always understood in all transactions in which the individual had a part. The town records of the seventeenth century are full of votes limiting individual freedom.

That which was true of the towns was true of the commonwealth also. Before the coming of the charter and even more so afterward, the higher government was in the hands of very few men. It was a combination and a commonwealth, and later a corporation, that was largely divorced from the inhabitants as a whole and did not regard all of them as necessary to its existence. It worked through the towns rather than through the people who resided in them, though it did not hesitate to control, punish, and penalize the individual, whenever the interests of the colony demanded that it do so, without

1. This is the sub-title of Johnson's widely read little volume on Connecticut in the American Commonwealth Series, which unfortunately has done much to mislead the public regarding the early history of the colony.

regard to whether the individual had political rights or not. In the political creed of the Connecticut Puritan the essentials of modern democracy—the rights and liberties of the individual and the sacredness of popular representation and majority rule—had no place.

Thus the men who drew up the Fundamental Orders had a perfectly definite idea as to what the words "inhabitants" and "people" were to mean in the practical business of running towns and commonwealth. And just as they disclosed their mind in that direction, so they made known their conviction regarding the relative importance, in another direction, of deputies and magistrates. There was to be no "negative vote" or "negative voice" in Connecticut as there had been in Massachusetts.[1] The deputies were to be supreme in matters of legislation and their will was not to be overridden by magisterial opposition. But as time went on and the administration settled down to a working routine, fear of the magistrates lessened and they tended to increase in dignity and prestige as well as in judicial authority. They obtained no enlargement of political powers, unless the reduction of those necessary to constitute a general court and their right to preside at its meetings in the absence of governor and deputy governor may be so considered. But they received noteworthy extensions of privilege in other directions. In the first place, with the governor and his deputy, they composed the particular court—court of magistrates or quarter court—which was a "tribunal for the settlement of differences and the establishment of just rights between particular persons, in distinction from the general court, which dealt with matters pertaining to the rights and benefit of all the inhabitants."[2] It was a common law court with a jury,[3] which

---

1. Above, Vol. I, 451–452.

2. *Particular Court Records*, preface. The court did a certain amount of probate business also. The proceedings of the court, which probably sat for the first time in 1637, are printed, as far as extant to December, 1649, in the first volume of the *Connecticut Colonial Records*. Those from 1650 to April, 1663, were discovered in 1861 by Charles J. Hoadly in the possession of a private family in New York.

3. A grand jury was instituted in 1643. For the oath, *Particular Court Records*, p. 131, and for a presentment, pp. 136–137. The members of the jury seem to have been none too desirous of serving, and so unsatisfactory were their verdicts that in 1649 arbitration was suggested in some cases and in others the magistrates were instructed, "if they doe not conceave the Jury to have proceeded according to the evidence," to give the parties a second trial and then if the verdict was still unsatisfactory to impanel another jury. In one instance the magistrates advised that there be a "forbearance of any persecution of each other for the future . . . and they do advise to a loving carriage to each other." It is likely that in more cases than one the jury in default of evidence returned the case "up to the bench" (*ibid.*, pp. 196, 198). The

was supplanted after 1664 by the county courts and the court of assistants, the latter being superseded in 1711 by the superior court.[1] In the second place, in addition to their duties as judges, the magistrates were authorized also to commit incorrigibles to prison, to swear in juries, to render judgment in case a jury was deadlocked, to mitigate or increase damages awarded by a jury, to give bills of divorce,[2] occasionally to grant licenses for the sale of liquor, to exercise discretionary power, should it be necessary, in punishing Quakers or sending them to prison,[3] and to superintend the disposal of servants. They could perform the marriage ceremony, as could also the deputies and the magistrates' assistants in the more remote towns, who were chosen by the towns to hear cases of less than forty shillings, with right of appeal to the particular court. They could make freemen, give the oath of fidelity to all males over sixteen years of age, press men and munitions for a defensive war, appoint days of thanksgiving and humiliation in the intervals between the sessions of the general court, serve as commissioners representing Connecticut at the meetings of the New England Confederation, and perform other diplomatic duties. The respect in which they were held appears from their being freed from all military service, exempted from all ferry dues, and granted the right to be entertained during the sittings of the particular court.[4] Thus the magis-

bench could vary and alter at will "according to equity and righteousness." Juries as few as six were allowed, and if four out of six and eight out of twelve agreed the verdict stood.

1. *Connecticut Colonial Records*, 1636–1665, pp. 72, 78, 85, 128, 138, 139 (293), 151, 275, 283, 284, 315–316, 324, 330, 335. For the court of assistants, pp. 186, 281, 435. After 1665 there were four county courts (*idem*, 1665–1678, pp. 34–35), presided over by assistants or commissioners. The term "magistrates," "assistants," and "commissioners" for a time seem to have been used interchangeably.

2. Divorces were looked on with disfavor, but they were granted even at this early date for desertion, "sinful, unworthy, unnatural carriage," and "upon good consideration and solid reasons and evidence," which probably included adultery and fraudulent contract (*idem*, 1636–1665, pp. 275, 301, 352, 362, 379; 1665–1678, pp. 129, 292, 293, 322, 326, 327, 328; Love, *Colonial History of Hartford*, p. 281).

3. The Quaker issue did not arise until 1656, when the Quakers appeared in Boston and the commissioners of the New England Confederation recommended that measures be taken against them. Connecticut accepted this recommendation on the ground that "the people of the Commonwealth must not be possessed in their judgment and principles by these loathsome heretics" (*Connecticut Colonial Records*, 1636–1665, pp. 283, 303, 308, 324).

4. In a case of appeal from the county court of New London the magistrates, sitting as a court of assistants, were allowed, at the expense of the colony, their breakfasts, dinners, and suppers, with beer, white wine, cider, spirits, rum, and sack. They

trate in Connecticut, though never considered divinely guided as was his fellow magistrate of Massachusetts, won, through his service as a member of the particular court and his usefulness as an agent of administration, a position of influence superior to that of the ordinary "freeman" and deputy, though both of these might at any time aspire to be magistrates themselves, should their fellow "freemen" choose to elect them as such.

Coincident with the advancement of the magistrates a reverse movement was taking place affecting the status of the "admitted inhabitants" and their deputies. This reverse movement would seem to indicate a loss of confidence on the part of the general court in the worthiness of those whom the towns were admitting to a share in local government and to the privilege of electing deputies. Perhaps for the same reason stress was laid more frequently than before on "honest conversation" as a qualification for "admitted inhabitants" and the towns were required to give certificates testifying to the "peaceable and honest conversation" of those whom the general court was willing to admit as "freemen."

At any rate something was happening to the social and moral standards of the Connecticut communities. The particular court records are filled with entries which show the presence in the colony of an undesirable element, neither better nor worse than appears elsewhere, but sufficiently filled with evil intents ("instigated by the Devil") to show that Connecticut during these years was not an abode of saints only. As was the case in other colonies, most of those charged with wanton dalliance, fornication, lying, drunkenness, blasphemy, robbery, and breaking the laws of the colony were apprentices and servants, of whom there were many in Connecticut as elsewhere bound to labor for a term of years. But some of these delinquents were clearly of the better classes, goodmen, misters, and esquires. Among them were those charged with contemptuous words and insolent carriage toward court and commonwealth, threatening and malicious speeches, defiance of authority and law, and the slighting of court orders. Men, and women too, were brought before the magistrates and juries in suits for debt, damages, trespass, extortion, slander, defamation, and offenses of all sorts "against the law." The court was called upon to regulate very minutely the personal con-

also had lodging and attendance and "horse-meat" (Connecticut Archives, Private Controversies, I, 23–24; *Connecticut Colonial Records*, 1665–1678, p. 210).

duct and domestic welfare of the people of Connecticut during the years before the coming of the charter, and to take cognizance of such matters as using tobacco, drinking and selling liquor, playing cards, working and traveling on the Sabbath, marriage and divorce, and not infrequently, relations between husbands and wives, fathers and children, masters and servants. Some twenty or more cases of witchcraft or "familiarity with the Devil" are recorded for Connecticut and New Haven before 1663, with at least ten hangings.[1] Two women were executed for other reasons, one for poisoning her husband and the other for saying that "Christ was a Bastard and she could prove it by Scripture."[2] There were others too whose utterances, if not as blasphemous, were to say the least disrespectful of the clergy and the New England way of ecclesiastical polity and procedure. The troubles that arose between 1650 and 1660 in the churches of Windsor, Wethersfield, Hartford, and Middletown gave opportunities for a good deal of free speaking. The Rev. Mr. Stow of Middletown was called a contentious, pestilent person by several people, one of whom charged him with saying "that those that were not in the visible covenant" were "dogs and among dogs and in [the] Kingdom of Sathan and at Sathans command."[3] As a result Stow was relieved of his pastorate by the general court, though allowed to continue preaching if he could get anyone to hear him.

Whether there was any connection between the limitation of the franchise and the troubled state of the colony during these years it is impossible to say. Newcomers were undoubtedly thrusting themselves into the towns, religious disturbances were increasing

1. On witchcraft in Connecticut before 1663, *Particular Court Records*, pp. 56, 93, 131, 188, 238, 240, 251, 258, 259; Connecticut Archives, Towns and Lands, I, no. 8; *Connecticut Colonial Records*, 1636–1665, pp. 220, 573; *New Haven Colonial Records*, II, 78–88; Mather, *Magnalia* (1702), bk. VI, 67, 71; Stiles, *Ancient Windsor*, I, 444–450, and, the same, *Ancient Wethersfield*, I, 680–682; Love, *Colonial History of Hartford*, pp. 283–286; Taylor, *The Witchcraft Delusion in Colonial Connecticut*, chs. v, xi; Levermore, "Witchcraft in Connecticut," *The New Englander*, 1885, pp. 788–817. The list is as follows: executed, Alse Young, Mary Johnson, the Carringtons, Goody Bassett, Goody Knapp, the Greensmiths, Mary Barnes, and Mary Sanford; possibly executed, Lydia Gilbert; jury divided, the Jennings and Andrew Sanford; acquitted, Elizabeth Garlick, Seager, Goodman, the Bayleys, and Meaker. Others were suspected, some arrested, a few fled from the colony. No executions took place after 1662, which for some reason or another was the year of greatest excitement. The case of Katherine Harrison of Wethersfield, who was acquitted, came up in 1668. Stiles, *Wethersfield*, I, 682–684; Paltsits, *Executive Council Minutes of New York*, I, 53, 54, 55.

2. *Particular Court Records*, pp. 194, 268.   3. *Ibid.*, pp. 182–183.

ill will, controversy and disorder were troubling the magistrates (if the records of the particular court are to be accepted as reflecting the spirit of the times), and the witchcraft mania was approaching its height. Certain it is that in 1646, 1657, and 1659, for reasons not specially disclosed, steps were taken to bar undesirables from having any part in the government and, seemingly, to rebuke the towns for letting down the bars of admission and the "freemen" for their want of orderliness at the courts of election. As we have already seen, all these alterations in the law of the colony were made by fiat of the court in the regular course of its legislative business, without reference to the "freemen" for their approval.

In 1646 the court decreed that anyone who had been fined or whipped for a scandalous offense, if legally convicted, should be disfranchised, and such an order proves that the offenders so punished were not servants or apprentices who had no vote, but men in the higher walks of life who could vote under the colony rule. In 1657 the court further decreed that no one was to be admitted a "freeman" unless he could present "an affirmative certificate under the hands of all or a major part" of the deputies of his town to the effect that he was of "a peaceable and honest conversation."[1] Later in the same year it forbade the towns to accept as an "admitted inhabitant" anyone under twenty-one years of age or who had not at least £30 estate, thus restricting materially the meaning of the term "admitted inhabitant," as used in the seventh fundamental. Finally in 1659, in order to prevent, if possible, the "tumult and trouble" that had disturbed the courts of election, it ordered that no one be made a "freeman" or have the privilege of freemanship conferred upon him unless he was twenty-one years of age, had borne office, was possessed of £30 of "proper personal estate," and was a man of honest and peaceable conversation. In these measures there is ample evidence to show that the ideals of Hooker, as presented in his sermon and commonly interpreted, whether at any time they had actually been put into practice or not, had become completely discredited within twenty years of the adoption of the Fundamental Orders.

---

1. The term "a major part" could apply only to the three original towns, each of which till 1662 sent four deputies to the general court. In the Cromwellian Instrument of Government of 1653 (§xvii), those elected as members of parliament had to be "person of known integrity, fearing God, and of good conversation," twenty-one years old.

An explanation in part of these measures lies in the fact that the colony was extending its jurisdiction and facing new conditions as one by one additional plantations came into existence. Alien peoples were drifting in and larger areas of territory, some of it adjoining the coast as well as the rivers, were scattering more widely the activities of the commonwealth and bringing unexpected problems in its train. The Connecticut colony was pushing its jurisdiction eastwardly toward the Pequot country and westwardly toward the Dutch at Manhattan. The former region had been known to the English for a long time, for it was familiar to the coasting vessels going to and from Boston and had served as a rendezvous for the Connecticut soldiers during the Pequot War. John Winthrop, Jr., returned from England in May, 1643, and after spending a year or two in Massachusetts, gained the consent of the Connecticut general court to make a plantation on the west side of the Thames River. The plantation was organized May 6, 1646. In 1650 fourteen families arrived as a covenanted church from Gloucester, with their minister, Richard Blinman, and, uniting themselves with those already there, became the first church of the community. In 1658 the name of the place was changed from Pequot to New London.[1]

Just as Winthrop was the founder of New London, the leader and director of the people there, so Roger Ludlow was the pioneer to open the coast region to the west. Having taken part in the swamp fight against the Pequots near Southport in 1637 he had recognized the possibilities of the region. In September of 1639 he obtained permission from the general court to promote a plantation at Pequannock and for that purpose purchased land of the Indians there. From this purchase and the subsequent settling of peoples sprang the towns of Stratford and Fairfield, in the latter of which Ludlow lived for fourteen years.[2] For a while these two plantations acted jointly in judicial and financial matters, but after 1650 they appear separately in the colony's list of estates. Ludlow removed from Windsor probably in 1640, took up his residence in Uncoway (Fairfield) and remained there until 1654, when he returned to England, as did many others who were attracted by the successes of the Puritans there and the offers of positions and honors. He made his way

---

1. Caulkins, *New London,* pp. 44–45, 66–67.
2. Schenck, *History of Fairfield;* Taylor, *Roger Ludlow;* Coleman, *Roger Ludlow in Chancery,* pp. 16–17.

to Dublin, where in all probability he died.[1] He had been influential in promoting the settlement of Norwalk also, which was started about 1650 and made a town the next year.[2] Settlers continued to move westward along the coast, coming into contact with the Dutch moving eastward, but Connecticut made no effort to extend her jurisdiction there until just before the absorption of New Haven, when she endeavored to draw away Stamford and Greenwich from their allegiance to that colony. Interpreting the terms of her charter as giving her all land south and west of the forty-second degree of northern latitude she attempted in 1663 to annex also the English towns of western Long Island and the town of Westchester in the present state of New York.[3]

Expansion in the neighborhood of the original river towns was slow, partly because of the sufficiency for the moment of the arable land and partly because of the dense woods that stretched to the east and west on both sides of the great river. Enterprising traders had moved up the Tunxis or Farmington River, engaged in tar-making and in locating favorable places for settlement. Projects for removal were entertained as early as 1640 and finally led to the planting of Farmington and its recognition as a town in 1645. Movements farther north but down the course of the meandering stream began soon after, and in 1664 Massaco or Simsbury was permanently settled, as an appanage of Windsor, and in 1671 was made a town.[4] This was the farthest point inland from the great river to be occupied for many years.

There was no settlement to the southward, between Wethersfield and the mouth of the Connecticut until 1647, when enterprising men, overcoming their fear of the Indians, began to interest themselves in a certain attractive locality which they must have passed frequently on their way up and down the river. Once begun the plantation there grew rapidly and was sufficiently populated to receive recognition as the town of Mattabesect in 1651, a name that was changed to Middletown two years later. Norwich, where Jona-

1. Coleman, pp. 39–41. Mr. Coleman has exploded the myth that Ludlow went to Virginia. The one that went was his brother George.

2. Hall, *History of Norwalk*, 1650–1800, p. 14. The early deeds are printed on pp. 30–37.

3. *New York Colonial Documents*, II, 485–486.

4. Porter, *History of Farmington*, p. 58; Phelps, *History of Simsbury*, pp. 11, 13–14, 22, 75.

than Brewster had located his trading house, was settled by a migrating church congregation from Saybrook, and after various vicissitudes was accepted by the general court as a town in 1663.

Thus without including the towns of Southampton and East hampton at the eastern end of Long Island and of Setauket and Huntington, about the center of the north shore, which were under Connecticut's jurisdiction for only a short time, there were in 1662 Hartford, Wethersfield, Windsor, Farmington, Middletown, New London, Norwalk, Stratford, and Fairfield, with Norwich, Stonington, Killingworth, Haddam, and Simsbury. The New Haven towns were soon to come. In a day when traffic was difficult and almost entirely by water, these Connecticut towns, unlike those of Massachusetts, were situated so far apart as to render communication and transportation infrequent, a condition that had a marked effect in slowing down the tempo of the colony and developing that spirit of local independence and self-reliance always so characteristic of the Connecticut communities.

One town has not been included in the list given above—Saybrook, for the circumstances in its case call for a somewhat fuller treatment. Starting as a blockhouse within a palisaded tract of land built by Lion Gardiner under Winthrop's direction in 1635, it gradually grew into a settlement. By 1641 it had lost much of its military character, but there was no church organization until 1646, though John Higginson was there as minister for four years.[1] Fenwick was the only one of the lords and gentlemen ever to reside there, as he did with the exception of a few years (1636–1639, 1645–1647) until 1648.[2] When it became quite evident that the English grantees had given up all intention of using the place as a retreat, the Connecticut

---

1. *Proceedings*, Massachusetts Historical Society, 1902, p. 46.
2. Two Fenwick letters from Saybrook, of date 1642 and 1643, are in *Hoadly Memorial*, pp. 1–5. Two of the grantees—Humfry and Pelham—and two of the associates—Hopkins and Fenwick—came to America, but only Fenwick went to Saybrook. Hopkins is thought to have had charge of the business in England until 1636 when the English grantees began to lose their interest and soon abandoned their project and their claim. He came to New England in 1637, in company with Davenport and Theophilus Eaton, his father-in-law. There is a close connection between all these men. Davenport and Hugh Peter were instrumental in persuading Lion Gardiner, a military engineer, who had served under the Prince of Orange in Holland and had married a Dutch wife, to accept Winthrop's offer to go to Saybrook (*Collections* Massachusetts Historical Society, 3d ser., III, 136; *Original Narratives, New Netherland*, p. 202), and there is some reason to believe that Davenport obtained permission of the grantees to negotiate with Connecticut regarding land within their grant.

leaders, who were undoubtedly kept posted on the situation by Edward Hopkins, one of the associate grantees, began negotiations for a "treaty of combination," to which Fenwick in 1639 agreed, as far as the fortification and the land about it were concerned, the question of boundaries and jurisdiction being left open. Connecticut offered to help financially in the repair and upkeep of the fort and in 1643 made Fenwick a "freeman" and magistrate of the colony. Then on December 5, 1644, a formal agreement was drawn up, according to which Connecticut allowed Fenwick certain duties on goods, furs, and livestock passing out of the mouth of the river, while he in return made over the fortification and the land, but not the jurisdiction which he could not convey, to the use of the people of the colony, to be enjoyed by them forever. He promised to transfer also all the territory named in the Warwick deed, lying between the Connecticut River and the "Narragansett River" (presumably Narragansett Bay) "if it came into its power." This agreement was merely a bill of sale of land, the ownership of which was assumed to be vested in Warwick, the grantees, and their associates, though it is doubtful if Fenwick had a legal right to alienate any part of the land without the formal consent of the grantees, which, as far as we know, he never obtained. Much less could he transfer the remainder of the land together with the jurisdiction, thus conveying powers of government over the whole territory. Legally it made no difference that the lords and gentlemen had abandoned their claim, at least as far as Fenwick's right of disposal was concerned.

Fenwick went finally to England in 1648[1] and was there continuously until his death in 1657. Why he did not obtain a renewal of the patent while there in 1645–1647 or after 1648 or secure the consent of the lords and gentlemen, some of whom were still living, to the transfer of land and jurisdiction such as Connecticut desired, is difficult to understand, unless it be that no copy of such a patent could anywhere be found.[2] Doubtless consent could have been ob-

1. Fenwick's name appears in the list of magistrates, December 1, 1645, but it does not appear again until May 20, 1647. It has been thought that he went to England in 1645 and returned in 1647. As his name appears in the list for May 18, 1648, he must have remained at Saybrook in the colony until the death of his wife, Lady Boteler, in that year when he went back to England for the last time. Gates, *Saybrook* (1936), pp. 60–64; *Connecticut Colonial Records*, 1636–1665, pp. 149, 163.

2. When, in 1646, the question of the ownership of the Pequot country became an issue between Massachusetts and Connecticut, and the latter claimed it by virtue of a patent from the king, Winthrop recorded in his journal that such patent "was never

tained if it would have done any good to have it, but it seems reasonable to believe that by that time the true inwardness of the patent had been realized and Fenwick had discovered that it was not in his power to make the transfer. This cannot have been due to his inability to find a copy of the patent or the deed. The former, had it ever existed, could have been obtained from the patent books of the council or from Warwick himself; the latter from some one of the grantees, just as John Winthrop, Jr., later found a copy among the Hopkins papers. There was, as Mrs. Cullick, Fenwick's sister, said in her petition, "a total failure" on Fenwick's part "respecting his procuring of a Pattent for the Colony." It was all a "great disappointment."

Fenwick's death in 1658 left the question of land and jurisdiction exactly where it was before, except for the fort and land at Saybrook, which Connecticut, whether legally or not, had taken under her direct control. Immediately on hearing that Fenwick had died and finding that they had profited but little from their negotiations with him, the Connecticut authorities demanded of his executor, Captain John Cullick, who had married Fenwick's sister Elizabeth, the return of a part of the £1600 already paid (as Connecticut estimated it) before letters of administration would be granted. Cullick promised to return £500, a sum that had not been entirely paid in 1663, when Mrs. Cullick petitioned for a remission of the amount still due—about £150. This request was refused by the general court. The balance was eventually paid in full, in 1673, from money obtained by selling a piece of land belonging to Fenwick's estate in Saybrook. It is quite certain, therefore, that this Fenwick money was never available for the purpose of meeting the expense of obtaining the charter, as has sometimes been said.[1]

Thus in 1644 Saybrook came into Connecticut's possession and from this time forward was reckoned one of Connecticut's towns. In 1654 the population was rated at fifty-three taxable persons and the value of the estates there higher than those of either Middletown

showed us, so it was done de bene esse, quousque, etc." (*Journal*, II, 275). Warwick was still living, as were also Saye and Sele, Saltonstall, Haselrig, and others.

1. That the court hoped to use the Fenwick money for meeting the expense of obtaining the charter is clear (*Connecticut Colonial Records*, 1636–1665, pp. 369–370), but in its instructions to Winthrop and in its letter to the Earl of Manchester it expressed its fears that the total sum would never be paid. The final payment is recorded in the Saybrook Land Records, I, 31, as of date June 25, 1673 (Gates, *Saybrook*, p. 88).

or Norwalk. The settlement must have prospered in this interval of twenty years. In 1663 it was rated above these two towns and above Norwich also, showing that the habitable lands outside the fort and the palisade were gradually increasing in extent as more people came in and that the whole was beginning to take on the form of a town of the usual type. It was granted representation in the general court in 1651, placed in the list of towns "within this jurisdiction" in 1654, and shared all the burdens and obligations, including jury duty and military service, as would any other town. In 1659 its church congregation, under the leadership of the Rev. James Fitch, dissatisfied, it may be, with the uncertainty of land titles there, migrated as a body to settle the plantation of Norwich at the head of navigation on the Thames. A new church was erected to take its place.[1]

The powers of the towns were carefully defined by the general court in October, 1639. They could dispose of all lands undisposed of within their boundaries and could traffic freely in their own commodities. They could choose their own officials, with power to look after the prudential affairs of the community, make orders not repugnant to the general laws of the colony, impose penalties for the breaches of these orders, levy fines, and distrain for their payment. They could select the magistrates' assistants whom the general court required to hold court in minor cases and were ordered to keep books for the recording of lands, the entering of the estates of deceased persons, and the registering of the ear-marks of cattle. Additional laws were passed from time to time concerning weights and measures, hogs at large, and other local concerns. The central government kept a watchful eye upon its towns and plantations, but did not often interfere in their affairs unless requested to do so. It expected each settlement to stand on its own feet, to pay without grumbling its share of the colony's running expenses, and to keep the peace among its own inhabitants and with those of the neighboring towns. The general court did not encourage new settlements or grant town privileges until certain conditions had been fulfilled that would reasonably assure the meeting of these expectations.

The towns, after having heard the colony laws read publicly at town meeting, were supposed to copy them into a town law book

1. *Connecticut Colonial Records*, 1636–1665, pp. 30, 31, 95, 99, 113, 266–272; Connecticut Archives, Towns and Lands, I, no. 3; Hart, "History of the Early Settlement of Saybrook" (*Saybrook Quadrimillenial*), pp. 1–13.

provided specially for the purpose, though there is no evidence to show that anything of the kind was done before 1650. Aroused by the efforts of the Bay colony to prepare a code of law to meet the demands of the inhabitants for a more certain knowledge of what the laws were all about, the general court in 1646 requested Ludlow "to take some paynes" in making an abridgment of laws already passed. This Ludlow did. The results were approved in May, 1650, and issued in manuscript copies as the code of that year. Transcripts were sent to the towns, headed by the Fundamental Orders, and this code remained the "town law book" for more than twenty years. In 1671 a revision was called for, which was accepted the next year and ordered to be printed (1673), with a preface written by the governor and the assistants containing this sentence, "Being willing that all concerned by this Impression may know what they may expect at our hands as Justice in the Administration of our Government here, we have endeavored not onely to ground our *Capital Laws* upon the *Word of God,* but also all other *Lawes* upon the Justice and Equity held forth in that *Word* which is a most perfect Rule."[1]

The colony thus settled in the wilderness had necessarily to provide itself with the means of subsistence and growth, and its efforts to develop its resources are worthy of examination as those of a settlement largely dependent upon its own efforts for maintenance. Life was agricultural and pastoral and only to a small extent concerned with industry and traffic in furs. The people ("about three thousand" in 1643)[2] were engaged for the most part in raising corn and other grains and were busy with the breeding of horses, cattle, swine, sheep, and other livestock, none of which were indigenous to the country, but in the beginning had to be brought from England or the Continent. Horses were used but little as draft animals, because for ploughing and other similar purposes they were found less serviceable than oxen. They were chiefly employed for transportation, were small in size, and were probably brought originally from England, Ireland, or Holland.[3] Neat cattle were essential to Connecticut's prosperity. They furnished the inhabitants with flesh for

1. *Connecticut Colonial Records,* 1636–1665, pp. 138, 154; 1666–1678, pp. 153, 190, 232, 246, appendix xv; 568; Acorn Club, vol. 12, pp. 12–14, Bates, *Bibliography of Connecticut Laws* (1900).

2. So stated in the petition of 1643, for which see p. 82, note 1.

3. Phillips, "Horse Rearing in Colonial New England" (*Memoir,* Cornell University Agricultural Experiment Station, no. 54).

food, hides for leather, and strength for ploughing and hauling, and their possession was an index to the owner's personal rating. In their garden plots the householders raised small amounts of tobacco, flax, and hemp; from the woods they obtained timber for building, pitch and tar for their boats, and pipe and hogshead staves and headings for export.[1] To facilitate local exchange a market was held at Hartford in 1643 and, following the English custom with which the colonists must have been thoroughly familiar, two fairs were arranged for at which business transactions of all kind might be carried on. Of sea-going traffic there was little, the people of the colony, even as late as 1681, "having neither license nor ability to launch out in any considerable trade at sea."[2] Pinnaces and sloops, built in the colony, of small tonnage on account of the bar at the mouth of the Connecticut,[3] passed up and down the rivers and out into the Sound, and early made their way along the coast to Boston and the Dutch at Manhattan and later on to the West Indies.[4]

Corn was the commodity most frequently exported, always under restrictions laid down by the general court, in order that the colony might not be deprived in periods of scarcity of its most necessary staple; but biscuit, bread, beaver, pipestaves, and livestock were also shipped away to Boston, New Amsterdam, Long Island, the Delaware, and by enterprising captains, to Barbados and the Leeward

1. For tobacco, *Connecticut Colonial Records, 1636–1665*, pp. 53, 153, 558. No one under twenty, or any other who was not already accustomed to its use, was to take tobacco at all, and no one was to smoke in the fields, highways, woods, barnyards, etc.

2. Connecticut Archives, Foreign Correspondence, no. 21. From the statement in the petition of 1643 I infer that the petitioners were planning to hire or build a ship large enough to go to England for the purpose of bringing provisions directly back to the colony at a time of great scarcity (*Connecticut Colonial Records*, 1636–1665, p. 100). The embargo in England made such petition necessary. The petition was, however, not granted and the project fell through.

3. The same petition says that the plantation of Connecticut "lying upon a river that is barred, noe ships or vessels of burden can come to trade wth them, and thereby the planters there are deprived of those supplyes wch other plantacons have by shipping that comes to them from these parts."

4. Dongan of New York in 1687 informed the Lords of Trade that Connecticut had "but a small trade, what they have is to the West Indies, Boston and this place. They have not above a Ketch or two and about six or seven sloops belonging to the Place" (*New York Colonial Documents*, III, 397). In 1696 Captain John Hamlin, a prominent Connecticut merchant, landholder, and deputy from Middletown, sent his sloop, *Supply*, to Charles Town, South Carolina, laden with 100 barrels of cider, which were admitted custom free (*Journals*, Common House of Assembly, South Carolina, 1696, p. 18).

Islands.¹ Out of this traffic, in vessels owned in Connecticut and elsewhere, arose the beginnings of a custom service, finding its origin in the collecting of dues at the mouth of the river—the "Fort rate"—to discharge the obligations incurred by the agreement with Fenwick in 1644. We meet with the equivalent of clearances, entrances, naval officers, forfeitures, collectors, and searchers in rudimentary form.² Rules were laid down concerning the dumping of ballast, the prevention of Sabbath Day sailings, and the conduct of incoming mariners and sailors, who made much trouble for these Puritan communities, whether in Massachusetts Bay, Connecticut, or New Haven. The medium of exchange was chiefly the products of the soil, though payments were made in wampum and beaver also. There was less wampum or sewan, as the Dutch called the Indian substitute for money, in the river towns than in the coast towns of Connecticut and in Rhode Island, New Haven, and New Amsterdam, where the shell supply was nearer at hand. There are traces of coins—nobles, angels, crowns, and marks—probably brought from England, and of Spanish dollars and Dutch guilders, which were acquired in trade.³

There seems to have been neither great wealth nor extreme poverty among the people at large, though there were men in Hartford who possessed goodly estates in England or who brought a measure of wealth, either in money or goods, with them into the colony. Pynchon of Springfield owned many houses and lands in the parishes of Writtle and Widford in Essex; Edward Hopkins was a wealthy man; the Eatons of New Haven were men of property before they left England; and Hopkins bequeathed money for educational purposes in the colony.⁴ Captain Richard Lord had an estate

---

1. *Particular Court Records,* mention of Barbados, of muscovado sugar, of a Connecticut vessel taken by Prince Rupert in the West Indies, of the *Duck* of Milford, pp. 130, 137, 172, 201, 248, 249, 250.

2. *Ibid.,* pp. 120, 121, 131, 134, 135, 258.

3. Nettels, "The Beginnings of Money in Connecticut" (*Transactions,* Wisconsin Academy of Sciences, Arts, and Letters, XXIII, *passim*). In Winthrop's petition to the king in 1661 or 1662 he asked for "immunity from Customs as may encourage the merchants to supply our necessities in such commodities as may be wanting here for wᶜʰ we have neither silver nor gold to pay, but the supply in that kind may enable in due time to search the bowels of the earth for some good minerals, whereof there seem to be fair probabilities." This is a characteristic Winthrop touch, for his interest in mining is well known. Connecticut Archives, Foreign Correspondence, I, pt. 1 no. 1.

4. Davis, History of the Hopkins Grammar School (manuscript).

valued at £3000; James Lord one of £8000. Both Haynes and Wyllys were rich and spent money in subduing the wilderness and building houses, Wyllys's mansion being one of the finest, if not the finest at the time in New England.[1] But facilities for accumulating money were few and far between. Staple products were insufficient to furnish a surplus for export that would pay for the commodities needed from abroad; means of transportation were limited almost entirely to water travel, as highways for horses and carts were almost unknown even among the river towns, though there must have been a certain use of the Indian paths down the river and toward Quinnipiac, for cattle were driven both to Saybrook and New Haven. Such transit was, however, slow, arduous, and infrequent. Because of these difficulties of travel distant towns were allowed to vote by proxy at the court of elections and the time and expense involved in travel led to the suggestion regarding the reduction in the number of deputies to the general court in 1661.

The colonists lived in a world heavily wooded, though because of the river bottoms the forests were probably less dense than had been the case with Massachusetts. The river Indians were never a serious menace, but those in the neighborhood of some of the coast towns now and then threatened uprisals and the government kept a strict watch over them, everywhere and at all times.[2] Wild animals were dangerous and continued to be so throughout the century. The gray wolf was a "pernicious creature" and a constant threat to the lives of the planters and the peace of the plantations. Less common were bears, panthers ("painters"), and lynxes ("wild cats"), but they also made trouble because like the wolves they destroyed sheep. Towns and colony paid bounties for wild animals killed and wolf-pits were dug both within and without the settlements. Beaver were everywhere and "beaver brooks" and "beaver meadows" are still so called in local nomenclature. The red fox, members of the weasel tribe—otters, fishers, martens, mink, wolverines, and skunks (Indian "seqanku")—muskrats (Indian "musquash"), Norway or wharf rats—all abounded. Moose, too, raccoon (from which coon-caps were made), squirrels, woodchucks, etc., were everywhere. The streams

<hr>

1. Seymour, *Hale and Wyllys,* pp. 78–104. For similar conditions in Massachusetts, above, Vol. I, 502–503.

2. At Hartford the Indians lived in wigwams thickly planted in the great meadows toward the southeastern part of the town and along the banks of the Connecticut River. In New Haven they lived to the eastward across the Quinnipiac.

were full of fish and in the Sound and tributary waters and harbors
were hair-seals—from which came the seal caps of the colonists—por-
poises, and right whales which furnished oil and whalebone. Whales
were caught by Connecticut seamen as early as 1647. Some parts of
the clothing of the early settlers was fashioned from the skin of the
white-tailed deer, which ran through the woods and in severe sea-
sons penetrated the settlements themselves.[1]

Such was the general situation in the commonwealth when in the
year 1660 news came of the restoration of Charles II to the throne
of England. The news was disconcerting to all the Puritan colonies,
who looked to the ascendancy of the Puritan minority in England
for their continued security and freedom from interference. To Connecticut, which had no certain legal standing as a colony, it was particularly disconcerting. However much the leaders may have placed
their trust in the validity of the Warwick deed, they must have come
to realize by this time that it would not stand the test of legal scrutiny. They had been unfortunate in their attempt to obtain a patent
from the Long Parliament,[2] as Roger Williams had done in 1644,
and Fenwick's failure to do anything for them in England and his
manifest inability to carry out his promises must have shown them
that something was wrong with their title.[3] Except for the slight

1. S. W. Adams, *The Native and Wild Animals of Connecticut* (1896).

2. In 1644 Connecticut joined with the New Haven jurisdiction in authorizing
Fenwick to undertake a voyage to England for the purpose of obtaining a patent
from parliament, but when Fenwick for some reason could not go, or was unwilling
to go, the colony accepted New Haven's choice of Gregson, who sailed in the
"phantom ship" in January, 1646, and was lost at sea (*New Haven Colony Records*,
I, 511; II, 519–520; *Connecticut Colonial Records*, 1636–1665, I, 126, 128). It is an
odd fact that Fenwick should have returned to England on his own business in 1648.

3. The facts regarding the Warwick Patent are these. Warwick planned to take
out a patent from the Council for New England as early as 1630, in the interest of
his Puritan friends in Essex and elsewhere. He apparently saw no reason why he
could not obtain it, as he was president of the council and had one or more of the
seals in his possession. He therefore made out a deed of conveyance, March 19, 1632,
to the Puritan lords and gentlemen, three months before he formally put in a request
for a patent to the council. Not until June 21 was the draft of such a patent prepared
and a committee of the council appointed to consider it. No entry appears in the
records of the council of any action on this draft and no mention of a patent is
made later in its proceedings. Eight months afterward Warwick lost the presidency.
Gorges having suffered one serious defeat at Warwick's hands in the grant of the
charter to the Massachusetts Bay Company did not propose to allow Warwick to injure him further by obtaining a patent for another large section of the territory of
the Council for New England which Warwick undoubtedly intended to hand over to
a second Puritan group. Gorges, if he could help it, would allow no more of the
council's land to fall into the hands of the Puritans. Therefore he bent his efforts to

protection that the transfer of the Warwick deed gave them, and for their moral claim to exist as a colony of honorable men, which they believed themselves to be, they stood defenseless in the presence of the new king. If the authorities in England should be inclined to be unfriendly and ready to take the severe measures that some of the colony's opponents in New England wished them to do,[1] these same authorities might advise the king to receive the colony into his own hands and for good and sufficient reasons get rid of the Puritan governments altogether. The king might even place a governor general over them, as Massachusetts had feared would be done as early as 1635 and was actually done when the Dominion of New England

prevent the draft from being perfected. Warwick had waited a little too long (above, Vol. I, 403–404).

Regarding the deed itself two comments may be made. First, it contains no recital of title or even a phrase to show by what right Warwick made the grant. Consequently, the question may be raised whether such a deed could be valid in law. Secondly, a deed of land cannot carry jurisdictional rights. Had a patent actually been sealed rights of jurisdiction would have been vested in the lords and gentlemen as joint-tenants of the crown with Warwick himself. Therefore, in any case the lords and gentlemen would have been unable to transfer such rights without Warwick's co-action with them. The deed of conveyance carried no rights of government, though the lords and gentlemen, believing that a patent had been duly issued, appointed Winthrop governor at Saybrook. Fenwick never received formal authorization to act on their behalf from the lords and gentlemen and much less from Warwick, who was still alive in 1644 and might have straightened things out, if he had believed that he could.

No one has ever seen a copy of the patent and Winthrop said in 1646 that no such patent was ever shown him to support Connecticut's claim to the Pequot country (above, p. 121, note 2). Massachusetts two years later challenged Connecticut to produce either patent or deed but without success (Hutchinson, *History*, Mayo ed., I, 131–132). Inability to produce the document caused the colony some embarrassment afterward. In 1664 the Hamilton claimants demanded it but got no satisfactory reply (*Connecticut Colonial Records*, 1648–1689, p. 334, §2; *Calendar State Papers, Colonial*, 1661–1668, §735; 1696–1697, §§992, 993). In 1667 under-secretary Williamson said that "the old pretended patent to Lord Say etc. never passed the seal" (*ibid.*, 1661–1668, p. 533) and in 1700 Rhode Island said frankly "we know not of any Patent granted to the Lord Say and Lord Brook in 1631[2] and purchased by Connecticut as they say" (*ibid.*, 1700, p. 749). The subject is discussed adversely to the existence of the patent by R. V. Coleman in *The Old Patent of Connecticut* (1636).

I am sure that at first the Connecticut leaders acted in entire good faith, but that later they came to have their doubts as to the strength of their position. Fenwick's telling them that he would try to make their title valid, when they thought it was valid already, must have given them pause and have led to their saying dejectedly to the Earl of Manchester, "We are as naked as before, having neither Patent or Coppy of it." It is not enough to say that there must have been a patent because of the high character of the men who believed in it. Such an assertion has no weight as evidence.

1. For Maverick's advice to Lord Clarendon, *Collections*, New York Historical Society, 1869, pp. 21, 25–26, 31–32, 35.

was set up under Andros in 1686. Connecticut's leaders knew that
the colony was helpless in the presence of this danger and they laid
their plans to meet it by the best means at their command. As events
were to show, these plans were shrewdly and even audaciously conceived and successfully carried out. The man who obtained for
Connecticut her first charter and consequently her first legal right
to exist as a corporate colony was John Winthrop, Jr., whom the
freemen of Connecticut, with considerable adroitness, had drawn
away from New Haven, where he was residing at the time, by offering him the governorship of the Connecticut colony in 1657.

John Winthrop, Jr., the eldest and most worthy son of all the children of the governor of Massachusetts, was born in 1606 and was at
the time of the king's restoration fifty-four years of age. He had
been educated at Trinity College, Dublin—though he did not graduate—was a member of the Inner Temple, and in early years had
been a traveller of wide experience. He was a gentleman of many
personal contacts, not only among the East Anglian Puritans but
also among the leading men of the day in England. He never practiced law but early developed an interest in colonization, and after
some delay joined his father in Massachusetts Bay in 1631. Returning to England for a brief sojourn, he accepted in 1635 the offer of
the lords and gentlemen to start a settlement at the mouth of the
Connecticut River, later known as Saybrook. Remaining there but a
year he returned to England but soon came back to America, sailing
for Boston in 1643, with the idea of promoting an iron-work in
Massachusetts in conjunction with Dr. Robert Child, the remon-
strant. As this undertaking did not prove successful, he withdrew
in 1645, having already been attracted by opportunities elsewhere.
In 1640 he received from Massachusetts a grant of Fisher's Island
"against the mouth of the Pecoit [Thames] Ryver, as far as is in our
power, reserving the right of Conectecot and Saybrooke,"[1] and
though at the time he made no effort to occupy and improve it, its
possession called his attention to the Pequot country, where, as we
have already seen, he began a plantation as a "curb to the Indians,"
under the auspices of Connecticut. Her title to the territory having
been confirmed by the New England Confederation, he was appointed a local commissioner in 1648, to exercise justice there according to the Connecticut laws and the rule of righteousness. In
1651 he became a "freeman" of the colony. After a year's residence

1. *Massachusetts Colonial Records*, I, 304.

in New Haven, where he was attracted by the project for an iron-works, he decided to throw in his lot permanently with Connecticut and accepted an election as governor in 1657, an opportunity which was later made more palatable by the change of tenure effected in 1660.

When the news of the Restoration came to the colony in 1660, Winthrop called a hurried meeting of such magistrates and deputies as could be assembled, who agreed to recommend to the next general court, that of March, 1661, the duty and necessity of despatching a speedy address to "our Soveraigne Lord Charles," declaring that the inhabitants were "his Highness loyall and faythfull subjects" and asking for "the continuance and confirmation of such privi-ledges and liberties" as were essential for "the comfortable and peace-able settlement" of the colony. At the next court, that of May, a committee was appointed to perfect the address, drawn up mean-time by the governor, and to frame a petition for presentation "to his Matie," together with letters to such "noble personages" as might be thought favorable to their request. Though many of those in England friendly to the Puritan cause in New England were either dead, in poor health, in retirement or concealment, or in prison, there were a few upon whom the colony believed it might call in this emergency. Among them were the Earl of Manchester, lord chamberlain, who had married as his second wife the daughter of the Earl of Warwick, was connected with the Essex group, and felt strongly inclined toward the Puritan party, even though he had played an important part in the restoration of the king; Lord Saye and Sele, lord privy seal, who for forty years had befriended the New England settlements; Lord Brooke, the son of the grantee; and a few others. The petition was accompanied by a hurried and in-complete statement of what the colony wanted. At the same time a body of instructions was prepared that presented in greater detail sundry matters of a more particular nature. These documents were communicated at the meeting of the court in June and approved. As Winthrop was to be the colony's agent in transacting the business in England, the court gave him a fairly free hand to do as he thought best, allowing him to write additional letters and to offer any further petitions that he thought necessary. It appropriated £80 for his expenses and £500, in the form of a letter of credit (dated June 16, 1661)[1] upon London merchants, to meet the legal costs and

1. *Hoadly Memorial* (Connecticut Historical Society, XXIV), p. 7.

such perquisites and gratuities as might be necessary. He was expected to obtain, if possible, a confirmation of the Warwick Patent, which the colony still hoped was somewhere in existence, and to secure in its stead a royal letters patent or charter, containing such additions and enlargements as the colony wanted. Winthrop was specially enjoined to see that the "liberties and privileges inserted in the Patent" should "not be inferiour or short to what is granted to the Massachusetts."[1]

Winthrop, bearing the address, petition, and letters, sailed from New Amsterdam with the Rev. Samuel Stone, in the ship *De Trouw,* to Holland, where he arrived September 6, 1661. He proceeded by way of Harwich to London, taking up his residence with William Whiting in Coleman Street, next door to the church of which John Davenport had been the vicar, and more than two miles from Whitehall where most of his work was to be done.[2] In the course of his activities he was probably advised that the address written in the colony was not in satisfactory form, and therefore drafted, or caused to be drafted, another and more suitable text, in which he prayed for a "Renual of the said [Warwick] Pattent under your Maties great Seale."[3] But there is no reference to a Warwick patent in the charter as there is to the New England Company's

1. *Connecticut Colonial Records,* 1636–1665, pp. 367, 369, 370, 579, 585; 1665–1677, pp. 340–341. For these and other documents that Winthrop carried, Bates, *The Charter of Connecticut,* pp. 12–14.

2. *Collections,* Massachusetts Historical Society, 5th ser., I, 594; *Proceedings,* 2d ser., I, 126.

3. This petition, the original of which was found by the writer among the Rawlinson manuscripts in the Bodleian (A. 175, f. 109) and printed in *Report,* Connecticut Historical Society, 1904, and in Bates, *The Charter of Connecticut,* pp. 15–16, is a strange document to bear the signature of John Winthrop, Jr. It contains what the colony and Winthrop himself must have known was not an accurate rendering of the facts in the case. It says (1) that Fenwick had conveyed the whole territory, which he had not; (2) that he had conveyed it with the rights of jurisdiction, which he had not done and could not do; (3) that the lords and gentlemen were "incorporated" with the said patent "about the twelfth yeare" of the reign of Charles I, which was not only untrue as to fact but a bad guess as to date, making the year of the deed 1636, the year after Winthrop himself became governor at Saybrook; (4) that the lords and gentlemen had transported at "great expense some hundreds of families," a gross exaggeration as Winthrop well knew; and (5) that Connecticut had built "several towns and villages" in the territory, when at most only New London had been so planted before 1661 and its founding was not due to any authority obtained by virtue of the Warwick deed. That Winthrop wished to make out the strongest case he could is natural and easy to understand, but that he deliberately falsified the evidence seems hardly in accord with his character. The finding of this document

patent in the Massachusetts Bay charter. This fact in itself is fairly conclusive evidence that no such patent ever existed.[1]

Winthrop was highly thought of in England, where he was known not only to the survivors of the original grantees but also to many a prominent man outside the Puritan fold. He had corresponded for some years, at various times, with Robert Boyle, the governor of the Society for the Propagation of the Gospel in New England and the most representative member, if not the founder, of the Royal Society; with Sir Kenelm Digby, whose connection with the Winthrops has already been noticed;[2] with Samuel Hartlib, the author of numerous pamphlets on husbandry and a great variety of other topics, educational, social, and religious; and with William Brereton, son of Sir William, the latter of whom had died before Winthrop reached England. The younger Brereton, knowing Winthrop's great interest in the medicine and science of the day, proposed him for membership in the Royal Society and he was admitted January 1, 1662. While in England he took an active part in the proceedings and read a number of papers. Though he found Saye and Sele too ill to be of much use to him, he learned that the Puritan lord had already written to the Earl of Manchester and through him had communicated with Lord Chancellor Clarendon in his behalf and was able to give him useful introductions. He was presented by Hartlib to Dr. Benjamin Worsley, who had been officially concerned with colonial affairs for a decade and he renewed his friendship with William Jessop, former secretary of the grantees and for many years identified with Puritan enterprises.[3] The letter which he bore to the Earl of Manchester must have been of great assistance to him.

raises more problems than it solves. Even Winthrop's statement of the burning of the fort, which he evidently based on information obtained from his father (Winthrop, *Journal*, II, 328), is doubted because unsupported by any other evidence (Gates, *Saybrook*, pp. 100–101). But as Hubbard, in his *History*, has the same story and adds details not found elsewhere, it is difficult to believe that such a report could have got abroad if there had been no truth in it.

1. Connecticut laid a great deal of stress on the phrase in the king's letter of April 23, 1664, which called the granting of the charter of 1662 "a renewing of our charter," that is, of the Warwick deed (*Connecticut Colonial Records*, 1678–1689, p. 336; *Calendar State Papers, Colonial*, 1661–1668, §719). This phrase simply shows that in writing the letter the king or Secretary Bennett (who probably prepared the original draft) followed the wording of Winthrop's petition. It proves nothing as to the actual existence of a Warwick Patent. The omission of any such statement of renewal from the charter itself is a much more significant fact.

2. Above, Vol. I, 393, note 2.

3. *Collections*, Massachusetts Historical Society, 5th ser., I, 394. Jessop had been

Despite his personal influence and the influence of his friends, Winthrop realized that his path to success was not to be without obstacles. In England the Puritan cause was not in favor and the Puritan colonies had also many enemies in America. The spokesman of these was Samuel Maverick, who had the ear of Clarendon and during the year 1661 had written him from New Amsterdam many letters on the subject. Returning to England he had followed up these letters with personal interviews, in which he sought to check-mate the Connecticut request. "The two sowtheren Collonyes Conec-ticott and Newhaven [he wrote] have no Pattents that I know but govern by Combination amongst them selves, but in a strange con-fused way, and in this Confusion [are] the governments in New England at present, and I conceive will be no otherwise untill his Maies^{tie} be pleased to call all againe in to his owne hands, and dis-posall . . . [reduced] under his Maties obedience."[1] Though Maver-ick's strictures were chiefly directed against Massachusetts they were aimed at Connecticut also, and Maverick would have been glad to see the latter's petition for a charter denied and a governor general placed over all the colonies in New England. But Lord Saye and Sele also had the ear of the lord chamberlain and the chancellor and Maverick had to acknowledge that there were influential men in England who had "no desire that these persons in New England should be reduced." Their insistence and Winthrop's dexterous di-plomacy had the desired effect. Winthrop's final petition presented some time before February 6, 1662, was received by Sir Edward Nicholas, one of the principal secretaries of state, and by him re-ferred to the attorney general. The latter's report being favorable, the secretary acting under instructions from the king in council, caused a warrant to be issued under the royal sign manual authorizing the attorney general to prepare the text of the charter, based on Win-throp's own version which the crown's legal advisers put into proper official form. These preliminaries having been completed, the char-ter passed rapidly through the seals and, in the form of a writ of privy seal, dated May 10, 1662, was enrolled in the Six Clerks' office

the secretary of the Providence Company, of the lords and gentlemen, of the War-wick commission, and later clerk of the Council of State under the Commonwealth, in daily contact with Milton. He died in 1675. He is not mentioned in the *Dictionary of National Biography*, as he ought to have been.

1. *Collections*, New York Historical Society, 1869, pp. 21, 32.

in Chancery Lane. It received the great seal on the same day, as is evident from the entries in the accounts of the clerk of the Hanaper and from Winthrop's own report of proceedings.[1]

There is no possible way of finding out how much it cost Winthrop to obtain the charter. Roger Williams, in a moment of what appears to be gross exaggeration, said that Rhode Island paid about one thousand pounds and Connecticut about six thousand pounds for their charters,[2] but these figures cannot possibly be accepted. It may be that Williams, recalling the circumstances nearly twenty years after the event and when seventy-eight years of age, was either forgetful or careless. He wrote in thousands when he should have written in hundreds. Six hundred pounds would be nearly correct, if we include the amount appropriated for Winthrop's expenses. Winthrop, when writing home, May 13, 1662, expressed the hope that the colony would be "well satisfied about the charge that had been necessary for the affecting and prosecuting a business of such consequence"; and had he run over the £500 allotted he would doubtless have heard from the colony about it and some record would remain. That he used some of his own money to meet the costs of living in England for nearly twenty months is likely, but that he kept within the limits set by the colony in spending the money furnished for fees and perquisites seems evident from the accounting that followed. He borrowed the £500 of three merchants of London—Cowes, Silvester, and Maskeline—and he and his son made themselves responsible for the payment. He agreed with the merchants that, toward the end of November, 1662, the colony should pay the £500 in the form of 2000 bushels of wheat at 3s 6d a bushel and 1200 bushels of pease at 2s 6d. As the Fenwick money was not available, the colony levied this amount on the towns, bidding them send the wheat and pease, in carts, boats, and canoes, at their own charge to New London, where it was to be stored until the arrival of the *John and Robert,* a flyboat of London despatched by the merchants for the purpose of carrying the cargo back to England for sale. The cost of sending the vessel on a voyage of five

---

1. *Collections,* Connecticut Historical Society, I, 52, note; Bates, *The Charter of Connecticut,* p. 25.

2. *Narragansett Club Publications,* VI, 401–402 (no. 11). "No charters are obtained without great suit, favor or charge. Our first [that of 1644] cost a hundred pounds (though I never received it all); our second about a thousand; Connecticut about six thousand." January 15, 1681.

or six weeks each way must have been considerable, when the charges for wages, food, and insurance are taken into account, but the merchants evidently expected to recover their costs as well as their loan from the prices received in the London market. The whole financial transaction was completed by October, 1663, when Winthrop and the colony formally acquitted each other of all further claims in the premises.[1]

Winthrop did not bring back the charter himself, as he was not returning at once to New England, but despatched it and its duplicate by the hands of two Massachusetts agents, Bradstreet and Norton, who arrived in Boston, September 3, 1662. From there it was brought to Hartford by the Connecticut representatives at the meeting of the commissioners of the New England Confederation, where it had been presented and examined before being sent to the colony.[2]

---

1. *Connecticut Colonial Records, 1636–1665,* pp. 385, 389–390, 392, 397, 400, 415, 416; *Collections,* Connecticut Historical Society, I, 52–55; *Hoadly Memorial,* p. 7. In Clarke's letter to Winthrop, November 17, 1662 (*Proceedings,* Massachusetts Historical Society, 1869–1870, pp. 344–345), we read, "And o[r] great care hath bene to effect the payment according to yo[r] order w[ch] we doubt wilbe issued to satisfaction by o[r] time; the Riv[r] having sent away their proportion and all parts willing and ready to performe, though troublesome at this season of the year to thrash . . . M[r] Stone hath likely accompanied M[rs] Winthrop to N. London to the ship that is to receive the Corne." See also *Wyllys Papers* (Connecticut Historical Society, XXI), p. 146. It is of course quite possible that the colony was called upon to make up any deficit incurred, as Talcott bound the colony to do in the letter of credit, but there is no record of this having been done.

2. Bates, *The Charter of Connecticut,* pp. 20–21. Some uncertainty exists as to whether the "duplicate," or second original charter, was sent to the colony at this time. Mr. Bates believes that it was retained in London until it was brought over by Fitz John Winthrop in 1697 (*ibid.,* pp. 24, 30, 60); on the other hand Mr. George Dudley Seymour argues that the second original was received at the same time with the first and that the document in London was not an original but an exemplification or attested copy (*Hale and Wyllys,* appendix T). It is difficult to believe that so important a document as a royal letters patent bearing the great seal could have been left for more than thirty years in the hands of "an inferior officer in the custom house"—one Porter, who was reported to the colony as "a very unfitt person" to be its agent (*Hoadly Memorial,* pp. 37–39). The interpretation by Mr. Bates of the word "duplicate," as used in two connections (Bates, pp. 22, 60; *Connecticut Colonial Records,* 1636–1665, p. 407; *Proceedings,* Massachusetts Historical Society, 1869–1870, pp. 344–345), is open to a reasonable doubt. Daniel Clarke, the secretary of the colony, in writing to Winthrop from Windsor, November 17, 1662, can mean but one thing when he says, "We have receaved the Chart[r], the duplicate and the old Coppy of the former Charter." The natural inference from these words is that both copies of the charter were brought over at the same time. "Duplicate" here cannot refer to a second copy of the "former Charter" (that is, the Warwick deed), for the only copy of that document which came to the colony is the one found by Winthrop among the Hopkins papers and now in the Connecticut Archives. The document

On October 9, 1662, it was publicly read "in audienc of the Freemen and declared to belong to them and their successors," after which both it and its duplicate were entrusted to the care of three of the magistrates for safe-keeping, though the documents themselves were given over to Lieutenant John Allyn, who became secretary of the colony the following year. He retained them in his possession until in 1687 Connecticut became a part of the Dominion of New England and the famous episode of the hiding of the charter in the oak tree on the Wyllys estate was enacted.[1]

Under the charter of 1662 Connecticut became a corporate government, legally and royally recognized, with authority vested in the governor and company, the members of which were the "freemen" of the colony. The people of Connecticut were for the first time given official security and their relations with their sovereign across the seas, who was now no longer ignored as he had been in the Fundamental Orders and the Code of 1650, were carefully defined. Henceforth they were the king's loyal subjects and as such were to have and enjoy all the liberties and immunities that were possessed and exercised by the free and natural subjects within any of the king's dominions. In their turn they, as "freemen formally incorporated into this civil society," took an oath of supremacy such as was required by the charter and, thirty years later, an oath of allegiance in which every member of the general assembly was obliged to swear that he would "bear true allegiance to his own protestant king" (William III). The oath of fidelity was still required of all "admitted inhabitants" of the towns and a new "oath of freedom" of all who were granted the freedom of the company, in which, as far as we know, there was no mention of either obedience or alle-

in London was an exemplification or attested copy, which John Winthrop, Jr., caused to be made and placed in Porter's hands before he left England in 1663. It was brought into use for royal or judicial inspection after 1689, when the question of the validity of the Connecticut charter was raised in the colony and became an issue in England. Porter mentions this copy in 1690, and in 1693 Fitz John Winthrop was instructed by the colony to make use of it in his address to the king (*Hoadly Memorial*, pp. 27, 39, 58). We read of a copy of this copy as having been made in 1697 ("from a copy lent by Maj. Gen. Winthrop"). This copy of a copy is now in the Public Record Office. It contains omissions and interlineations that preclude the possibility of Winthrop's copy being an original. The omissions are curious and are manifestly not mere clerical errors (C. O. 1:16, no. 47).

1. This episode has become legendary in Connecticut. For a discussion of the points at issue see the writings of Bates and Seymour as above. The questions involved are rather antiquarian than historical, and their settlement, either one way or the other, hardly affects the course of Connecticut's history.

giance.[1] Though justice was to be rendered as before according to the Word of God and the law of righteousness, the colony declared in 1673 that it was not its "purpose to repugn the Statute Laws of England, so far as we understand them, professing ourselves always ready and willing to receive Light for Emendation and Alteration as we may have opportunity."[2] Henceforth all writs ran in the king's name and later a king's or queen's attorney was appointed for "impleading in the law all criminal offenders."[3] Now that Connecticut had a royal charter and was determined not to lose that charter by any ill-advised or incautious acts, she was willing to go a long way in the direction of accepting English authority and English law. As long as she could retain and exercise the power of self-government, she was willing to make any reasonable concession that did not infringe on this fundamental right or that would enable her to avoid any inquisitorial investigation into her affairs by the authorities at home.

The essential parts of the charter were based on the Fundamental Orders and on the laws passed and practices tested since that time. The terms had undoubtedly been carefully drawn up by Winthrop in his final petition and they expressed in formal legal language, with here and there a modification, the determination of the Connecticut leaders to retain the government as it had been carried on since 1636. Thus the charter did little more than set the seal of the king's approval on what the colony had already done and its acquirement made little difference in the actual machinery and routine of administration. The colony, nowhere in the charter called a com-

1. The "oath of allegiance," properly so called, seems to have been required only of the members of the assembly (*Connecticut Colonial Records,* 1689–1706, p. 282), but the governor in addition was required to swear to obey the acts of trade and navigation, which he did for the first time early in the eighteenth century. The "oath of freedom," as phrased in 1704, obliged the freeman to declare that he would be "true and faithful to her Majestie Queen Ann and to her lawful successors, and to the Government of her Majesties said Colonie as established by charter" (*ibid.,* p. 483). Apparently the "admitted inhabitant" who was not a "freeman," that is, was not a member of the Company (and there were hundreds such) did not have to swear either allegiance or obedience. On the subject in general, one should notice the language used when the general assembly in 1684 passed the law required by the crown regarding privateers and pirates (*ibid.,* 1678–1689, pp. 150–151, and for comments on the law, *Calendar State Papers, Colonial,* 1697–1698, §§310, 628).

2. *Ibid.,* 1665–1678, p. 568.

3. *Ibid.,* 1689–1706, p. 468. For the relations between Connecticut and the British government during the colonial period, see my introduction to *Fane's Reports on Connecticut Laws* (Acorn Club Publications, 1915, reprinted in the Tercentenary Series of Publications, no. 1).

monwealth as the founders had styled it, continued to have its governor, deputy governor, and assistants, chosen as before by the "freemen" from among themselves; its two annual assemblies, with not
more than two members elected by each of the towns from among
the "freemen" of the colony; its power to make laws, no longer
unlimited but restricted by the phrase "not contrary to the laws of
England"; its right to erect courts of justice, though the indefinite-
ness of the language made uncertain the inclusion of vice-admiralty
courts under the civil law; full freedom to carry on trade, to bring
in or send away such of the king's subjects or strangers as were
willing voluntarily to enter or migrate, to impose fines, imprison or
otherwise deal with offenders, to pardon such if desired, and to convert the heathen. It was to have a common seal, for the first time
legally,[1] but it was not exempted from the payment of custom duties
in England, as Winthrop had so ardently hoped would be the case.
Its lands were to be held in free and common socage as of the king's
manor of East Greenwich in Kent;[2] and as was the case with all the
trading companies, it paid no quit-rent to the crown other than a
fifth part of all the gold and silver found within its limits. Nor was
it ever required to send its laws to England for the king's confirmation or disallowance.

Henceforth, on the governmental side, Connecticut was one body
corporate in fact as well as in name, with right of perpetual succession, capable of pleading and being impleaded, of answering and
being answered, of defending and being defended in all suits and

1. Quite apart from the tradition that Fenwick handed over to the colony the seal
of the Warwick grantees (for which see statement by Charles J. Hoadly in the *Connecticut State Register and Manual* for 1889), and the actual presence of a seal (il-
legible) upon a commission of October 27, 1647, to John Winthrop, Jr., it seems clear
that the colony had a seal of some kind from the imprint on the letter of credit issued
by John Talcott (*Hoadly Memorial*, p. 7). See Baldwin, "The Seal of Connecticut,"
Papers, New Haven Colonial Historical Society, VIII, 82–108.

2. On the meaning of the phrase "as of the manor of East Greenwich," above, Vol.
I, 86 note. To the illustrations there given may be added others, demonstrating still
further the fact that this phrase had only a legal and constructive value. Land was
held by a Wiltshire yeoman "as of the manor of East Greenwich" (*Wiltshire Inquisitions*, p. 111). Lands were held in two cases in Gloucestershire in free and common
socage "as of the manor of Hawkesbury" and "as of the manor of Frampton on
Severn" (*Gloucester Inquisitions*, I, 133; III, 81), while in the Berkeley Hundred,
Gloucestershire, lands were held of the king "as of the manor of East Greenwich in
free and common soccage by fealty only," "as of [George Lord Berkeley's] castle of
Berkeley" or "as of his manor of Berkeley," or "as of his manor of Home" (*The
Berkeley Manuscripts*, III). The Hudson Bay territory and the Bahama Islands were
both held by the same tenure, not immediately of the person of the king, but mediately
as of some honour or manor within the realm of England belonging to the crown.

causes whatsoever. She was secure against aggression or interference within the bounds of her jurisdiction.

"Within the bounds of her jurisdiction!" The story of Connecticut's land claims is neither a simple nor an inviting subject to deal with. It begins with the extent of land mentioned in the draft of the Warwick patent handed in to the Council for New England, June, 1632, but never acted on by the council. In that draft Warwick solicited land stretching southwesterly from Narragansett River (presumably Narragansett Bay) for thirty miles along the coast and fifty miles into the interior, thus asking for nothing west of the Connecticut River.[1] But in the deed, which he had already issued to the lords and gentlemen three months before, he granted them a territory running for one hundred and twenty miles along the coast and west to the south sea, which was then thought to lie just over the western mountains. How are we to account for this extraordinary discrepancy and who was responsible for it? These are questions that we cannot answer. But we do know that when the general court of Connecticut drafted its instructions to Winthrop it bade him apply for all the territory named in the deed and in addition for enough more to carry the eastern boundary to the Plymouth line, the northern boundary to the Massachusetts line, and the western boundary to the Delaware, thus rounding out by enlargement in three directions the land granted by Warwick to the lords and gentlemen. In his second petition Winthrop improved a little on this instruction, seeking land from Narragansett Bay on the east, to the Massachusetts line on the north, to the Sound on the south, and to the south sea on the west, with all the islands thereto adjoining. These are the boundaries of the charter, and, literally interpreted, as Connecticut insisted on interpreting them then and afterward, wiped out completely all other claims to soil within their limits. In thus "crowding on," Connecticut took advantage of the weakness of Rhode Island and New Haven, whose titles were defective, and of the insecurity of the Dutch on the Hudson, with whom her relations had been none too friendly, and following the precedent set by Massachusetts Bay dared all that she could. For the moment she was successful, though the committee of the Privy Council said later "that King Charles the Second was surprized in his grant to Connecticut as to the boundaries."[2] If this statement is to be believed

---

1. *Proceedings,* American Antiquarian Society, 1867, pp. 106, 107.
2. *Acts Privy Council, Colonial,* III, p. 14.

then how did the boundaries get into the charter, particularly in view of the fact that the English authorities in granting the charter, as later events were to show, had apparently no intention of destroying the independence of either Rhode Island or New Haven, for there is nothing to prove that in the latter case, the treatment of the regicides had anything to do with the matter. Winthrop, too, when he went to England had no thought of infringing on New Haven's liberties in carrying out the objects of his mission. William Hooke in his letter of February, 1663, to John Davenport, his former coadjutor in the New Haven church, speaks of spending a forenoon "with Mr Winthrop, Major Tomson (who hath bought Mr Whitfield's house and land at Gilford), also Captaine [John] Scott of Long Island, and Mr. Nath: Whitfield, in debating the business of your colony. They all came unlooked for, or undesired by me, to the place of my present abode [Hooke was in hiding]." In the course of the conversation "Mr. Winthrop apologizeth for himself, that it was not his Intention you should have been thus dealt with by his neighbours at Connecticut, nor that your Liberties should have been in the least infringed and that it is his desire that yet you may injoy them as much to the full as ever you did."[1]

1. Letter from William Hooke to John Davenport, February, 1663, calendared in part, *Calendar State Papers, Colonial*, 1661–1668, §422; *Domestic*, 1663–1664, pp. 63–65, 98 (12), 117 (16–18). C. O. 1:15, no. 81. Hooke's letter was seized in transmission and was probably never seen by Davenport. The English authorities deemed it "seditious" (*Calendar State Papers, Colonial*, 1661–1668, §§430, 440). The Major Thompson, here mentioned, was the brother of Maurice Thompson, the merchant, a man widely engaged in colonial trade and one of the Kent Island partners.

The attitude of the Connecticut fathers toward Winthrop, both as governor and as agent, is characteristic of the Connecticut Puritan's political philosophy, which subordinated the individual to the greater welfare of the community. Outside the colony, in England during and after the negotiations for the charter and in New Amsterdam at the time of the surrender, Winthrop exercised great personal influence and his opinion in each case carried the day. But at home, among his fellow Puritans at Hartford, he was merely one man among others. The magistrates ignored his opinions whenever they deemed those opinions in conflict with the higher interests of the commonwealth, as they saw them. They repudiated Winthrop's compromise with Rhode Island, they paid no attention to what he thought about the boundaries and the controversy with New Haven, and when in 1663 they heard the Dutch envoys cite him against themselves they cast the citation aside with the remark "the Governor is but one man" (also *ibid.*, 1700, p. 739). Having got their charter, with its boundaries written down in black and white and sealed with the royal seal, they refused to listen to any interpretation of those boundaries that circumscribed the colony's opportunity for territorial expansion. There are times when one feels a little uncomfortable regarding the application in Connecticut of the much vaunted "law of righteousness," just as one feels equally uncomfortable regarding Massachusetts' insistence on her "liberties."

With Winthrop and the king both disclaiming any intention, in granting the charter, of curtailing the liberties of New Haven, a question of considerable difficulty arises regarding the circumstances attending the drafting and issue of that instrument and the overthrow of New Haven's independence. The story of Connecticut's beginnings is not fully told until the relations of Connecticut with New Haven, which led to the absorption of the latter colony in the years from 1660 to 1665, are accurately and impartially narrated. To the founding, growth, and fall of the Puritan colony on Long Island Sound we must now turn our attention.

NOTE: Connecticut's system of self-government was so carefully thought out, intelligently written down, and wisely applied, the most advanced and lasting of all the Puritan systems, that it seems a pity and wholly unnecessary (merely as a matter of state pride) to misrepresent it, as many have done, by giving it a modern dress and using such modern terms as "the first written constitution," "the first written constitution of modern democracy," and "the first fixed formal and established expression of government for, by and of the people to be governed." The following objections can be raised to such usage.

(a) These terms are not descriptively accurate. The Fundamental Orders are not a constitution in any commonly understood sense of the word, and they have no connection with modern democracy or with any democracy. Connecticut's government was in a limited sense popular but never democratic. The Puritans in that colony would have repudiated Lincoln's phrase, "for the people, of the people, and by the people," even if they had understood it, which is doubtful, as affirming something in which they did not believe. They would have amended it to read "for, by, and of those who were the godly, that is, the approved Christian people to be governed" and even in using this phrase they would have preached something they did not literally practice.

(b) The use of these terms has led writers to believe in such fanciful statements as "The Fundamental Orders of Connecticut became the model for all constitutions that have since been adopted in the United States and for those beyond the seas" (Mills, *The Story of Connecticut*, p. 124). There is not a word of truth in that statement.

(c) It has led writers to introduce into the interpretation of early Connecticut history such terms as "Constitution," "Constitutional Convention," "Approval of the People," "Democracy," "Popular-Sovereignty" and other similar accompaniments of modern constitution making, which have no place there, either in fact or in theory.

(d) It has led many people to believe that Connecticut had something peculiar that the other New England colonies did not have. In scarcely any essential did the Connecticut practice differ from that of the other colonies. In fact Connecticut copied her governmental system from that of Massachusetts in its main structural forms, though she differed from Massachusetts in one or two very important particulars, the nature and significance of which we have already noticed. We must not forget that Plymouth, Massachusetts, Rhode Island, and New Haven were all self-governing colonies.

(e) It has led to the assumption that Connecticut had something more nearly akin to modern democracy than had any of the colonies out of New England and that the Fundamental Orders contributed more to American political ideas and governmental practice than any other colonial system. Such assumption is unfair to the other colonies. Virginia (1619), Bermuda (1620), and Barbados (1639) all had representative popular assemblies and partial self-government as early as did Connecticut, and because the right of their people to participate in government did not rest on a religious foundation their systems were more nearly popular and "democratic" than was that of Connecticut. What the latter colony had was complete self-government, which was earlier in origin and lasted longer than in any other colony or state. In the development of American political ideas and social practices, the influence of the popular assembly, in the eighteenth rather than in the seventeenth century, is the most potent single factor underlying our American system of government. It cannot be shown that the Mayflower Compact, the Fundamental Orders, or any of the so-called "liberty" documents of the seventeenth century had any influence on later events.

The Fundamental Orders cannot be taken out of their Puritan setting and away from their Puritan background and studied *in vacuo,* as is done by many a modern lawyer and student of political science, who in their interpretation of these orders have introduced a great many modern ideas that do not belong there.

CHAPTER V

THE RISE AND FALL OF THE
NEW HAVEN COLONY

DURING the years when Connecticut was laying the foundation of its government and expanding into a commonwealth, a new experiment was being tried on the shore of Long Island Sound, forty miles to the southwest of Hartford, Wethersfield, and Windsor. The defeat of the Pequots had removed the danger of Indian aggression in that quarter and had brought the whole coast within the scope of settlement by Englishmen. Until 1638 the seaboard was a wilderness frontier, unoccupied save by the inhabitants of the fort and lands at Saybrook and by the Nehantics, Quinnipiacs, Hammonasetts, Menuncatucks, Paugassetts, and other native tribes stretching eastward toward the Narragansett territory. This eastern stretch of coast had become known to those who had taken part in the Pequot wars and to others seeking opportunities for trade with the Indians. Its lands were remote from the communities already settled but were easily approached by water, as their harbors, though often blocked by silt, were more open than was the mouth of the Connecticut River. The Dutch, sailing along the shore in their visits to Buzzard's Bay and Plymouth harbor, had noted promising ports and rivers, offering favorable sites for forts and trading houses and there is reason to believe that they had planned to erect stations at advantageous points, fronting the harbors at Fairfield, Milford, and Guilford, and the river mouths at the entrance of the Quinnipiac, Connecticut, and Pequot rivers, as well as upon the islands in Narragansett Bay. But the only outcome of their efforts was the House of Hope which was established in 1633 on the southern side of the rivulet flowing into the Connecticut at Hartford. However promising the shore lands may have been for commercial enterprise because of the water connections, they were not well suited to agriculture and stock raising because they were only moderately fertile and varied greatly in value and availability for farm purposes.

The year 1635 in England was fraught with discouragement for

Puritan and parliamentarian alike. The writs of ship money had been issued and the trial of Hampden was under way. The Laud Commission was beginning what was feared would be a work of inquisition at home and in the colonies, and the courts of High Commission and Star Chamber were being charged, probably un-justly, with illegality and oppression. In general the outlook for a restoration of the parliamentary system was discouraging. The writ of quo warranto against the charter of Massachusetts Bay had been issued and there were fears of worse things to come. Migration to New England increased. The Puritan lords and gentlemen, begin-ning to think seriously of crossing the seas, sent over John Win throp, Jr., to prepare a refuge in America at the mouth of the Connecticut River for them and possibly for others among the par liamentary leaders. Groups of the nonconforming clergy and their followers were yielding to the necessity of leaving England, and were going either to Holland or to New England.[1] This impulse was strong among those who were feeling the weight of Laud's displeas-ure and who, already rebelling against the ritualistic tendencies of the Church of England, saw in Laud's efforts to beautify the church service and to enforce the religious uniformity required by the act of 1559 an offense against the organization of the primitive church as set forth in the Bible. Every vicar of an English parish church was potentially a plantation builder, for he was more than the spiritual head of his flock, he was a participant also in the prudential and secular affairs of his parish. The administration of an English parish gave to vicar, vestry, and parishioners just the sort of experience needed to prepare them for founding a settlement on New England soil, so it is not surprising that the New England villages should have reproduced in their local practices and methods of adminis-tration many of the details of organization and land distribution with which their founders were familiar in their previous life at home.

The history of the colony of New Haven[2] begins with the vestry

1. Many of the nonconforming clergy went to Holland, partly because it was a nearby refuge and partly because it was religiously sympathetic. But not all were able to remain there. Burroughs, Nye, Goodwin, Bridge, and Simpson, the "dissenting brethren" of the Westminster Assembly, held on, but others preferred exile in the wilderness, left Holland, and came to New England.

2. I wish to express my indebtedness in all that relates to Davenport's early career and the early career of the various settlements to the admirable work of Miss I. M Calder, *The New Haven Colony* (1934).

meetings of the church of St. Stephen, Coleman Street, London, of which for nine years the Rev. John Davenport, Bachelor of Divinity of Oxford,[1] was the vicar and influential head. He had been the curate of the neighboring church of St. Lawrence Jewry, under the eaves of the Guildhall.[2] The selection of a vicar was in the hands of the parishioners, with the approval of the Bishop of London, but the parish vestry by an ingenious adjustment of salary was able to neutralize the bishop's influence and to control the situation themselves.[3] This position of independence gave to the parish considerable experience in handling its own business and to Davenport and his leading laymen an apprenticeship that stood them in good stead when they came to America. During his first years in the ministry at St. Lawrence Jewry, Davenport adhered sympathetically to the ordinances and discipline of the established system and though not entirely above suspicion obtained a reputation for conformity. At St. Stephen's he added to his popularity as a preacher, with the ability to attract followers, particularly among the "common and mean people" as well as among the successful merchants of Coleman Street Ward. St. Stephen's was situated in the midst of a prosperous and strongly nonconformist community, a veritable Puritan stronghold, where lived or forgathered many of those who were interested in the activities of the Virginia and Massachusetts Bay companies, and were closely associated with the mercantile interests of the day. After studying the environment in which Davenport and his associates lived and worked, one need not wonder that the New Haven colony took on a mercantile character or that trade and commerce should have been in their minds the chief concern of the new settlement.[4] Unlike the promoters of other plantations in New England

1. Dexter, *Historical Papers*, p. 38; *Collections*, Connecticut Historical Society, XXI, 127.

2. Maitland, *History of London*, II, Cheap and Coleman street wards, with cuts of both churches as they were rebuilt after the Great Fire.

3. Freshfield, "Some Remarks on the Book of Records and History of the Parish of St. Stephen, Coleman Street," *Archaeologia*, L, 18. The regular salary was placed at £11, a sum too small for the vicar to live on, but a nominee of the parish received an addition of £39.

4. Old Jewry is in Coleman Street Ward, hardly a stone's throw from St. Stephen's. Among the leading merchants of St. Stephen's parish were Maurice Abbot, brother of George Abbot, Archbishop of Canterbury, and, after the death of Sir Thomas Smith, perhaps the leading merchant in London; also Sir Isaac Pennington, who as well as Abbot became a lord mayor of the city, and Owen Roe or Rowe, the regicide. None of these went to America, though Rowe sent over his son with Davenport in 1637. There was also Theophilus Eaton, who was identified with the Eastland and the

these men were not born and reared amid the manors and fields of old England and never took to farming as a natural and familiar vocation. Neither did the New Haven people ever succeed in becoming successful agriculturists.

Davenport was interested in the Virginia Company of London and although he may actually have become a member, the identification of the name is far from certain. However he did become a member of the Massachusetts Bay Company, contributed £50 toward the procuring of its charter, and took an active part in that company's proceedings.[1] There is nothing to show that at this early date (1629) he was interested in any plan of migration, though he showed his sympathies by serving as clerk of the meeting of the company at which Winthrop was elected governor and was present on at least one later occasion. Theophilus Eaton, whose father had baptized Davenport at Coventry, became an assistant of the company and contributed £100. Others, also, of St. Stephen's parish were members—Spurstowe, Rowe, Aldersey, Crane, White, and Bright—so that the intentions of the signers of the Cambridge Agreement to transfer company and charter to America must have been well known to him. It is but natural that when the time came he and those who went with him should at first have looked nowhere else than to Massachusetts Bay.

As early as 1627 Davenport had begun to attract the attention of the ecclesiastical authorities and was brought, with three other ministers, before the Court of High Commission for printing an appeal for funds to aid the persecuted Protestants of the Upper Palatinate,[2] a citation that cannot have increased his affection for the Church of England. He fully expected to be deprived of his pastoral charge

Massachusetts Bay companies. Sir Richard Saltonstall and Samuel Aldersey lived in Swan Alley in the parish and Theophilus Eaton took over Saltonstall's house after the latter vacated it in 1630. Mathew Cradock and George Foxcraft were both near by. Robert Seely, afterward of Connecticut and New Haven and a participant in the Pequot War, also lived at one time in Coleman Street. In Coleman Street lived William Whiting (d. 1699), son of William Whiting of Connecticut. Freshfield calls attention to the fact, which may be true or not, that at the Star in Coleman Street, Cromwell, Hugh Peter, Nathaniel Fiennes, and others were accustomed to meet and that there was plotted the death of Charles I (Freshfield, pp. 31–32).

1. *Massachusetts Colonial Records*, I, 37ᶜ, 37ᵉ, 47, 49, 50, 56, 57, 59, 61, 386. Roger Conant, who in 1625 migrated to Plymouth and later founded Salem, was one of Davenport's parishioners at St. Lawrence. He is an ancestor of President Conant of Harvard.

2. Dexter, *Historical Papers*, p. 39.

even then, but the blow did not fall, for Laud, whose influence in Davenport's life began with his elevation to the See of London in 1628, was not inclined to trouble himself with minor infractions of the rubrics, and it was not until he found the Puritans engaged in buying up ecclesiastical benefices in lay hands and appointing to them incumbents of their own persuasion that he took action. Davenport was one of those engaged in this business and Laud saw in it an attempt to undermine the strength and unity of the Church of England. Convinced that eventually this attempt would fail and that reform from within the church was hopeless, together with growing doubts about conformity, Davenport, in the years 1632 and 1633, joined the group of the nonconformists to which Cotton and Hooker belonged. It is reasonably clear that Cotton was instrumental in shaping Davenport's opinion and it is quite likely that Hooker had a hand in it also. Cotton had fled from Boston in Lincolnshire in 1632 and joined Davenport in London, thus beginning that long friendship between the two men which was to display itself so richly during their life in New England.[1]

Though Davenport was not ready to resign his vicarship, he was fast reaching the conclusion that his services for St. Stephen's were over and that, because of his conversion to nonconformity,[2] it would be necessary for him to leave England. Unwilling to cause any public disturbance and much perplexed as to the lawfulness of conformity, he wanted to free himself from his former connections with as little trouble as possible and, as far as he could, without affecting the peace and prosperity of his parishioners. Laud became Archbishop of Canterbury in 1633, and unlike his predecessor George Abbot, brother of Maurice Abbot of Coleman Street and St. Stephen's, he had no Puritan sympathies. When Juxon succeeded Laud as Bishop of London, Davenport saw the High-Church world closing about him. Cotton and Hooker were ready to leave. Withdrawing for the moment, for a brief period of retirement, he finally offered his resignation, which the vestry unwillingly accepted, and in mid-November, 1633, left England for Holland. Although at first he had every intention of returning to England when the storm had blown over, he soon offered himself as co-pastor with the Rev. John

1. Davenport, *An Apologetical Reply*, pp. 107–108; Young, *Chronicles of Massachusetts Bay*, pp. 432–433.

2. *Collections*, Massachusetts Historical Society, 4th ser., VI, 492; *An Apologetical Reply*, as above.

Paget, minister of the English church at Amsterdam.¹ But Paget
and Davenport fell out over the question of the baptism of the
children of unbelievers and the dispute, heightened by the hostile
efforts of Stephen Goffe, chaplain in the Netherlands of the English
regiment under Vere, rendered it certain that he would not receive
an unconditioned call to the co-pastorship of the church. After he
had aided Paget for five months and preached privately for four, he
removed to Rotterdam as Hugh Peter's assistant. There it was that
the project of the Puritan lords and gentlemen for the settlement of
Saybrook came under discussion and there it was that Peter and
Davenport persuaded Lion Gardiner to enter the service of the
Warwick grantees, while Peter himself accepted the agency with
John Winthrop, Jr., and the young Harry Vane. Conditions in old
and new England must have been frequently discussed between
them, and when Peter left on his mission, Davenport remained as
his substitute. Still pursued by the demands of his opponents that he
be dismissed, he became convinced that even Holland was no place
for him, and in order to escape an inquiry into his religious views
by Sir William Boswell, the English resident there, he returned to
England in April, 1636, two years and a half after his departure
therefrom.²

While in Holland Davenport undoubtedly reached a decision as
to his future movements. He determined to follow Cotton and
Hooker to New England, there to find freedom from the "extremi-
ties" of Laud in England and of Sir William Boswell in Holland.
Concealing himself from the authorities in the disguise of a country
gentleman, he set about gathering a group of his former parishioners

---

1. Laud learned of Davenport's departure indirectly through a letter from Stephen
Goffe, preacher of the English regiment in the Netherlands, of which Lieutenant General Vere was the head. Regarding this departure Laud wrote the king, "Since my
return out of Scotland Mr. John Davenport, vicar of St. Stephen's in Coleman Street
(whom I used with all moderation, and about two years since thought I had settled
his judgment, having him then at advantage enough to have put extremety upon
him, but forbare it) hath now resigned his vicarage, declared his judgment against
conformity with the Church of England and is since gone (as I hear) to Amsterdam"
(*Works*, V, 318–319). Goffe wrote that Davenport got away "by the connivance of
Mr. Stone, a merchant in Coleman Street. He was disguised in a grey suit and an
overgrown beard, and at his landing was presently with his complice put on horse-
back, and before all were well landed was got to Rotterdam [the Rev. Hugh] Peter
was there," etc., *Calendar State Papers, Domestic, Charles I*, 1633–1634, pp. 324,
413, 449; 1634–1635, p. 469; 1635, p. 151.

2. Davenport's return to England was probably hastened by the fact that in 1635
he had sent his wife and son (born in Holland) back to the hospitable home of Lady
Vere.

and others who were willing to accompany him, and found his chief ally in his former schoolmate and parishioner, Theophilus Eaton. Eaton had been involved in the quo warranto proceedings against the Massachusetts Bay Company, being one of the ten members of the company that appeared before the court of king's bench and disclaimed the charter in 1635, and he was also one of those who had been placed in charge of the joint-stock of the company on the departure of the main body to New England.[1] Davenport was aided by others also: the Rev. Samuel Eaton, brother of Theophilus; Edward Hopkins, Theophilus' son-in-law and one of the Warwick grantees; David and Thomas Yale, sons of Mrs. Eaton; John Evance, and others from the neighborhood of Coleman Street.

The vessel that bore the company to America was the *Hector*—Ferne, master—a boat of about two hundred and fifty tons burden, which had already gone once to Boston, where the mate, Miller, had been committed to jail for "certain seditious and opprobrious speeches" regarding the failure of the colony to display the king's colors at the fort in the harbor.[2] The St. Stephen's group probably hired the vessel, on its return from Boston in 1636, evidently contracting with a few separate passengers, of whom the only one named was Lord Ley, a young man nineteen years old, the only son and heir of the second earl of Marlborough, who went to see the country.[3] Delayed for a time by the government's impressment of the vessel,[4] the passengers, some two hundred and fifty in number, including many servants, finally got away in late April or early May and reached Boston on June 26. There Davenport found himself among old friends, for though Hooker had gone to Connecticut, Peter and Cotton were at hand to welcome him. He took up his residence at Cotton's house; Lord Ley stopped at the common inn;

1. Above, Vol. I, 398–399.

2. *Massachusetts Colonial Records*, I, 176. What these speeches were can be discovered in Winthrop, *Journal*, I, 181–182.

3. Lord James Ley returned in August, 1637, with Harry Vane, after a stay of only six weeks. The next year he became the third earl of Marlborough. For his later career see Vol. III, index.

4. *Calendar State Papers, Colonial*, 1574–1660, p. 245. The owners of the *Hector* petitioned for release, saying that the vessel was first going to New England "for a plantation there" and then to divers parts abroad for a cargo; that "most of the passengers had engaged their whole estates and all was ready for the voyage, when the ship was pressed for the King's service and that upon the vessels return His Majesty will receive 3,000 *l* at least [that is, in customs dues] on the goods imported." The petition in full is printed in Atwater, *New Haven*, p. 48.

the others probably found lodging and employment where they could, all awaiting the eventual decision as to their future course. That they were expected to constitute a plantation in Massachusetts, as other similar groups had done, is evidenced from the tax twice levied upon Eaton by the general court, the amount in the first instance being what he could pay and in the second £20.[1]

There can be little doubt that the leaders fully intended to remain in Massachusetts, for they spent the summer and autumn considering the opportunities that the situation offered and the locations that were placed at their disposal. The general court bade them select any site that appealed to them. The Charlestown people invited them to make their home there. Those of Newbury, who had already decided to leave their homes and cross the river to Winnacunnet (Hampton, New Hampshire) where the land was more fertile, offered them the tract upon which they were then settled.[2] Plymouth too made them offers. But they would have none of these. Eaton and others among them were merchants, who had their minds set on a place for trade and they could find no harbor along the Massachusetts coast that was not already occupied. The water frontage was overcrowded and the interior, involving a laborious clearing of the forest, did not attract them. Other reasons weighed heavily in the balance. The company had reached Boston at a critical time when the excitement over the Antinomian controversy was at its height and when the struggle between Winthrop and Vane was involving the colony in one of its most troublesome domestic conflicts. Also the news from England threatening the loss of the charter was very disturbing, and they were still fearful that a governor general might be imposed upon them. Davenport played his part in the trial of Anne Hutchinson and probably brought about the conversion of Cotton to orthodoxy just as formerly in England Cotton had helped to convert him to nonconformity, but he could have had little desire to enter into competition for place among the clergy or to help in unraveling the tangle of theological opinion in which the colony had become involved. However much God's providence may have designed Massachusetts for those who were already there, Davenport and Theophilus Eaton were willing to believe that the same "wise God whose prerogative it is to determine the bounds of

---

our habitations" had other designs for them. Another country, as yet unoccupied, might well come within the scope of the divine plan. Hugh Peter who had been with Fenwick at Saybrook may well have told Davenport what he saw and heard there. Israel Stoughton had accompanied Mason, Ludlow, and Seely in pursuit of the Pequots as far as the Quinnipiac in July, 1637, and had written favorably of the region, recommending its settlement. Richard Davenport, a lieutenant in the Pequot War, had likewise given glowing accounts.[1] Consequently on August 30, only a little more than two months after their arrival, Theophilus Eaton and others of the company set out for Quinnipiac, their minds fully intent on leaving Boston and finding a place for a plantation on the shores of Long Island Sound.[2] It had taken them but a short time to discover that the Massachusetts Bay colony was no suitable place for the carrying out of the purposes which they had in view.

Eaton returned from Quinnipiac to Massachusetts in the autumn, leaving seven of his companions to occupy the ground which they had selected as the site of their future settlement. These men remained through the winter, losing one of their number by death. They probably kept in touch with their associates in Boston, dispatching reports and receiving instructions, for it is hardly credible that they should have been left there without occasional communication and the receiving of provisions. The larger body continued to live in Massachusetts until the unfavorable season had passed and the weather had become propitious for migration. Davenport continued his activities, preaching sermons, engaging in theological discussions, and endeavoring by one means or another to induce others than those who had come in the *Hector* to join in the new venture. He almost persuaded Vane and Cotton to go with him, but the former decided to return to England and the latter, hesitating because he thought that his influence in Massachusetts had been impaired by his sympathy with the Hutchinsonian party, finally cast in his lot with Massachusetts.[3] Davenport, however, succeeded in

1. Winthrop, *Journal*, I, 226; the same (Savage ed.), I, appendix D; *Collections, Massachusetts Historical Society*, 5th ser., IX, 2.
2. Winthrop, *Journal*, I, 230–231.
3. *Narragansett Club Publications*, II, 81. That others in Massachusetts were contemplating a similar removal is evident from Cotton's words, ". . . which I discerning, it wrought in me thoughts (as it did in many other sincerely godly Brethren of our Church) not of a separation from the churches [as had been the case with Roger Williams] . . . but of a removal to New Haven, as being better known to

adding to his number Peter Prudden, who with a group of Hertfordshire families had arrived in Boston, July 31, 1637, five weeks
after Davenport's arrival;[1] Captain Nathaniel Turner of Lynn; and
later he welcomed to New Haven Captain George Lamberton of
the Ezekiel Rogers group of Yorkshire men. The latter company
under the leadership of Rogers, the friend of Hooker while living
with the Barringtons in Essex, crossed the water in 1638. Some of
its members went to New Haven, but a majority remained with
Rogers and founded Rowley in Massachusetts.[2] Turner and Lamberton were destined to play exceedingly prominent parts in the
later history of the New Haven colony.

On March 30, 1638, the reorganized company, differing in some
important particulars from the body that crossed in the *Hector,* set
sail from Boston, rounded Cape Cod, coursed along the southern
New England coast, past the fort at Saybrook, and on to the capa-
cious harbor, larger than it is today, into which flows the Quinnipiac River. There they found the six men who had survived the
winter and who may have done something in the way of gathering
materials and erecting structures against their arrival. But the preparations could not have amounted to much, for Michael Wigglesworth from Yorkshire, who with others came the next October,
reports in his autobiography that during the following winter his
family "dwelt in a cellar partly underground covered with earth,"
which proved so unsatisfactory a protection that, as he says further,
"one great rain broke in upon us and drencht me so in my bed

the Pastor [Davenport], and some others there, than to such as were at that time
jealous of me here."

1. Calder, *The New Haven Colony,* p. 47. That the Prudden company came from
Hertfordshire and not from Herefordshire, as is commonly stated, appears from two
documents, "The Several Answers of Edward Tapp, one of the defendants to the
bill of Comp[lt] of Richard Barber als Griggs Comp[lt]" (obtained by Miss Calder from
the Public Record Office, Chancery Bills and Answers, Charles I, B 93/34), which
definitely locate Tapp, a member of the Prudden company, at Bennington, Hertfordshire. Hubbard, *History of New England,* p. 319, says "Another company from
Hartford . . . came over with Mr. Peter Prudden." On the Prudden company in
Boston, see Morison, "Peter Prudden's Company and Colonial Affairs in 1637 and
1638," *Publications,* Massachusetts Colonial Society, 17, pp. 244–248; Winthrop,
Journal (Savage ed.), I, 311–312, 484–486.

2. Winthrop, *Journal,* I, 298. Rogers was quite disturbed by Lamberton's desertion
of his party. "Mr. Lamberton did us much wrong. I expected his coming to the Bay,
but it seems he sets down at Quinnipiac: yet he hath a house in Boston. I would
humbly crave your advice to Mr. William [Richard] Bellingham about it, whether
we may not enter an action against him" (*Collections,* Massachusetts Historical Society, 4th ser., VII, 208, and for further relations with Quinnipiac, *ibid.,* 209, 217).

being asleep [he was seven years old at the time] that I fell sick upon it." Others had similar uncomfortable experiences. Pits dug in the ground, six or seven feet deep, encased with timber, with plank floors and roofed over were not unknown elsewhere, and this cellar may have been something of that sort. A few of the cellars were probably buildings of fair size, for we read of them as still occupied in 1642.[1] But as the numbers of the settlers increased, with the arrival of newcomers from Boston and elsewhere, who continued their wanderings until the tide of emigration from England began to ebb, the settlers laid out the town, apportioned home lots, distributed the adjoining fields and meadows, planted crops, and built houses and barns. The town plot was a rectangle, divided into nine squares, of which the square in the center, larger than the others, was set apart as a green or market place. The plot was cut by ways or paths that ran north and south, east and west. Progress was rapid and soon the cellars and shacks must have been supplanted by houses of a more substantial character.[2] Gradually the settlement fell into the ordinary ways of a plantation.

The Davenport company came to Quinnipiac without royal patent or any certain legal warrant authorizing them to occupy a part of the king's domain. Even if they had reached some understanding with Peter or Fenwick, acting on behalf of the Warwick grantees, whereby they received permission to locate on a part of the Warwick grant, such understanding could have had no legal significance. They bought this land of the Indians, as a group of purchasers or

1. Atwater, *New Haven*, p. 532; *New Haven Colonial Records*, I, 31, 32, 41, 46, 47, 70, 218, 233, 234, 258, 420. *New York Colonial Documents*, I, 368. Some of these "sellars" were probably merely the foundations of houses, as the word implies, but when Lamberton was granted "a yard to his sellar by the West creeke" in 1640, on condition that he "sell both house and lott at what time and only to whom the court shall approve of" (*New Haven Colonial Records*, I, 41), the cellar is manifestly some sort of a dwelling.

2. The description of four of the houses, those of Davenport, Eaton, Gregson, and Allerton, built during these early years in New Haven, that is given in Stiles, *History of the Judges*, p. 63, Lambert, *History of the Colony of New Haven*, pp. 52-53, Hubbard, *History of New England*, p. 334 ("they laid out too much of their stocks and estates in building of fair and stately houses"), must be looked on with suspicion and has not gone unchallenged. Mr. George Dudley Seymour in *Hale and Wyllys*, pp. 90, 91-92, 104, 174-175, after an examination of the inventories, from which he insists there is no appeal, reduces the "fabled mansions" of thirteen, nineteen, and twenty-one fireplaces and many "apartments" to the proportions of substantial but not elaborate dwellings, such as might have been built by men of means with servants at their disposal. Johnson, *Wonder-Working Providence*, p. 176, says simply, "very faire houses and compleat streets."

proprietors, and in several successive transactions extending over a series of years gradually enlarged the area of their possessions. Afterward they made a number of efforts to rectify the situation by obtaining a legal warrant for their claims. In 1644 Theophilus Eaton asked Massachusetts for a copy of her charter, thinking to use it to justify the colony's right to settle on the Delaware, but when the general court of the jurisdiction realized the uselessness of the document for that purpose, it set about obtaining a royal patent of its own. It instructed Thomas Gregson, one of the most influential and wealthy merchants in the colony, to go to England, and agreed to furnish him with £200 to meet all charges. As Roger Williams had just received from the Warwick committee of the Long Parliament his patent for Rhode Island, it seemed a propitious time for New Haven to do likewise. Gregson was advised to join with Connecticut to procure a joint patent for the two colonies. But the effort came to nothing. Gregson was lost in the "phantom ship" and Connecticut deferred action until 1645 when she asked Fenwick to obtain an enlargement of the Warwick grant in the form of a royal confirmation, but said nothing about a joint patent to include New Haven. Fenwick, as we know, did not make the attempt, probably realizing that he had no sufficient warrant for the application, as neither he nor anyone else could show the crown lawyers or the parliamentary committee any copy of an original Warwick Patent. This fact is significant inasmuch as Warwick himself was the head of the parliamentary commission on plantations before whom such application would have to be made.[1] Seven years later New Haven asked Edward Winslow to petition the Council of State for a patent covering the Delaware region, encouraged perhaps by Coddington's successful effort the April before to obtain a commission as governor of Aquidneck. The petition was referred to the Council of Trade of which Sir Harry Vane was the president and then to the committee for foreign affairs, but nothing came of it.[2] After the Restoration a further attempt was made and it was generally believed in

---

1. Above, p. 128. Winthrop, *Journal*, I, 160–161; *New Haven Colonial Records*, I, 149, 211; II, 519–520; *Connecticut Colonial Records*, 1636–1665, pp. 126, 128.

2. *Calendar State Papers, Colonial*, 1574–1660, p. 373; *Plymouth Colonial Records*, IX, 183, 199; *Collections*, Massachusetts Historical Society, 4th ser., VII, 548–550, 552–553. It is strange that neither Warwick nor Vane should have shown any interest in the New Haven colony, particularly when we know what Warwick did for Massachusetts and Vane for Rhode Island. Was there anything in Davenport's extreme orthodoxy and the political limitations of his colony that repelled them?

New Haven that Winthrop in his mission of 1661 was to ask for a joint patent, but, as will be noted later, Connecticut had no intention of instructing Winthrop to do so. This want of a patent of any kind was a source of great weakness to the New Haven jurisdiction and gave excuse to the Dutch for calling it "a pretended colony."

Thus the settlers of New Haven, like the Pilgrims of Plymouth, were obliged to erect their civil government upon the uncertain foundation of a title obtained from Indian purchases. Both Davenport and Eaton had their own ideas of what such a civil government should be, for both had lived long enough in Massachusetts Bay to study the working of the system there. Davenport had lived for nine months in the same house with John Cotton and must not only have talked with Cotton about his plans but have got from him certain notions also as to the best form of government to erect. It is quite likely that he took advantage of the opportunity to study the contents of the code "Moses his Judicials," which Cotton had drawn up at the request of the general court in 1636 and presented to that body the October following.[1] We know that a copy of that code was sent by Winthrop to New Haven, probably before 1643.[2] This code was not based upon the Bible, despite its marginal references to the Scriptures, which were added after the code was written, but was, in brief form, an outline of the government and law of the Massachusetts Bay colony, based on the charter, the common law of England, and, in capital cases, the Mosaic code. New Haven as a plantation or town, and even more as a jurisdiction or colony after 1643, followed contemporary models in all its essential parts, for no system founded on the Old Testament could possibly have proved adequate to meet the needs of a political community in the seventeenth century. Not one of the New England governments was in any exact and literal sense of the phrase a "Bible Commonwealth."[3]

1. Above, Vol. I, 455.
2. "New Haven's Case Stated," *New Haven Colonial Records*, II, 518. The statement reads, "And by voluntary consent among themselves upon such fundamentals as were established in Massachusetts by allowance of their patent, whereof the then governor of the Bay, the Right Worp[11] Mr. Winthrop sent as a coppie to improve for our best advantage." What Winthrop sent was not a copy of the charter, as has sometimes been said, but of the Cotton code. As Miss Calder points out there was no copy of the charter in the New Haven colony before 1644, when Eaton asked Winthrop to send one (*Journal*, II, 161). That it was the code which was sent and not the "Body of Liberties" is clear from the fact that the "Liberties" was merely a body of law, while the code contained the outline of a frame of government.
3. One of the most interesting features of Cotton's "Moses his Judicials" is the

It is very probable that Davenport, Eaton, and others among the leading men of the company had reached some understanding, even before the arrival at Quinnipiac, as to what should be the main features of the political and ecclesiastical edifices they proposed to build. But it was not for a year after they set foot on New Haven soil that they took definite action. Finally, in June, 1639, all the free planters, some seventy in number, gathered according to tradition in a large barn (built by the leading carpenter of the colony, William Andrews, and belonging to Robert Newman) and there began the dual work of establishing "such civill order as might be most pleasing unto God, and for the choosing the fittest man for the foundation work of a church to be gathered." A formal plantation covenant had already been solemnly entered into on "the first day of extraordinary humiliation" which the settlers had appointed after their arrival, and this covenant had sufficed until the time came for the more orderly structure. That time had now come.

Before any definite steps were taken, Davenport raised the fundamental question as to the qualifications of those who might best be entrusted with matters of government and fortified his recommendations with citations from the Old and New Testaments.[1] The motion that all free burgesses should be church members—either of the church in New Haven or of one or other of the approved churches in New England—was not carried without dissent, for after the vote was taken, one man at least, name not known, arose to object. A discussion ensued but without altering the final decision, which they profoundly believed expressed the mind of God. Hence the rule was established, similar to that laid down in Massachusetts

ingenious way in which the compiler, following a practice common to the Puritans, justified as much of the code as he could by references to the Old Testament. The "Moses his Judicials" was made first and the references were added afterward. The same was true of the New Haven Code of 1656. To have built a political structure or a body of law out of the passages cited would have brought into existence an extraordinary political organization for an English colony in the seventeenth century. On the influence of "Moses his Judicials" upon the organization of the New Haven colony see Calder, *The New Haven Colony,* ch. VI. On the question of the authorship of *A Discourse about Civill Government,* see the same writer in the *American Historical Review,* XXXVI, 267–269. It is reasonable to believe, as Miss Calder states, that Davenport, who brought about the publication of this pamphlet in Cambridge in 1663, should have been better informed as to its authorship, which he ascribes to Cotton, than would Cotton Mather, who thirty years later ascribed it to Davenport himself.

1. Exodus 18:21; Deuteronomy 1:13, 15, 17; and 1 Corinthians 6:1–7. These are taken directly from the Cotton code.

and embodied in the Cotton code, that church members only should have the right to choose magistrates and officials, to transact public affairs, to make laws, divide inheritances, to decide all differences that might arise, and to do all other things of a like nature.

This having been decided, the church was next organized by the selection of twelve men (actually eleven), who chose seven among themselves, as those most fit for the foundation work, the seven pillars of the structure.[1] These seven pillars, adding to themselves nine more—and later others from time to time, formed a "general court" of the town. This court elected a magistrate and four deputies, whose duties were largely judicial, while the duties of the court itself (a kind of town meeting) were prudential. Theophilus Eaton was the magistrate for the first year and was annually reëlected a magistrate until his death. It was he who was responsible for the rejection of jury trial in the colony, apparently because he had no faith in other judgments than his own and those of the magistrates. Davenport was the pastor, but Eaton, headstrong and determined, was in large part the dictator of the settlement until his death in 1658. This was the general form of the government for the first four years, from 1639 to 1643, when, the church system remaining unchanged, there was superimposed upon the town government a larger and more elaborate organization, that of the colony or jurisdiction. The circumstances that led to this enlargement were as follows.

During the years following the close of the Pequot War in 1637, the coast region saw the founding of many new settlements. Connecticut was promoting the plantations at Stratford and Fairfield; and New Haven also, as the Dutch expressed it, was "hiving farther out." A second purchase in 1638 carried the latter's possessions as far to the east and west as to constitute an area thirteen miles in length and ten in width, ample acreage for a single plantation, but insufficient in Puritan eyes to meet the demand for expansion. Hardly was the work of organization well under way than the "hiving" began. In the late summer or autumn of 1639, the Rev. Peter Prudden, with his band of faithful followers from Hertford-

---

1. The church thus organized elected Davenport as its first pastor and he held the office during the lifetime of the colony. He was assisted by William Hooke as teacher from 1644 to 1656, when Hooke going back to England was followed by Richard Blinman as assistant but not as teacher. Blinman remained only a year and in 1659 Nicholas Street became first the teacher and finally the pastor.

shire and others from Wethersfield, under the guidance of an experienced Indian fighter, Thomas Tibbals, started westward through
the woods to found a town, later called Milford, ten miles away.
Prudden had long desired, as had many a leading Puritan minister
of the day, to have a settlement of his own. There is nothing to
show that he and his company had ever intended to remain permanently in New Haven or that any dissatisfaction with Davenport
was the cause of their removal. They had already, February 12, 1639,
acquired land beyond the New Haven second purchase and before
starting on the new pilgrimage had organized themselves as a
church body, choosing their own seven pillars, and fashioning their
own church covenant. On November 29, either in New Haven or
Milford, probably the former, they set up a government of five
judges or magistrates and made provisions for a town meeting and
the distribution of lots, and agreed that in all their doings they would
be guided by the written word of God.[1] In nearly all essentials they
copied New Haven, but relaxed in some measure the rule regarding
church membership, for there were ten men among them sharing
in the management of local affairs who were not covenanted Christians. Four of these entered the church before 1643, but six remained
outside, suffering thereby no loss of political privileges.[2]

1. Lambert, *History of the New Haven Colony*, p. 92.
2. The date of the settlement of Milford rests on no certain documentary evidence. That the church of which Peter Prudden was the pastor was organized in
New Haven, August 22, 1639, and continued to function there until its removal to
Wepowaug or Milford the following February or March admits of no doubt. But
there is doubt as to whether or not men of the Prudden company went to the site
of the proposed plantation in the summer or autumn of 1639 and there began the
laying out of a town, preparatory to the removal of the women and children and
the transference of the church. Should this have happened then Prudden must have
gone back and forth, performing church duties at one end and plantation duties at
the other, for a period of some months, a not impossible feat, as Prudden was young,
only thirty-seven years old. Such a conclusion does not prove, however, that the civil
organization of November 20, 1639, referred to in the text, was brought about on
Milford soil. It might equally well have been effected in New Haven, just as the
church organization had been.

Is there any evidence of a Milford occupation in 1639? Several references may be
cited. Winthrop, under date, July, 1639 (*Journal*, I, 308), says that "Two other
plantations were begun beyond Quilipiack, and every plantation intended a peculiar
government." This statement is made in connection with the arrival of the Fenwick
ship at New Haven and seems to imply a New Haven not a Connecticut venture, as
would be the case if the plantations were Stratford and Fairfield, as is usually thought.
Also the words "peculiar government" point rather to New Haven than to Connecticut. De Vries, writing under date, June 15, 1640 (*New Netherland*, Original Narratives, p. 205) says, "Sailed this day four leagues passed Roode-berg [New Haven] and

Eastward of New Haven and forming part of the second purchase was the locality known as Totoket, which in 1640 was allotted to Samuel Eaton for a plantation of his own and of a company that he was expected to gather in England and bring to America.[1] Eaton, who had accompanied his brother and Davenport to New Haven and had lived there as a free burgess and householder for two years, returned to England for the purpose of gathering his company. But satisfied with conditions at home and probably none too well content with what New Haven offered him he never returned,[2] and the proposed plantation at Totoket failed to materialize. Its place was taken later by another settlement, started, as we shall see, by a group of planters from Wethersfield and elsewhere, well hardened and acclimated, who began the plantation and town of Branford in 1644.

Ministerial leadership was a conspicuous factor in the founding of towns in the New Haven colony, as is seen in the settlement of Guilford. Stimulated by the example of Hooker, Cotton, and especially Davenport, the Rev. Henry Whitfield, who was a friend of Hooker and had given him shelter at his rectory at Ockley in Surrey, finding it impossible, with his growing nonconforming views, to remain longer in England, gathered about him a group of his own family, friends, and parishioners, sold his property in Surrey, and prepared to migrate to America. He was never a separatist, even in the Massachusetts limited sense of the term, and found no difficulty, after his return to England in 1650, in taking up again his duties as

came to a river where the English had begun to make a village and where fifty houses were in proces of erection and a portion finished." This village may be Stratford on the Housatonic, but again it may be Milford, if the "few leagues" is to be taken literally. More conclusive than either of these is the entry in the *Connecticut Colonial Records*, I, 36, where under date, October 19, 1639, certain Connecticut commissioners at Stratford were instructed "to speake with Mr. Prudden, and that Plan[tačon] that the difference between them and Pequannocke [Stratford] may be peaceably decided." If this means what it seems to mean, then a Prudden plantation in some form was well started in October, 1639.

Two other comments may be made. A number of Wethersfield people joined the Prudden company in New Haven in the summer or autumn of 1639 (Stiles, *Wethersfield*, I, 138). It seems unlikely that such restless people (among whom was Thomas Tibbals himself) would have remained in New Haven, inactive, for a whole winter, living on their friends, with land ready for occupancy so near by. Then, too, a migration of the whole company would hardly have been begun in February or March, unless housing had been provided beforehand. To prepare houses and sow winter wheat demanded the presence in Milford of a considerable body of able-bodied men at least as early as the autumn of 1639.

1. *New Haven Colonial Records*, I, 40, 45, 199-200.
2. Below, Vol. III, index.

a minister of the Puritanized Church of England. He was intimate with Fenwick, who had gone home the year before and, wishing to return, joined the Whitfield group for the voyage. In this way Whitfield learned much about the country and was able to obtain from Fenwick permission to locate within the bounds of the territory given the Puritan lords and gentlemen by the Warwick deed, receiving later a grant from Fenwick of a piece of land to the west of Hammonasset, though not a part of the section upon which the town was later to be located. Fenwick and his wife aided the expedition, sharing the cost of both vessel and supplies. Embarking on a ship of two hundred and fifty tons, the name of which is not known, about May 20, 1639, this company set out for New Haven, on the first transatlantic voyage directly to a harbor on the northern shore of Long Island Sound.[1]

Adopting a plantation covenant during the passage, just as the Pilgrims had done in Plymouth harbor, this noteworthy company, consisting very largely of young men, some unmarried, others with wives, children, and servants, soon left New Haven, as Prudden and Samuel Eaton were thinking of doing, to found an independent plantation of their own. They bought land of the Indians at Menuncatuck, which they found "low, flat and moist, agreeable to their wishes," and there they remained a self-sustaining community and an independent republic for four years. Unlike both New Haven and Milford, they confined political privileges not only to church members but to the members of their own particular church, thus creating the narrowest political franchise to be found anywhere in New England. This limitation of privilege was somewhat eased by a willingness to allow the nonfreemen or "planters," as was done in both Massachusetts and New Haven, to take part in town meetings but not to vote for town officials. Their teacher under Whitfield was the same John Higginson who had been Lady Fenwick's chaplain

1. *Collections*, Massachusetts Historical Society, 4th ser., VI, 365; Steiner, *History of Guilford*, pp. 22–23. Whitfield was born at Greenwich, Kent, in the summer or autumn of 1592 (information obtained from the registers of Winchester College and New College, both of which Whitfield attended). Besides Whitfield and others from Kent, Surrey, and Suffolk, there were on board Fenwick and his wife, Lady Alice Boteler, William Leete, who afterward became governor of Connecticut, Samuel Desborough, who later returned to England and rose to high office under Cromwell, and Davenport's young son, who had been left behind with Lady Vere. A brief account of the voyage is given by Davenport in a letter to Lady Vere, September 28, 1639, printed in *The New England Historical and Genealogical Register*, IX, 149.

at Saybrook.¹ In their organization of government and in their management of town affairs they followed very closely the New Haven model.

Two other plantations were soon started. It happened that Captain Nathaniel Turner, in the summer of 1640, acting on behalf of the planters of New Haven, had purchased a section of land lying to the west along the coast beyond Fairfield at a place called Toquams or Rippowams, extending sixteen miles inland and eight miles from east to west. It lay some thirty miles from the Quinnipiac settlement. In the same year, owing to ministerial difficulties in the town of Wethersfield, a group of men there made up their minds to find a home elsewhere. At their head was the Rev. Richard Denton, one of the contentious clergymen, who had come from Halifax, England, and located in Wethersfield in 1638, and among its members were Matthew Mitchell, Andrew Ward, Richard Coe, and Richard Gildersleeve, the last named of whom had got into trouble with the Connecticut authorities for casting out "pernitious speeches, tending to the detriment and dishonnor" of the commonwealth. The company having determined to remove found it difficult to decide where to go and listened willingly to overtures made by Davenport (who had already endeavored to bring peace to the Wethersfield church) that they should occupy the newly acquired territory. In the agreement finally made with New Haven² the Wethersfield men bound themselves to reimburse that plantation for what it had already spent, to acknowledge the authority of the New Haven government, and to accept the system there established both in principle and form. Thus in 1641 was brought into existence the plantation and town of Stamford, never a completely independent community, for it was always subordinate to New Haven, from the first sending deputies to the general or town court and accepting such of their own number as magistrates and constables as that court saw fit to select.

1. Baldwin, "Sketch of the Life of the Rev. John Higginson, 1619–1708," *Proceedings*, Massachusetts Historical Society, 1902, pp. 478–521, especially, pp. 489–490; Lechford, *Plain Dealing*, p. 98. Higginson was the son of the Rev. Francis Higginson of Salem and married Sarah, one of Whitfield's daughters.

2. Winthrop, *Journal*, I, 307–308; *New Haven Colonial Records*, I, 45 (where the terms of the agreement are given); Huntington, *History of Stamford*. For Richard Gildersleeve, see Andrews, "By-Path through Early New England History," *New England Magazine*, February, 1892, pp. 702–709; *New York Colonial Documents*, III, 999.

Another town settled before 1643 was Southold, at the eastern end of Long Island, facing the Sound. In 1640 New Haven, always on the watch for opportunities to extend her territory, purchased the Yennicock region, where Southold was afterward located, of James Forret, agent of the Earl of Stirling, who had received Long Island by grant from the Council for New England. As far as we know the grant was never confirmed by the crown.[1] There New Haven established a small company of men, women, and children, led by the Rev. John Youngs or Yonges, which had come to New Haven from Salem in New England the same year. She retained title to the soil until in 1649 the Southold people cleared off their indebtedness and received the territory in their own right. In all particulars they followed the New Haven way, and in 1642 recognized New Haven's right to appoint their constable, until some further course should be taken "to settle a magistracy there according to God."[2]

Totoket or Branford, which Samuel Eaton had promised to make the seat of a new plantation, did not become a part of the New Haven jurisdiction until after 1643. Because the region was being encroached upon by unauthorized squatters, New Haven, who owned it, in 1644 extended an invitation to some Wethersfield people to occupy it, provided they paid the cost of the purchase, joined in one jurisdiction with New Haven, and accepted the fundamental agreements upon which that jurisdiction was based. Shortly afterward the group from Wethersfield was joined by Abraham Pierson from Southampton, Long Island, and the place was called Branford, a popular corruption of Brentford, a London suburb on the Thames River opposite Kew. The plantation was slow in getting started, for there appears to have been no formally organized church there until after 1650. Permanent town government must have come into being soon after.[3]

1. *New Haven Colonial Records*, I, 463; Calder, "Stirling and Long Island," *Essays in Colonial History*, p. 86, note 36; *The New Haven Colony*, pp. 58, 75.

2. *New Haven Colonial Records*, I, 70, 463; Whitaker, *History of Southold* (enlarged ed. 1932). There is no doubt of the fact that Youngs went from Southwold in Suffolk, England, first to Salem in Massachusetts and from there, with other members of his family, to Long Island, *Salem Records*, pp. 54, 98; Akerly, "Southwold, the English Home of Rev. John Yonges, of Southold, L. I." (*New York Genealogical and Biographical Record*, April, 1904); *Collections*, Massachusetts Historical Society, 4th ser., I, 101 ("removed to New England").

3. *New Haven Colonial Records*, I, 84, 126, 199–200, 275–276; II, 2, 4. The early history of Branford is obscure because of the loss of the colony records from 1649 to 1653 and the incompleteness of the records of the town.

Thus did New Haven "hive farther out." The town had brought under its control Stamford, Southold, and later Branford. In its immediate neighborhood were Milford and Guilford, two independent self-governing communities, each of which had been settled under New Haven's auspices and was in sympathy with the principles governing her method of rule. All remained as they were, six separate plantations, with New Haven the center and most important member of the entire cluster, until in 1643 a situation arose that called for further action. In that year was formed the New England Confederation, a combination of jurisdictions, not of plantations, to which New Haven was admitted because she could bring with her two subordinate settlements, over which she was able to exercise a measure of control. Before 1643 New Haven was a town, with a town organization and government, but after that date she became a jurisdiction, a colony, because she was exercising, somewhat hesitatingly but effectively, an influence that extended from eastern Long Island to the region where the Dutch and Swedes were already building forts on the Delaware or Great South River. As the New England Confederation did not admit independent plantations, such as were Southampton, Milford, and Guilford, it became necessary for their own protection that these towns yield some part of their independence and combine with an already established jurisdiction. For this reason Southampton joined Connecticut, and Milford and Guilford joined New Haven—Guilford on July 6, 1643, and Milford the following October.[1]

Thus within the short space of five years, the town of New Haven had become the jurisdiction of New Haven, and the bounds of the colony had been expanded from the eastern line of Guilford to the western boundary of Milford and thence, leaping over the intervening Connecticut towns of Stratford, Fairfield, and Norwalk, to the western line of Greenwich, which by agreement with the Dutch in 1650 had become a part of the town of Stamford.[2] The northern boundary was never exactly drawn but it ran some ten or fifteen miles from the coast except at Paugassett, the modern Derby. Though the jurisdiction made efforts to extend its authority to Long Island and hoped that the settlement of Huntington, which had been established under New Haven's guidance, would come into the fold, it never succeeded in obtaining a footing there except at

1. *Ibid.*, I, 96, 110–111, 199–200.   2. *Ibid.*, 144–145, 176, 185, 215–216.

Southold. Southampton, Easthampton, Oyster Bay, and Huntington all eventually threw in their lot with Connecticut, to New Haven's dismay.[1]

This transformation from a single town into a colony and from a group of towns into a federation demanded a reshaping of the machinery of government and the superimposing of a colony jurisdiction upon the separate organizations set up by the towns. In New Haven itself until 1643 the officials were a magistrate and four deputies and the "general courts" were in all essentials the equivalent of town meetings. All the householders or free planters were present at these meetings, but only those who were church members, had been admitted by the court as free burgesses, and had taken the freeman's charge could vote.[2] As New Haven acquired additional territory and new towns such as Stamford and Southold came into existence, these dependent communities were given representation in the "general court" of the town, a kind of hybrid arrangement that was halfway between the organization of a town and that of a colony.[3] Not until after the admission of Guilford (July 6, 1643) and Milford (October 23, 1643), was the first step taken toward the formal fashioning of a federative system, by the drawing up of a fundamental agreement or frame of government for the entire jurisdiction. On the 26th a governor and deputy governor, secretary and marshal were elected for the jurisdiction and magistrates for New Haven, Milford, and Stamford. On the 27th a regular general court was held for all the towns.[4] This court, which was the court of the jurisdiction and consisted of the governor, deputy governor, and magistrates and two deputies each from New Haven, Milford, Guilford, and Stamford, concerned itself entirely with colony, not town, business. The fundamentals or frame of government of the jurisdic-

1. *Ibid.*, 377; II, 237–238; *Connecticut Colonial Records*, 1665–1678, pp. 95, 548. New Haven claimed jurisdiction over Shelter Island, but the claim was disputed and was never made good. Oyster Bay and Setauket (Ashford and Brookhaven) retained for the moment a position of independence.

2. One cannot but be struck by the similarity of the political methods employed in all the New England colonies. They are the methods of the incorporated borough or company. Davenport in *An Apologetical Reply*, p. 312, hints at this when he says, "Now the liberties of a city or of a house, every man knoweth, are peculiar to those who are incorporated into that city or family."

3. This curious arrangement appears in the meeting of April 6, 1642, when it was ordered that a general court be held at New Haven "for the plantations in combination with this towne." *New Haven Colonial Records*, I, 70. Also 79, 119.

4. *Ibid.*, I, 112–116.

tion followed closely the Massachusetts model as set down in the Cotton code.[1] From this time forward town government and colony government were distinct and the records of the latter were kept in separate books. Unfortunately the volume carrying the entries of the jurisdiction to 1653 has disappeared, but its successor, covering the years from 1653 to 1665, still exists and has been printed as the second volume of the so-called *New Haven Colonial Records*.

The New Haven jurisdiction was a loose confederation of towns, scattered and lacking in unity, held together by a general court, each member of which took an oath of fidelity, while the church members in the towns took both an oath of fidelity and the freeman's charge.[2] The general court sat as a single house, without a speaker, and passed orders or laws, some new, others amendments of or additions to the Code of 1656. These laws were read in the local town meetings and all the inhabitants, church members, free planters, and others were expected to obey them. Even if one could not read he was required to know and remember the law when read in his hearing.[3] The court did a certain amount of judicial work, but justice, generally on appeal, was handled by the court of magistrates, which was heavily burdened with the duty of ferreting out cases of misconduct and dealing with admiralty and probate business. New

1. Calder, "John Cotton and the New Haven Colony," *New England Quarterly*, III, 82–94, where the passages common to the Cotton code and the New Haven fundamentals are cited.

2. *New Haven Colonial Records*, I, 115 (4thly), 130, 137–141; II, 17, 51, 52, 57, 98, 402, 616; *New Haven Town Records*, I, 136, 141, 204, 212, 449, 520–521, 524. The oath of fidelity was first required in 1643, administered in 1644, 1647, 1648, and reinforced in 1654, at a time when disaffection was beginning to appear, and given again in 1657 and 1660. The freeman's charge was required of church members in all the towns, who had been admitted as free burgesses or freemen, but it is probable that the free planters took only the oath of fidelity. There were undoubtedly some who took neither of the oaths. The records are not clear on this point.

3. *New Haven Town Records*, I, 32, 74, 177, 186, 204, 426. The first suggestion of a code of law was made in 1643 when the general court ordered that the laws of a lasting nature be examined and made the subject of a report (*New Haven Colonial Records*, I, 155). This was done in 1645 and the report approved (*ibid.*, 191–219). Nothing further took place until in 1655 Governor Eaton recommended the drawing up of a code to be printed (*ibid.*, II, 146–147); the draft was read and approved and sent to England (154). The printed copies were received in 1656, distributed, and later added to or amended (186, 198, 219, etc.). This Code of 1656 is reprinted in the second volume of the records, pp. 567–616. Five hundred copies were struck off and distributed as follows, the numbers allotted showing the relative size and importance of the towns: New Haven, 200; Milford, 80; Stamford including Greenwich, 70; Guilford, 60; Southold, 50; Branford, 40 (*ibid.*, 154–155, 186).

Haven was unique among the New England colonies in refusing to allow trial by jury in the courts of either the town or the colony.

This was the simple form of civil and judicial organization that prevailed in the New Haven colony until its submission to Connecticut in 1665. But that this arrangement was not expected to be permanent, had the Delaware venture succeeded, is evident from the statement made in 1654 that "when God shall so inlarge the English plantations in Delaware as that they shall grow the greater part of the jurisdiction . . . then due consideration shall be taken for ease and conveniency of both parts, as that the governor may be one yeare in one part and the next yeare in another, and the deputy governor to be in that part where the governor is not, and that generall courts for makeing lawes may be ordinarily but once a year [instead of twice as in the jurisdiction], and where the governor resids; and if God much increase plantations in Delaware and deminish them in these parts, then possibly they may see cause that the governor may be constantly there and the deputie governor here, but that the lesser part of the jurisdiction be protected and eased by the greater part, both in rates and otherwise."[1] But God did not enlarge the New Haven plantation on the Delaware, and this dream of a larger New Haven jurisdiction was never fulfilled. To the colony's interests on the Delaware we must now turn our attention.

Those who founded the plantation of New Haven in 1638 had before them the vision of an expanding commercial enterprise, which should utilize the shores of Long Island Sound, Long Island itself, and the region of the Delaware as the sphere of its energies. But they reckoned without any adequate knowledge of the obstacles that lay in their path. At no time were they able to occupy even a tenth of the world of their ambition. Almost from the start they were hedged in by the growing Connecticut commonwealth, which early took advantage of the victory over the Pequots to establish settlements along the coast. They could not expand eastwardly beyond Guilford because Saybrook blocked the way. They were prevented from controlling Long Island by the unsympathetic attitude of the eastern and central towns already there, from Easthampton to Oyster Bay. On the Delaware the Dutch and Swedes were in possession and were disputing the attempts of all others to intrude upon the region. Both were working under trading companies which were

1. *Ibid.*, II, 131.

organized at home for promoting trade in the New World and were sending over ships and men to found posts and factories for traffic with the Indians. The Dutch, first in the field (the Dutch West India Company was chartered in 1621), had built a fort on the southern point of Manhattan island, another, Fort Orange, up the Hudson, and a third, Fort Nassau, on the Delaware near the mouth of Little Timber Creek.[1] The last named was early abandoned,[2] so that when in 1637 the New Sweden Company was chartered and two vessels under Peter Minuit, with a company of colonists, were dispatched across the ocean they found the banks of the river unoccupied and laid claim to the territory in the name of the company.[3] On Christina Creek (modern Wilmington) Minuit erected a fort, Christina, named after the reigning queen, daughter of Gustavus Adolphus. Under Johan Printz an aggressive policy was adopted, new forts were built, and the region was claimed from the upper end of the bay to the Delaware Water Gap. The Dutch returning to the river established trading houses, bouweries, and plantations at various points and disputed the Swedish claim. The contest between the two lasted for eighteen years, until in 1655 the Dutch subjected the Swedes and retained possession until they in turn were driven out by the English in 1664.

But in 1640 the Swedes and Dutch had hardly got more than a

1. *New York Colonial Documents*, I, 283–284. In the "Remonstrance" of 1649, the deputies from New Netherland claimed that a fourth fort, the House of Hope, had been constructed on the Connecticut in 1623 (above, p. 70, note 4), but the Dutch West India Company was not in a position to operate before 1623–1624 and it was not until the latter year that Fort Orange and Fort Nassau were begun. New Amsterdam was settled in 1626. That Dutch vessels sailed up the Connecticut as early as 1623 is probable and that they landed at Dutch Point is possible, but the fort itself was not built and occupied until ten years later.

2. "But as the natives there [on the Delaware] were somewhat discontented, and not easily managed, the projectors abandoned [Fort Nassau]." *Documentary History of New York*, III, 27.

3. Amandus Johnson, *The Swedish Settlements on the Delaware*, 1638–1664, two vols. (1911); *The Swedes in America*, I (1914), a brief popular account, never completed. Johnson has also edited Lindestrom's *Geographia Americae* (1925), and *The Instructions for Governor Printz*, with introduction, notes, and appendices, including letters from the elder Winthrop and the minutes of courts sitting in New Sweden (1930). There is an article by Kidder, "The Swedes on the Delaware and their Intercourse with New England," in *The New England Historical and Genealogical Register*, XXVIII, 42–50, and a brief popular work by Ward, *The Dutch and Swedes in the Delaware*, 1609–1664 (1930). Documents relating to the Dutch occupation are in *New York Colonial Documents*, I, 271–318, XII, *passim*; and *Documentary History of New York*, III, 27–63.

foothold in the territory; consequently the Davenport company, which had probably heard of the country during their own residence in Boston, determined to see what the place was like. "Some particular persons at their own charge," with the approval of the town, organized a "Delaware Company" and sent an expedition, under Captain George Lamberton and Captain Nathaniel Turner, to explore the river. With the consent of the Swedes they occupied land on the east side of the river, at Varkenskill or Salem Creek, intending to set up a plantation "for the advancement of the public good as in a way of trade, also for the settling of churches and plantations in those parts in combination with New Haven."[1] The area of occupation was widened by a further purchase of land from the Indians at the mouth of the Schuylkill, nearly opposite Fort Nassau, and the beginning of a fortification there. The Dutch, aroused by the menace of an English invasion, sent an expedition, seized Lamberton and others, and destroyed the fort,[2] and it was only after an imprisonment at New Amsterdam that the prisoners were sent back to New Haven. Though the settlement at Varkenskill was unmolested, its occupants, consisting of some twenty families, suffered so much from sickness and death that in 1643 most of them gave up the enterprise and returned to New Haven. A few, however, remained and Lamberton himself went back to trade with the Indians along the river, trafficking, as the Swedes claimed, under the very shadow of Fort Christina. Governor Printz, remarking that the English were "evil neighbors," called a halt to Lamberton's activities, and instituted a court inquiry into the circumstances. The court decided against the English claim and against Lamberton's right to trade, and the latter went back to New Haven filled with indignation at the treatment he had received. The matter was brought to the attention of the newly formed New England Confederation and was, in part at least, responsible for its formation in that year. At the first meeting of the confederation the issue came up for consideration and after debate Governor Winthrop was instructed to write to Printz demanding satisfaction. Printz reopened the case, and at an examination of witnesses in January, 1644, obtained a complete exoneration. Amicable relations were restored and when Governor Eaton and the Delaware Company obtained from the

1. *New Haven Colonial Records*, I, 56–57.
2. *New York Colonial Documents*, XII, 23–24.

confederation a commission authorizing Captain Turner to revive the plantation and to continue trading in the Delaware Bay and River, Printz promised to recognize it. But as far as we know no further colonization was attempted at this time.[1]

With the growth of the town and the expansion of the jurisdiction of New Haven after 1643, interest in the Delaware region was revived. Eaton wrote to Stuyvesant protesting against the duties levied at New Amsterdam upon goods imported into New Netherland and demanding freedom for the English trading at Manhattan and their right to pass the Dutch town, without interference, on their way to and from the Delaware and points south. He also reasserted New Haven's claim to lands purchased on the river. Stuyvesant had already written both to Governor Bradford of Plymouth and to Governor Endecott of Massachusetts—who had succeeded Winthrop in 1647—saying that the Dutch had a "lawful right" to all the territory and would maintain it by force if necessary. Naturally, therefore, he answered Eaton to the same effect.[2] Though the New England Confederation refused to have any part in the undertaking, it informed the New Haven leaders that they could "dispose, improve or plant the land they had purchased . . . as they shall see cause." New Haven construed this as permission to go ahead, and at a town meeting, March, 1651, on the ground that the town was overcrowded, decided to continue the Delaware project "for the good of posteritie."[3] Before formal action was taken by the town various private efforts were made. Lieutenant Seely of Pequot War fame, carrying the commission of 1644, attempted to go down the Sound and through the East River to the Delaware, but was stopped by Stuyvesant and imprisoned. When others tried to do the same

1. The circumstances are given in a deposition by John Thickpenny, mariner, who was on the *Cock* with Lamberton (*New Haven Colonial Records*, I, 106–108). Lamberton's "relation," mentioned by Winthrop, has not been preserved. The action of the confederation is in *Plymouth Records*, IX, 13, and Winthrop, *Journal*, II, 141–142. Winthrop calls Printz "a man very furious and passionate, cursing and swearing, and also reviling the English of New Haven as renegades," but he changed his opinion later and after 1644 the relations between the two men became more cordial. Winthrop had great admiration for Gustavus Adolphus and Printz performed a kind act when in 1644–1645 he sent to New Haven and thence to Boston certain Indians who had murdered seven Massachusetts men who had gone to the Delaware to trade (*Journal*, I, 92; II, 210–211).

2. *New York Colonial Documents*, XII, 50–53. The use of force is clearly implied in these letters. See *New Haven Colonial Records*, I, 184–185, 280.

3. *New Haven Town Records*, I, 54, 66, 86.

Stuyvesant threatened "force of arms and martial opposition even to bloodshed" against them unless they desisted from their undertakings.[1]

The danger seemed so much greater than the expected profit from the venture that for the moment Stuyvesant's threat was heeded, but the pressure of those wishing to go was too strong to be resisted and on November 2, 1654, the business was again agitated. Still fearful of trouble the New Haveners postponed the decision until the 27th. Some said they would go if Davenport would go with them, but he declined on the ground of health. Eaton gave an evasive answer. His son, Samuel, and Francis Newman, two of the magistrates of the jurisdiction, were willing to take the matter into consideration. Despite this want of alacrity, the feeling prevailed that enough had been done by the town to bring the proposal to the attention of the jurisdiction, and at a general court, January 30, 1655, the town asked that the court "afford some incouragement to help forward so publique a work" for "the enlargement of the Kingdom of Christ, the spreading of the Gospel, and the good of posteritie therein, that they may live under the wings of Christ." Though the court took no definite action, the plan was debated at a town meeting, April 8, 1655, at which time the authorities made it perfectly clear that if a plantation were settled on the Delaware it would have to be based "on the same foundations of government as were at first laid in New Haven" and to remain "a part or member of this jurisdiction."[2]

The Delaware project of 1654–1655 was quite different from the earlier effort, which had trade rather than settlement as its object. At that time a few venturesome sea captains and migrating families were concerned, now a group of men and women, not only from New Haven but from other towns as well and even from Massachusetts and Connecticut, were proposing to go as a body and set up a permanent home on the Delaware River. The movement was watched with considerable interest by many outside the New Haven boundaries, for it was an early phase of that expansionist urge which had sent Hooker to Connecticut, Davenport to New Haven, Prudden to Milford, Denton to Stamford, Whitfield to Guilford,

---

1. *New York Colonial Documents*, XII, 69–70. Atwater and Seely went apparently with the knowledge of the town (*New Haven Town Records*, I, 200). The overpopulation of New Haven in 1650 is indicated in *ibid.*, I, 54.

2. *Ibid.*, I, 223, 225–227, 236–237; *New Haven Colonial Records*, II, 128–131; Johnson, *Swedish Settlements*, II, ch. XLVI.

and was to send Russell to Hadley, and Fitch to Norwich. The fact that Davenport, the pastor, and Hooke, the teacher, were both invited to lead the company and that Samuel Eaton and Francis Newman consented to take part as magistrates shows that the migrating group was to be an organized company, with ecclesiastical and judicial unity. Furthermore, it was to become a small edition of New Haven both as town and church. But in the end nothing whatever came of the effort, though New Haven did not relinquish her claim to the territory, even after she ceased to be an independent colony.[1]

At the outset New Haven was possessed of considerable wealth, a fact upon which contemporary writers are all agreed. Edward Johnson, writing before 1653 in his *Wonder-Working Providence,* said that "many of [the settlers were] well experienced in traffique and had good estates to manage it"; and Hubbard, less than half a century later, wrote of them as "Merchants of Considerable estates and dealing in the world [who] propounded to themselves the setting up a place of trade for which they were most fitted."[2] Some of the town's leading men had had mercantile careers in London and had accumulated a certain amount of capital, which either they brought with them in the shape of goods rather than money or left in England in the form of landed possessions from which they received financial returns. The drain upon this capital must have been heavy during the first few years in the history of the settlement. The hire of the ship, the preliminary outfitting in goods and equipment, the living during the winter in Boston, the purchase of the lands from the Indians, and the expenditure, as they themselves said, of "great estates in buildings, fencings, clearing the ground, and in all sorts of husbandry"[3] must have eaten up an appreciable part of the resources brought with them. Also, the early Delaware venture, which cost the undertakers £1,000; the loss of the great ship, which was sent to England in 1646 but foundered at sea; the wasteful expenditures on the ironworks located between New Haven and Branford[4]—all these enterprises called for heavy disbursements without

---

1. *New York Colonial Documents,* III, 82.

2. Johnson, *Wonder-Working Providence,* p. 247; Hubbard, *History of New England,* p. 318.

3. *New Haven Colonial Records,* II, 518.

4. The ironworks became the nucleus of the later village, borough, and town of East Haven. No iron was produced there until the very end of New Haven's independent career and then only for a short time. Eventually the undertaking was given up. Governor Saltonstall of Connecticut came into possession of Furnace Farms, about

any corresponding returns either of principal or profit. All the ambitious plans of the leaders had come to naught during the first fifteen years in the history of the colony and the Delaware failure was
the final blow. William Hooke wrote to Cromwell in 1653 in the
following disconsolate vein, "Trade is obstructed, commodities
(especially cloathing) very scanty; great discouragements upon the
most, if not all; many still looking toward Ireland . . . and a continual dropping away there from us, and fears of great dissolutions
and desertions . . . our cure is desperate, if the Dutch be not removed . . . so that we and our posterity (now almost prepared to
swarme forth plenteously) are confined and straitened, the sea lying
before us and a rocky rude desert, unfitt for culture and destitute
of commodity, behind our backs, all convenient places for accommo-
dations on the sea coast already possessed and planted."[1]

It was during this period of depression that Cromwell endeavored
to persuade the people of the colony to migrate first to Ireland—an
effort that was at an end before 1654—and then to Hispaniola or
Mexico, both of which Spanish possessions he expected to take in
the famous expedition under Penn and Venables. But the New
Haveners, though some of them considered Ireland favorably, finally
refused to go, just as later they refused to go to Jamaica after the
seizure of that island in 1655. They were willing to go to the Delaware but nowhere else, and they wanted war with the Dutch, in
the hope that by this means the latter would be removed from New
Amsterdam and the Delaware, and the way opened to a westward
enlargement. They were much cast down when in 1653 Massachu-

a hundred acres on the east side of the "great pond" or Furnace Pond, by his marriage with Mary, daughter of William Rosewell, the proprietor at that time of the
iron furnace, and in 1708 built a house there of considerable size and architectural
attractiveness. There he resided until his death in 1724. The name of the pond was
changed to Lake Saltonstall and the house, sadly fallen from its high estate, was
finally destroyed by fire on November 30, 1909.

The colony undoubtedly suffered from the experiment not only in pocket but also
in the damage done to the adjoining lands, highways, and fences, by the dam at
the works and the disorders that arose from the laborers sent in by Captain Thomas
Clarke of Boston, the lessee of the works. This disreputable crew and the seamen
who frequented the town were a constant menace to the peace of the Puritan community (*New Haven Town Records*, II, 133–134, 138, 146, 223, 275–276).

1. Thurloe, *State Papers*, I, 565. John Higginson of Guilford wrote, October 25,
1654, to Thomas Thatcher, "God seems to provide in a gradual way for a supply of
clothing by the multiplicity of sheep, there being many thousands in Rhode Island"
(*Collections*, Connecticut Historical Society, III, 318–320). There are other references
also to sheep-raising in Rhode Island.

setts refused to coöperate in such a war (possibly because Massachusetts found profit in the Dutch trade), and made a number of direct appeals to Cromwell, until peace with Holland stopped all further efforts in that direction.[1] "The apprehension of such a thing as being removed thither [to the West Indies or the Spanish Main], or of a trade, doth for the present stop and stay many in these parts," wrote John Higginson in 1654,[2] and it is quite clear that the New Englanders had little sympathy with Cromwell's plan of driving out the Spaniard and making room in the conquered territory for such of them as would go there. New Haven wanted only the Delaware, but the leaders of the colony were already beginning to grasp the unwelcome fact that as long as the Dutch remained in New Netherland the erection of a larger jurisdiction on a commercial and trading basis was impossible. They may even have begun to realize that the resources of the colony, already depleted, would not stand the strain of further enterprise along mercantile lines.[3] After 1650, movements were in the interest of colonization rather than of trade.[4]

1. Thurloe, *State Papers*, I, 564–565; *New Haven Colonial Records*, I, 37–38, 100–102; *Calendar State Papers, Domestic*, 1653–1654, p. 189; *New England Historical and Genealogical Register*, XII, 356. John Evelyn thought that the reason why Massachusetts was unwilling to join the others in ousting the Dutch from New Netherland was because she had good trading connections with New Amsterdam. Historical Manuscripts Commission, *Pepys*, p. 270.

2. *Collections*, Connecticut Historical Society, III, 318–320.

3. Regarding the shrinkage of estates in New Haven during these years, statistics are unreliable but may be given for what they were worth. Taking the list of personal estates of 1643 (*New Haven Colonial Records*, I, 91–93) and omitting all entries of less than £100 we reach an average of £440 each for 76 planters. Over against this average we can place that obtained from the inventories, before 1660, of 55 planters of over £100 estate and obtain an average of £375. In some cases the shrinkage was considerable. Theophilus Eaton's property fell from £3000 to £1440; that of Francis Brewster from £1000 to £555; that of Thomas Gregson from £600 to £500, and that of Edward Tapp from £800 to £713. Evance left the colony in 1652 financially embarrassed, Goodyear died heavily in debt; Allerton's estate was probably insolvent or at least seriously involved: Davenport started at £1000, in 1648 he had only "a good visible estate." Later inventories show appraisals of as low as £6 and £2.

On the other hand, some estates had increased in value. Peter Prudden's rose from £500 to £924; Wigglesworth's from £300 to £401; Newman's from £160 to £430. The colony may have been despondent but it was far from bankrupt, and hardly in the deplorable condition sometimes credited to it.

4. Following the Restoration and the fears that event aroused for the future of the colony, the Delaware project was taken up again with the idea of going under the Dutch jurisdiction (*Collections*, New Jersey Historical Society, VI, Supplement, 13–18, 158–162). After the capture of New Amsterdam, August 27, 1664, William

Nevertheless, to a limited extent trade flourished in the colony, as must inevitably have been the case among a people living in towns on the shores of Long Island Sound, with harbors that were available for shipping and with leaders who had been merchants at home and were more familiar with mercantile transactions than with agriculture. But progress could not be maintained. The loss of Lamberton, Turner, and Gregson, all of whom with nearly seventy others went down with the "phantom ship" on its voyage across the Atlantic, was a terrible blow to the infant colony for it removed three able men, who, had they lived, might not have given up easily the plans of the founders. No one appeared to take their places. Allerton and Goodyear were not successful businessmen in the later days of the colony. Prudden, Eaton, and Newman died, and Whitfield, Samuel Eaton, Hooke, Desborough, and others returned to the old country. Though a tide of immigration set in for a short time after 1660 and the numbers in the colony increased, very few of the second generation equaled the founders as leaders either in politics or in trade.

None of the towns of the jurisdiction ever became important shipbuilding or ship-using communities, but all of them had trading interests and in some of them were individuals, who, as sea captains and mariners, came into contact with the wider world of the north Atlantic basin. Canoes, skiffs, shallops, and lighters or floats were early in use for purposes of local communication and transportation, and pinnaces, ketches, barks, and sloops of more than fifteen tons engaged in distant traffic. They crossed to Long Island, coasted along the north shore as far as New Amsterdam and the Delaware on the west, and Rhode Island and Massachusetts Bay on the east, and even went on to Newfoundland, Virginia, and Barbados. Yet the number of vessels in service cannot have been large, and most of those of any size must have come from outside the colony, either Dutch- or English-built. How early the colonists constructed their own boats it is difficult to say, for the building of any ship is not certainly recorded before 1645. That small craft were fabricated before that date is attested by the presence of ship carpenters, who may

Jones, in the name of the general court of New Haven, wrote to Governor Nicolls, asking that New Haven's just claim to the territory it had purchased and settled on the Delaware be admitted (*New York Colonial Documents,* III, 82). Evidently New Haven still hoped to recover her lands and perhaps to open a trade there. But nothing was done until after the submission of New Haven to Connecticut, when Newark was founded in 1666.

have been employed in house construction also and have done boat-building as need arose. Private wharves and warehouses appear as conveniences for landing and storing—the wharves for the small craft of their owners or for the landing boats of larger vessels from Massachusetts, New Amsterdam, Virginia, Barbados, and England lying in the harbor. These outside vessels brought manufactured goods, hardware, canvas, rum, sugar, cotton, salt, tobacco,[1] and wines, while the New Haven towns shipped provisions, cattle, horses, and a variety of sundries, though a surplus of such staples was always limited, and in times of war or the fear of war, as in 1653, foodstuffs were placed under embargo.[2] The one effort that was made to open up a direct trade with England was a disastrous failure, for the vessel, perhaps the first large boat built in New Haven, promoted by Theophilus Eaton, Goodyear, Malbon, and Gregson in 1645, commanded by Captain Lamberton, and laden with an elaborate cargo, foundered at sea and was never heard of again.[3] All the ventures, running from £50 to £80, which were put

1. Tobacco was obtained from Rhode Island and even from Saybrook, though efforts were made to raise it at home. Certain men of New Haven offered to experiment with its cultivation if twelve acres of land might be given them for the purpose. *New Haven Town Records,* I, 207.

2. For the cargo of a Salem ship, *New Haven Colonial Records,* II, 346–347. For the prohibition of 1653, *ibid.,* 23.

3. The statement made by the Rev. James Pierpont to Cotton Mather many years later (*Magnalia,* bk. I, 25) that the "great ship" was a vessel of 150 tons and built in Rhode Island cannot be accepted as even probable. Winthrop, who had better facilities for knowing the facts, puts the tonnage at 80, while the evidence for the place of construction shows conclusively that the vessel was built in New Haven. There is not a word of contemporary reference to a Rhode Island origin. The vessel was promoted by a group of New Haven co-partners who awarded the construction of the hull to four contractors or "feoffees"—John Wakeman, Richard Myles, Joshua Atwater, and Jasper Crane—all well-known New Haven men. As the rigging was supplied in New Haven, one wonders how the hull without the rigging could have been brought from Rhode Island if it had been built there as Pierpont says. In a law case tried November, 1647, regarding the payment for a "suit of blocks for the great ship" the language used proves that the vessel was the same as that in which Gregson and Lamberton were interested, that is, "the great ship," for Lamberton gave the dimensions of the blocks and Gregson ordered them, showing that both men were in New Haven at the time and had not started on the voyage. As Lamberton commanded the ship (which sailed in January, 1646) and he and Gregson went down with her, the law suit can have had nothing to do with the *Fellowship* (not launched until October, 1647) as the index to the *New Haven Colonial Records,* I, has it. Furthermore, the reference to the launching of the *Fellowship* does not read as if this was the first launching in the colony. The years 1645–1648 were a time of experimenting with shipbuilding in New Haven on a larger scale than before, evidently in anticipation of an expanding trade. This fact is amply attested by the building of the

into this, the "phantom ship," and into the *Fellowship* of 1647 (another New Haven venture) were either lost entirely or were greatly depreciated in value.[1]

That the promotion of trade during the first twenty years had not met the expectations of the merchants concerned is evident from Davenport's remarks made in 1659 and 1662. Speaking in town meeting on the question of granting East Side (Fair Haven) and South End (East Haven) the status of villages he said that "if the town did not consider of some way to further trade, how would they subsist he saw not." In 1662 he said further that unless the town could do something "to bring shipping yearly from England . . . and so rayse manufacture" its inhabitants could not long subsist.[2] He wished by making liberal grants of land to encourage merchants from other colonies or England to come to New Haven for the encouragement of trade. The effort was not successful, as but one merchant, Samuel Bache of Boston, came to New Haven and set up a warehouse, and that too not until just before the time when New Haven gave in its submission to Connecticut.[3]

The simple truth is that despite the ambitions of the founders, the towns of the New Haven jurisdiction never were more than small agricultural communities in a region that was not well adapted for agricultural purposes. Their layout and the methods followed in the distribution of their lands differed only in detail from those of other New England plantations and the life of the great majority of the people was closely and intimately connected with the soil. In order of size New Haven came first, followed by Milford, Guilford, Stamford, Southold, and Branford, with two dependent communi-

---

"great ship" (nowhere given a name, but called by Johnson, *Wonder-Working Providence*, p. 178; "Mr. Lamberton's ship," because Lamberton was its captain), the *Fellowship*, the *Swallow* and possibly the *Susan*, and later the *Adventure*. We read of four ship carpenters brought from Boston to work on a ship "hear built" in 1648 (*New Haven Colonial Records*, I, 341, 344, 393–394), and these men might well have come originally to aid in building the "great ship" in 1645. As the first large vessel experimented with, the latter might well have proved cranky and unseaworthy.

1. *New Haven Colonial Records*, I, 449.

2. *New Haven Town Records*, I, 393–394; II, 4. Davenport was much concerned about the town mill, which was a constant source of trouble and up to that time (1659) had been rather a loss than a benefit. It was twice burned down (1662, 1679) and its use and abuse were constantly under debate. At one time the inhabitants had to go to Milford to have their corn ground.

3. The other Boston merchant, Davis, finally decided not to come (*Collections, Massachusetts Historical Society*, 4th ser., VIII, 202–203).

ties, Paugassett (Derby) and Hashamamock (near Southold).[1] The people inhabiting these plantations were mainly English, with a few Frenchmen, Dutchmen, Scotsmen, Negroes, and Indians, the last named of whom in New Haven lived on the east side across the Quinnipiac River. In status these inhabitants were freemen or church members, free planters, indentured servants, and apprentices, and in vocation, merchants, mariners, farmers, artisans, and hired laborers. There was also a transient element among them, not much wanted but very much needed, made up of wanderers from other colonies and seamen brought in by the ships frequenting the harbors, a roistering, rowdy lot that made New Haven as well as Massachusetts a great deal of trouble.

All these people were carefully watched over by the local town meetings which kept a vigilant eye on the affairs of their respective communities. They looked after fences, cattle, swine, sheep, and horses, doing something but not much for fences and highways, and endeavoring, with considerable effort and frequent prodding, to build and repair bridges, of which there were many. They provided, with difficulty because of frequent neglect, for ward by day and watch by night, guarding against fires within and attacks from without. To protect themselves further against fires they required householders to keep ladders at hand and to have their chimneys frequently swept, the chimney sweeps to wear canvas frocks and hoods. They regulated the cutting of timber for building and firewood, and frequently complained of the "stinking and noxious weeds"—henbane, nightshade, and pokeweed—that grew along the roadsides and in the fields. Each town had its trainband, though training was none too popular, worked out with discrimination exemptions from the service, and struggled with the disorders that regularly arose on training day. There was a view of arms four times a year and a training at least six times and oftener if necessary.[2]

While agriculture and its incidents occupied a large part of the time and attention of the people in the various towns, industry remained in a very primitive state. There were gristmills everywhere,

1. *New Haven Colonial Records*, II, 108, 219, 221. The colony was opposed to the erection of villages for three reasons: the danger of disorders; the loss of rates to the mother town; and the weakening of the influence of the ministry. Some of the arguments seem to be much the same as those presented by Bradford against the expansion of the New Plymouth colony.

2. This account of local conditions is based largely on the town records of New Haven, but the state of things in the other towns was not essentially different.

but no sawmills, sawing being done in the simple way of a saw pit. The gristmill in New Haven—an overshot affair—was a subject of endless concern, both as to maintenance and supply of water, and when it was burned down in 1662, the proposal was made to change its construction to that of a windmill and horsemill, such as was known to exist at Easthampton. There were a number of tanneries or tanyards, but at best leather was poorly prepared, shoes were insufficient in supply, inexact as to sizes, and badly made, and both tanners and shoemakers came in for considerable abuse. Probably much of the artisan work of bakers, hatters, blacksmiths, coopers, carpenters, ropemakers,[1] wheelwrights, dishturners, and the like was done at the houses or barns of the workmen or in shops on the premises. The bakers were often charged with underweight loaves and so serious had this offense become that an assize of bread was inserted in the Code of 1656. This was the London assize, which New Haven adopted, just as she adopted the London assize of hogsheads, Winchester measures of dry and liquid volume, avoirdupois weight, and the London steelyard. There were shops also in private houses and there were stores where a variety of goods was sold, such as could not be produced at home and had to be brought from abroad. Liquor was available at the ordinaries and in limited quantities at private houses, and the licensing problem was one of periodic perplexity. Manufacturing activities were of necessity infrequent because of the scarcity of raw material. The only manufacturing industry known to the colony was that of the ironworks at East Haven, though we hear of a promise of steelmaking emanating from Southold in 1655.[2]

Business transactions of every kind must have been greatly hampered by the want of a convenient and flexible medium of exchange. Hard money, whether in the form of English shillings, Dutch guilders, or Spanish pieces of eight, was always scarce, though there must have been a certain amount brought in by ships from England or gained in traffic with New Amsterdam and Barbados. There is no mention of silver in the records of the colony until 1651 when contributors to the church funds were urged to pay in silver or bills because the wampum was so bad that "the officers who receive it

1. Flax for weaving and hemp for rope were raised to a small extent in the "gardens." Proposals were advanced for the preparation of tar but nothing came of them.
2. *New Haven Colonial Records*, II, 153, 175.

can make litle of it," and until 1654 when the widow Wigglesworth loaned the commissioners going to Boston five pounds.[1] Even after these dates we come on very few instances of its use. In the early years black and white wampum was almost the sole medium, particularly in private transactions, until it became so poor in quality that it would not pass current and so much of a drug in the market as to lose much of its value, despite the efforts of the general court to stabilize it. Barter and payments in kind became increasingly common—corn and other grains, cattle, wool, pease, beef, pork, bread or "biskit," and even brass and iron passed at local prices fixed by the Boston traders. Rates, taxes, and imposts were met by "good currant country paye at cuntry price" determined by the authorities. In 1657 Winthrop paid for his house £100 in goats from Fisher's Island, the town to send a ship to carry the "cash" to New Haven.

But while land, fences, debts, and prudential affairs generally were matters of concern to the town fathers, manners and morals, having to do with the peace of the community and the problem of sin, weighed most heavily on their minds. Drunkenness and sexual misdemeanors were "horrible miscarriages," for which those guilty were held accountable before God as well as the courts, and they were inquired into with a minuteness of scrutiny that has made it necessary, in the case of sexual misdeeds, for the editors of the town and colony records to omit from the printed pages several portions of the original text. Such offenses were bad enough when committed by a nonfreeman, but when a church member was involved, whether in fornication or drunkenness or in disrespect toward an assembly where "the holy God and the holy Angells were present," the act was construed as scandalous and the offender was reprimanded by bell, book, and candle. The ultimate end of justice was the reformation of man and the averting of the wrath of God, and its immediate purpose the preservation of peace and righteousness, the prevention of disorder, and the settlement of differences among neighbors. The attainment of such results was worthy of the utmost vigilance. Many lesser indulgences, such as cardplaying, dancing,

---

1. *New Haven Town Records*, I, 98; *New Haven Colonial Records*, II, 102. Following the Massachusetts law, the general court in 1643 fixed the price of a piece of eight at five shillings (*ibid.*, I, 86). This order was followed in the laws of 1645 (*ibid.*, I, 211) but was not included in the Code of 1656. Some silver must have been in the colony from the beginning.

and singing, were frowned on and in part at least forbidden, because they tended to the corruption of the youth and the "mispense of precious time," but they were enjoyed on the sly by those who had known the merry life of old England and were repelled by the cheerless atmosphere of the Puritan colony. Smoking was allowed but not in public, and one man who was found "taking tobacco" near the meetinghouse was promptly fined.[1] A large number of the sinners were servants and seamen: the former always an unmanageable lot, generally in some sort of mess, thieving, cursing, swearing, drinking, and quarreling, and guilty, a few of them certainly, of bestiality and other abominable crimes; the latter given to intoxication, disorder, and profanation of the Sabbath. The laws were vigorously enforced and persons were executed for adultery[2] and for deeds of "unspeakable filthiness." Occasionally one or another would be banished for good and sufficient cause from the jurisdiction, while those guilty of ordinary misdemeanors would be punished by stocks, pillories, fines, whipping, imprisonment (where they were "kept to a prison diet"), and by such humiliating public penances as the wearing of a halter for a given length of time.

On the cultural side education alone received attention. Davenport very early expressed his interest in a school and a college and wanted to gather books for the use of the ministry and the town. In 1641 it was proposed to set up a free school, the cost of which was to be met out of the common stock of the town. This was done, a schoolhouse was built, and a schoolmaster engaged.[3] But the experiment languished. The ambitious programme for the teaching of English, writing, and especially Latin dwindled to a course of spelling and reading; the number of pupils fell as low as six or eight and then five and six; and the results were not commensurate with the trouble. In 1659 it was proposed to erect a "Colony School," and at first the plan seems to have been to set up feeding schools in each of the plantations, but this was soon seen to be beyond the resources of the colony. Then it was decided to create only a single "Colony School or College," for the teaching of Latin, Greek, and Hebrew, and to locate it at New Haven. For this purpose Edward Hopkins

1. *New Haven Colonial Records*, II, 366–367; *New Haven Town Records*, I, 443, 487, 488, 494; II, 25–30, 42.

2. There was at least one case of execution for adultery, *ibid.*, II, 32.

3. *New Haven Colonial Records*, II, 471–472; *New Haven Town Records*, I, 473–474.

made his famous bequest of his estate in New England and £500 from his estate in England, "for the service of God in Church and Commonwealth," from which in time were to arise the Hopkins grammar schools of New Haven, Hadley, and Hartford, the whole amounting to £1,000, four hundred of which was to go to Hartford. But at best this was only a grammar school, and despite Davenport's efforts a bona fide college did not appear until the next century, then to bear the name not of Davenport but of Elihu Yale. The suggestion made in 1664 that a library building be erected for the "many books belonging to the town" was never carried out. The books were probably those left in New Haven by Samuel Eaton and later given by his brother Theophilus "for the use of a college," but which reverted to the town on the failure of that project. It constituted what may be called "the first public library in New Haven."[1]

On the architectural side we have little reliable information regarding the buildings in which the householders lived, beyond the contemporary statement that many of the merchants' houses were pretentious. The meetinghouse on the green in New Haven was fifty feet square, with a tower and a turret, and casement windows with glass panes. It was in constant need of repair and its various vicissitudes find frequent reference in the records. It had a platform, with rails and banisters, built upon its roof in 1653, for "one to stand upon to make discovery of danger that might be neere," and within were the seats, a large gallery with a little gallery adjoining, and a high pulpit with stairs. Built in 1640 it began to show signs of decay by the end of the decade and by 1657 was called very defective— groundsills and timbers, ceiling, tower and turret, doors and windows needing constant attention. Nothing was done beyond repairs until 1670 when a new structure was put up. Upon its door, as was the custom with the parish churches of England, all public notices were posted—for the town as yet had no signpost—and near by in the market place stood the drummer to summon the inhabitants to meeting on lecture days, days of humiliation and thanksgiving, and the Sabbath.

Until 1660 the position of the town and jurisdiction of New Haven was strong despite its economic weakness and legal insecurity,

---

1. *New Haven Town Records,* II, 85; Dexter, "The First Public Library in New Haven," *Historical Papers,* pp. 223–224.

though its inhabitants were not all living in perfect harmony. There had been murmurings as early as 1653 and 1654, at the time of the threatened war with the Dutch. Inhabitants of Stamford, Southold, and Milford voiced their discontent with the form of government under which they lived, demanding an extension of the suffrage, the admission of English law, and the right of appeal to England. Robert Basset in the Stamford town meeting declared that he would obey no authority except such as came out of England, and he and others dubbed the jurisdiction a tyrannical government, under which no justice could be obtained. The ringleaders at different times were haled before the general court of the jurisdiction and charged not only with disturbing the peace of their respective towns but also with words and carriage against the colony at large. They were accused of attempting to undermine, overthrow, and alter the foundations of authority, to turn things "upsidowne" in church and commonwealth, and to stir up rebellion, thus breaking their oaths of fidelity. All were reprimanded in language that was severe unto righteousness—the language of the pulpit—and were heavily fined and put under bonds to answer before the court of magistrates. All submitted and acknowledged their sin and the trouble was over.

The general court took advantage of the opportunity to see that all the people in the jurisdiction were bound by oaths of fidelity and that the deputies from the towns to the general court of the jurisdiction took a special oath to "doe Equall right and Justice in all cases" that came before them, using their "best skill and knowledge according to the wholesome laws here established."[1] Thus did they hope to make the colony watertight against further disaffection, and for the moment they succeeded, though financial conditions did not improve, and efforts to expand the area of the jurisdiction by the inclusion of Southampton, Huntington, and Oyster Bay ended in failure.[2] New Haven's dream of a colony that should embrace Long

1. The deputy's oath is printed in the *New Haven Town Records*, I, 534. The leading objectors were Thomas Baxter, Robert Basset, John Chapman, Jeremiah Jagger, and William Newman of Stamford; Captain John Youngs, son of the founder of Southold; Edward Hull of Milford; Nathaniel Sylvester of Shelter Island; and Henry Robinson of Stratford, the last named of whom brought charges in the Connecticut court against Newman of New Haven and for this strange proceeding was called "a universal disturber of the peace." *New Haven Colonial Records*, I, 92, 93–95, 96; II, 26–28, 48–49, 51–57, 309–310, 367–369; *Southold Town Records*, I, 468.

2. There seems to have been difficulty at this time in gathering rates and getting debts paid. New Haven was incurring additional expenses for school house, mill,

Island within its limits went the way of its dream of a commercial center and capital on the banks of the Delaware. By the year 1660 the jurisdiction was probably already on the downward grade— less ably manned, less economically prosperous, and less united in the fundamentals of religion and government than it had been in the period immediately following the reorganization of 1643.[1] It was badly prepared to meet the crisis which now arose.

In 1660 Charles II returned to the throne of England. Davenport refused to believe the report of this when it was brought to his attention and could only exclaim, when he could no longer doubt its truth, "Our comfort is, that the Lord reigneth and his counsels shall stand."[2] With apprehension and dismay he heard of the execution of such old friends as Peter and Vane, of the deaths in the Tower of Pennington and Rowe, and of the persecution and flight of his former colleague in the church at New Haven, William Hooke.[3] He viewed with alarm the new migration which now took place from England, bringing to the colony not only many who echoed Hooke's remark, "I know not what will become of us, We are at our wit's end," but others also such as the regicides Edward Whalley, Hooke's brother-in-law, and William Goffe, who had been exempted from the act of amnesty passed by parliament in 1660. The flight of these men to America was followed by orders from England for their apprehension brought over by agents instructed to ferret out the fugitives. In consequence the New England Puritan colonies were placed in the embarrassing situation of either repudiating their former friends or disobeying the royal command. Massachusetts with a somewhat unexpected but shrewd display of wisdom, declared her abhorrence of all who would aid those "convicted of

meetinghouse, watch house, and gun house, and was also in debt to the jurisdiction (*New Haven Colonial Records*, II, 472; *New Haven Town Records*, I, 462, 473–474.
The three Long Island towns had all been assisted in their settlement by New Haven and were expected to join the jurisdiction. Negotiations were entered into to that end but failed owing to differences regarding fundamentals, particularly the limitation of the franchise. *New Haven Colonial Records*, II, 98, 144, 236–238, 299; *Connecticut Colonial Records*, I, 112, 348, 377, 379, 566–568.

1. Except for the addition of Greenwich to Stamford, of Hashamamock to Southold, of the plantation of Paugassett, and the possession of a disputed claim to Shelter Island (*Calendar State Papers, Colonial*, 1661–1668, §52) the jurisdiction had not added an acre to its territory or an ounce of weight to its authority in seventeen years.

2. *Collections*, Massachusetts Historical Society, 4th ser., VII, 515–516.

3. *Ibid.*, VIII, 177, 179; Palmer, *Rev. William Hooke, 1601–1678*, pp. 13–14.

having a hand in the execrable murder of the late king" and ordered the arrest of the two men. The latter left the Bay hurriedly and passing through Connecticut went directly to New Haven, where Davenport, with more conscientiousness but less wisdom, was ready to receive them.¹ Though the royal agents, Kellond and Kirke, warned Governor Leete that in protecting the "two traitors they would do themselves injury and possibly ruin themselves and the whole colony,"² New Haven and Milford harbored the regicides and in so doing hampered the agents in their efforts to find them.

All the New England colonies, after some delay, recognized Charles II as king of England, but only Massachusetts, New Haven, and Rhode Island formally proclaimed him in a public demonstration. The other two, Connecticut and Plymouth, contented themselves with votes of acknowledgment only, perhaps for the reason that no order to make a public proclamation was ever sent over by the Privy Council.³ But all of them felt the imperative necessity of taking advantage of the royal amnesty issued from Breda and of soliciting the king's favor, each in its own behalf. Massachusetts had many charges lodged against her, for her enemies rose up in this emergency to call her contumacious and perverse, and she in particular needed to act promptly. She sent over Simon Bradstreet and John Norton, with an address written by Governor Endecott. It was couched in characteristic Puritan language and in a spirit of unctuous humility that would certainly have amazed Charles II, had he ever read it, as undoubtedly he never did.⁴ Connecticut fol-

1. *Calendar State Papers, Colonial,* 1661–1668, §§66, 80, 96; *Collections,* Massachusetts Historical Society, 3rd ser., X, 37–39.

2. C. O. 1:15, no. 59, inadequately calendared in *Calendar State Papers, Colonial,* 1661–1668, §96. The only adequate history of the regicides is that of Lemuel Welles, *History of the Regicides in New England* (1927), which supersedes Stiles, *History of the Judges,* published in 1795. The importance of the story of the regicides has been greatly exaggerated by writers on New England history. It cannot be shown that their treatment by New Haven had anything to do with the ending of that colony's independence.

3. Neither Connecticut nor Plymouth ever publicly proclaimed the king. Connecticut passed a vote, March 14, 1661, acknowledging her loyalty and allegiance and declaring that her people were "his Highness loyall and faythfull subjects" (*Connecticut Colonial Records,* I, 361). New Plymouth recognized the king's authority as early as March 5 (*Plymouth Records,* III, 210, also 220 and IV, 7), and soon after June 5, petitioned the king for a confirmation of her privileges (C. O. 1:15, no. 61, greatly abbreviated in *Calendar State Papers, Colonial,* 1661–1668, §102). Though the petition was signed by Governor Prence, there is no reference to it in the printed Plymouth records.

4. *Massachusetts Colonial Records,* IV, (2), 30–33. Earlier addresses to the king

lowed suit, sending John Winthrop, Jr., to plead her cause, but New Haven, who perhaps more than any of the others had reason to fear the weight of the king's displeasure, was in no position to follow the lead of her sister colonies. She was too poor to meet the expense of an agency and not sufficiently sure of her own record to approach the throne with a petition for royal privileges. Therefore, she first turned to Massachusetts, explaining her delay in proclaiming the king and asking that Massachusetts would present her case to the crown. She suggested the appointment of a common agent, offering to bear a part of the expense.[1] We do not know the Massachusetts answer, but it was probably unfavorable. Then Governor Leete turned to Connecticut with the proposal that Winthrop should say a good word for her in England and obtain, if he could, a single patent that would cover both jurisdictions and contain for New Haven a grant of land "beyond Delaware."[2] In this way she hoped to gain what she had been unable to obtain for herself, that is, a foothold on the Delaware, and to throw upon the mother country the burden of ousting the Dutch from their possessions on the river. Unfortunately Winthrop had already sailed in July and Governor Leete could do no more than send the letter to Boston to be forwarded to Winthrop in England. It is doubtful if the latter ever received it.

The Connecticut authorities had already instructed Winthrop to ask for a grant of territory that should extend from the Massachusetts and Plymouth boundaries to "the Delaware River South," thus completely ignoring the claims of Rhode Island on one side and of the Dutch on the other. Whether also at this time they were deliberately planning the extinction of the independent jurisdiction of New Haven cannot be said, but at any rate it is strange that in neither of the instructions to Winthrop (for there were two) is there any mention whatever of New Haven, though the boundaries asked for included the territory of this friendly and autonomous Puritan state, Connecticut's fellow member in the New England Confederation. Whatever else can we think but that as early as 1661 Connecticut had determined to absorb New Haven if she could? In her

and houses of parliament were drafted December 10, 1660, at even greater length (ibid., IV (1), 450–454). These, though less unctuous, are scarcely less obsequious in their attitude toward crown and parliament.

1. *New Haven Colonial Records*, II, 421–422.
2. *Collections*, Massachusetts Historical Society, 4th ser., VII, 548–550.

letter to the Earl of Manchester she speaks only of her own need of a patent to strengthen herself "against such as may oppose oᵣ pʳsent interests in civil policy," and in all the negotiations that were carried on in England, as far as they have been recorded, neither she nor Massachusetts said anything about New Haven's claims. Winthrop, petitioning on Connecticut's behalf, asked for a patent for Connecticut only and for the territory bounded "on the south by the ocean."[1] Why was New Haven so entirely ignored? Were her people "such despised ones," as Leete meekly called them, that they were beyond the consideration of their neighbors, or were they out of sight and consequently out of mind because unrepresented by an agent of their own at Whitehall? These questions can never be satisfactorily answered, but it is a suggestive fact that of the four colonies without charters in 1660, the two that got no charters were those which were too poor to send agents to England. This may be a sufficient explanation, but the suspicion will always be latent that Connecticut had made up her mind to adopt an aggressive policy from the start and to emulate Massachusetts not only in obtaining like privileges and liberties but also in adding to her territory at the expense of her nearest neighbor. Massachusetts was extending her jurisdiction to the north, why might not Connecticut extend hers to the southward as well, as far as she could?

From the beginning New Haven's position was hopeless. As news of the Restoration came to the malcontents in the towns of the jurisdiction, opposition once more became vocal. One Francis Browne uttered many contemptuous and reproachful speeches against the government, denying the magistrates' authority now that the king was proclaimed, and refusing to obey laws that had not come out of England.[2] There were others too of like minds, who not only questioned the legality of the jurisdiction but chafed under the limitations of the suffrage and looked with longing eyes toward the wider privileges of Connecticut. In October, 1662, a month after the latter colony had received its charter, a majority of the inhabitants of Southold withdrew from the New Haven jurisdiction and submitted their persons and estates to the authority of the newly chartered government. Several people of Guilford followed suit and Stamford and Greenwich went over bodily. Connecticut accepted

1. *Calendar State Papers, Colonial*, 1661–1668, §229.
2. *New Haven Town Records*, I, 491–492.

these overtures and appointed constables for the revolting towns.[1] Within the jurisdiction, men were refusing to accept office because of "the distraction of the time" and the uncertainties of the future.[2] Many arguments were used by those who were endeavoring to hold the jurisdiction together, but "they prevailed not." The general court realized "that there was a great discouragement upon the spiritt of those that were now in place of magistracy," but it knew of no other remedy than to summon the obdurate persons before it for examination and to bind them over to appear before the court of magistrates as disturbers of the peace.[3] By the end of 1662, the jurisdiction had shrunk to but a fragment of its former size, for only Milford, Branford, and New Haven remained, and even in those towns there was discontent. Milford did not break away until 1664, Branford remained loyal to the end, and in all the towns there continued to exist groups of those who still adhered to the fundamental principles upon which the colony rested. Officially the jurisdiction was still alive and possessed of sufficient strength to resist the Connecticut demands, New Haven and its leaders refusing "to breake or conclude anything that may have tendencie to change of the present government."[4]

The struggle that ensued lasted for nearly two years, from the issue of Connecticut's ultimatum in October, 1662, to the arrival of the royal commissioners in July, 1664. During this time, with all the play of Puritan controversialists, mingling loving words with the recriminations of attack and defense, the two contestants waged the battle back and forth. Connecticut, standing immovable on the terms of her charter, demanding the last pound of flesh; New Haven, with Davenport and Leete as spokesmen, with equal firmness

---

1. *Connecticut Colonial Records,* I, 386–390, 405.

2. Had Winthrop premonitions as early as 1656 regarding New Haven's fate? In that year he had taken a house in New Haven in order to be near the ironworks, and there is no doubt that he would have been elected governor of the New Haven jurisdiction to succeed Eaton had he remained. But Connecticut shrewdly drew him away in 1657 by offering him the governorship there, later changing the tenure of the office in order to make it more attractive. Winthrop, sensing the situation, accepted the offer as the one with the more certain future. This event was of significance in the history of the two colonies, for with Winthrop governor of New Haven, affairs might have turned out differently.

3. *New Haven Town Records,* I, 474–475, 479, 484–485, 492, 520, 521; *New Haven Colonial Records,* II, 429–430, 454–456 (the case of Bryan Rossiter and his son of Guilford, for which see also, *ibid.,* 512–514, footnote), 457.

4. *Ibid.,* II, 453.

opposing the union, saying that they could do nothing against conscience, that the freemen had already voted (November 4, 1662) to uphold the status of the colony, and that in any event they could make no final answer until the results of an appeal to the king had been received.[1] This appeal had been embodied in an address to the king, which was to be presented if other means failed, but Winthrop, who knew all the details of the situation, opposed it, because he was in the midst of his controversy with Clarke over the Rhode Island boundaries and wished to avoid, if possible, "a tedious and chargeable trial and uncertain event" such as would happen if the appeal were handed in. He wrote to Deputy Governor Mason of Connecticut deprecating the course Connecticut was following and implying that he had never intended that New Haven's rights should be disquieted or prejudiced by the issue of the Connecticut charter. Afterward Connecticut denied that Mason had ever received this letter.[2] She acted all along with little regard for Winthrop's opinion, taking the ground, as she did later in her controversy with Rhode Island, that once the charter had passed the seals Winthrop had no further connection with it and his feelings in the matter might be safely disregarded.[3]

A further exchange of queries and answers took place in August, 1663, but in no way advanced the progress toward a settlement of the difficulty.[4] It became evident that the issue would have to be brought before the commissioners of the New England Confederation, because New Haven charged Connecticut with violating the terms of that union by continuing to interfere with the New Haven towns. At their meeting in Hartford in September, the commissioners reviewed the circumstances, and the delegates from Massachusetts and Plymouth (the others naturally not voting) decided that because New Haven was recognized in the articles as distinct from Connecticut she could not have her jurisdiction encroached upon.[5] Encouraged by this decision and the manifest sympathy of the Plymouth delegates, New Haven wrote Connecticut bidding

1. In New Haven's reply to the proposals made by Connecticut, March 20, 1663 *Ibid.*, II, 475–477.

2. *Collections,* Massachusetts Historical Society, 5th ser., VIII, 77–80, 80–81; *New Haven Colonial Records,* II, 498–499. For Connecticut's denial, *ibid.*, 534.

3. Above, p. 141, note 1.

4. *New Haven Colonial Records,* II, 491–492, 493–494.

5. *Plymouth Colonial Records,* X, 309–310; *New Haven Colonial Records,* II, 495–496.

her withdraw from all attempts to exercise authority outside her own bounds. Connecticut's answer to this letter was to ignore the act of the commissioners and to demand, categorically and without reserve, New Haven's submission according to the tenor of the charter.[1] Thoroughly aroused by this unfriendly and peremptory reply, the New Haven court of October 22 considered various possibilities and came to the conclusion that it would be best to appeal to England for a letter of exemption from the king and if possible to obtain a patent of her own, which should spike Connecticut's guns. In the meantime the colony was to hold a day of solemn and public thanksgiving "that the Lord by his mercifull providence hath been pleased to give them some breathing time in the enjoyment of present liberties, notwithstanding their fears."[2]

As Connecticut refused to yield and continued during the winter of 1663–1664 to pursue her aggressive tactics, New Haven, further encouraged by an order of the Privy Council of June 24, 1663, directing the jurisdiction of New Haven (among others) to obey the navigation acts[3]—an order which certainly recognized New Haven as still independent despite the Connecticut charter—appointed a committee on January 7, 1664, to prepare a statement of the colony's case.[4] This statement, drawn up by Davenport and Street, is a review of the whole situation from the founding of the colony and contains several items of information, otherwise unsupported, of considerable importance. Among them is the assertion that before Winthrop went to England he certified in two letters to a friend that Connecticut had no intention of extending the boundaries of the desired patent to include New Haven and was willing to agree that New Haven should be left free to join Connecticut if she wanted to, otherwise not. Also that New Haven trusting in this promise had

---

1. *Connecticut Colonial Records*, I, 415. Winthrop was not present at the meeting of the general court of Connecticut (October 8, 1663) that adopted this curiously curt and offensive resolution.

2. *New Haven Colonial Records*, II, 502–503.

3. *Acts Privy Council, Colonial*, I, §601; *New York Colonial Documents*, III, 44–46; *New Haven Colonial Records*, II, 511.

4. *Ibid.*, 514. In February, Connecticut in a more chastened mood instructed a committee to go to New Haven and offer that colony all the privileges it desired, not repugnant to the tenor of the charter. To which Leete and others replied that they would not treat further until Connecticut "redintigrate the colony" by restoring to New Haven the members from Stamford and Guilford, "which they had soe unrighteously took from us." In reply Connecticut "agreed that they [the inhabitants of Stamford and Guilford who had accepted the jurisdiction of Connecticut] be ordered to submit to the same authority with their neighbors in those places." *Ibid.*, 515–516.

felt secure against Connecticut's aggression and had made no effort to obtain a patent of her own. If Davenport's and Street's statements are to be received at their face value, then it seems clear that the English authorities, in consenting to the issue of Connecticut's charter, did not realize that they were encroaching on New Haven's jurisdiction and without intending to do so had given Connecticut legal warrant for her aggressive policy,[1] a warrant that her leaders took advantage of to the full. If the committee's facts are correct, it is not strange that Davenport and Street should have charged Connecticut with a breach of faith and with taking "a praeposterous course in first dismembering this colony and after that treating with it about union, which [they said] is as if one man purposing to treat with another about union, first cut off from him an arme and a legg and an eare then to treat with him about union." In an extraordinarily unfair and self-righteous reply Connecticut characterized this paper—"New Haven's Case Stated"—which cannot be considered as other than honest and well reasoned, as "bluster," and the references in it to Winthrop as a very ungrateful return for his "great courtesy and tender respect . . . his love, favoure and tenderness."[2] Just why New Haven should be grateful to Winthrop it is difficult to see.[3]

1. This view of the case would seem to be borne out not only by the order in Council of June 24, 1663 (already noted), but also by the royal letter of June 21, sent to the governor and assistants of Massachusetts, Plymouth, New Haven, and Connecticut regarding the Atherton Company (*Calendar State Papers, Colonial,* 1661–1668, §494). If king and Privy Council had intended to wipe out the New Haven colony in May, 1662, by the grant of the charter to Connecticut, why were a royal letter and a Privy Council order sent to that colony in June? The same question can be asked in the case of Rhode Island, which territorially, according to Connecticut's interpretation, was also in large part wiped out by the same charter, yet itself received a charter the next year. There is something mysterious about the boundaries inserted in the Connecticut charter, just as there is something mysterious about the issue of the charter itself.

If we are to believe that king and council knew little or nothing about the contents of the Connecticut charter and so unwittingly made it possible for Connecticut to bring to an end the New Haven colony then it is quite clear that New Haven's attitude toward the regicides did not enter in as a factor in the case.

2. *New Haven Colonial Records,* II, 517–537.

3. In his letter to Mason of March 3, 1663, Winthrop says that he had given assurances to the English authorities that Connecticut never intended "to meddle with any other towne or plantation that was settled under any other government." How he was able to reconcile this settlement with the instructions he received from the colony or with the territory asked for in his petition is far from clear. He must have known what was written in his own petition as regards both New Haven and Rhode Island.

The controversy might have been drawn out interminably but for two occurrences of the year 1664: first, the royal grant of March 12 to the Duke of York; and secondly, the sending over of the four royal commissioners, two of whom arrived in Boston, July 20. The grant invested the duke with the proprietorship of eastern Maine and of the Dutch territory of New Netherland (not yet conquered) extending easterly to the Connecticut River, thus estopping Massachusetts from further expansion to the eastward, taking the region of the Hudson and the Delaware from the Dutch, and handing over to the duke all lands west of the Connecticut River together with Long Island, which meant the New Haven territory and half of Connecticut. It was an astonishing grant, particularly when studied in the light of the charter of Connecticut and the controversy between that colony and New Haven, and also it raises the question as to who was responsible for the boundaries inserted in the Connecticut charter, upon which alone Connecticut based her claims against her neighbor colony. Conditions at Whitehall, in the council chamber, the seals offices, and the chancery, must have been at loose ends if a grant of 1662 to Connecticut could be so completely negatived by a grant of 1664 to the Duke of York, thus throwing Connecticut's claim to the territory of the New Haven jurisdiction completely into the discard. The second event, the sending of the royal commissioners to capture New Netherland and to investigate New England threatened the existence of all the New England governments, for the commissioners were instructed to report on the general situation among the Puritan colonies with an eye to their possible reorganization.

The emergency was a serious one for all concerned. Massachusetts immediately sent word to Connecticut and New Haven to settle their dispute and Connecticut sent agents to New Haven to demand her submission and to take over the control of the colony.[1] There was nothing else for New Haven to do, unless she removed her people as a whole to the region of the Hudson or to the Delaware (for the overthrow of New Netherland had been effected in the summer of 1664), but this step was blocked by the duke's grant of the Jerseys to Berkeley and Carteret, three months after the issue of his charter and a month before the capture of New Amsterdam

1. *New Haven Colonial Records*, II, 545; *Connecticut Colonial Records*, 1636-1665, p. 437.

Of course the towns of the jurisdiction might remain as they were and go under the duke's proprietary authority, but such a plan appealed to the New Haven people less than did a union with Connecticut. It took the general court a long time to reach a decision, but when in September, 1664, the commissioners of the New England Confederation changed their minds and agreed that under the articles New Haven could be represented by the delegates from Connecticut and on November 20 the royal commissioners decided that Connecticut's southern boundary was Long Island Sound—though how they squared their verdict with a literal interpretation of the duke's grant is difficult to see—then New Haven gave up the struggle. The matter was settled December 15, 1664, though the formal act of submission was not passed until January 5, 1665.[1] In yielding to her fate, New Haven refused to recognize the justice of Connecticut's actions and disclaimed all responsibility for the blow struck at the integrity of the confederation. In testimony of her loyalty to the king's majesty and in deference to the verdict of the king's commissioners she agreed to capitulate "as from a necessity brought upon us by their meanes of Connecticut, but with a salvo jure of our former right and claims, as a people who have not yet been heard in point of plea." Thus ended as an independent government the jurisdiction of New Haven, the towns of which, from this time forward, became a part of the Connecticut colony and conformed in all respects to the fundamental rules that that colony had established for itself in the Fundamental Orders, the laws that followed, and the charter of 1662.

The failure of the colony as a commercial enterprise—a failure largely due to the insufficiency of the available area of supply—the impossibility of territorial expansion, and the unfortunate location that it occupied on a semi-inland waterway, blocked in some measure at each end, resulted in grave economic weaknesses and eventual

1. *Plymouth Colony Records*, X, 318–319; *New Haven Colonial Records*, II, 551, 555, 556. On that day, January 5, James Bishop, secretary of the New Haven jurisdiction, wrote to the Connecticut committee announcing the vote, but referring in caustic terms to Connecticut's way of doing things, sending "forth yor Edict from Authority upon us, before our Conviction for submission was declared to you." "We scope not," he added, "at reflections, but conviction & Conscience satisfaction, that soe brethren in the Fellowship of the gospell might come to a Cordiall and regular Closure, & soe to walke together in love & peace to advance Christ his interest among them, which is all o^r designe. But how those high & holy ends are like soe to be pinoved [*sic*] between us, wthout a Treaty for accomodation, we have cause to doubt." *Bulletin*, Connecticut Historical Society, no. 7.

poverty and discouragement. The rigid limitation of the franchise, confined as it was to church members only, and the refusal of the leaders to allow in any degree a liberalizing of the system and a consequent widening of the political foundation alienated many of its people. As time went on more and more of the inhabitants looked with envy upon those who enjoyed the broader privileges of Connecticut and were ready to take advantage of the opportunity to break away from an allegiance that became increasingly irksome with the years. More important than all else was New Haven's want of a legal title to exist, for the lack of a charter left her defenseless at a time when her northern neighbor, possessed of greater strength, determination, and diplomatic sagacity, was able to obtain royal privileges, which, however secured, were to serve, at least in her own mind, as a sufficient legal warrant justifying her attack on New Haven, in the interest of her own expansion in rivalry with Massachusetts. The absorption of New Haven left but two Puritan colonies in New England, which with Rhode Island and New Hampshire made up this section of the colonial area during the eighteenth century.

Whatever one may think of Connecticut's method of bringing about the submission of her Puritan neighbor and the complete overthrow in this manner of an independent jurisdiction, the fact remains that the continuance of New Haven as a separate political and religious institution could have been of no advantage to New England or to the English colonial world. The weakness of the colony was manifest and its continued success as a going concern problematical. Hemmed in by powerful neighbors, its towns scattered and without unity, its territorial contour broken and irregular, it always suffered from want of cohesion and unity. The federation of towns that composed the jurisdiction was always loosely knit and though all were held together by laws, oaths, and a common adherence to certain fundamental Puritan ideas in church and state, its tendencies were centrifugal and there were always among its people a considerable number that were dissatisfied and discontented.

THE
PROPRIETARY GOVERNMENTS

AMONG the many colonies in America founded by Englishmen in the seventeenth century the greater number were at the outset proprietary in form and manner of government, the patentees of which often enjoyed by virtue of their charters prerogatives more absolute even than those of the grantor, the king of England himself. Why such a system, outworn at home, should have been revived for America in the earliest charters issued to sixteenth century adventurers and have continued to be so revived on to the end of the seventeenth century is not difficult to understand. America was a frontier territory, occupied by warlike Indian tribes, possession of which was disputed by rival nations, Spaniards, French, and Dutch. To meet the dangers incident to so distant and perilous a country exceptional powers had to be conferred upon those who were willing to run the risks involved. The policy underlying these grants was the same as that which had been employed in England in medieval times when, in order to defend the kingdom against hostile attacks, palatinates had been erected along the Welsh and Scottish borders, the heads of which were allowed to exercise almost regal authority. These powerful territorial lords were largely independent of royal control and within their allotted boundaries were, feudally speaking, supreme. Their counterparts in America, legally vested with similar powers, were never in the long run able to make good their pretensions, because the times were no longer medieval but were becoming modern and the people inhabiting these proprietaries were English subjects, claiming all the rights and privileges of their fellow subjects at home. Nevertheless, the colonial proprietors, most of whom never visited their possessions and in only a few instances attempted to govern their people in person, demanded from the beginning full recognition of their proprietary rights in the soil and, to a greater or lesser extent, varying with the different colonies, exacted bonds of obedience and fidelity to themselves as the absolute governing lords of the territory. Inevitably accompanying such a revival of feudal prerogatives there was to be found in the landed and social life of each propriety a reproduction, often crude and sketchy and never complete, of many of the time-honored and familiar customs and incidents of the seignorial and manorial life in England.

These proprietary and tenurial aspects of our early colonial life are not negligible features of American history. Before the colonists could enter upon the great struggle of the eighteenth century against the continued exercise in America of the royal prerogative, they had to war against the proprietary prerogatives that were enforced in a number of the most important of England's colonies. In this effort they were aided by the policy which the English government itself formulated toward the end of the seventeenth century, that of abolishing the private colonies and centering colonial administration in the hands of the crown. The "march of democracy," which has too often formed the sole topic presented by many in the past who have viewed the colonial period as merely the prelude to the history of the United States, was no simple and easy advance and followed no smooth, even, and unobstructed path. Rather it involved a constant struggle with reactionary and conservative factors that were religious, proprietary, aristocratic, and monarchical. All these factors, save such as were religious, were derived from constituted authority in England and represented the customs, usages, and laws of the homeland from which the colonists had come.

Thus in their progression toward a freer and more independent life the colonists had to contend with other obstacles and restrictions than those imposed by the navigation acts or enforced by royal or parliamentary authority. Outside New England, and even there to a greater extent than is commonly realized, they were engaged, consciously or unconsciously, in ridding themselves and their institutions of many rules and practices, precedents, and legal obligations which hampered freedom of action and government and a natural development of ideas which were slowly becoming rather American than English. The separation from the mother country was more than a matter of revolutionary warfare for eight years. It was a century-long process, without dates and without boundaries, whereby, little by little, features of English law, constituted authority and precedent, land tenure, and other conditions ingrained in the minds and habits of the Englishman at home, such as were neither needed nor wanted in the colonies, were being one by one altered, reduced, or eliminated altogether. In that way and for that reason independence of the mother country had been won in many directions long before the treaty of Paris in 1783.

CHAPTER VI

THE PROPRIETIES: INTRODUCTORY

INTERESTING and absorbing as are the New England colonies in the seventeenth century, because of the personalities presented and the problems involved, their history forms but a small part of that great complex of conditions which underlay English expansion in the New World. The story of that growth and development is no continuous narrative. Its presentation, as of a panorama, requires that the observer, often by a shift in the scene before him, bring within his purview the widely differing circumstances that attended the efforts of Englishmen to find a place on American soil or to derive profit from the possession of landed property there. The colonial expansion of England, of which our first three volumes treat, must be dealt with in all its parts and the colonial policy of the mother country, to be dealt with in volume four, must be adequately understood before we are ready to trace the growth of those ideas and institutions that we call American and that led, in their slow and painful development, out of a great variety of beginnings and in the face of an even greater variety of obstacles, to the establishment of a new order of civilization—our national heritage. Furthermore, a thoroughgoing analysis of the social and political life in the homeland, which made expansion possible and even inevitable, prepares us for a better understanding of the later history of England itself, during the century and a half before the American Revolution, and so to secure, what should be the aim of every writer on our colonial history, a proper treatment of the forces in mother country and colonies that in their gradual and often discordant divergencies provoked on both sides misunderstanding, ill will, and, finally, resistance, coercion, and conflict. We cannot hope to have any real knowledge of colonial history, at least before the middle of the eighteenth century, until we have made a determined effort to familiarize ourselves with the background, environment, and provincial outlook which characterized the average Englishman of that day.

Trading companies and groups of religious dissenters were not the only English agencies that had to do with settlement in the New

World. There were the proprietors also. The planting of colonists on the soil of Virginia and Bermuda was the work of commercial organizations with business profit as the main end in view. The rapid populating of the coast and river regions of New England was, it is true, the outcome of a religious restlessness on the part of groups of men and women in the mother country, who wished to be free from the entanglements of ecclesiastical tradition and practice, and who saw only persecution in the attempts made in England "to correct them for disobedience to the lawful ceremonies of the established church."[1] But with the settling of these regions the influence of commerce and religion as dominant colonizing factors came to an end and from then on all efforts on an extended scale to enlarge the area of English control in America had a proprietary origin and coloring. The normal interest of the average Englishman during the seventeenth and eighteenth centuries was neither commercial nor Puritan, because neither mercantile enterprise nor religious dissent were characteristic of England's past or typical of the way in which the bulk of England's population lived and worked. On the contrary Englishmen were still agriculturally minded, and land not trade, Anglicanism not dissent, manorial organization not city life, governed the thought and conduct of the vast majority of those who constituted the privileged classes at home during these years.

At the time of the settlement of America England was a kingdom where possession of the soil was still the hallmark of quality and where, in social prominence and in the opportunities enjoyed for preferment in the field of politics and administration, the gentry were far more important than were the mercantile and trading classes. As yet few merchants had found their way into the halls of parliament or into official positions under the government, and the laws regarding the tenure, transfer, occupation, and incidents of real property were among the most binding that concerned the English landholder, lawyer, and conveyancer. These men were slow to change their minds and they adhered as long as they could to the traditional rules and precedents that prevailed in the domain of territorial possession. Inevitably changes had come and were coming, for even English conservatism could not withstand the pressure of an expanding and growing population, but in the face of dogged

1. Historical Manuscripts Commission, *Coke*, I, 56 (1605).

resistance the modifications were gradual and often imperceptible The lawyers and justices on the bench might still appeal to Magna Carta, Bracton, Glanville, Fleta, Littleton, and Coke to sustain theii arguments and decisions, but even they had to recognize and accept the new conditions that were altering the face of the land and intro- ducing a new era in the history of property control. Just as it has been necessary for us to characterize briefly the background of the commercial and religious movements that led to the occupation of Virginia, Bermuda, and New England, so it will be necessary to say something about the proprietary conditions that environed the life of influential Englishmen during our entire colonial period and that had much to do with -determining England's attitude toward the colonies down to the Revolution. A survey of the history and mental demeanor of the landed classes will also go far to explain why so many from among them were eager to obtain land in America, from which to reap such profit as they could to compensate in a measure for losses sustained at home.[1]

England of the seventeenth century was a land of manors—though never of a manorial system—where seignorial rights and privileges, local customs, and agricultural practices, though varying greatly in detail, were everywhere pretty much the same.[2] The lords of these manors might be of any rank or class, noble or commoner, from the king down to the country squire, who had the fee. All these lords, ex- cept the king himself, and even he in some instances not as king but as landholder, held by forms of tenure that were still feudal in part and were legally, though not often actually, in force in England at the time of the first settlement of America. These strictly feudal tenures were four: frankalmoin, a spiritual service, including inter- cession and prayer, rendered only by ecclesiastical persons and al-

1. Little or no work has been done to throw light on manorial conditions in Eng- land during the seventeenth and eighteenth centuries. Until many studies are made of the type of Miss Davenport's *A Norfolk Manor* and Professor and Mrs. Gras' *Economic and Social History of an English Village* [Crawley in Hampshire], *909– 1928,* conclusions are bound to be provisional. Even in the two cases mentioned the evidence is far from complete for the times and places in question. The work of the Webbs (*The Parish and the County,* 1906, *The Manor and the Borough,* 1908) is chiefly of value for the later period, and that of Johnson, *The Disappearance of the Small Landowner,* is devoted almost entirely to enclosures.

2. These manors and courts and groups of villagers were still visibly and vitally alive when Leland wrote his *Itineraries* (Smith ed., 1907–1909) in the middle of the sixteenth century.

ready much out of use;[1] grand serjeanty, a personal service to the king, which was rendered and is still rendered at the time of the coronation exercises; petty serjeanty, a lesser personal service to the king, which had already got commuted for a token or money pay· ment and was rapidly losing itself in the prevailing tenure of free and common socage;[2] and, lastly, knight service, which had long lost its military character and continued to exist only because it carried with it certain rights that had a money value.[3] These rights had to do with scutage, marriage, wardship, and the like, the right of wardship covering guardianship of an "infant" under age, the business relating to which was transacted in the court of wards and liveries, where at one time John Winthrop and Emmanuel Downing were employed as attorneys.[4] The old knight service payments had already dropped to merely nominal amounts and in some cases had ceased altogether. All of these strictly feudal tenures, as well as the court of wards and liveries, were finally done away with in 1660, and became merged in the one great tenure of free and common socage. All feudal aids and incidents were abolished also and only two obligations remained, the payment of a fixed rent or quit-rent and the taking of an oath—of allegiance in the case of the king and of fidelity (*per fidem fiducius*) in the case of a lesser lord.[5] This tenure because of its simple, certain, and practical nature was better adapted than were the older forms to meet the needs of a changing civilization, the increasing mobility of which demanded a less cir-

1. Kimball, "Tenure in Frank Almoin and Secular Services," *English Historical Review*, XLIII, 341–353. Miss Kimball shows that though frankalmoin was a spiritual service it did not always free the holder from demands of a secular nature, similar to the obligations resting upon those who held land of the crown by military service. Exemptions, however, could generally be obtained at the exchequer by the bishop or abbot on the score of his tenure, though the king generally demanded an equivalent in the form of *dona* or voluntary gifts.

2. The name of this tenure continued to prevail. Valentine Carey wrote to Sir John Coke in 1621, "I possess a little land which I bought as holding *de domino rege per servitium parvae sergeantiae*," Historical Manuscripts Commission, *Coke*, I, 110.

3. Knight service, or in the language of the grant, service *in capite*, still had a sort of military flavor when applied to grants in America. This is the case with the grants to Stirling (1621), Calvert (Avalon, 1623), Carlisle (1627), Montgomery-Pembroke (1628), Heath (Carolana, 1629), Kirke (Newfoundland, 1637).

4. Above, Vol. I, 384 note 3. The court was abolished in 1646 by the Long Parliament (Firth and Rait, *Acts and Ordinances of the Interregnum*, I, 833; II, 1043, 1057), but as none of the ordinances of the Interregnum had legal standing after 1660, it was revived only to be abolished again in that year (12 Charles II, c. 24).

5. Many lands were held of mesne lords in free and common socage. The tenure first arose within the manor and spread until it had swallowed up both petty ser-

cumscribed and more flexible method of acquiring and retaining possession of the soil.

The manor thus held—by one lord or sometimes by two or more jointly—was rather a jurisdiction than a compass of land, though corporeally it had to be identified with a fairly definite area of occupied and cultivated territory. It might embrace one or more villages or towns and even parts of towns, but usually it coincided with a single town, the home of laboring villagers and the seat of a busy agricultural life. Each manor was divided into two parts: one, the lord's demesne, made up of the lands which the lord himself cultivated, itself threefold—the home farm (nucleus of the demesne), the lands let out to copyholders, and the waste or such part of the original demesne as had not been brought into use; the other, the lands of the customary tenants or freeholders, who held their tenancies of the lord by a fixed payment, either in service or in money, the former at this period having in large part ceased to be rendered. The freeholders were freemen, whose status was higher than that of the copyholders and whose holdings and rents were matters of bargaining with the lord, having nothing to do with the custom of the manor according to which the copyholder held his lands. They had a standing in the common law courts even against the lord himself, a privilege and right which in the early seventeenth century was under certain conditions extended to the copyholders also. The freeholders were of the rank of yeomen, below the esquires but above the copyholders. As a rule they were independent farmers, often of wealth, whose value to the lord lay in the rents paid, which in their case as sometimes also in the case of the copyholders came to be known as quit-rent, whenever there were quittances of service due. The tenancies of the freeholders were separate from and outside the demesne, of which the holdings of the copyholders were an integral part, and therefore the freeholders could have no use of the waste, which the copyholders shared in common with the lord. The freehold tenancies, taken altogether, were larger in extent than the demesne, but the rights attached to them were, as a rule, inferior to

jeanty and the burgage tenures. At the beginning of colonial settlement only two tenures of importance remained—knight service and free and common socage—and of these only the latter had any vitality. Frankalmoin and grand serjeanty were never in socage, and being at this time only ceremonial tenures did not count. For lands held of mesne lords in free and common socage—"as of the manor of Hawksbury" and "as of the manor of Frampton," exactly as were manors and lands held of the king, "as of the manor of East Greenwich," see above, p. 139, note 2.

those of the copyholders. As the open fields and commons slowly gave way before enclosures and improved farming methods, the old freeholders as a class began to decline in some quarters, both in strength and numbers, and before the end of the eighteenth century were already entering upon their transformation.[1]

According to the law books there could be no "real" manor without at least two freeholders, but, in fact, there were so many manors in which copyholders only were to be found that the *lex maneriorum* had chiefly to do with copyhold problems.[2] The law was very complicated and full of difficult and debatable points and for that reason cases were constantly arising that were irritating and expensive for both lord and tenant. Problems of tenure, descent, alienation, surrender, service, rights of common and commoning, and procedure in the manorial courts—all varied in different quarters and had to be settled by different laws and precedents. First of all there was custom—the *leges loci*—itself not an infallible rule, as there were "good" customs and "bad" ones; secondly, immemorial usage according to the established principle that "a long and uninterrupted enjoyment is a great evidence of a right";[3] thirdly, the decisions of the judges in the common law courts; and lastly, the acts of parliament relating to landlords, tenants, and farmers, of which there were many from the time of Edward IV to that of James I and his successors.

Upon the manors were stewards, bailiffs, and beadles of the lord's appointment, some of whom, such as the stewards and the bailiffs, may have had several manors in charge. There were also reeves and constables elected by the copyholders in the leet court—often called

1. Chambers, *Nottinghamshire in the Eighteenth Century*, p. 205; Johnson, *The Disappearance of the Small Landowner*, ch. VI.

2. Coke, *The Compleat Copyholder* (1630 and later editions) and Calthorpe, *The Relations between the Lord of a Mannor and the Copy-Holder, his Tenant* (London 1635) should be compared with Jacob, *Complete Court Keeper* (1713, many editions) *The Landlords Law: or, the Law concerning Landlords, Tenants, and Farmers* (6th ed., 1720), Nelson, *Lex Maneriorum* (1733), *Tenant Law, or the Laws concerning Landlords, Tenants and Farmers* (London, 1737), and John Paul, *Every Landlord or Tenant his own Lawyer* (London, 1775), to grasp some of the changes which had taken place during this period of more than a hundred years.

3. Historical Manuscripts Commission, *Middleton*, p. 502 (1703). There were frequent disputes, even at this early date, over the right to use the commons, which the lords as a rule claimed for themselves. One such case was taken into the court of ward and liveries, though why this should have been done is not clear from the evidence furnished (the same, *Salisbury*, XVI, 89), as the case apparently had nothing to do with wardship.

the lord's tourn—and so representative of the villagers as a whole, a fact which largely explains why of all these officials the constable was the only one that survived in the colonies. The reeve was the most important man in the medieval village and the one who managed the estate on the agricultural side, but in America there was no place for him. Later he often leased the demesne and in so doing became the farmer of it after his duties as reeve were no longer required. The other officials were possessed in the main of ministerial rather than executive or judicial functions, though the steward, who at this time was generally a lawyer or a person who possessed at least a knowledge of the law, had certain judicial responsibilities also.

The maintenance of the lord's household depended partly upon the substance received from the cultivation of his own acres and partly upon the payments in kind which were made by his copyhold tenants. But far-reaching changes were already taking place. "Base" tenure, involving service and payments in kind, was passing away and villeinage was freeing itself of its "servile" obligations.[1] The increasing mobility of labor was leading to the withdrawal of tenants—notably artisans—to the towns and seaports, resulting in the depopulation of the country districts and the decay of dwellings, of which one reads much in the letters of the period. The larger centers were invaded by the migratory poor, for the enclosure movement, which broke down the old open field system, helped to recruit the army of vagrants that battened on the country in the seventeenth and eighteenth centuries. Tenants were shaking themselves free of their old "servility" and were refusing to conform to some of the time-honored usages.[2] Inevitably, therefore, the customs of the manor became relaxed and the burden of payment lightened, a situation that worked rather to the disadvantage of the lord than of the tenants, because the copyholder was personally free to move wher-

---

1. Naturally the lords resisted this movement as long as they could. Professor Gras says that the Bishop of Winchester was a saviour of souls but an equally "zealous shepherd when it came to freemen services owed to him. He clung tenaciously to the servitudes his tenants bore in his favor." *The Economic and Social History of an English Village*, p. 79.

2. Historical Manuscripts Commission, *Finch*, p. 37. On the decay of villeinage see Davenport, *A Norfolk Manor*, p. 97 and chapter IV, and the same writer's "Decay of Villeinage in East Anglia," Royal Historical Society, *Transactions*, new series, XIV. Also Savine, "Bondmen under the Tudors," *ibid.*, XVII, and Popham's letter to the Privy Council, Historical Manuscripts Commission, *Salisbury*, XVI, 180–181

ever he liked, provided he surrendered his land to his lord. In cases of dispute or of ill treatment he could bring a complaint in law and enjoy the protection of the common law courts. Consequently, for the tilling of his acres the lord became more and more dependent on hired labor, which was often difficult to obtain and when obtained was transient and unreliable.[1]

Other influences were at work. The use of the manor by the central government of the kingdom as a local administrative unit was bringing into prominence the town or vill beneath it, because the town organization fitted better into the national plan than did that of the manor which was never used for administrative purposes. This policy of the government hastened the transformation of the lord, as an owning and ruling seigneur, into the proprietor of a country estate, a process that was the outstanding feature of English agricultural and social life at the time of the settlement of America.[2] The process was slow and irregular and was not completed in some parts of England until well on in the nineteenth century. Undoubtedly it was hastened by the selling of ecclesiastical and royalist estates during the Interregnum and the introduction into the class of manorial lords of many to whom the traditions and practices of a seignorial past were foreign and unfamiliar. Though large numbers of these estates were returned after the Restoration others remained in the possession of the purchasers and on these the old customs were greatly relaxed.[3]

Side by side with the alteration in the status of the manorial lord went the enfranchising of copyhold land and the turning of copy-

1. With the decay of the system of bondage in the sixteenth century many of the servile payments ceased. Miss Davenport says of Forncett in Norfolk that the returns from 1528 to 1605 fell from £77 to £50 and with the decrease in the value of money the rents became less adequate to the lord and the returns to the courts less profitable, pp. 58–59.

2. That the old manorial organization was breaking down at the time of the settlement of America is clear, but I think that Professor Cheyney has gone much too far in saying, in his *History of England*, II, 397, that at the end of Elizabeth's reign "the term manor may be largely disregarded, because it was fast becoming a forgotten or disregarded institution." The term was not so disregarded in the statutes (for example, 22–23 Charles II, c. 25, 1670), in the writings of the law compilers (above, p. 204, n. 2), or in local nomenclature (for examples of continued usage after 1600, Historical Manuscripts Commission, *Middleton*, pp. 322 ff.). John Evelyn was lord of the manor of Stalbridge, Dorset, in 1674, the same, *Pepys*, p. 268.

3. The position of the copyholders became worse during the Interregnum, when in the change of masters, due to the sale of forfeited estates, many were evicted and other laborers put in their places. Lands were sold to the highest bidders and the

holders into freeholders, in the hope of increasing the revenues from the estates. Payments from copyholders were always uncertain and at this time were heavily falling off, while those of the farmers and lease-holders were fixed and fairly stable, even though the shilling was decreasing in purchasing power. This issue was not so much one of land as of status, for the copyholder had no vote in the counties where the freeholders were the only ones with the franchise, and in some quarters the movement was resisted on this account. The steps taken in the process were hesitating and full of perplexities, for many a copyholder held at "fee farm," that is, in freehold, just as many a freeholder was the possessor of land in copyhold. Thus the distinction between freehold and copyhold was often difficult to determine and recourse had to be had to the manor rolls, the testimony of oldest inhabitants, and the decisions of the judges.[1] Hence the conversion proceeded very slowly and did not reach its culmination until the twentieth century.[2]

This confusion in estate-status was greatly increased by the practice of leasing the demesne lands to a tenant farmer and of re-leasing smaller holdings which had fallen in, on surrender, forfeiture, expiration, or death of heirs, to either copyholders or freeholders. It was also increased by the practice of many a "gentleman"—knight or baronet—becoming a farmer on his own account, holding a manor in farm, rather than in fee, of one of higher rank than him-

purchasers, new men frequently, introduced an arbitrary control for the purpose of making the new acquisitions easy and profitable sources of revenue. These conditions formed a part of the discontent which gave rise to the Leveller Movement.

A suggestive pamphlet on the subject is *Considerations concerning Common Fields and Enclosures, A Dialogue* (London, 1654). It was written partly to answer some passages which were thought to make against enclosures in general, presented in a work by John Moore, minister of the church of Knaptost in Lincolnshire, entitled *The Crying Sinne of England of not Caring for the Poor*. The *Considerations* have much to say about the discharging of tenants and cotters and defends enclosures entirely on agricultural grounds, while Moore deems them the "Canker of the Commonwealth" because leading to depopulation, the decay of tillage, the making of beggars, the rise in the price of land, and the "flaying the skin off the poor."

1. Professor Gras says that this distinction between freehold and copyhold did not become prominent at Crawley until the nineteenth century. For resistance to the transformation of copyholders into freeholders, Historical Manuscripts Commission, *Tenth Report*, appendix, IV, pp. 310–311, *Coke*, I, 293–294; II, 249. In 1634 Sir Francis Nedham bought "the capital messuage and manor of Alton as freehold; it now proves to be copyhold of the king's manor of Wirksworth," p. 71.

2. The final step in the abolition or enfranchisement of copyhold was taken in 1925, when was passed the Administration of Estates Act, which went into effect January 1, 1926.

self, whenever he was barred from holding in fee by the statute of Quia Emptores.[1] On this account the lot of the steward-lawyer was far from an easy one and even the judges of the common law courts sometimes got lost in a maze of doubts. The whole manorial organization and practice, which eventually was to emerge simplified and fairly symmetrical, was at this period in confusion because manorial law was passing through a transition state of fluidity and change.

The lord's money returns came from the rents of his tenancies and leases and from the casual revenues that arose from the seignorial relationship. The latter, never large in amount, were from deodands,[2] forfeitures, waifs and estrays,[3] the goods of felons[4] and suicides,[5] the contents of mines of coal and quarries of stone, amercements and fines of many sorts from the leet court of the copyholders, imposed for default of attendance, or for contempt, disturbance, and breaches of law, custom, and the king's peace. Among the most lucrative of these revenues were the payments on admittance to the tenement, known as "reliefs," which were predial payments due only from a freeholder of full age. Similar payments were made on the alienation and surrender of freeholds. This payment, the "heriot," though not a money settlement, since it was a personal not a predial obligation, may be placed in the same category. It was a very old charge still exacted at this period and consisted of the best beast—ox, cow, or sheep—or on some manors the best goods or piece of plate that the tenant—freeholder or copyholder—possessed at the time of his death. Though properly a payment in kind, it was occasionally compounded for or made in a form readily convertible into money. The lords clung to these revenues, many of which were exacted in the proprietary colonies in America, because they realized

1. Gras, as above, pp. 99–101.

2. "Any moveable inanimate, or a Beast which is animate," which "Causes the untimely Death of a reasonable Creature without the Will [that is, by mischance] on the Land but not on the Sea," Nelson, Lex Maneriorum, p. 96.

3. Waifs were goods stolen or left by a felon, on his being pursued, for fear of being apprehended, which were forfeited to the king or lord of the manor. Estrays were beasts, not wild, found within the bounds of a lordship or manor.

4. Sir Edmund Carey petitioned in 1624 "for confirmation of his right to the goods of a felon convict tenant in his manor of Danby (Historical Manuscripts Commission, Coke, I, 171). In 1604 Sir Thomas Monson applied for the office of "surveyor of the goods and chattels of all felons, and all that fly [that is, escape], or against whom any exigent shall be awarded for felony; also of all heriots due to the king." The same, Salisbury, XVI, 449.

5. Nelson, Lex Maneriorum, pp. 107–111.

that the profits from their estates were dwindling and that they had to be sure of every penny which could be wrung from their tenantry. The modification that was taking place in the passage from a service to a money system was rendering these lords peculiarly sensitive to fluctuating and shifting monetary values and made an increase of their incomes, either from land or some other service, a matter of imperative necessity.

Many of the manorial lords lived away from their estates, under circumstances that made economy the harder to endure. Some had town houses in London and the nearby suburbs, extending from the Strand to St. James Square and as far north as Highgate. Others had lodgings near the court at Whitehall, where they spent part of their time in the service of the king. Still others had in town both houses and lodgings, and all were away from their country estates for months at a time.[1] Consequently these estates were looked after by agents—stewards, secretaries, overseers, managers, or bailiffs, whose business it was to administer the manor or manors and transmit the income to their lords.[2] The stewards were important personages, often of knightly rank in the case of royal manors, and their duties were exacting and burdensome. They presided over the customary court or court baron of the freeholders, if there happened to be such a court in the manor of their stewardship, which was held every three weeks or less frequently in some cases, and where, by the homage jury, presentments were made of deaths and defaults, admittances and surrenders, and other matters dealing with the use and abuse of the tenancies. They were the judges also in the lord's tourn or court leet of the copyholders, held once or twice a year, where the jury made presentments relating to offenses against the peace of the realm. Sometimes the two courts were held together as a "court leet and general court baron," with the steward in charge. Though meeting at the same time these courts did not constitute a single body but functioned separately.[3] The court baron was not a court of record because it was a private manorial institution concerned with

1. Many of the younger sons also betook themselves to London, where they became, some of them, men of substance in the City, members of the livery companies, lawyers, and merchants. In London and its neighborhood they lived in Lincoln Inn's Fields, Bloomsbury, Paternoster Row, etc., *Orlebar Pedigrees*, supplement, pp. 308–321.

2. Edward Laurence, *Duty of a Steward to his Lord* (London, 1727).

3. Historical Manuscripts Commission, *Various*, VII, 304–307; *Extracts from the Court Rolls of the Manor of Wimbledon, Edward IV to 1864, passim;* Gras, pp. 511–

local tenurial problems, but the court leet was a court of record because it was a king's court dealing with the king's peace and deriving its authority from the crown through the lord of the manor. These courts were still active in the sixteenth century but tended to lose their jurisdiction over criminal matters and to confine their energies more and more to the intricacies of the management of property. The leet court, which was longer-lived than any of the others—borough or manorial—was gradually supplanted by the justices of the peace, to whom, from Elizabeth's time onward, was entrusted a constantly increasing variety of functions. These functions became a part of the regular duties of the lords of the manors who served as justices in their respective localities.[1]

The steward or bailiff, who received a fixed sum for his services,[2] returned to the king or other absentee lord what he could from the profits of the manor, though the total amount at this period was distinctly diminishing. In order to understand why this was so it is necessary to remember that in number and amounts the customary payments were growing smaller, owing to the withdrawal of many copyholders from the manors and the unwillingness or inability of those that remained to meet their usual obligations. In consequence the sums due were either wanting altogether or else were badly in arrears.[3] The purchasing power of the money received from the fixed rentals of the freeholders had lessened, leading to an absolute loss

518. The Duke of Chandos once said (1735) that he had not held a court at Shawhall (which he rented) since he had been in possession, for the legal estate was not vested in him and he doubted if he could do so. He said that the tenants were getting uneasy about it and he had written to his solicitor to know the law in the case. Letter Book (Huntington Library), 45, p. 44.

1. The leet courts were, however, sufficiently important in the eighteenth century to call out many lawyers' books descriptive of their functions: Sir W. Scroggs, *The Practice of Courts Leet and Courts Baron, containing full and exact Directions for holding the said Courts* (London, 1728); William Greenwood, *Authority, Jurisdiction and Method of keeping County Courts, Courts Leet and Courts Baron* (London, 1722). Courts leet continued to be held well on in the nineteenth century.

2. Historical Manuscripts Commission, *Gawdy*, p. 4.

3. Earl of Suffolk and Folk Greville to Sir Edward Watson, steward of H. M. Manor of Ketthering, August 7, 1615, "His Majesty is resolved not to suffer that part of his Revenues which consist of copyhold to be so unprofitable unto him as it hath been in times past, but to make some just improvements thereof." The writers follow up this statement with an outline of remedies, together with strict injunctions to the steward, and mention certain "printed instructions." They complain of the "pretended customs" of the tenants and the neglect of the stewards and insist on the necessity of seizing lands in case of default. They too speak of the possibility of enfranchisement. Historical Manuscripts Commission, *Buccleuch*, III, 185.

of income in that direction also, and even the king himself after 1660 was quite unable to maintain his household from the revenues of his manors. Tenants were not easy to find and in order to obtain them adjustments had to be made, the evidence showing that renting was slow and that many tenements were standing vacant.[1] Commodities were increasing in cost, their transportation by carriers was becoming more expensive, and building materials (a matter of consequence at a time when many a manor house was old and ruinous and the quarters of its tenants were in decay, wet, cold, and comfortless) were growing scarce and high priced. To these disadvantages, which weighed heavily against the lords, must be added the development of a market for land which made selling attractive to impecunious owners; the appearance of the gentlemen-lessees; and the turning of the arable into sheep pastures.[2] There was also a prevailing tendency toward depopulation in the rural districts and a great insufficiency of money in certain parts of England,[3] for with money as with men the drift was toward the cities and seaports, where capital derived from commercial exchanges was rapidly accumulating.[4] Lastly, may be noted the injuries wrought by the royal rights of purveyance and hunting. It was no small burden for lord and tenant alike to have to provide food and lodging for king and retainers and provisions for hunting horses and hounds,[5] and to put up with the gaming laws, of which complaints were frequently made by the farmers for the loss of their wheat and by the gentlemen for the loss of their partridges.

1. "We have let no more goods nor are certain of our tenants," wrote Marie Coke at Hale Court to Sir John in London, March 3, 1623 (the same, *Coke*, I, 131; for further particulars, 374). For adjustment of rents in the endeavor to reconcile old rentals with new, *Salisbury*, XVI, 58 (1604).

2. "All these tendencies [the enclosing and converting of arable farms to pasture] strengthened the movement for large scale pasturing, for the taking over of leases and copyholds by the landlord, the absorption of small farms by large ones, resulting in the relative decline of the small grain-growing yeoman farmer, who, less than half a century before, was regarded as the rock upon which the commonwealth was built." Chalmers, *Nottinghamshire*, p. 13.

3. Sir John Popham to Viscount Cranborne, September 16, 1604, "I never knew these western parts so bare of money, as I hear now it is—the want of money seems to be very great," *Salisbury*, p. 308.

4. The rebuilding of country houses of a scale that was often elaborate during the Elizabethan and Jacobean periods was made possible not by money from the estates themselves, but by the profits of capital investment and the holding of government sinecures.

5. Historical Manuscripts Commission, *Coke*, I, 126–127.

Nevertheless the period was one of widely expanding interests, when new undertakings were in progress and when men dependent on their incomes from land were reaching out to supplement their diminishing returns from the soil by revenues obtained from other sources. Then, too, it was a time when titles to property were in question, when lords were forced to part with portions of their estates to meet debts or to invest what they had or could borrow on mortgage in any enterprise that looked financially hopeful. The possession of land without money to maintain it was a burden not a benefit and phrases of the day show the trend of men's thoughts "Money is the Heir of Fortune and the Lord Paramount of the World"; "Dea Moneta is the goddess of the world"; "A man's heart is upon his half-penny." These and similar sayings current at the time were peculiarly applicable to members of the gentry who saw their manorial estates in decay and were unable to meet their deficits by improving old-time methods.[1] They were putting their money into the stock of trading companies, during the period of prosperity after 1575,[2] and the great profits made by such corporations as the East India Company and by some of the newly established industries that began to make money with the revival of trade after the peace with Spain in 1604 led to an improvement in the standard of living and to an increased demand for the means wherewith to maintain their standing in the social and political world.

Men of all ranks sought to obtain exclusive control of the manu-facture or importation of such commodities as saltpetre, gunpowder, alum,[3] wines, logwood, starch, silk, and others of like nature. In

1. A clue to one aspect of the situation in the middle of the seventeenth century may be found in the following entry: "Water bailiwick of Severn—little use of such office, but to keep the fishermen in order—that is (according to the abuses of these times) to make them tributary to him & then [compel] them [to] do as they list." *Ibid.*, I, 163.

2. In the East India Company there were fifteen peers, thirteen titled ladies, and eighty-two knights. In the Virginia Company of 1609 there were twenty-one peers and ninety knights, and in the reorganization of 1612 there were twenty-four peers and one hundred and eight knights. One hundred knights underwrote the list for enlarging the funds in 1610 to meet the expenses of the great expedition of De La Warr.

3. On the royal alum works, Historical Manuscripts Commission, *Various*, VIII, preface, and on the general subject Scott, *Joint Stock Companies*, I, ch. VII, and Price, *English Patents of Monopoly, passim.* Sir George Calvert (and others, executors of Robert Cecil, Earl of Salisbury) was granted a letters patent, October 4, 1613, for a yearly pension of £3000 for twenty-one years, payable out of the customs and subsidies of velvets, satins, cambrics, lawns, etc. Historical Manuscript Commission, *Laing*, I, 192; *Calvert Papers*, I, 50.

their eagerness for gain and in their need of obtaining as great a surplus as possible over the specified amounts that were to be paid to the crown, these men became adepts in the art of corrupt practice, able "to fat themselves with the fleece of the friendless and poor."[1] They responded with the utmost eagerness to the lure of mines of silver, copper, iron, lead, coal, and zinc, which were being opened in Wales, Cumberland (Keswick),[2] Yorkshire, and Scotland, and they watched eagerly for promising investments in the stock of companies organized to work them. They became suitors to the crown not only for such unusual offices as the surveyorship of felons, receiver of the king's heriots, keeper of the register book for the dioceses of Canterbury and York, and farmer of the tax upon all that came into playhouses, but also for annuities, pensions, rewards, and sinecures, which depleted heavily the royal resources. It was a time when, as a contemporary said, "every man sought to benefit himself by suits" for privilege and office and thronged Whitehall, where the "saints of the court" demanded not only "adoration but intercession" also. They wanted positions under government, some of which they held in person, others by deputy, the latter too often being sinecures with large profits.[3] They wanted appointments as

1. Sir Giles Mompesson was proclaimed in 1620 for his abuse of monopoly-patents affecting inns and gold and silver thread. He and two others had been nominated commissioners in October, 1616, for the licencing of inns. They could charge what fees they liked provided four-fifths of the sums received were paid into the exchequer. Mompesson performed his duties recklessly, charging exorbitant fees and extracting heavy fines. For so doing he was ordered to be apprehended four years later.

2. Brathwait (*The English Gentleman*, 1630, 2nd ed. 1633) who lived in Westmorland, speaks of the copper mines about Keswick, worked by Dutchmen, who had to go deep into the bowels of the mountains, digging out the metal with incredible pains and labor from a region "steepe, ragged, and cliffie" (p. 126). The allurement of mines remained potent with the country gentlemen for another century. Derbyshire lead mining is whimsically described by Manlore in his *Rhymed Chronicle*, which deals with the customs of the wappentake of Wirksworth, one of the royal manors.

3. Historical Manuscripts Commission, *Salisbury*, XVI, 215, 227, 324, 339, 402. What some of these offices were, with the emoluments allowed, can be learned from the same, *Coke*, II, 67. See Scott, *Joint Stock Companies*, I, 137 note. The Duke of Lenox made suit for the alnage of cloth; the Earl of Dunbar for the monopoly of logwood and on the surrender of his patent received £2000; the Duke of Chandos was paymaster of the forces, a most lucrative post, from 1707–1712 and what it meant can be inferred from his later longing for the good old times when "I rolled at that time in money" (July 11, 1734). He held also the clerkship of the hanaper (1728), and by subletting it was able to pocket £4000 a year. He had control in part of the sixpenny-writ office, from which he expected to make £200 a year, an amount which he thought quite insufficient.

ambassadors, consuls, and foreign agents,[1] and pulled many wires in their efforts to secure such positions.

The result of this shift from the country to the town and the city and from an agrarian to a capitalistic economy was to carry a long step farther on the transformation of the lord and the manor. The former was gradually becoming little more than a country gentleman and the latter a country estate with farms and leases and a few remaining copyholders on the old arrangement, who because of an inherited right could not be dispossessed or absorbed into the new system. The capital messuage or manor house became the home of the esquire and the gentleman, who with their fellows made up the "quality"—the landed gentility, owners of wide domains and leaders of provincial society.[2] To this home they could retire in their declining years, as did such men as Sir John Coke, William Blathwayt, and the Duke of Chandos (to take the names of three men from the beginning, middle, and end of a period of one hundred and fifty years, 1610–1760). There they might spend their days in little else

---

1. *Coke*, II, 103.

2. Treatises now begin to appear on the legal obligations of a country gentleman, such as Meriton, *Landlord's Law: a Treatise very fit for the Perusal of all Gentlemen and others, being a Collection of several Cases in the Law concerning . . . Matters which often happen between Landlord and Tenant* (London, 1665).

"Gentility" was determined, not by arms or ancestry alone, but by the possession of an estate which local society felt to be an establishment suitable for a gentleman. Such estate was to be in land not money, though wealth from trade could easily be converted into land. Wealth acquired from "plentiful merchandize," such as trade in cloth, was carefully distinguished from that obtained from "common buying and selling," that is, from retail trade. It must be remembered that during this period there was taking place a constant replacement of the old families by new ones, the heads of which had gained their wealth not only from the right kind of trade, but also from the practice of law, advantageous marriages, and positions at court. These men bought out the old families, some of which had died out, while others had become bankrupted by the failure of the income from their estates, by gambling, high living, hard drinking, and unsuccessful investments. The new "gentility" was made up of yeomen rising from below, merchants from the cities with social and political ambitions, nabobs from India, and absentee landlords from the British colonies in the West Indies. The dignity of knighthood, once a sacred order of chivalry conferred for brave feats of arms, had become greatly cheapened by the lavish conferment of the honor by James I. Elizabeth had made few knights, but James made 900 during the first year of his reign and before his death 2323 (W. A. Shaw, *The Knights of England*, pp. 100–188). Among those so knighted, who were required to accept the honor of knighthood or compound, if possessing £40 a year in lands, was Sir Richard Saltonstall. This subject has been discussed by the writers of two doctoral dissertations, now in the library of Yale University: Squire, "The English Country Gentleman in the Early Seventeenth Century," and Ralph, "A Critical Edition of the Diary of Sir Humphrey Mildmay, 1633–1652," introduction.

than "killing fat does and hearkening after a kennel of dogs that makes a good cry," breeding hounds and horses and "indulging in the primitive plenty which enjoined full habits and increased the size of the apothecaries' bill with its purges and boluses and pills and powders."[1] Some gave themselves up to more intellectual pleasures, as did Richard Brathwait, who owned the manor of Catterick and found enjoyment in the reading of history, "the sweetest recreation of the mind";[2] or as did the Duke of Chandos, a century later, who after a life of financial success and ultimate failure retired to his estate at Shawhall, where he lived "very contented and quiet." "I smoak my pipe regularly [he writes] after dinner and supper. I seldom see anybody, spending my time in writing and reading—a life not very unpleasant to one naturally lazy—have fallen into the humour of reading mathematics."[3]

Many of these men rented or erected houses architecturally impressive, and they beautified the grounds within which these houses stood, laying them out in the form of sumptuous and spacious parks, with noble trees, wide velvety swards, enclosures for deer, and warrens for rabbits. They planted orchards of apricot, cherry, pear, and plum trees, raised grapes, early and late varieties, and frequently exchanged grafts with each other. They laid out gardens containing plants and small shrubs native to the soil and occasionally experimented with exotic specimens sent by friends and correspondents in the East Indies, Madeira, Barbados, Jamaica, and the southern continental colonies. Among these specimens were the plants, slips, or seeds of pineapples (ananas), shaddock, coffee, oranges and

1. *Orlebar Pedigrees*, pp. 91–93.
2. *The English Gentleman*, p. 220. Compare William de Britaine, when he said "No learning makes a man more judicious than history." Both Brathwait and de Britaine inveigh against the prevailing habit of the country gentlemen of devoting themselves to hunting, hawking, and fishing. For Lord Cottington's estate at Hanworth in 1630 and his and Lady Cottington's activities there, see Earl of Strafford, *Letters and Despatches*, I, 51, 141.
3. Letter Books, 43, pp. 140–141. Shawhall was half a mile north of Newbury, a manor house that came into Chandos' hands in 1729 (the same, 44, pp. 6, 327; 45, pp. 45–46). Chandos wrote in 1735 that he was out of all public business and was living in the country where his time was taken up with looking after his own concerns (51, April, 1735). As William de Britaine puts it in *Human Prudence* (p. 193), "in retirement there is no slavish attendance, no canvassing for places, no making of parties, no envy of any man's favour or fortune." John Evelyn wrote in 1674, "I am neither statesman nor statesman's sonne, but a plaine country gentleman, whose idle moments having afforded him so much leisure as now and then to dip into books," Historical Manuscripts Commission, *Pepys,* p. 268.

lemons, often accompanied by paroquets, macaws, land turtles, and in one instance by a "tackawiney" or diminutive lion "no larger than a rabbit."[1] Here and there was a physic garden, modeled after that of the Apothecaries' Company at Chelsea, of which Philip Miller, author of the *Gardener's Dictionary,* was the undergardener and gardener in the eighteenth century. From Miller's book members of the gentry obtained information how to manage a garden and from Miller himself they received many plants and seeds and occasionally a trained gardener. These improvements in agricultural methods began early in the seventeenth century and gave rise to the great estate in England, which with its house, park, gardens, and other accompaniments became one of England's most conspicuous features down to the twentieth century.[2] There has never been any parallel to it in America that had permanence, and this landed environment of the most influential social and governing class in England has to be reckoned with in understanding England's attitude toward her colonies in the eighteenth century.

Thus while the old manorial system was undergoing important modifications in its internal structure and in the status of its villagers and tenants, the lord himself was losing his seignorial trappings and becoming the head of a landed estate. In common parlance he was still the lord of the manor, the owner of freehold and copyhold, and the receiver of rents from his tenants. His manor was still there, with the greater part of its lands in copyhold held at the common law, in fee or in tail, as fixed inheritances. Many of the lord's rights and privileges were still extant in law and many of the old customs were still in full force.[3] England of the seventeenth and eighteenth centuries, though rather aristocratic than seignorial, was still proprietary and manorial. There was a tendency also toward an oligarchical concentration of powers, for the lords as justices of the peace acquired that position of judicial importance which marks the

1. Historical Manuscripts Commission, *Portland,* II, 205, 206.

2. Many a modern English estate traces no farther back than to the reign of George IV, who according to his recent biographer (Fulford) started by his own example every nobleman and country gentleman throughout the land rebuilding their houses, laying out lawns and gardens, buying pictures, filling libraries, and acquiring new sets of furniture in the latest style.

3. Nelson writing his *Lex Maneriorum* in 1733 has sections on "Manors in General" and "Manors and the Lords of Manors," in which he makes this point perfectly clear and shows the conditions under which a manor existed and was expected to continue (pp. 201–204).

history of the country magnates in the eighteenth century, a position retained until the period of reform, 1825-1835, and the later local government acts of 1888 and 1894.

But the lord was becoming something else that his medieval predecessor was not—he was becoming the member of a social caste or breed of gentry, known as the "squirearchy," with habits and conventions of its own. What these conventions were is admirably illustrated by the writings that appeared during the period, stressing often in great detail the qualifications that such an English gentleman should possess, the recreations that he should engage in, and the temptations that he should avoid.[1] As even a yeoman was "a gentleman in ore" and might rise to the ranks of the better sort, it was deemed desirable to define the distinguishing marks of "gentility." These writings are codes of character, collections of precepts, and definitions of conduct such as should govern the lives and thoughts of so important and influential a group of men and particularly of their children. The wives also were included, for Brathwait's *English Gentlewoman* informed the mistress of the household "What Habitants doe best attire her, What Ornaments doe best adorne her, What Complements doe best accomplish her."

I know of no treatises of this kind before the middle of the sixteenth century and only a very few as early as that time. They were called into being not only as guides to behavior and etiquette, but even more as warnings against what the authors considered the corruption, profligacy, and idleness which were beginning to appear in

1. Among the most important of these writings are: Henry Peacham, *The Compleat Gentleman* (London, 1622), the standard authority of the time on etiquette and originally prepared for Lord Arundel's youngest son; Richard Brathwait, *The English Gentleman* (London, 1630, 2d edition, 1633), and *The English Gentlewoman, drawn out of the full body* (London, 1631); Francis Osborn, *Advice to a Son* (London, 1658, in two parts and many editions); *An Address to the Hopeful Young Gentry of England* (London, 1669); William Ramesey, *The Gentleman's Companion: or a Character of True Nobility and Gentility* (London, 1673, preface dated 1669); Joseph Dare, *Councillor Manners, His last Legacy to his Son* (London, 1673); *The Courtier's Calling, showing the Ways of making a Fortune* (London, 1675); Nicholas Cox, *The Gentleman's Recreation: In Four Parts, viz. Hunting, Hawking, Fowling, Fishing* (London, 1677); William de Britaine, *Human Prudence, or the Act by which a Man may raise Himself and his Fortune to Grandeur* (London, 1689, 10th edition, 1710); *Essay of Particular Advice to the Young Gentry* (London, 1711). A recent work dealing with this subject along quite different lines is Mason, *Gentlefolk in the Making, Studies in the History of English Courtesy Literature, 1531–1774* (1935), which looks at the subject from the standpoint of education, conduct, manners, and etiquette.

social, financial, and political life. These authors saw men making money easily and quickly from the opportunities offered in the world of commercial and industrial enterprise, from favoritism at court, and from the grants of sinecures and monopolies. They laid stress upon the prime duties of the lord as the owner of a landed estate and upon the method necessary "to preserve his estate and greatly to increase it." William de Britaine has many recommendations to offer not only as to the handling of money and servants but also as to the proper conduct in official life, warning his reader that honors and preferments are rarely the reward of virtue but rather the result of possession and interest.[1] Ramesey says in much the same strain that "if a gentleman will keep within compass and avoid the many cheats of servants, he must have an in-sight, nay, a diligent eye into his own estate," must be courteous to his inferiors, mindful of his tenants, and the enemy of idleness, the badge, far too often, of the high life of the day.[2] Generally speaking many of these writings contain little else than moral maxims, but they are symptomatic of the changes which had come upon the upper classes of the English people and it is impossible to think of them as having been written in early Tudor times.

Thus the old relationship between lord and tenants, which had been determined by ties that were personal and social and only in a lesser degree economic, was passing away. The old manor as a collective unit, bound by custom and long standing usages, was already disintegrating; the old lordship was becoming a capitalistic affair, a matter of finance and administration, and social standards were influenced rather by money than by "ancientry." A different social and political class was coming into existence, that was showing itself very proud of its own gentility and had only disdain for the moneyed but landless class as such. During the first half or three-quarters of the eighteenth century these country gentlemen tended to become narrow, stupid, and intolerant and increasingly prudish, formal, and punctilious. Though in the seventeenth century they had life and vitality, courage and resource, they later became stereo-

---

1. William de Britaine, pp. 104–105, 211.
2. Ramesey, pp. 59, 88–91, 124–128. Sir William Mildmay found domestic servants becoming poor, unreliable, and drunken, requiring frequent dismissals and changes. Slingsby in his *Diary* (Parsons ed. London, 1836) deemed the higher servants much more reliable and dependable, serving often as agents and factors. Evidence of this appears in early colonial New England (Vol. I, 500, note 4).

typed, class-conscious, and convinced of their own superiority. They were intensely individualistic, concerned rather for their own individual comfort and salvation than for any general improvement of the human structure within which they lived, and though deeply reverent they never profaned their religion by fussing about it. They were self-contained, self-determining souls, pursuing their own happiness, doing their own duty, enjoying the society of their equals and eschewing all unnecessary contact with others inferior to or unlike themselves, and cut off as most of them were from the rest of the civilized world they remained satisfied with institutions that they could not change and were unaware of the need of doing anything to better other members of the human race. Men were entering upon that state, peculiarly characteristic of the eighteenth century, when they were "afflicted by too much good taste and too many superstitions about being 'ladies and gentlemen' to form a correct idea of the realities and material of life." Not until late in the century and after the American revolt had dismembered the empire did the great philanthropic and humanitarian movements begin their beneficent work of transforming the intellectual, social, and industrial life of England.[1] Until that time the country gentlemen as a class had no clear idea of the obligation of man to be his brother's keeper or of his bounden duty to take some part in alleviating a world full of suffering and evil. It is a strange but illuminating fact that the great philanthropist Thomas Coram, in his appeal on behalf of the foundling hospital, should have had to wait seventeen years before he could overcome the suspicion that he was a profligate whose aim was to make vice easy. Similar appeals in other directions a century later found popular support almost at once.[2]

The pride of place and social prestige which the country gentle-

1. The conditions that prevailed during the first three quarters of the eighteenth century were gradually changed by three transforming movements. These were, first, the weakening of the idea that the privileged classes alone possessed the prerogative of reason, the unprivileged being actuated only by feeling and instinct. Secondly, the Wesleyan religious upheaval, which concerned the common, neglected classes. And, thirdly, the industrial advance, beginning with the use of steam, which brought about, among other changes, the elimination of the restrictive measures placed by the landowners of the past upon the free movement of laborers. No one of these movements had begun during our colonial period.

2. Of course there are a great many exceptions to the general statements made in the text. Many private individuals were engaged in charitable and philanthropic enterprises, of which examples could easily be given. But such enterprise was individual and relatively on a small scale.

men felt during these years was increased by the fact that as magistrates and justices of the peace they looked after county affairs and administered the poor law in all its aspects.[1] Parliament in the eighteenth century was not a legislative body in any modern sense of the term. Its members did little more than act as a check upon the crown and pass laws that met the needs and remedied the grievances of the nation in its larger relations. They left local government in the hands of the country gentlemen. As the manors within which these men lived were the one stable and enduring form of local and rural life in England that defined the relation of the mass of the people to their superiors in rank and gentility and as these men were also the ones who controlled the offices and formed the majority in parliament, we can understand somewhat the insular and provincial state of mind that determined and was responsible for England's colonial policies down to and during the American Revolution. The descendants of these men, though influenced by the democratizing movement of the last hundred years and the infusion of new and often vulgar blood, comprise in largest part what has been called "that fluid and impregnable class or caste [in England] which is one of the most remarkable phenomena of the world today." This class, the squirearchy, is, however, now slowly dying out.

This brief description of manorial England is designed to throw light on the conditions that surrounded the life of the Englishman of the privileged classes and to disclose the influences at work shaping his ideas regarding the world outside his own country. As a rule he was provincially not nationally or internationally minded. He did not look often beyond his own local sphere. He might dabble in the market and have a hand in financial ventures, but it was at court or on his country estate that he loved to live and his acres were his pride and his possession. His heart lay in the country, and not in the city or the counting house, and his notion of the way the

1. The justices of the peace were at the height of their power in the seventeenth and eighteenth centuries—the "rulers of the county" as they have been called, that is, the local authorities who judicially and administratively aided the Privy Council in governing the realm. In their halls of justice and quarter sessions courts they brought law and order into the chaos of local life. If one wishes to know something of their duties and the efficiency with which they performed them and thus to obtain some idea of the highly concentrated local activity of many a man who held office and sat in parliament during our colonial period, one should study the county and quarter sessions records now in process of publication in England. Those for Middlesex, Warwick, Surrey, Buckingham, and Hertfordshire altogether run to many volumes.

world should be run was fashioned by the manorial and proprietary environment in which he spent so large a part of his time. He knew no other way than his own of holding and cultivating the soil and it is not surprising that when he thought of lands in America he should have invested their ownership with the terms and practices with which he was most familiar. He did not realize that nowhere in English America could these conditions be fully reproduced, but that he was willing to attempt their reproduction the remainder of this chapter will show.

Among these country gentlemen, particularly those about court with estates in the southern counties, the desire for additions of land was as keen as the desire for office or for profits from investments. Those that were "unthriftie and decayed" wanted land from necessity; those already possessed of acres wanted more because they were land hungry and ambitious for the social prestige that land conferred. At home they were experimenting with the redemption of the marshes by drainage and of the barrens by irrigation. They bought up the forfeited estates seized by parliament during the Interregnum[1] and applied for lands in Ireland under the so-called Cromwellian settlement of 1652.[2] But before these forfeited estates and Irish tribal lands became available (except on a much smaller scale in the occupation of Ireland under James I and Charles I)[3] they saw in the wide spaces of America and the islands of the West Indies amazing and tempting prospects. All those who subscribed to the stocks of the Virginia, Plymouth, Bermuda, and other com-

1. 1651 and 1652, Firth and Rait, *Acts and Ordinances*, II, 520–545, 623–652. Ashley, *Financial and Commercial Policy under the Cromwellian Protectorate*, pp. 40, 41, 93; Chesney, "The Transference of Lands in England, 1640–1660," *Transactions*, Royal Historical Society, fourth series, pp. 181–210.

2. Firth and Rait, II, 598–603, An Act for the Settlement of Ireland, August 12, 1652.

3. Sir William Boswell, who had been England's representative in Holland, "humbly" asked in 1635 if he might not be "a petitioner to his Majesty for 2000 or 3000 acres, at so reasonable a rent as I may find with good husbandry some relish of my master's most gracious bounty in the same. The sense I cannot avoid of my present fortunes (which your Honour [Sir John Coke] knows to be yet in herba though the winters of my age be drawing on) makes me look about," etc. *Coke*, II, 98. During the next few years many others sent in similar petitions. Boswell in 1630 had agreed with others to promote the settlement of Carolana and in 1632 had been granted (with others) the office of "Receiver General hereditary of the augmented revenue arising in America" (*Calendar State Papers, Colonial*, 1574–1660, pp. 115, 140, 144). The unproductiveness of these ventures may have been the reason for the petition mentioned above.

panies were promised land in part return for their investment and some of them took up their allotments and sent over servants to occupy them. Others received the equivalent in the form of private plantations and proceeded to build up miniature colonies of their own. Still others became members of the Council for New England, not with the desire in most cases to promote colonization, but in the expectation of land grants that would give them claims to areas of territory in the New World. How the Puritan gentry felt about land has already been narrated, but their attitude can be further emphasized by the plea which Sir Richard Saltonstall made to Emmanuel Downing in 1632, when he wrote that "if gentlemen of ability would transport themselves, they might advance their own estates and might improve their talents and times in being worthy instruments in propagating the Gospel."[1]

The interests and activities of these men of the proprietary classes, in all that concerned land in the New World, were many and continuous and while the effects were in most cases of short duration, in others they left so deep an impress upon our colonial history that they can be neither neglected nor ignored. From 1622 to 1639, beginning with the Scottish grant of Nova Scotia to Sir William Alexander and ending with the grant of Maine to Sir Ferdinando Gorges we have a series of proprietary patents that are strikingly indicative of the desire of the nobility and lesser baronetage of England to find overseas opportunities for the enlargement of their estates and the increase of their revenues. Conspicuous among them were members of that group of closely related families, Lenox, Arundel and Surrey, and Calvert, all of whom became participants in the Council for New England at its formation in 1620 and received a grant of land in 1622, to be called "New Albion."[2] Henry Lord Maltravers (1608–1652), son of the second earl of Arundel and Surrey, had married the daughter of the Earl of Lenox[3] and in 1632 bought of Sir Robert Heath his patent to lands south of Virginia, planning to establish

1. Historical Manuscripts Commission, *Coke*, I, 449.
2. *Calendar State Papers, Colonial*, 1574–1660, p. 32.
3. This marriage stirred the anger of Charles I, who had planned that Elizabeth, the duke's daughter, should marry a son of the Duke of Argyle (Historical Manuscripts Commission, *Skrine*, pp. 50, 52–53, 54, 56, 72–73, 143). He caused the father, the Earl of Arundel and Surrey, to be imprisoned in the Tower, and in so doing brought on something of a constitutional crisis, because the House of Lords deemed the imprisonment a breach of its privileges. Eventually, Charles I had to give way and restore to the earl his freedom and his offices.

there several plantations within what was designed to be a feudal principality across the seas. Of this plan something will be said later. Calvert's ventures in Newfoundland and Maryland probably had something to do with inciting Maltravers to purchase the Heath patent. The Earl of Arundel and Surrey had taken shares in the Amazon Company as early as 1618 and together with Lenox and Calvert was often called upon for advice whenever colonial questions arose at court.[1] In 1637 Maltravers, while pursuing his plans for a settlement of "Carolana," was combining with others for the founding of a West India Company, the object of which was to invade the Spanish islands and to distribute the conquered territory among themselves and others,[2] thus anticipating Cromwell's expedition of 1654. The many schemes of this powerful group, which had suffered heavily because of the attainder of the first earl and the forfeiture of his ancestral estates, had accomplished nothing more than to give the name of Norfolk to a county in Virginia. The place of the Earl of Southampton in the business of settling Virginia has already been recounted and it is only necessary to add that he too left his name on the American map in both Virginia and Bermuda. The important part which was taken by the earls of Carlisle, Pembroke, and Montgomery in the settlement of the islands in the Caribbean will be dealt with in the next chapter. The Earl of Holland, brother of the Earl of Warwick, was nominally the head of the Providence Company, though he took little interest in any colonial ventures and invested no money in company stock. With the avarice characteristic of many a peer of the day, he hoped to share in the profits without putting down the stakes. As his biographer says, "he preferred monopolies and crown grants as a quicker method of improving his fortunes."[3]

Among the futile enterprises of this period, comparable with those of Alexander and Hamilton in the persistence with which the claim was followed up, was the grandiose effort made by Sir Edmund Plowden in 1632 to found a palatinate on the soil of America. This effort was based upon a patent of doubtful legality, issued in 1634

1. *Calendar State Papers, Colonial*, 1574–1660, pp. 23, 26.
2. *Ibid.*, p. 257.
3. *Dictionary of National Biography;* Newton, *Colonizing Activities*, p. 61. Holland, with David Kirke, the Marquis of Hamilton, and the Earl of Pembroke, was one of the proprietors of Newfoundland, but he took no part in the despoiling of the Baltimores (above, Vol. I, 311).

by Lord Strafford, lord chancellor of Ireland, for land in the region of the Delaware River—covering the present territory of Long Island, New Jersey, eastern Pennsylvania, and parts of Delaware and Maryland—to be held of the king as of the crown of Ireland. Aroused by the success of Sir George Calvert and his son Cecilius, both of whom he knew well, Plowden, a Roman Catholic, obtained the coöperation of a number of gentlemen, and, gathering a collection of servants under various forms of indenture,[1] went himself to America. He lived in Accomac and Northampton counties, Virginia, for seven years, 1641–1648, while his followers built Fort Eriwonick on the east side of the Delaware in what was later to become Gloucester county, endeavoring persistently but vainly to obtain possession of his domain in the face of determined Swedish opposition. In the end his palatinate and his hopes alike vanished and his title of earl palatine proved as illusory as had Alexander's title of proprietary lord of Nova Scotia.[2]

Of all the claims based on the distributions by the Council for New England in 1634, only four had had enough vitality to survive in any form. These were the claims of Captain John Mason, which in conjunction with his earlier Laconia grant from the council was destined to give birth to the independent colony of New Hampshire; that of Sir Ferdinando Gorges which received confirmation at the hands of the crown in 1639; that of Sir William Alexander, Earl of Stirling, which, though without royal confirmation, became the basis of the later patent to the Duke of York in 1664 and the origin of a number of land titles in Long Island;[3] and that of James,

1. Some of the terms of these indentures may be found in *Maryland Archives*, IV, 210, 224, 358.

2. The petition to the king is in the Earl of Strafford's *Letters and Despatches*, I, 73 (1632); *Calendar State Papers, Colonial*, 1574–1660, p. 154. For further information see Keen, "Note on New Albion," Winsor, *Narrative and Critical History*, III, 457–468; *Collections*, New York Historical Society, 1869, pp. 213–222. See also *Maryland Archives*, IV, 205; V, 454. There is a small quarto, *A Description of the Province of New Albion*, by Beauchamp Plantagenet, printed at London, 1648, regarding which see Taylor, *Late Tudor and Early Stuart Geography*, pp. 173–174. The name of the writer is suspiciously romantic and clearly fictitious, but the tract is illuminating as showing one Englishman's notion of an ideal colonial life. The work contains also what is probably an authentic letter from Captain Evelyn. For an estimate see Paltsits, "Founding of New Amsterdam in 1626," *Proceedings*, American Antiquarian Society, April, 1924, pp. 42–44. See also *Memoirs*, Pennsylvania Historical Society, IV, pt. 1. The *Description* has been reprinted in Humphrey's *Tracts*, 1898.

3. This subject has been well treated by Miss Calder in "The Earl of Stirling and

third marquis of Hamilton, who claimed lands in southern New England—eastern Connecticut and the Narragansett country—a claim that was revived after the Restoration by his heirs and made the authorities of Connecticut considerable trouble.[1] The Hamilton demand was dismissed by the Privy Council on the recommendation of the Board of Trade because the board believed that "the revival of all the dormant titles under the grants of the Council of Plymouth would lead to unspeakable disturbance and confusion."[2] This decision ended all further attempts to obtain proprietorships in America, based on the distribution of 1635.

Other efforts were equally unsuccessful. Lord Culpeper, whom we shall meet again in connection with the Fairfax proprietorship, took part in the affairs of the Atherton Company in 1680, in the hope of obtaining eventually a share of the Narragansett country, which he and others of the company wished to hold of the crown as a proprietary domain.[3] Richard Wharton of Massachusetts, a leading land engrosser of the colony and a member of the Atherton Company, sought in 1683 to secure land in Maine whereon to erect a manor, and with others of the colony to advance an undertaking on the Merrimac River, known as the Million Purchase, for which they sought a patent from the crown which should invest them with extensive rights and privileges on payment of a quit-rent to the king.[4] In these enterprises, which partook of a proprietary character,

the Colonization of Long Island," *Essays in Colonial History*, pp. 74–95. The grant of 1664 to the Duke of York was made up of three parts—the Dutch territory of New Netherland, Maine, and Long Island: the last named the duke, with £3500 borrowed of the Earl of Clarendon, bought of John Lord Berkeley and Stirling's son.

1. Bond, *Quit-Rent System*, p. 41 note, where the present writer has given a brief outline of the case based on the *Calendar of State Papers, Colonial, 1661–1668*, §§735, 1089; 1696–1697, §§962, 992, 993, 995, 1234; *Connecticut Colonial Records*, III, 136, 333–336; Trumbull, *Connecticut*, I, appendix xv.

2. C. O. 5:907, pp. 221–238; *Calendar State Papers, Colonial, 1696–1697*, §1234 (p. 579). Anne, Duchess of Hamilton, daughter of the first duke and duchess in her own right, was at the same time endeavoring to recover her title to certain properties and arrears in France (Historical Manuscripts Commission, *Bath*, III, 118), and we know that her grandson, James, the fifth duke (son of the fourth duke killed in the duel with Lord Mohun [1712] as narrated in Thackeray's *Henry Esmond*), was desirous of reviving his claim to the lands in New England as late as 1722 (*Board of Trade Journal*, 1718–1722, p. 344).

3. *Calendar State Papers, Colonial, 1685–1688*, §§1594, 1695; the representation of the Lords of Trade is in C. O. 5:905, pp. 8–9; Barnes, "Richard Wharton," *Publications*, Colonial Society of Massachusetts, 26, pp. 245–247.

4. *Ibid.*, pp. 247–250. William Blathwayt apparently accepted a share in the Million Purchase, in return for his influence at court. Miss Jacobsen, in *William Blath-*

the undertakers had little trouble in persuading Englishmen of influence to aid their cause on promise of a share in the venture.

Even in the eighteenth century the hope still remained strong in the minds of titled men in England of financial profit from lands in the New World. In 1717 Sir Robert Mountgomery of Shilmore, Bart., a Scotsman, prompted by a desire for revenue from tenancies and rents, acting in conjunction with Abel Ketelby, a landgrave of Carolina, obtained from the Carolina proprietors a grant of land lying between the Savannah and Altamaha rivers, including the "Golden Islands" of San Simón, Zapala (San José), and Santa Catalina, whereon he proposed to erect a seignory to be known as the margraviate of Azilia, a title undoubtedly selected because of the seignory's frontier character as a buffer colony between the Spanish and English possessions. This margraviate was to be quite distinct from the province of South Carolina and independent of its laws, and of it Mountgomery was to be the governor for life, subject only to confirmation by the crown. He issued a "Discourse" concerning the proposed settlement and in a memorial to the Board of Trade and a further elaboration of his scheme at a hearing before that body he explained the conditions of settlement and organization. He did not propose to depend entirely on the subscriptions of land purchasers, but was already assured of the coöperation of others—relatives, friends, and investors—who had increased his own private stock to a total of £30,000. He opened land-books at the Carolina Coffee House, near the Royal Exchange, where after August 1, 1717, he was prepared to enter the names of any who desired to migrate, and he felt confident that in carrying out his project he would be doing something of great advantage to the kingdom, particularly in protecting the southern frontier against Spain.[1]

---

wayt, pp. 463–466, discusses the various charges of covetousness brought against Blathwayt and finds little legitimate basis for them. The Revolution of 1689 in England and America brought all these schemes to naught.

1. *A Discourse concerning the Design'd Establishment of a New Colony to the South of Carolina, in the most delightful country of the Universe* (London, 1717). The large folding map, which accompanies this pamphlet, shows the proposed plan of settling the districts or county divisions. For an understanding of Mountgomery's scheme, the pamphlet should be supplemented by Mountgomery's memorial to the Board of Trade (*Calendar State Papers, Colonial,* 1717–1718, §389) and by his remarks at the hearing of February 25, 1718 (*Journal, Board of Trade,* 1715–1718, p. 343). A very imperfect abstract of the contents of the pamphlet is given in Winsor, *Narrative and Critical History,* V, 460. For Aaron Hill's connection with the Mountgomery scheme see Brewster, *Aaron Hill,* pp. 50–59.

On presentation from the Carolina proprietors the terms of the grant came before the Privy Council, because of the requirement that the proprietor's appointment of Mountgomery as governor for life be ratified by the king. The committee of the council sent the presentation to the Board of Trade, which despatched it to Attorney General Northey for an opinion as to the legality of the grant. Northey reported that the grant was in the form of a lease and release (similar to that of 1664 from the Duke of York to Carteret and Berkeley), and while he saw nothing in it prejudicial to the rights of the crown, should the king approve a governor for life, nevertheless he doubted whether the Carolina proprietors could divide the powers granted them and hand over a part of these powers to another proprietor as the head of an independent government. He suggested that the only legal remedy was the surrender of the Carolina charter and the issue of another embodying the changes.[1] The question in Northey's mind was entirely one of government and not of tenure or of seignorial rights, to which naturally he had no objection. When the matter came again before the Board of Trade, the latter based its recommendation of April 9, 1718, upon Northey's opinion but added a further and important objection of its own. It opposed any increase in the number of charter and proprietary governments because of the difficulties which the English authorities experienced in compelling all private owners to conform to the trading interests of the kingdom, an opinion similar to that already expressed by the earlier members of the board in 1697. The Privy Council accepted the recommendation and in an order in council issued before July 24 dismissed entirely the plea of the Carolina proprietors.[2]

After the Treaty of Utrecht in 1713, the uncultivated lands of the smaller islands of the Caribbean had an irresistible attraction for those in search of vacant territory that might be used for the advancement of trade and the making of profit. British merchants were

1. Northey's opinion is in *Calendar State Papers, Colonial*, 1717–1718, §459.
2. *Ibid.*, §493. The representation of April 9, 1718, is in C. O. 5:1293, pp. 145–147, abstracted in *Calendar State Papers, Colonial*, 1717–1718, §493. Oddly enough the order in council is not given in *Acts Privy Council, Colonial*, but we know that it was issued from an entry in the *Board of Trade Journal*, 1715–1718, p. 415. That Mountgomery was having financial troubles and probably difficulties also in attracting emigrants appears from his request, made in August, 1718, that he be allowed to erect a lottery in Edinburgh or in any one of the Scottish royal boroughs for the purpose of raising a fund. *Calendar State Papers, Colonial*, 1717–1718, §671.

opposed to enlarging the number of islands engaged in the production of sugar as likely to injure the interests of sugar planters in the other British possessions, but they recognized the usefulness of new lands for the raising of such other commodities as cocoa, indigo, and anotto, which at the time had to be purchased largely from the French. As such purchase was contrary to the dictates of mercantilism, the Board of Trade was ready to listen to any reasonable request looking to the improvement of the situation. Many suggestions were advanced for the disposal of the lands of St. Lucia, St. Vincent, and Tobago.[1] But as nothing was done and as the proposed grants were to be made to others than Englishmen and were in no way different from similar forms of allotment elsewhere they do not concern us here. More important was it that in 1722, John, second duke of Montague, should have petitioned the king for a grant of these islands, proposing to erect them into a seignory and manor, with the usual privileges of a lord, such as he was accustomed to exercise on his manor of Bewley at home.[2] The board was favorably impressed and the grant was made June 22, 1722.[3] In the same year

1. *Ibid.*, 1720–1721, §§87, 143, 666, 721, 724. For the attempts of the dukes of Courland to occupy the island of Tobago, see H. I. Woodcock, a former chief justice of Tobago, *History of the Island of Tobago* (1867), II, 26–31. The island was settled in 1630 but the settlement was broken up by the Spaniards in 1634. In 1642 it was granted by Charles I to the elder duke, James, who made a beginning there at Great Courland Bay. This settlement was taken over by the Dutch during Courland's troubles with the Swedes and a regrant was made in 1664 to James, who arranged with Captain Pointz to reoccupy the island (Blome, *Present State*, pp. 253, 259–262). After James' death, Frederick Casimir, the younger duke, requested in 1683 a renewal of the grant, asking that the claim be recognized by Charles II (*Calendar State Papers, Colonial*, 1681–1685, *passim*). In the same year he issued two pamphlets, *Present Prospect of the Famous and Fertile Island of Tobago* and *Proposals to all such People as are minded to Transport or Concern themselves in the Island of Tobago* (these were apparently the same proposals as those of Captain Pointz above), but without result. In 1686 the duke sent Baron Blumberg to England to press his claim, but after a year's consideration Charles II, acting on the advice of his attorney general, rescinded the grant, because the duke would not hold the island as a fief of the English crown. There is a description of Tobago in Sloane, 3662, which is printed in *West India and Guiana* (Hakluyt Society, Series II, Harlow ed.), pp. 103–108.

2. *Acts Privy Council, Colonial*, VI, §589; C. O. 29:14, pp. 289–290.

3. Representation of February 1, 1722. In this representation the Board of Trade said, "These are two of your Majesty's Windward Charibbee Islands at present comprehended in the Commission of your Majesty's governor of Barbados, but as they have neither of them been hitherto settled they produce no revenue to the Crown, nor any advantage to these kingdoms. It would therefore undoubtedly be for your Majesty's service that the same should be effectually settled and planted, and so much the rather because the French have heretofore made several attempts to possess them to the manifest Prejudice of your Majesty's Title."

Montague sent out Captain Nathaniel Uring with seven ships containing five hundred settlers with their families, but both at St. Lucia and at St. Vincent the French prevented their landing. Montague is said to have spent £40,000 in the undertaking.[1]

Driven from St. Lucia and St. Vincent, the duke renewed his petition in 1728, but this time asked for Tobago only, as a seignory and proprietary settlement, within which to erect manors and bailiwicks and to enjoy the rights of a lord and proprietor. But the board, though recommending that the petition be granted, refused to agree to the concession of seignorial and proprietary privileges and insisted that Tobago be erected into a crown colony of the usual type. It made the following pertinent comment, "We have found by experience that all proprietary colonies, where the government is not in the Crown, are highly detrimental to your Majesty's service and to the welfare of Great Britain. . . . In case your Majesty should be pleased to grant the Island of Tobago to the Duke of Montague, it will be requisite that particular care be taken to reserve to your Majesty and to your Heirs and Successors the absolute sovereignty, dominion and government of Tobago, in as full and ample manner as your Majesty does now or may exercise the same in Barbadoes."[2] This enunciation, taken in conjunction with previous and similar utterances of the board, which we have already noted, is of great significance as showing the determination of the British government

1. *Relation of the late Intended Settlement of the Islands of St. Lucia and St. Vincent in America in the Right of the Duke of Montague, and under his Grace's Direction and Orders in 1722,* with maps and plans, two volumes in one (London, 1725). Also *Voyages and Travels of Capt. Nathaniel Uring* (London, 1726). This work includes "A Voyage to Boston in New England and the West Indies, in which Voyage he was again taken by the French; with a short description of New England, their Trade and Product, and the Nature and Manners of the Indians." There is a brief account of St. Lucia in 1655, in *Venables Narrative* (Camden Series, 1900), p. 147.

2. The first report of the Board of Trade is in C. O. 29:14, pp. 286–290; and the second in the same pp. 434–438. An abstract of the latter is in *Acts Privy Council,* VI, §401.

Nothing further was done about Tobago. These smaller islands remained a subject of dispute between Great Britain and France until Dominica, St. Vincent, Tobago, and Grenada were ceded to the British crown in 1763. St. Lucia was given to France, but in 1803 was captured by Great Britain, after years of terrific fighting, during which it is said that more British and French blood was spilt on the slopes of Morne Fortuné than on any other spot of the same size in the world. In the readjustments of 1814 the island was finally recognized as belonging to Great Britain. A very vivid description of some of this fighting is in Willyams, *An Account of the Campaign in the West Indies in 1794, with the Reduction of the Islands of Martinique, St. Lucia, Guadeloupe, Marigalante, Desiada, etc.* (1796).

to centralize colonial administration and to prevent any further increase in the number of private proprietary colonies. Even in the case of Georgia, founded in 1732, the trustees were to remain in control for only twenty years, after which the colony was to revert to the crown. Connecticut, Rhode Island, Maryland, and Pennsylvania were allowed to remain in largest part because their charters conveyed franchises that could not be taken away except by due process of law. By 1722, therefore, we can say that British policy as far as it concerned the status of the colonies in America and their relations with the mother country had at last taken definite and permanent form.

The least known of all these unsuccessful attempts of Englishmen to obtain lands in America whereon to erect English estates, with their accompanying tenancies, leases, and rents, is that of the Duke of Chandos in the years from 1731 to 1738.[1] Chandos had heard from Francis Harison of New York (collector of customs there, for a short time judge of vice-admiralty, and a persistent and a none too honorable applicant for political and monetary favors of any kind), of certain lands that had come into the hands of the crown. These lands, amounting to some 62,000 acres, were ceded to New York as the result of an agreement between New York and Connecticut, whereby a strip along the western boundary of the latter colony was given in exchange for an equivalent number of acres forming the rectangular block at the southwestern corner of the present state of Connecticut. The duke, financially embarrassed at the time, saw an opportunity to obtain possession of this strip, as an addition to his home estates, and so to provide for the future of his family. He was led to believe that the region was favorable to the production of hemp, pitch, tar, and other naval stores and well situated for trade with the Indians. He saw there also possible mines, minerals, and veins of saltpetre and he looked to the lands as likely to bring in a

---

1. The Chandos case is interesting as disclosing the ideas that prevailed in the minds of a group of Englishmen regarding the value of lands obtained by grant in America. The evidence in the case is unique in that from the Chandos Letter Books (Huntington Library, particularly volumes 35–53) one can obtain the entire history of the enterprise in great detail. They show the difficulties met in securing the patent, the offices visited, the authorities solicited, and the delays encountered. I know of nothing comparable with this evidence as throwing light not only on the transaction in question but also on office seeking in general, together with the life and troubles of a peer of the realm and the estates and revenues of a country gentleman of high rank.

profit of at least £10,000 a year. He was enamored with the idea of having a property of his own in the New World and at one time in the course of the negotiations he thought of going to America himself and even toyed with the notion of obtaining a commission as governor of New York. But Lady Chandos' health forbade and he was "growing old and become useless."

At first Chandos considered the possibility of obtaining the grant in the usual way from the governor of New York, but fearing prolonged delay and possible failure, he decided to appeal directly to the crown. Unwilling to make the appeal openly, he entered the application in the name of four of his friends, Sir John Eyles, Jonathan Perrie, John Drummond, and Thomas Watts, all members of parliament and men of influence in the business life of the City of London.[1] The grant was obtained on May 15, 1631. A month later and before news of the royal patent had reached New York, a group of New York and Connecticut men obtained from Governor Montgomerie a provincial patent for 50,000 acres within the same area. It is impossible to narrate here the history of the contest that followed between the two groups of patentees. The issue got mixed up

1. Sir John Eyles was the brother of Sir Joseph Eyles and the son or nephew of Sir Joseph Eyles, lord mayor of London, who had been chosen mayor in September, 1688, then turned out with all the aldermen in October by James II, and finally reinstated the following year by William III. The members of the Eyles family were all interested in the Barbados trade and held various offices under government. Joseph was concerned with the settlement of Georgia, was at one time in service under the paymaster of the forces, and later became one of the postmasters general; John had been a director of the South Sea Company and was mixed up with the South Sea business. Nearly all of the Eyleses were loyal supporters of George II and Walpole. Perrie was the son of Edward Perrie, formerly the surveyor general of Barbados, was one of the London members of parliament, and a great trader in the West Indies, specializing in the importation of Spanish tobacco. John Drummond, the chairman of the patentees, and interested in the Hamburg Company and the fisheries, was the brother of Andrew Drummond, member of parliament from Scotland, one of the East New Jersey proprietors, and a great friend of Governor Montgomerie of New York. Andrew was at one time the treasurer of the group. Watts was connected with the Sunfire Assurance Company and acted for a time as treasurer in place of Andrew Drummond. He had a brother in Tower Street who taught business accounts and took lodgers. He was the "contact" man for Chandos, doing much of the drudgery of soliciting at the offices and employing brokers. Colonel Martin Bladen, a neighbor of the Eyleses, whom Chandos calls "the oracle of the Board of Trade," was frequently consulted but refused to join. John Sharpe, the solicitor (brother of Joshua, the clerk of the Privy Council), Sir Mathew Decker (a great friend of Chandos'), Colonel Samuel Robinson, chamberlain of the City of London (influential "behind the curtain"), came into the picture on the English side, and Governor Cosby, George Clark, and others on the New York side. Ferdinand John Paris was the agent in England for those in New York who opposed the royal grant.

with the wrangling already taking place between the prerogative and popular parties in the province. Conspicuous among the New York patentees were James Alexander and William Smith, two of the ablest attorneys in the colony, whom Chandos characterized as "a couple of dangerous fellows"—as they were from his point of view—and their argument in the case as "one of the closest and shrewdest papers I have met with." Distance, bad advice, and poor service prolonged the litigation until Chandos became thoroughly tired of the unexpected difficulties encountered. "That we have been grossly abused in the management of the whole affair [he wrote in 1738] is the opinion of everyone I have heard speak of it." Regarding Harison who got him into the mess, he said, "I never saw him to the best of my remembrances in all my life; I never had any acquaintance with him; I know not what became of him; and it would have been very fortunate for me if I had never heard from him." Increasing charges and growing uncertainty as to the outcome finally brought Chandos to the mood of not caring whether he succeeded or not. By 1740 he had allowed the case to go by default, and we hear no more of the matter.

The last of these unsuccessful attempts made during our colonial period to fasten an English seignorial system upon the soil of America and certainly the most extraordinary exhibit that we have of the working of the English mind on the eve of the Revolution is that of John Percival, second earl of Egmont, in 1763. Egmont petitioned the king for a grant of the island of St. John (Prince Edward Island), for the purpose of erecting there a military and tenurial settlement of an extreme feudal type. We pay attention to Locke's Fundamental Constitutions of Carolina, largely because some of its provisions were put into actual operation, but no one has ever discussed Egmont's fantastic scheme, although many prominent Englishmen of the time thought well of it and underwrote it. This fact alone is of historical importance, not for the destinies of America but for the Englishman's outlook on the colonies and his ideas regarding the disposal of the lands newly acquired as one result of the treaty of Paris. Egmont estimated these lands at 1,200,000,000 acres, and wished to divide them into sixty-two provinces, each larger than Pennsylvania. He formulated a plan which he believed would contribute greatly to the strength and safety of his Majesty's empire in America, insure the settlement of North America and the sugar islands, serve to prevent all clandestine trade with the French islands, which he feared was increasing, and lead all to coöperate in excluding the French and confining the commerce of America and the West Indies to Englishmen only. There is no need of expounding here in detail the proposed organization of these sixty-two provinces or Egmont's elaborate scheme for his own island of St. John, with its baronies or hundreds, manors, freeholders (no copyholders are mentioned), courts baron and leet, quit-rents and services, burgage and socage tenures, lord paramount, capital lords and lords of manors. What he advocated was in full accord with English common and statute law and with English tenurial practices at the time, more so indeed than was Locke's more academic and artificial arrangement of nearly one hundred years before.[1] As a combined military and tenurial plan for the protection and development of the American frontier it deserves study, if for no other reason than to show how little prominent and influential men in England understood the forces that were behind what is called the Western Movement in America. Even the best of these men were unable to conceive of any other conditions than those with which they were familiar at home or to think of these lands except in terms of their value to England only. Happily the members of the Privy Council had sense enough to see how utterly futile the whole plan was and how incapable it was of execution in view of the state of British finances at the close of the Seven Years' War.[2]

In two instances, however, proprietary ownership, in which the

1. *To the King's Most Excellent Majesty, the Memorial of John,* [2nd] *Earl of Egmont* [1711–1770], *most humbly showeth, that the said Earl desires from his Majesty a grant of the whole Island of Saint John's in the Gulph of St. Lawrence, to hold the same in Fee of the Crown for ever, as one entire County* (London, 1763, reprinted 1765), 32 pages. The work has no title page. It begins as above on page 1 and is inscribed on the lower margin *"For Perusal of Thomas Earl of Kinnoul, P. C. only."*

This exceedingly rare pamphlet, a copy of which was recently offered for sale at ten guineas, was privately printed for distribution only among officials and others who might be interested in the scheme. On pp. 21–22 there is an explanatory footnote outlining the plan in seven paragraphs. At the end is a list of officers, merchants, and others desirous of taking part in the enterprise and engaged to assist the earl in settling the island. Among those enlisted are Admirals Knowles, Saunders, Townshend, and Rodney, Generals Townshend, Monckton, and Oglethorpe, Colonel Tarleton, and many others. I know of no copy of the pamphlet in this country. For an abstract and in part transcript of the copy in the British Museum I am indebted to my friend and former student, Miss Elizabeth E. Hoon.

2. *Acts Privy Council, Colonial,* IV, §542; VI, §§585, 639, 722; C. O. 218:6, pp. 268–273; *Board of Trade Journal,* 1764–1767, index, *s.v.* "Percival."

landlord had only title to the soil and, unlike the proprietors of Maryland and Pennsylvania, no rights of government did get established in the colonies and lasted until after the Revolution. These were the instances of Lord Fairfax in Virginia and of Lord Granville in North Carolina.

The great Fairfax proprietorship, a vast domain of some five million acres lying between the Potomac and Rappahannock rivers and stretching back through the wilderness to the first springs of these rivers, had its origin in a grant by Charles II in 1649. The king, then in exile,[1] desirous of compensating certain of his loyal adherents for the loss of their forfeited estates in England and of furnishing them with a refuge, should they need it, in America, patented the unsettled portions of northern Virginia to Ralph Lord Hopton, Henry Lord Jermyn, John Lord Culpeper, Sir John Berkeley, Sir William Morton, Sir Dudley Wyatt, and Thomas Culpeper, a cousin of Lord Culpeper.[2] This territory, known in its lower section as the Northern Neck, was not immediately utilized by its grantees, because the province of Virginia was taken by the Commonwealth fleet before anything could be done. But immediately after the Restoration the claim was renewed, only to be bitterly opposed by the Virginians, who had begun to settle in the region and who feared a repetition of the Maryland grant and a further loss of territory. The claimants appealed to the king and a compromise was reached whereby the patent of 1649 was surrendered and a new one issued, May 8, 1669.[3] This patent was ratified in Virginia and land grants in the region ceased to be made in the colony.

At this juncture the whole matter was given an unexpected turn by the action of Charles II in granting, February 25, 1673, to the Earl of Arlington and Thomas Lord Culpeper, eldest son of the original proprietor, the whole of Virginia, as far as soil and regalities were concerned.[4] The grant was for thirty-one years at the yearly

---

1. For the king's residence at this time at St. Helier's, Isle of Jersey, Clarendon. *Life of Himself,* I, 199–200, 201. Lord Hopton was a prominent Somerset royalist, of whom something will be said later. He died in 1652.

2. On Culpeper and the Culpeper genealogy see Fairfax Harrison, "The Proprietors of the Northern Neck, Chapters of Culpeper Genealogy," *Virginia Magazine,* April, July, 1925; January, 1926.

3. *Acts Privy Council, Colonial,* I, §611; *Calendar State Papers, Colonial,* 1669–1674, §§63, 145, 146. The ratification is in *Virginia Council Minutes,* I, 247, 281, 296.

4. *Calendar State Papers, Colonial,* 1669–1674, §769; Hening, *Statutes,* II, 569–578.

rent of forty shillings. This unforeseen event alarmed the Virginians largely because of the fears entertained as to the extent of the regalities that might be demanded. There was no opposition in the colony to the king's grant of the quit-rents and no intention in the mind of the king of removing the territory from under the control of the colony's government, as had been done in the case of Maryland, but the extensive powers named in the patent promised to make trouble.

Culpeper was the manager of the whole affair. He secured the aid of Arlington, at that time one of the principal secretaries of state, in order to obtain recompense (as William Penn did later) for £12,000, which the Culpepers had loaned the king.[1] In 1681 and 1683 he bought out the other claimants, Arlington and the survivors among the patentees of 1649, and became himself sole proprietor and the receiver of the quit-rents. In 1680 he had become governor of the colony, thus combining in himself both the governorship and the proprietorship of the soil. His failure as governor led to his return to England in 1683 and there he sold to the crown (May 27, 1684) all his rights, except those to the Northern Neck lands, in return for £700 down and a pension of £600 a year for twenty-one years.[2] The Northern Neck was confirmed to him as sole owner and

---

1. The will of John Lord Culpeper, made July 3, 1660, contains this clause, "Whereas His Majesty in answer to my petition of 27 June last hath engaged his royal word for payment of £12000 out of his first receipts for clearing of my paternal estate and toward paying fortunes to my younger children, I beg His Majesty, toward redeeming of my distressed family and Estate from ruin, His Majesty will take order with his Court of Exchequer that the whole debt of £12000 may be punctually paid to my executor, my eldeste son and heir Thomas Culpeper to be executor." "Proprietors of the Northern Neck," *Virginia Magazine*, XXXIII, 243–244. This learned article (in three parts), *Virginia Land Grants* (privately printed, 1925), and H. C. Groome, "Northern Neck Lands," *Bulletin*, Fauquier Historical Society, August, 1921, are indispensable aids to an understanding of the Fairfax proprietorship.

2. *Calendar State Papers, Colonial*, 1681–1685, §§1289, 1395, 1771, 1815; *Acts Privy Council, Colonial*, II, p. 143, Blathwayt Entry Books, Treasury 64: 88, pp. 122–133, 193, 226–240, 254–256, 303–304; *William and Mary Quarterly*, VI, 222–226; *Calendar, Treasury Books*, IX, part IV, 1503–1504. Culpeper's pension was charged against the budget of the military establishment and was paid to him until 1689 and, after his death in that year, to his younger brother, John, third Lord Culpeper, until April 24, 1700, when it ceased. Sometime in the year 1702 the fifth Lord Fairfax, who had married Catherine, daughter of Thomas, second Lord Culpeper, and was the executor of the third lord, sent in a memorial, saying that on June 9, 1702, there was due £1550, and he asked that payments be continued until 1705, which would mark the expiration of the twenty-one year period, either out of the military establishment or out of the Virginia quit-rents. Probably nothing more was ever paid. The Fairfax memorial is among the Blathwayt Papers, "Virginia," in the Hunting-

to his descendants and assigns by a patent issued September 28, 1688, without limitation of time and with a new definition of the boundaries. For "heads" of the rivers was substituted "first heads or springs," a change that was to make a great deal of trouble later.[1]

Culpeper died in 1689 and his interest went to his wife, Margaretta, with their daughter, Catherine, as heiress. The latter married the fifth Lord Fairfax. Now it happened that a cousin, Alexander, as the son of Thomas Culpeper, had received from one of the original patentees of 1649 a sixth part of the Northern Neck, and this right had been confirmed by James II in 1688, independently of the Culpeper patent of that year. The claimants were, therefore, four: Lady Margaretta, Catherine, Lord Fairfax, and Alexander Culpeper, all of whose rights were confirmed by order in council, January 26, 1693, to the great dissatisfaction of the Virginians, who had hoped that William would buy out all the claims.[2] The four were reduced to one by the death in 1694 of Alexander, who left his sixth to Margaretta; of Thomas Lord Fairfax, in 1710, who left his interest to his wife Catherine; and of Margaretta in the same year who left the sixth part received from Alexander to her grandson Thomas, the sixth Lord Fairfax. From 1710 to 1719 Catherine and her son were joint proprietors. In 1719 Catherine died and Thomas became the sole lord of the propriety.[3] From this time forward he controlled the estate, at first with Robert Carter as his agent, whose zealous regard for the proprietor's rights[4] stirred up a good deal of resentment in

ton Library. There is also in the same library (Bridgewater-Ellesmere, 9574) a paper on the "Lord Fairfax and Lady Culpeper case," which shows how difficult it was for an Englishman of the period to conceive of the possession of land in the colonies except in terms of his own tenancies.

1. *Virginia Magazine*, XV, 392–399, especially notes, pp. 393–394, and for the rewording, p. 396.

2. *Calendar State Papers, Colonial*, 1693–1696, §34. In 1708 the fifth Lord Fairfax rejected the suggestion that he exchange his share of the estate for the "Lott and Cape and office of Bergmaster in the Wapentake of Wirksworth in the county of Derby." Blathwayt, Entry Book, II, 401; *Acts Privy Council, Colonial*, VI, §225, *Virginia Magazine*, XXXIV, 23–24.

3. *Virginia Magazine*, IX, 31–33; *Journals House of Burgesses*, 1690–1693, p. 371; *Acts Privy Council, Colonial*, II, §404; *Calendar State Papers, Colonial*, 1689–1692, §1514; 1693–1696, §34. Thomas had one share of his own and the other five shares as beneficiary under his mother's will in trust.

4. In a letter from Carter to William Cage (for whom see *Virginia Magazine*, XXXIV, 25 note) July 25, 1725, the former insists on Fairfax's right to the deodands ("I was in possession of them all along in my first agency"), the goods of felons ("were entirely given up to me"), fines and forfeitures, and the belongings of a felo de se ("the matters in difference . . . which Mr. Attor⁷ is very sanguine in although

Virginia and led to an attempt on the part of the colony to wrest from Lord Fairfax a portion of the territory by refusing to accept his interpretation of the boundaries.

Into this dispute it is impossible to enter.[1] The point at issue was how far up the Potomac and the Rappahannock the Fairfax property extended and what were the "first heads or springs." The suit lasted from 1733 to 1748 and was finally decided in Fairfax's favor, more than doubling his estate. With this matter settled Fairfax returned to Virginia and took up his permanent residence in the colony. About 1751 he built a modest house in the Shenandoah valley, which he called Greenway Court, after an ancestral manor in Kent. He died there in 1781.[2]

The Fairfax estate was neither a palatinate nor a proprietary colony, for Fairfax had no powers of government, being wholly under the authority of the colony of Virginia in all save the rights and incidents of property. His was a great landed domain, within which were reproduced many of the tenurial features characteristic of the manorial system at home. While confirming the titles to all lands which had been granted within his territory by the governor and council of Virginia, he made his own grants in fee to applicants at his land office, following much the same procedure at that time adopted by the proprietors of Maryland and Pennsylvania. All the lands allotted carried a quit-rent of one shilling for fifty acres. Fair-

my lawyer is as positive against him"). "These things," he adds, "are not very considerable at present, but it may happen that in time they will be worth struggling for." Other letters, November 18, 1724, and December 16, 1727, says that the point in controversy was the ownership of the fines imposed in the county courts, which "according to the lawyer's phrase are 'franchises in the Crowne.'" Brock Papers, Huntington Library.

1. Fairfax first petitioned the crown in 1733. In 1735 he came to the colony for a year and entered into a kind of treaty-compromise with Virginia (Hening, *Statutes*, IV, 514–523; VI, 196). This agreement was confirmed by the Privy Council (*Acts Privy Council, Colonial*, III, p. 853) and validated titles. Next the boundary question was taken up and a commission appointed from England to make a survey (*ibid.*, §281, pp. 385–386). The decision was favorable to Fairfax and the colony finally accepted it. The Board of Trade then recommended that the Privy Council confirm it, which it did (pp. 386–391). Then the House of Burgesses also confirmed it in 1748, and the suit ended. The itemized bill, which Ferdinand John Paris, the solicitor for the crown, handed in for "business done and money laid out," from April 30, 1739, to May 6, 1742, amounted to £142. 19. 9 (Treasury 1: bundle 335, fo. 95). Paris was probably paid eventually, but he waited a long time for his money.

2. Groome, *Fauquier during the Proprietorship*, pp. 73–77. For the later history of the proprietorship see the same, pp. 218–240; *Virginia Land Grants*, pp. 117–121; and Beveridge, *Life of Marshall*, II, IV, index.

fax was authorized to erect manors, the title to which was to remain in himself, and he did so in three instances—Greenway manor where he lived and of which he retained the seignorial title, holding there a court baron of the freeholders, with himself as the presiding head; the manor of Leeds on the eastern slope of the Blue Ridge; and the South Branch manor on the west side of the valley. Lands within these manors were leased on easy terms for three lives (of the lessee and any other two persons the latter desired to name), or for a term of years. The lease was renewable at the expiration of the term on payment of a fine (relief) or one year's rent, which usually amounted to twenty shillings for a hundred acres. The tenants on the manors were responsible for all the colony rates and taxes, but not for the quit-rents, which were paid by the grantee of the manor.

Similar in principle but entirely different in the way it worked out was the Granville grant in North Carolina.[1] At the time of the surrender of their charter in 1729 the Carolina proprietors, one of whom was John Carteret (later, 1744, first earl Granville) refused to give up his claim to the soil, so that only seven-eighths of the territory of North and South Carolina and Georgia came under the proprietary control of the crown. Until 1743, one eighth of the quit-rents were always reserved for Carteret,[2] but in 1742 the Board of Trade recommended that the eighth part be laid off as a propriety. By order in council, on September 15 of that year, this recommendation was embodied in the king's instructions to Governor Johnston, issued April 25, 1743,[3] under whose direction the survey was begun. A line was drawn separating an area sixty miles in width (26,000 square miles in content, constituting the northern third of the col-

1. Coulter, "The Granville District," *James Sprunt Historical Collections*, XIII, no. 2; *North Carolina Colonial Records*, III, 32–47; IV, 655–663; V, lv–lxi; *History of North Carolina*, I, "The Colonial and Revolutionary Periods," by R. D. W. Connor, pp. 222–227; H. G. Connor, "The Granville Estate and North Carolina," *University of Pennsylvania Law Review*, 62, no. 9; Bond, *Quit-Rents*, pp. 76–82.

2. The following is the form of receipt given by the receiver general, "North Carolina. Received this 20th Day of *April*, 1742 of *John Hodgson, Esqr* the sum of *Fourteen pounds Currcy* being for *Three Years'* Quit-Rents due to the Crown the Twenty-fifth Day of March last, for *Three hundred and twelve* Acres of Land holden by the said *Hodgson* at *4/ pro[clamation money] per 100* and scituated in *Chowan* County.

"I say received for the Use of His Majesty and Lord Carteret." The portions italicised are written in, the remainder is a printed form.

3. C. O. 324:37, pp. 212–217.

ony) from the rest of North Carolina, the proprietary rights of which but not the government was handed over to Carteret. At first the line stopped at Bath, then in 1746 it was extended to the northeast branch of the Cape Fear River, where for a time it ended, because, as the commissioners reported, the region farther west was little settled and the difficulties of forage and housing were too great to make a more prolonged survey feasible.[1] The one-eighth part of the quit-rents had covered all three colonies, but the propriety was taken solely from North Carolina, a manifestly unfair arrangement. It is worthy of note, however, that when a few years later the quit-rents of that colony proved insufficient to meet Governor Johnston's salary, those of South Carolina were drawn on for the purpose, because it was felt that South Carolina was morally bound to bear some of the loss incurred by the setting off of the Granville section. It is also worthy of note that the locating of the Granville grant in North Carolina was a factor taken into account when the line between the two colonies North and South Carolina, was drawn farther south than might otherwise have been the case had it not been felt necessary to compensate North Carolina for the injury done her.[2]

Under the letters patent issued September 17, 1744, Lord Granville was confirmed in his grant and was authorized to receive all such rights, rents, revenues, and remainders as belonged to a territorial lord. His position was exactly the same as that of Lord Fairfax, except that he himself never came to the colony and was so deeply involved in political affairs at home as to pay little attention to his property overseas.[3] Consequently he never received anything like the same reward. Eventually he opened a land office in Eden-

1. The line started from a cedar post set up at the seaside, six and a half miles south of Chickinacomack Inlet and was carried westwardly just north of Bath Town and along the southern borders of the counties of Chatham, Randolph, Davidson, Rowan, and Iredell, where the line, forming the southern boundary of these counties, can be traced today. In 1766 it was extended to Rocky River in Rowan County and in 1774 to the Blue Ridge Mountains.

2. *North Carolina Colonial Records*, V, 383–384.

3. It is significant that neither in the article on Granville in the *D.N.B.* (1886), in Ballantyne's *Life of Carteret* (1887), nor in the recent life by W. Baring Pemberton (1936) is Carteret's possession of property in North Carolina so much as mentioned. Carteret had a barony also in South Carolina, granted in 1718, known as Hobcaw on Winyah Bay, which he held for twelve years. By deeds of lease and release he sold this barony in 1731. During these twelve years he made no effort to improve or cultivate his Hobcaw estate and apparently took no interest in it (Smith, *Baronies*, pp. 91–92; *Board of Trade Journal*, 1754–1758, pp. 151–152).

ton, and appointed, one after another, a series of agents who served him none too well. The land office was closed in 1765. Settlement of the territory was delayed by gross neglect and abuse on the part of the agents, by the difficulties placed in the way of obtaining grants, and by what the provincial assembly claimed were excessive fees. Complaints proved useless, for the colony had no proprietary control over the region and the discontent of the holders of the Granville land-scrip, though menacing at times, played but a minor part in the history of the province,[1] except as far as it had something to do with bringing on the Regulators' War.[2] Unlike the proprietorship of Lord Fairfax, which was never seriously disliked in Virginia, that of Lord Granville in North Carolina was a constant source of irritation and trouble. It led to quarrels and disputes, uncertainties of title, controversies with governor and council, and a widespread dissatisfaction within the district itself.

The only remedy would have been the purchase of Granville's rights by the crown and such a course was recommended by every governor and assembly from Dobbs to Martin, with the approval of the second Lord Granville.[3] Tryon said that the proprietary privileges, covering an area of thirteen entire townships, could be bought for £60,000 sterling, but the British government, trying at the time rather to extract money from the colonies than to spend money in the colonies, was neither willing nor able to meet any such outlay. The matter was not settled even with the coming of the Revolution, for not until November 15, 1777, was the property confiscated by the state. Later the Granville heirs made strenuous efforts to recover their lands. The case went to court, the suit lasting for five years, until in 1805 the jury decided for the defendants, that is, for the men who had bought land in the district after the confiscation and based their titles on grants made by the state of North Carolina in 1788. The peremptory instruction of the judge to the jury contained, however, no satisfactory judicial opinion as to the legal issue involved. It was based solely on the inequity of handing over to the claimants so vast a territory, occupied and cultivated by a people to whom the very name of Granville was anathema.

1. *North Carolina Colonial Records*, V, 1016–1017, 1042–1043, 1044, 1088–1094; VI, 292–296. For the best known of the agents, Francis Corbin, see *Journal of a Lady of Quality*, appendix vii.

2. Bassett, in *Report*, American Historical Association, 1894, pp. 140–212.

3. Dobbs (*North Carolina Colonial Records*, VI, 1025); Tryon (VII, 513–514); Martin (IX, 261); Assembly resolution, 1773 (530, 580); Historical Manuscripts Commission, *Fifth Report*, p. 218.

CHAPTER VII

FAR FLUNG BARBADOS

WHILE the colonies of Virginia, Bermuda, and New England were finding lodgment on the soil of coast and islands of the northern Atlantic, the lands and waters of the West Indies and the Caribbean Sea were becoming the scene of adventurous activity and international rivalry. In the language of the day there was no peace below the line—the tropic of Cancer—for there lay the seat of Spain's colonial power and the routes of her ships and galleons. The story of the Caribbean during the years from 1600 to 1659 is one of the struggles of Dutch, Danes, English, and French to obtain a footing upon Spanish colonial soil and in that region to break the monopoly of the Spanish crown. This story, often told, is one of romantic adventure, reeking of the blood of cruel and hazardous undertakings, producing reckless and often great personal prowess, and above all else exhibiting the bitter strife of conflicting nations and the determined efforts of the enemies of Spain to wreak a vengeance on the despoiler of the world's peace, "that cruel and insolent nation," more greedily thirsting "after English blood than after the lives of anie other people of Europe." So wrote Sir Walter Raleigh, and few better than he knew whereof he spoke, the feeling toward Spain of the people of England.

With the treaty of 1604, the enmity of England for Spain subsided at least officially, trade revived, and the era of English settlement in America began. But there was no cessation of privateering and piracy and no end to the half-legitimate, half piratical commerce which had been engaged in by men of the Warwick-Cumberland type. There was a new enthusiasm for regular exploration, colonization, and trade, which found expression in the expansion of trading companies, search for the northwest passage, and the founding of Virginia and Bermuda. Expeditions, large and small, went in one direction or another, looking for openings in the south and west that would bring success and a profit.

Spain was established in Central and South America and the

larger islands of the West Indies, but her settlements were little more than agencies for the advancement of the faith and the satisfaction of her greed for the metals. Portugal had known Brazil for a century, but had been accustomed to use Brazilian harbors largely as stopping places on her way to Africa and the East, where the riches of India whetted the appetite of her voyagers with much the same intensity as those of Peru allured the Spaniards. Her earliest form of occupation, the feudal dependency or captaincy, located along the coast from the Amazon to Rio de Janeiro, had suffered from neglect during the sixteenth century. By 1600 the king of Portugal had resumed control of all these feudal immunities and the population gradually increased. Greatly aiding in this development of the country were the Jews, who had fled from Portugal to Holland and thence to Brazil, where they took a leading part in the production of the chief staples, hardwoods and sugar, which soon became important factors in the trading life of the mother country. Regular ocean caravans went back and forth across the Atlantic, and though the Portuguese were always searching for gold and silver, they were forced by circumstances to lead an agricultural and a plantation life, a manner of living they engaged in without enthusiasm. It is an important historical fact that the cultivation of sugar in the New World was first begun in Brazil.

With the incorporation of the Dutch West India Company in 1621, which was to have a great deal to do with the founding of New Netherland on the Hudson and Delaware rivers, the men of Holland gradually obtained a footing on the coast of Brazil, from the river San Francisco northward around the nose of eastern South America, with Pernambuco (Recif) as their chief town. Though they were shut out from the lower Amazon, they occupied six provinces, and this position they held until 1654 when, weakened by the war with England, they were unable to retain their footing. By 1661, they had lost their control without hope of recovery.[1] Their

1. See articles on the Dutch in Brazil by Edmundson in the *English Historical Review*. Nothing permanent came of this occupation, but Holland acquired other territory later in the northern part of South America. The region from Surinam to the Orinoco was first settled from Barbados in 1650 and 1652 by Francis Lord Willoughby, who had great hopes of building up an important colony there (*Calendar State Papers, Colonial*, 1661–1668, preface, xl–xliii, §451; Harlow, *Barbados*, pp. 79–80). The Dutch seized the territory in 1666, but the English re-took it in 1667, only to surrender it to the Dutch by the treaty of Breda in the same year. This surrender was the cause of the famous century-long effort of Jeronimy Clifford and

occupation brought about a further migration of Jews from Holland, many of whom and their descendants went eventually in large numbers to the West Indies and thence occasionally found their way to the American continent, locating chiefly in South Carolina, New York, and Rhode Island.

Englishmen too were becoming interested in that part of the South American coast which lay to the north of the Amazon and as far west as the Orinoco. Though nearly all these early ventures came to naught, they served to call the attention of English merchants to the possible advantages of the region.[1] In 1605 a vessel, the *Olive Branch,* bearing settlers to Charles Leigh's colony on the Wiapoco, under stress of adverse winds and shortage of provisions, was compelled to put in at St. Lucia to land its sick and to obtain supplies. This first landing of Englishmen on a West India island, though followed by nothing but disaster for those who took part in it, has led to the belief, based on an interpolation in Purchas's account of the voyage and a deposition by a survivor who was still alive in 1688, that the landing was at Barbados, where the exact spot is today commemorated by a monument.[2] Other voyages followed, promoted

his heirs to obtain from the English government compensation for losses incurred (Andrews, *Guide,* I, 32, 53, 253). The Dutch kept the colony until 1781, when three of the four provinces, Essequibo, Berbice, and Demarara, were taken by the British and after many vicissitudes were finally secured to Great Britain by the treaty of Vienna in 1814. Thus Surinam is now Dutch Guiana and the other three provinces are British Guiana.

1. Above, Vol. I, 45–49.

2. The statement that Barbados was first occupied by Englishmen, April 12, 1605, is accepted as true by all loyal Barbadians and is repeated in every guide book to the West Indies. Williamson, *Caribbee Islands under the Proprietary Patents,* pp. 13–18, has thrown grave doubt upon it, as based on an interpolation in Purchas's account of the voyage, drawn from Nicholl, *An Houre Glasse of Indian Newes* (1607), which does not contain this particular item, and on *Memoirs of the First Settlement of the Island of Barbados, and other the Carribbee Islands . . . to the year 1642* (p. 2), extracted from the records, papers, and accounts of William Arnold, Samuel Bulkly, and John Summers, who were among the settlers of 1628. Summers was alive in 1688 and, at the age of 82, deposed that the settlement was made in 1605. But the information given by Bulkly and Summers so clearly belongs to the year 1624–1625 as to make the earlier date impossible of acceptance. Williamson and Harlow refer to an edition of the *Memoirs* bearing date 1742, but my copy is of 1743, with no reference to an earlier edition and with the last date in the preface, August 8, 1742. This work is valuable as containing material drawn from records now lost, including a list of the names of the inhabitants in 1638, numbering 766, holding more than ten acres each. On pp. 71–84 and in an appendix are remarks on the laws and constitution of the island. In Hall's *First Settlement of Barbados,* written in 1755 but first printed in 1924 (with a foreword by E. M. Shilstone), the matter is put thus: "It is said that in the year 1605 an English vessel touched here . . . But it seems to be

by London merchants, who were eager, now that the advantages of the islands were becoming known, to exploit them. But nothing of a permanent character took place until in 1624 Thomas Warner, a Suffolk man, an old friend of the Earl of Warwick, and a neighbor and friend of John Winthrop's, landed with a group of colonists of East Anglian stock on the island of St. Christopher. Warner had taken part in the ill-starred North expedition of 1620,[1] and at that time had learned of the possibilities of profit from the nearby islands. Returning to England he enlisted the aid of Ralph Merrifield, an enterprising merchant and promoter of London, who with the co-operation of a group of associates furnished and equipped a vessel and provided the necessary supplies and implements for starting a plantation.[2]

Thus was begun the first permanent English settlement on the West India islands. After a year's residence, during which trouble arose with the Caribs and a successful effort was made to raise tobacco for shipment to England, Warner returned home for the two-fold purpose of obtaining recruits and of securing the protection of the crown. In both particulars he was successful. In 1626 he went back to St. Christopher with an additional number of colonists, carrying with him a commission from Charles I, which recognized the new plantation, granted Merrifield and his associates liberty of trade from thence, and appointed Warner the king's lieutenant for life of the islands of St. Christopher, Nevis, Montserrat, and Barbados.[3] Thus Warner became the first governor of a group of four West India islands. As he was not the proprietor, an honor reserved at that time and afterward for titled courtiers only, he was in the pre-

generally agreed" that the year 1624 is the more reliable date, pp. 1–2. The historical portions of this little volume of 65 pages are drawn from Ligon and Dalby Thomas, but the analysis of the government, of industry, finance, etc., is based on the personal observations of the writer, who is well known as the editor of the first and very rare edition of the colony's laws.

1. Above, Vol. I, 48. Warner was a friend of Captain Roger North, who was a Suffolk man. Captain John Jeaffreson, who aided Warner, was an old schoolmate and comrade, living but a few miles away from Parham where Warner was born. The Willoughbys were also of Suffolk stock. Jeaffreson, *A Young Squire of the Seventeenth Century*, I, chs. I–III.

2. Aucher Warner, *Sir Thomas Warner, Pioneer of the West Indies* (1933), pp. 22–24; Williamson, *Caribbee Islands*, pp. 21–29; Smith, *Travels and Works*, II, 900–903; Egerton, 2395, ff. 3–26, 503–509[b] ("Relation of John Hilton," April 29, 1675, and several depositions of the same date, all printed in *West Indies and Guiana, 1623–1667*, Harlow ed., Hakluyt Society, Series II, LVI).

3. A facsimile and the text of the commission are given in Warner, *Sir Thomas Warner*, pp. 28–33. The date is September 13, 1625.

carious position of one whose powers might be revoked at any time should the king so wish and whose functions of office might be abrogated should a proprietary patent be issued to a peer of the realm. Nevertheless he retained his post until his death, long enough to coöperate in the settlement of Nevis, Antigua, and Montserrat (all of which had become established colonies certainly before 1636, and probably before 1632),[1] and long enough to see these four islands well started on their way from very humble beginnings to their final ranking as the Leeward Islands, a group of independent yet conjoined members, united under a common governor and forming a very important part of the English colonial system.

The island of Barbados was first occupied by men from the ship *Olive,* returning from Pernambuco, who, according to the story of survivors, landed at Holetown in 1625 and took possession in the name of the king. The captain of the vessel, John Powell, the elder, attracted by the tropical richness and beauty of the island, reported his discovery to Sir William Courteen (Dutch, Coerten),[2] a Netherlander, whose father had settled in England and become a rich trader there. The sons, William and Peter, one remaining in London, the other returning to Middleburg, combined English enterprise with Dutch knowledge and experience and in consequence prospered exceedingly. William became one of the richest men in London, able at this time and afterward to make large loans to the king for the ordinary and extraordinary charges of the crown. Deeply impressed with Powell's story, he organized a voluntary joint-stock company, Courteen and Associates, to furnish funds and take all the risks of settlement. During the next two years, 1627–1629, this company sent out ships, settlers, and supplies, until by the latter year there were from sixteen to eighteen hundred people in Barbados, all of whom were tenants of the company, paid and main-

---

1. Williamson, *Caribbee Islands,* p. 94. The dates when these islands were first settled are partly traditional, but all were occupied at a date nearer 1632 than 1636, Nevis probably as early as 1628 (*Calendar State Papers, Colonial,* 1574–1660, p. 146; *Acts Privy Council, Colonial,* I, 238, where the date is given as July 22, 1628). The promoters were Anthony Hilton ("How was Nevis first Settled," *West Indies and Guiana,* pp. 4–17), Thomas Littleton, Roger Glover, and other merchants of London.

2. He was probably related to Pierre Coerten of Middleburg, one of the twelve directors of the Zeeland chamber of the Dutch West India Company, which next to the chamber of Amsterdam was the most important of the five chambers that had charge of the capital of the company (for these chambers, Vol. III, 75). It is interesting also to note that his grandson William (who took the name William Charlton) was a botanist of distinction, whose collections, acquired by Sir Hans Sloane, became the nucleus of the later great accumulations of the British Museum.

tained by it and returning to it all the products of their labor.[1] The arrangement was similar to that adopted in Virginia, Bermuda, and Plymouth, and was characteristic of all the earliest settlements, because these settlements were begun by private initiative as business undertakings. With Barbados we have for the first time a colony established and for a while controlled by an unincorporated group of merchants, who recruited colonists of the usual sort, with no higher aim than financial advantage.[2]

The Courteen Associates had no royal grant of soil and government and to obtain one was essential if their possession were to be legal and permanent. Unfortunately, any means to that end which Courteen may have had in mind were forestalled and frustrated by the action of James, Earl of Carlisle,[3] a Scot and a notorious spendthrift and high liver, but a courtier near the king and possessed of considerable personal attractiveness and diplomatic sagacity. At this juncture Carlisle, urged on, it may be, by Warner and Merrifield, obtained, July 2, 1627, a proprietary letters patent, which covered all the Caribbee Islands from St. Eustatius to Barbados, under the name of the "Carlile Province" or "Cariola." The islands were to be held of the crown at a rental of £100 and the furnishing of a white horse whenever the king should come into those parts, which he was never likely to do.[4] There is some reason to think that Courteen was unaware of Carlisle's intention to include Barbados but supposed that he was aiming only at the Leeward Islands in order to give proprietary protection to what Warner had already done Whether this be true or not the fact remains that the "certain region or country" named in the grant was afterward interpreted to include Barbados, where Courteen's interests lay.[5]

Thus at the very beginning of the island's history a rivalry was

1. Hilton's "Relation," *West Indies and Guiana,* pp. 29–31.

2. One cannot but notice a likeness between the organization and purpose of Courteen and Associates and Weston and Associates who financed the Pilgrims. The difference of course lies in the religious character of the Plymouth colonists and the much smaller amount of money involved in the Plymouth settlement. Courteen and Associates spent, we are told, £10,000.

3. "James Lord Haye, Baron of Sully, Viscount Doncaster and Earl of Carlisle, Knight of the most honorable order of the Garter and one of his Majesty's honorable Privy Council."

4. Francis Lord Willoughby was granted the palatinate of Surinam in 1663 to be held of the manor of East Greenwich on payment of two white horses whenever the king or his successors should land in the country. *Calendar State Papers, Colonial,* 1661–1668, §451.

5. *Ibid.,* 1574–1660, pp. 85, 86.

created between two groups of London merchants, each seeking opportunities for investment in this newly discovered and promising world—Merrifield and Associates in St. Christopher and Courteen and Associates in Barbados. To complicate matters further and confuse the picture a third group appears, headed by Marmaduke Rawdon, also a London merchant, who had been one of those behind Carlisle in his effort to obtain a charter from the king. Carlisle was in debt to Rawdon and others and, after obtaining his propriety, in order to liquidate his obligation, made a grant to them, early in 1628, of 10,000 acres in the island of Barbados.[1] At about the same time, on March 29, he issued to one Charles Wolverston, whom the Rawdon Associates had chosen as their agent, a commission as governor, commander, and captain for three years, over "all such persons as the said merchants shall at their charge cause to be transported . . . doeing Justice, desidinge of controversies, keeping his Mat^s peace and punishing offenders according to the Lawes of the Kingdome of England." These were the powers of the governor of a private colony or plantation, similar to those we have already described as belonging to the grantees of a private plantation in Virginia.[2]

Courteen, seeing all his expenditures and plans imperilled by the unexpected activities of Carlisle and the Rawdon Associates, now in his turn sought a patron at court in order to equalize his chances with those of the other merchants. He appealed to Philip Herbert, fourth earl of Montgomery and afterward of Pembroke, the lord chamberlain, chancellor of the University of Oxford, and one who was deeply immersed in court and parliamentary politics.[3] Pem-

1. Hilton's "Relation," pp. 31–42.
2. A copy of this commission is in the Huntington Library (HM, 17). The names of the merchants there given agree with those printed by Williamson (p. 49), except that John Charles appears as John Sharpless, Swinnerton as Swinerton, and Farrington as Ferington. In the commission Rawdon's name is so spelled, not Raydon, and Carlisle's signature at the end is Carlile, which was probably the contemporary spelling (Historical Manuscripts Commission, *Pepys*, pp. 294–296). By his patent Carlisle was authorized to set up within the bounds of his province "plantations and collonyes" and to "constitute officers" for the government of the same. The 10,000 acres were laid out by Captain Wolverston (whose assistant was the young Henry Winthrop, John's son) and Captain Henry Wheatly from the Mangrove River to the Black Rocks, and so directly up into the land, and the grantees were to pay yearly to the proprietor five per cent of all the fruits, profits, and issues. These acres were later sequestrated by Lord Willoughby as royal demesne (Historical Manuscripts Commission, *Portland*, III, 278). The location is indicated on the map in Ligon's history.
3. Of the Pembrokes Miss Rowe writes in the *English Historical Review* (April,

broke was very probably induced to favor the appeal by an offer of money and possibly of a share of profits, and he willingly made application to the king for a charter covering Barbados. In characteristic fashion, the chancery, February 28, 1723, issued another patent which embraced somewhat the same territory as that allotted to Carlisle, territory to be known as the "Montgomery Province," an act of carelessness or indifference that was typical of the methods of the period in making grants to land in the New World. The patent created at once a conflict of titles that could be resolved only by judicial interpretation. To obtain such interpretation from the chancery Carlisle made a new application and received, April 7, 1728, a renewal of his charter in the form of an amendment and explanation, in which the right of the earl to Barbados was set forth in unmistakable terms and a victory was won for the Rawdon-Wolverston group. The claims of Courteen, who was in actual possession of the island, were ignored and the rights of Montgomery were entirely set aside.[1]

While thus the issue between the two courtiers and the two groups of London merchants were being settled at Whitehall, a more spectacular conflict was taking place in the island where rival groups of

1935, p. 256) "The two earls . . . are in many ways typical of the Stuart nobility. The third earl died with his lands heavily mortgaged to his secretaries and steward. Their court intrigues against more favored noblemen, their eagerness for office and the way in which they sought to extend their power to its farthest limits are also typical of the nobility at the time."

1. Just as Rawdon had turned to Carlisle and Courteen to Montgomery, so Warner and Merrifield at this juncture turned to James Ley, first earl of Marlborough and lord high treasurer. Marlborough obtained the promise of a grant which was probably never actually issued. He does not appear to have had any interest in colonization himself, but his grandson, at this time a young boy, who in 1638 became the third earl and heir to his grandfather's claims, was later to show considerable activity. He it was who as Lord Ley spent six weeks in Boston (Winthrop, *Journal*, I, 223–224) for the purpose of seeing the country. In 1645 he took a group of colonists to Santa Cruz, but the attempt at settlement failed and the survivors were inhumanly driven out by the Spaniards (*Calendar State Papers, Colonial*, 1661–1668, §§226, 1368, p. 473; below, Vol. III, index). He was an ardent loyalist and had the favor of Charles II, who wrote of him (probably about 1649) as "a Person of great honᵣ and abilities, of great experience and Interest in the Caribbo Islands and other plantations" (Historical Manuscripts Commission, *Pepys*, pp. 296–297). Marlborough later made a number of ventures in the colonizing field (*D. N. B.*). That he took his proprietary claim seriously, is evident from his insistence on the payment of the yearly rent charge of £300 from the profits of St. Christopher, Montserrat, and Nevis, for which his grandfather had exchanged his option before he died. That his grandfather had not pursued further the matter of the promised grant may have been due to Warner and Merrifield's belief that it would be better to come to terms with the Earl of Carlisle than to dispute further the Barbados title.

colonists were engaged in very realistic warfare. Though efforts were made to reconcile the contending parties and to persuade them to live together in peace the attempts were unsuccessful. On one side were the Courteen people under John and Henry Powell and on the other were more than a hundred settlers sent out by the Rawdon Associates. The Courteens resented the intrusion of the newcomers and fighting followed. Wolverston sent home a bitter complaint against the Powells charging them with the destruction of 30,000 pounds weight of tobacco and injuries to the Rawdon servants.[1] He wrote that if the London merchants did not speedily despatch more men and supplies they were in danger of losing their plantation altogether. The fighting continued. At first success lay with the Courteens, who seized Wolverston and sent him back to England. Then the Rawdon group appointed in his place Henry Hawley, brother of Jerome Hawley, afterward of Maryland[2] and of a family that had colonial connections with both Maryland and Virginia, who by high-handed methods recovered the ground that Wolverston had lost. The Rawdon Associates once more dominated the colony. Carlisle, at last sure of his title, now selected Sir William Tufton as his principal governor in the colony, with Captain James Holdip as steward and the receiver general of all the rents and revenues due himself as proprietor, but he enjoined Tufton not to exercise authority within the 10,000 acre colony of the merchants or to intermeddle in its affairs. The merchants, in their turn, December 20, 1649, elected Holdip as their agent and governor, thus demonstrating the entire independence of their private plantation. By these means the Courteen interests were effectually supplanted and nothing remained to Sir William Courteen to repay him for all his trouble and expense except a claim, which thirty years later was revived by his son, only to be dismissed by the Privy Council committee on foreign plantations in 1660.[3]

1. The story is told in great detail in the Chancery Proceedings, Bill of Complaint, dated, September 9, 1629, in connection with the suit which Carlisle, the merchants, and Wolverston brought against Courteen and the Powells for damage done. This bill of the plaintiffs and the answers of the respondents were discovered by Dr. Williamson and printed in his *Caribbee Islands*, pp. 218–229. Further information can be obtained from the *Memoirs;* from occasional documents in the reports of the Historical Manuscripts Commission (for example, *Fourth Report*, pp. 51 (2), February 11, 1641, 67 (1), May 25, 1641, 96 (1), August 12, 1641, the petition of the creditors); and from a paper or two in the Huntington Library.

2. Original Narratives, *Maryland*, index; *Maryland Archives*, III, index.

3. *Calendar State Papers, Colonial*, 1574–1660, pp. 488–489. The case was revived

From 1629 on Barbados was a proprietary colony, one of a number of islands, including the Leeward group, that came within the terms of the Carlisle patent. Tufton, an efficient but tactless governor, was ousted by Henry Hawley, his superior both in ability and brutality, after a successful uprising of the colonists. Tufton, protesting, was shot and three of his followers were hanged, and for a few years there was anything but peace in the island. In 1636 Carlisle died, leaving debts of £25,000, assets of £5000 and as tangled a skein of claims as is to be found in the history of any of the proprietary colonies. The aftermath of personal bitterness and prolonged litigation because of these claims continued, in one case at least, on into the eighteenth century, while the indirect influence of the proprietary title upon Barbados itself lasted even longer, for the four and a half per cent export duty, imposed in 1663 by the local assembly as a commutation in part of the proprietary rents and revenues, was not abolished until 1798.

At his death Carlisle left many creditors, a son, the second earl, and a board of three trustees. Under the last named, who were instructed to pay the creditors first, the island was governed until 1642. In that year the second earl leased his proprietary rights to Francis Lord Willoughby, for twenty-one years, from Michaelmas, 1646, to Michaelmas, 1667, and when he himself died in 1660, he left a share to his cousin, the Earl of Kinnoul, thus preparing trouble and a problem for Charles II and his advisers, which they deftly avoided by reaching an agreement with the claimants first and paying no attention to this agreement afterward.[1]

While all this quarreling over proprietary claims was entering on its first stage in England, the colony itself was beginning to prosper. The governors sent over by Carlisle until 1636 and by the trustees

later by the heirs and creditors, but as far as I know, it never came to a hearing. The nature and extent of the claims can be found stated in Thomas Carew, *Hinc Illae Lacrymae: or an Epitime of the Life and Death of Sir William Courten and Sir Paul Pynder, late of London, Knts* (London, 1681; Carew was the agent for the heirs, executors, and administrators of the dead merchant); and in *Several Advertisements concerning the Services and Sufferings of Sir* William Courten *and Sir* Paul Pyndar, *for the Crown of* England, dated October 21, 1680. As presented in these two privately printed papers, the first a folio, the second a shorter work of four pages, the indemnifications sought are four in number: for money loaned Charles I; for leases in Barbados; for depredations committed by the Dutch East India Company on Courteen's ships and factories; and for debts due Courteen in Holland and Zealand. The total reaches the enormous sum of £498,828.

1. See Note at the end of the chapter.

until 1642—Hawley, 1629, 1636–1640, Huncks, 1640–1641, Philip Bell, 1641–1649—were none too satisfactory, though Hawley was responsible for the first representative assembly of the freeholders (1639) and for important changes in the judicial arrangement, and Bell brought about "the consolidation and expansion of the executive and judicial system already in existence" and the enlargement of the elective body by granting it the right to initiate legislation.[1] From 1641 to 1655 Barbados was practically an independent colony doing pretty much as it pleased, without interference from outside. It had weathered its troubles arising out of the proprietary claims and the rivalries of the merchants and was entering on a period of prosperity. Its population grew rapidly from 1800 in 1630 to 30,000 in 1650 and although the Church of England was the established church of the colony its people enjoyed a large measure of religious toleration.[2] It had a well-developed governmental system, which Ligon, as of the years 1647–1650, describes as follows: "They Govern there by the Lawes of England, for all Criminall, Civill, Martiall, Ecclesiasticall and Maritime affairs. This law is administered by a Governour, and ten of his Councill, for Courts of ordinary Justice, in Civill causes, which divide the land in four Circuits; Justices of the Peace, Constables, Churchwardens and Tithing-men: five sessions a year, for tryall of Criminall causes, and all Appeals from inferiour Courts, in Civill causes. And when the Governour pleases to call an Assembly, for the supream Court of all, for the last Appeales, for the making of new Lawes, and abolishing old according to occasion, in the nature of the Parliament of *Englana,* and accordingly consists of the Governour, as Supream, his Councill, in nature of the Peers, and two Burgesses chosen by every Parish for the rest. The island is divided into eleven Parishes. No Tithes paid to the Minister, but a yearly allowance of a pound of Tobacco, upon an acre of every man's land, besides certain Church-duties, of Mariages, Christenings and Burials."[3]

Agriculturally the island was fertile beyond any others of the English group in the Caribbean. Originally heavily wooded, "grown over with trees and undershrubs without passage, except where the plant-

1. Harlow, *Barbados,* p. 25.   2. Stock, *Debates,* I, 191.

3. Ligon, *A True and Exact History of the Island of Barbados* (London, 1657), pp. 100–101. The introductory letter to the Bishop of Salisbury is dated from the Upper Bench Prison, July 12, 1653, but the observations were made in the years from 1647 to 1650.

ers have cleared,"[1] its surface yielded rapidly to the advance of the settlers, as one plantation after another was carved out of the jungle.[2] The labor, however, was heavy, for most of the trees, as Ligon says, were so "large and massie, as they were not to be salne with so few hands and when they were laid along, the branches were so thick and boysterous as required more help, and these strong and active men, to lop and remove them off the ground." Water was very scarce (the island being largely dependent on its autumn and winter rains) and fires were frequent, with the consequent losses extremely heavy. Yet despite drawbacks, labor had its reward in the richness of the soil, the salubriousness of the climate, and the profitable returns that began to accrue as the arable area was widened, champaign and savannah gave pasture for livestock, and a surplus for export began to find place in the island's economy. Ligon saw twenty ships in the harbor when he arrived there in 1647 and thought that not less than a hundred arrived yearly. Father White in 1634 was impressed with the island as "a granary of all the rest of the charybbies Isles" and tells us that the Maryland settlers took on some store of Indian corn before leaving there, which they needed to save "their English provision of Meale and Oatmeale."[3] The staples at this time were tobacco, cotton, indigo, ginger, dye woods, and corn. The earliest plantations were small and situated chiefly near the shore along the leeward or western side of the islands, in order to lighten the labor of transportation and shipping, and despite the rules laid down by the Privy Council trade was free and intercourse with other peoples than those of England was a common occurrence. The Hollanders were much in evidence and supplied the inhabitants with what they needed; the planters sold their produce to them and otherwise engaged in a direct trade with the European continent. Connection with New England and Virginia was still in its infancy, but it was slowly expanding and we know

1. Original Narratives, *Maryland*, p. 37.

2. Modyford said in a letter of June 20, 1655, that even at that date the timber was already disappearing ("when the wood is gon^, and that cannot be long first"). Thurloe, *State Papers*, III, 566. In addition to Ligon's description there are accounts of Barbados by Colt (1631), in *West Indies and Guiana*, pp. 65–71, 91–92, and by Hilton (1651) in *ibid.*, pp. 42–53. Others of slightly later date owe their origin to the Ayscue expedition of 1652 and to that of Penn and Venables of 1654–1655. Almost all the writers, who accompanied the latter expedition have something to say about conditions in Barbados at the time, especially Venables, I. S., and Barrington.

3. Original Narratives, *Maryland*, p. 75; *Calvert Papers*, I, 23.

that New England vessels were already frequenting the island and that Barbados was obtaining much of her provisions yearly from Maryland.[1]

The cultivation of tobacco began early but was never successful, for either the soil was unfavorable or the planters were unskilful. John Winthrop wrote his son Henry in 1629 that the tobacco he sent was "very ill conditioned, fowle, full of stalks, and evill coloured." Ligon calls it "earthy," the worst, he believes, that was grown anywhere in the world, and he implies that when a Barbadian wanted good tobacco for his pipe he had to get it from Virginia. That the tobacco was rank appears from his remark regarding the rooms of a Barbadian house, which he thought so low-roofed that what with the heat without and "so much tobacco and *killdevil* [rum] within," the building might well be set on fire. By 1650 the "soul of Trade" in the island was sugar, which was first introduced from Brazil in 1640–1641 by a Dutchman, Pieter Brower, and was experimented with by Colonel Richard Holdip on his plantation as a better staple than tobacco.[2] It took some time to bring the processes of planting, cropping, crushing or grinding, boiling, and potting to perfection, but before 1647 the planters had learned how to handle it. Its cultivation soon proved to be amazingly profitable, because an acre of sugar cane was equal to three acres of tobacco. Consequently by 1660 it had completely ousted its rival and become the staple of the colony, remaining so throughout the early colonial period. Whereas in 1647 tobacco was still the medium of money payment, by 1660 sugar had entirely taken its place.

During the civil wars in England, when the royalists there had other things to think about than the acquiring and looking after estates in America, the proprietorship in Barbados became a mere name, and during Bell's governorship, a position he held at first from the Carlisle trustees, the island was to all intents and purposes an autonomous state.[3] It was independent of interference on the part of proprietor, parliament, and king, and its planters were anxious that this favorable state of things should continue. With its assem-

1. Original Narratives, *Maryland*, p. 364.
2. Sloane, 3662, ff. 54ᵇ, 70 (John Scott's account).
3. In 1664 Willoughby, recalling old times, wrote to Secretary Arlington, "It is a new thing for the people to have the King's authority among them, for in the Earl of Carlisle's time it was Governor and people that did all, but little of my Lord of Carlisle's name, being very rarely and seldom used amongst them." *Calendar State Papers, Colonial,* 1661–1668, §792.

bly meeting more or less regularly,[1] its judicial machinery functioning smoothly, and its sugar plantations showing an increasing prosperity—largely because of the thriving trade with the Dutch—the
island, despite an occasional epidemic,[2] enjoyed peace and contentment and its leading planters, some of them prominent men of the
period—Drax, Walrond, Holdip, Modyford, Byam, and others—
were doing all that they could to profit by their opportunity. They
were satisfied to be free from the troubles at home and were ambitious to attain to that condition of wealth which the natural advantages of the place afforded. Though as yet few owned plantations of
large acreage[3] and simple though their lives might be, their self-
respect, social origin, and pride of gentility were high, and their
ancestral background was equal to that of any of the best county
families in England itself.

With the death of the king and the establishment of the Commonwealth, however, harmony disappeared and the same antagonisms
that had torn the English asunder for a decade now manifested
themselves with devastating effect. Broken cavaliers from England
flocked to the island and joining with those of royalist sympathies
there, chief among whom were Colonel Humphrey Walrond and
his brother Edward, they made it their business to set the islanders
by the ears, in the hope of repairing their own fortunes at the
expense of their roundhead opponents. For many months of the
years 1649–1650 the island was kept in an uproar and became the
scene of a struggle that approached very near to civil war. Governor
Bell, who had adopted a policy of strict neutrality during the English wars, was powerless to restrain those "well affected to Majesty,"
and the exultant royalists proclaimed Charles Stuart, King of England, obtained from the assembly laws confiscating roundhead estates, and adopted a programme of free trade with Holland and
Hamburg.

At this juncture, two days after the proclamation of the king,
May 3, 1650, Bell was superseded by Francis Lord Willoughby, as
lessee of the island and its revenues. Arriving on May 5, Willoughby

1. *Memoirs*, p. 24.
2. Harlow, *Barbados*, pp. 82, 97. In 1647 and 1648 the island was visited by an
epidemic, of which Richard Vines, formerly of Maine but at this time of Barbados,
writing to John Winthrop, April 29, 1648, called "very infectious and destroying, in
so much that [in] our parish there were buried 20 in a weeke, and many weekes
together 15 or 16."
3. *Memoirs*, p. 20. Fifty to one hundred each on the average.

presented his credentials as the earl's personal lieutenant general and the exiled Charles Stuart's governor of Barbados. Though an avowed royalist he was not welcomed by the Walronds, because he was supplanting them in their mastery of the island and was certain to disagree with their plans for the complete overthrow of the roundheads and the making of Barbados a royalist colony. In this they were right. Willoughby turned for allies to the moderate royalist group, whose members, led by Thomas Modyford and the recently arrived James Colleton, were Barbadians first and royalists afterward. They had no desire to see the prosperity of the island endangered by any wholesale proscriptions and confiscation of estates.[1]

But despite his wise policy of conciliation Willoughby did enough to draw down upon the colony the wrath of the Commonwealth for what appeared to be treasonable conduct to the ruling powers in England. Soon after his arrival he proclaimed the king for the second time, and thus placed Barbados in the same class with Antigua, Bermuda, and Virginia, as openly acknowledging its allegiance to the exiled heir to the throne and offering an asylum to his fugitive adherents.[2] Influenced by these manifestations of loyalty to the monarchy and urged on by the merchants of London, who regarded the free trade with Holland as inimical to their and England's best interests, the Commonwealth parliament—the rump so called—on October 3, 1650, passed the famous act prohibiting trade with the four colonies, on the ground that they were and ought to be dependent on England.[3] This pronouncement was in accord with the decla-

1. The whole story is well told in detail by Davis, in *Cavaliers and Roundheads, 1650–1652* (1887). His main sources of information are Foster, *A Briefe Relation of the late Horrid Rebellion acted in the Island Barbados* (London, 1650) and "A Brief Relation of the Beginning and Ending of the Troubles of the Barbados . . . set forth by A. B., a diligent observer of the times" (1653), in Egerton, 2395, ff. 48, both strongly anti-royalist. For a better balanced and more comprehensive account, Harlow, *Barbados*, pp. 45–82.

2. Three hundred and thirty refugees, including Colonel Henry Norwood, Major Francis Moryson, and other prominent royalists arrived in Virginia toward the close of 1649. Early in the following year, according to a doubtful tradition, Norwood was sent by Governor Berkeley to invite Charles Stuart to Virginia, and returned without the king but with two commissions, one confirming Berkeley in his office and another for himself as treasurer. Such is the story.

3. Firth and Rait, *Acts and Ordinances*, II, 425–429; *Calendar State Papers, Colonial, 1574–1660*, pp. 343, 345, 346, 347. On November 22, 1650, a group of merchants in England, Puritan in sympathy, recommended the displacement of Willoughby and the appointment of Edward Winslow, formerly of New Plymouth, as governor (below, p. 265, note 1). For the former Pilgrim leader, who had been governor of New Plymouth in 1633, 1636, and 1644, to be considered as a possible gov-

ration of 1649, which asserted the supreme authority of parliament over the dominions beyond the seas.

But the Council of State, instead of yielding to a demand in some quarters that Willoughby receive a parliamentary commission as governor, listened to the complaints that came from the merchants in London and the roundheads in the island and decided to send a punitive expedition under Sir George Ayscue to reduce the four colonies to obedience. Willoughby wavered for the moment as to his course, but finally decided on resistance. A contingent of horse and foot was raised, the forts were manned, and the stock of provisions and such other necessaries as horses and equipment were replenished from the Dutch ships lying in the harbor. By the time the fleet arrived in October, 1651, the island was well prepared to meet force with force, and Ayscue began to believe that his only chance of eventual success was to starve the royalists into submission.[1] But this desperate expedient was found to be impracticable, as the parliamentary fleet itself was insufficiently provisioned to conduct a prolonged blockade. Many of its own men were falling sick of the scurvy and later had to be sent to the Leeward Islands for recovery. Ayscue was well aware of his own weakness, but fortune was working in his favor. That which finally broke the back of the royalist resistance in Barbados was the news of the parliamentary victory in England at Worcester, September 3, 1651, and the defection of the moderates in the island, under Colonel Modyford, who was willing to accept the very advantageous terms which Ayscue was prepared

ernor of Barbados in 1650 is an unexpected turn in the career of a man who is usually identified only as a Pilgrim father. He had been born at Droitwich in 1595, had come into contact with John Robinson at Leyden, and had joined the Pilgrims on the *Mayflower* in 1620. In 1646 he returned to England and in 1650 was made, by act of parliament, one of the seven commissioners appointed to compound with delinquents. He was frequently consulted on overseas affairs and it was but natural that as a non-conformist and one experienced in colonial matters he should have been appointed, with Penn, Venables, Searle, and Butler, one of the commissioners in charge of the expedition of 1654. As Searle, appointed governor, stayed on in Barbados and Butler was an unreliable drunkard, Winslow was the head commissioner after Venables and Penn. He was influential, of an "always irresistable affirmative," and one "who wanted not to be contradicted." He more than any one else represented the religious aspect of the Western Design (for additional information, Vol. III, index).

1. *Calendar State Papers, Colonial,* 1574–1660, pp. 364–374. Many of the documents entered only in abstract in the *Calendar* are printed in full in Davis, where will be found other important texts given at length. Similar documents are to be found in the appendices to Schomburgk, *History of Barbados.*

to offer in case of surrender—terms the more generous because of Ayscue's conviction that "one month's war with two Armies on foot would have utterly ruined the place." Even the royalists realized that the future of Barbados hung in the balance, and Willoughby capitulated when he saw the uselessness of a protracted defense with its inevitable loss of lives and destruction of property.

Ayscue promised—and the promise as embodied in the articles of surrender, January 11, 1652, was ratified by parliament the August following—liberty of conscience, local control of taxation, justice and suits at law, restoration of estates for the roundheads in the island and for Willoughby and others in England, Scotland, and Ireland, and most important of all in the eyes of the Barbadians "as great a freedom of trade as ever . . . with all nations that do trade and are in amity with England."[1] In transmitting these articles to parliament Ayscue explained this last named clause to mean that trade was to be free "under such Restrictions and Limitations as are enacted by the Parliam^t of Engld," but the islanders interpreted the words literally and felt that they had been played upon and deceived when later they were required, as were the other colonies of the English mercantile world, to conform to the provisions of the navigation acts of the Restoration.[2] Some of the other articles also were not strictly observed afterward, for though the appointment of Daniel Searle in Willoughby's place as governor and the reorganization of the government after the model of the Commonwealth was provided for, the banishment of Willoughby, the Walronds, and half a dozen others among the royalist leaders was not in accord with the terms of the surrender, which promised by an act of indemnity a pardon to all who had resisted the parliamentary forces.

For the moment the reduction of Barbados probably did little injury to the plantation life or to the sugar industry of the island. When the Ayscue fleet withdrew, trade resumed its former channels and the prohibitory act of 1650 was deemed only temporary, as undoubtedly it was originally intended to be, and no longer operative after the surrender. For the greater part of the three years that fol-

---

1. The articles are printed in both Davis (pp. 250–255) and Schomburgk (pp. 280–283).

2. *Calendar State Papers, Colonial*, 1574–1660, p. 370. Dr. Harlow, p. 80, quoting from Tanner Manuscripts, 55, p. 141b, has furnished me with the evidence here. I saw these papers a number of years ago in the Bodleian Library but have not had access to them for the purpose of this work.

lowed the Barbadians raised sugar and engaged in a free and unrestricted commercial intercourse with Holland and Hamburg, despite the fact that the Council of State construed the act as still in being. The planters violated the act knowing the risk they were taking, but they could always point in defense to the free trade guaranteed by the articles as a sufficient plea in the premises. England was far away, the Dutch vessels were in the harbor, and the long arm of the Commonwealth had been withdrawn.

This happy state of affairs, however, was brought to an end by two events: the war with Holland of 1653–1654, and the despatch of the fleet under Admiral Penn in the latter year. The first of these events caused the Dutch to be wary and fearful for the loss of their ships, while the second brought the islanders face to face with a show of force that had as a secondary purpose the maintenance of the prohibitory act and the humbling of Holland as well as the despoiling of Spain.[1]

In the meantime the Leeward Islands were taking their place as factors in England's colonial expansion. These four distant islets at the northern turn of the crescent, occupied by English, Irish, and French settlers, were legally under the authority of the lieutenant general of the Caribbee Isles, though so far away from Barbados, where he resided, as to be practically independent of his power to interfere in their affairs. Antigua, similar to Barbados in its physical characteristics but with more and better harbors, was thinly populated and its planters, either controlled from St. Christopher or with a governor sent from thence to look after them, were on the whole less prosperous. It was a frequent port of call for merchant ships from England, and Willoughby had a plantation there which he occasionally visited and to which he retired after he was compelled to leave Barbados in 1652, before finally sailing for England. The island was liked by the Barbadians who then and afterward held

1. The seizure of Dutch ships both in the harbor at Barbados and on the high seas during the prosecution of the Western Design and the question raised as to what should be done with the prizes taken had two important future results: (1) they marked the beginning of the problem of vice-admiralty courts, the erection of prize offices, and the appointment of prize officers in the colonies in the seventeenth century and (2) they inaugurated the series of events that led to the capture of New Netherland in 1664. Their immediate effect was to start the quarrel between Penn and Venables which was to have such serious results later in their campaign (*Venables Narrative*, pp. 17, 54, 59; Historical Manuscripts Commission, *Portland*, II, 90). Vol. III, ch. I.

the place in high esteem and owned lands in it. Even after the execution of King Charles, Antigua, largely through the influence of Colonel Henry Ashton,[1] remained loyal to the monarchy, but was finally reduced by Ayscue to the authority of the Commonwealth. In the four years that followed that event it suffered from desertions and the cutting off of supplies and servants. Its governor, Colonel Christopher Kaynell, was appointed in 1652 and on his complaint to England of the weakness of the island, arms and ammunition were sent out and provision was made for a supply of servants.[2] The island had also a governor's council and an assembly of planters (Nevis had the same, a tiny gathering) and it had its quarrels also, largely of a political and domestic nature, of which complaint was made in 1656. Montserrat, where, as Father White said in 1634, was "a noble plantation of Irish Catholiques whom the virginians would not suffer to live with them because of their religion,"[3] was occupied largely by Irishmen, one of whom in 1654 was governor and an accessory in a serious homicidal affair, when he and his "Irish accomplices" in a "barbarous and inhuman" manner murdered one of the planters and confiscated his estate. All the islands were small in area and sparsely populated, the inhabitants being chiefly engaged in the cultivation first of tobacco and then of sugar.[4]

The story of St. Christopher, of which Sir Thomas Warner was the founder and governor and where he was buried after his death in 1649,[5] is more involved and dramatic. We need not enter into the troubles and anxieties of the great pioneer or into his dealings with the London merchants, the English proprietors, Carlisle and his successors, or the Caribs on the island. In his relations with all these he displayed the qualities of a great organizer and builder, energetic, resourceful, and at times ruthless, possessed of initiative and enterprise, and so impressing himself upon King Charles as to receive

1. Ashton proclaimed the king and endeavored to persuade the people of Nevis and St. Christopher to do the same, but without success. Willoughby from Barbados added his influence, but the islanders replied that they would "take neither partye, but allowe free trade to all commers" (Historical Manuscripts Commission, *Loder-Symonds*, p. 387. August 30, 1650).

2. *Calendar State Papers, Colonial*, 1574–1660, pp. 420, 439, 443, 445, 446.

3. Original Narratives, *Maryland*, p. 38; *Calvert Papers*, I, 29.

4. *Calendar State Papers, Colonial*, 1661–1668, §§751, 804, and for all the islands at this time, pp. 229–230.

5. Warner was buried in Middle Island Parish, the heart of the English section, where his tomb may still be seen.

the honor of knighthood in 1629. By that time, so well had he promoted immigration, there were 6000 people in the island, all busily
engaged in raising tobacco, the one great staple of this early period.
The cultivable area was not large, because the center of the island
was mountainous and unsuitable for agriculture of any kind but the
broad levels along the coast and on the higher ground under the
mountains were soon filled with plantations, the richest of which
were at the northwestern end, extending toward the southeast on
the leeward side.[1] The rapid increase of population, the limited area
of land fit for profitable cultivation, and the gradual crowding out
of the small holders by the more wealthy planters and merchants led
to frequent migration to neighboring islands and even to the American continent. The result was that in the eighteenth century, St.
Christopher, even to a greater extent than Barbados and Antigua,
became the land of large plantations, the owners of which, abandon-
ing their estates to the care of overseers and managers, spent their
fortunes in England, "where they [were] either overlooked entirely
or ridiculed for their extravagance."[2]

That which gives variety and color to St. Christopher's early history was the presence there for ninety years of the French as co-
inhabitants, sharing the island with the English. Arriving in 1625,
as a small body of thirty privateersmen under D'Esnambuc, a leader
possessed of some of the qualities of Warner himself, they had so
far increased under the fostering care of Cardinal Richelieu as to
effect a peaceful division of the island in 1627. The terms as agreed
upon by Warner and D'Esnambuc provided for four quarters, the
French taking those at the ends, the English those in the middle
with their headquarters at Old Road, Brimstone Hill, and Palmetto
Point, where they had already settled. Thus the French controlled
Basseterre and the peninsula or neck toward Nevis, where lay the
saltworks. These they shared with the English, the latter having a
path to them through the French quarter, with the right also to use
the roads through the western French quarter, in order to gain access
to the windward side of the island from which they were separated
by the mountains.[3]

1. Thurloe, *State Papers*, III, 505 (St. Christopher in 1655).
2. *Journal of a Lady of Quality*, pp. 92-93.
3. Map in Williamson, p. 73. The articles of agreement are in Egerton, 2395, pp.
3-26, bearing dates April 28 and May 13, 1627, and September 5 and November 8,

For many years the two peoples, with varying fortunes and under the constant menace of a Spanish attack—which in 1630 was successfully and devastatingly carried out—lived amicably enough side by side, bound together by fear of Spain. But with the Spanish power broken by the peace of the Pyrenees in 1659, the friendly relations were threatened, and in 1666 the French, aided by a fleet from home, seized the English quarters, only to have them restored by the treaty of Breda in 1667. Again in 1689, the French occupied the English sections, but were driven out by Governor Codrington, the elder. The *status quo* was reëstablished by the treaty of Ryswick in 1697. At the beginning of the War of the Spanish Succession the younger Codrington drove the French completely out of the island,[1] but in 1705-1706 the French fleet reversed the situation and inflicted so much damage on the planters of St. Christopher and Nevis that parliament had to appropriate more than £100,000 to cover their losses. The island was handed over to Great Britain by the treaty of Utrecht in 1713 and the French resigned permanently all their claims.

As early as 1667 the planters of St. Christopher sent in their first petition to be separated from the governorship of Barbados and to be given an independent government of their own. They based their request on the distance, on the indifferent interest which the Barbadian governor took in the northern islands, and on the value of an independent life as better conducing to the prosperity of the planters. The cause of the island was taken up in England by the Leeward Island merchants and the separation was finally effected in 1672, when Sir William Stapleton was sent out by the crown as governor general of St. Christopher and the rest of the Leeward Islands. The government was continued much as it had been before, the governors of the islands becoming lieutenant governors under the governor general, who later took up his official residence at St. John's, Antigua, each island having as before its own council and representative assembly. From this time forward the Leeward Islands—Antigua, St. Christopher, Nevis, and Montserrat—constituted one royal colony, differing from the other royal colonies only in its peculiar federative form.

1628. The final arrangement regarding Sandy Point is dated October 10, 1649, in the name of Charles II (f. 95).

1. Harlow, *Christopher Codrington, 1668–1710* (1928).

In the meantime Barbados was passing through a very strenuous and disturbing transitional period. In common with other colonies in that decentralizing decade of the civil wars in England when such colonies as had been settled were left largely to their own devices by the authorities in England, Barbados had gone her own way and until the year 1655, as we have already seen, was in a state of independence[1] almost as complete as had been Massachusetts Bay at the same time. Both roundheads and royalists, following the precedent in England in the early days of the Long Parliament, appealed to the liberties and privileges of free-born Englishmen against the interference of the mother country in the affairs of the island, and on February 18, 1651, the lieutenant general (Willoughby), the council, and the assembly joined in the issue of a famous declaration in which they insisted that the prohibitory act was contrary to "the freedom, safety, and well being" of the island, and if enforced would bring the inhabitants "into contempt and slavery." They raised a question that others were raising elsewhere at the same time, as to whether they should be bound by the laws of a parliament in which they had no representatives "there to propound and consent to what might be needful to us, as also to oppose and dispute all what should tend to our disadvantage and harm."[2] Apparently unaware as yet of the growing strength of the mercantilist idea, which was taking possession of the statesmen and merchants of the Commonwealth and Protectorate as it had those of the early Stuarts and, in more constructive form, was to influence those shaping England's policy in the years to come, they thought only of their own immunity, lib-

---

1. Edward Winslow to Secretary Thurloe, March 16, 1655, Thurloe, *State Papers*, III, 249.

2. This declaration is printed in full in Davis, pp. 197–200, and in Schomburgk, appendix. Three dates are given, February 18 and 20 and October 29, 1651. February 18 is that usually accepted. The issue of "liberty" versus "tyranny" appeared in one form or another throughout the colonies at this time—in Massachusetts Bay, Bermuda, and particularly in Maryland. This declaration has sometimes been cited as a precedent for the Declaration of Independence. The comparison seems irrelevant as the underlying principles in the two declarations are quite different, but this interpretation explains why the Barbados declaration was included, as a photostat facsimile, in the American Series issued under the auspices of the Massachusetts Historical Society in January, 1926.

Modyford, writing two years later, expressed the same idea regarding the representation of the colony in parliament when he said, "The people of Barbadoes would delight to have the same form of government as that of England and would like to have two representatives chosen in the island to sit and vote in the English parliament," *Calendar State Papers, Colonial*, 1574–1660, p. 373.

erty, and freedom and would not recognize the right of the mother country, whether ruled by Stuart or Cromwellian, to subordinate the colony's welfare to its own advantage and to the colony's injury as they saw it.[1] It was Ayscue's acceptance of this point of view, when he promised in the articles of capitulation to allow liberty of conscience, freedom of trade, and the continuation of the "ancient and usual custom" in all matters of administration and justice that finally led them to submit to the authority of the Commonwealth. The history of the ensuing ten years is one long and bitter struggle to make good, if they could, the terms of that surrender. Even though the Barbadian planters agreed to the appointment of a governor by the authorities in England, they tried to round out their programme of self-rule by insisting that the person named be one of themselves. Could they have attained all their ends their autonomy would have been complete. But they never attained them.[2]

Even before Admiral Penn at the head of the fleet and General Venables at the head of the troops on board entered the harbor of Bridgetown, January 29, 1655, the islanders had begun their protest against the act limiting their trade, and they were unremitting, both then and afterward, in their efforts to have it repealed. Trade with the Dutch and the Hamburgers had become indispensable to them, and its continuance, they said emphatically, was essential to their well-being, because the prices of the Dutch were lower, their commodities more varied and useful, and their credit periods longer. Therefore the colonists saw only disaster to their prosperity in the confinement of their market to England.[3] They could not under-

---

1. Apparently the Barbadians did not know that as far back as 1632 the Privy Council had forbidden the ships sailing from any of the English plantations to "goe into forraigne countries with their goods and Marchandize to his Majesty's great loss and prejudice in his Customes" (*Acts Privy Council, Colonial*, I, §292).

2. It should be noted that at this early period in the history of the colonies, the idea of a royal review of colonial legislation had not been conceived. In Governor Searle's commission, as in all other charters and commissions up to this time, laws were to be valid that were not contrary to the laws of England.

3. Captain Gregory Butler, who was one of the least useful of the five commissioners (p. 255, note 3), wrote to Thurloe, "Our English merchants trafiquing to these parts [are] generally great extortioners" (Thurloe, *State Papers*, III, 142); Winslow also was exasperated at the way the Barbadians courted the Dutch and ignored the English merchants (*ibid.*, 249–250); and it is worthy of note that both Lübeck and Hamburg protested as well as the Barbadians (*ibid.*, I, 537, 542–548; II, 94). But the Cromwellian government made no concessions. On March 1, 1655, five commissioners, headed by Modyford, were appointed "for putting in force the laws prohibiting foreign vessels from trading with Barbados to the prejudice of the

stand the complaint of the English merchants that "by the consequence of this unlimited trade those islands will in a short time be brought to desert English interests and become the treasure of other nations,"[1] or envisage the larger aspects of England's rivalry with the Dutch. They only saw that they were in danger of becoming "the merchants' slaves," and in the concessions that England offered, such as a virtual monopoly of the home market and certain tariff advantages, found no sufficient compensation for the anticipated losses. When the terms of the prohibitory act, no longer valid after the Restoration, were renewed in the navigation act of 1660, the Barbadians realized that their commercial freedom was at an end, and when these terms were embodied in the instructions to Willoughby in 1663, they gave up the struggle. "You are required," Willoughby was informed, "to defend the Rights, Priviledges and Prerogatives of the Crown in those Dominions . . . to apply yourself to all prudentiall meanes to advance [their] Wealth and Prosperity both within themselves, and rendering them usefull to England . . . [and] to put an Act of Parliament in execution," that is, the navigation act of 1660.[2]

Just as the Barbadians wanted freedom of trade so they wanted freedom of government, that is, home rule for themselves. Their determination to ward off all outside control or any undue amount of it, whether of parliament, proprietor, or king, was the inevitable consequence of the autonomy they had enjoyed during the years from 1640 to 1650, when Philip Bell was their kindly but not very efficient governor. The planters were not united on just what they wanted, for though all were agreed on the importance of an unlimited trade, they were not all of one mind when it came to the form of government under which they wished to live. There were even some who wanted a supreme parliament in the island, with the powers of a governor and council reduced to a minimum, and who would have been glad to reproduce in the colony the system

Commonwealth of England" (Historical Manuscripts Commission, *Portland*, II, 90. These five were in charge of the prize office, the first in English America).

1. Additional Manuscripts, 11411, f. 4a; Thurloe, *State Papers*, VI, 169; Egerton, 2395, f. 182. Dr. Harlow says (*Barbados*, p. 94), "the fact that after 1655 Barbados became a regular port of call for vessels on their way to the new colony of Jamaica were factors sufficiently deterrent to scare away all but the most daring of foreign adventurers. After 1655, therefore, it may safely be said that alien intercourse with Barbados dwindled to insignificance."

2. *Acts Privy Council, Colonial*, I, §598 (secs. 5, 11).

under the Commonwealth, without king or House of Lords. They were of the same mind and purpose as Righton in Bermuda and Fendall in Maryland, parliament men, who, some of them at least, had in view a "free state" similar to that of the New England colonies.[1]

This phase of the struggle brought out all the old party differences under new guises. Royalists and roundheads were transformed into die-hards, moderates, and republicans or commonwealth men, the first few in number, the second containing both royalists and round-heads and constituting by far the largest group, while of the last named there were not enough probably to form a government, though they were none the less vociferous on that account.[2] Searle, during the years of his governorship, could do little to check the animosities, for his commission, in common with other Puritan investments of authority, minimized the powers of the executive by denying him the right to veto legislation or to nominate the council, the members of which were appointed directly from Whitehall and continued to be so appointed until the Restoration. He was therefore at the mercy of the other two branches of the government,[3] and the first assembly summoned by him—the burgesses elected by the parishes and all sitting together—saw to it that the powers of the governor suffered no increase.

While the colony was endeavoring to hold its own against both the Commonwealth and the Protectorate and in matters of administration was looking after its own affairs, another movement was on foot to oust Searle from the government. He was the appointee of an outside authority and not of the colony, and for years the Barbadians had asked that one of themselves be selected as governor. Then too Searle was at the head of a minority party and was not wanted by the bulk of the planters, who had formed the backbone of re-

1. *Calendar State Papers, Colonial*, 1574–1660, pp. 384, 399; 1661–1668, §1017. These were the ones in the islands who wanted Edward Winslow as governor. Farmer, later speaker of the assembly, seems to have been in somewhat the same class, *ibid.*, 1661–1668, §§1017, 1036.

2. *Ibid.*, 1574–1660, p. 406 (9).

3. Searle's first commission is in Egerton, 2395, f. 117. It provided for a governor, council and assistants, acting "by and with the advice and consent of the Freeholders or their Representatives, chosen according to the customary course and manner of election to make constitutions, ordinances and bye-laws." The second commission was brought by Venables and is dated July 31, 1654. For the government under it for three years see Thurloe, *State Papers*, III, 499–500.

sistance to Ayscue and the Commonwealth fleet. Leading this movement was Thomas Modyford, himself a Barbadian planter and a lawyer used to the ways of politics and not unfamiliar with the usefulness of opportunism and expediency. He had been in considerable part responsible for the surrender of 1652 and though a royalist by tradition and sympathy was able in the same year to write Bradshaw, president of the Commonwealth parliament, "you have sweetly captivated my mind and clearly fixed it in a true affection to your service."[1] He became speaker of the Barbadian assembly in 1654, but lost a good deal of his popularity when he urged the islanders to support Cromwell's expedition of that year. This expedition got thoroughly disliked because, lying as the fleet did in the harbor for two months (January to March, 1655), it drained the island of both men and supplies. In consequence Modyford was defeated at the next election and in 1657 went to England to obtain the recall of Searle and his own nomination as governor. Nearly two years of intrigue followed, during which Searle's cause was upheld by a group of merchants in London led by Martin Noell and Thomas Povey[2] and that of Modyford by a coterie of Barbadian planters led by James Colleton and other "grandees" of the island. Conditions underwent such important changes on the death of Cromwell and the abdication of his son that Modyford was able to obtain his desire from the Rump Parliament, April 24, 1660.[3] His appointment represents the high-water mark in the colony's effort to win complete self-government, for though he was commissioned from without he was the first of the planters themselves to receive the office of governor. He held the position long enough to show the ease with which he could change his mind, when need be, for on hearing of the return of the monarchy, he turned royalist, proclaimed the king, and with the coöperation of the council swung the colony into the royal hands. With the accession of Charles II his commission ceased to have validity, but he clung to his post in the hope of a new patent from the crown. In this he was opposed by the Walronds[4] and

1. *Calendar State Papers, Colonial*, 1574–1660, p. 373.

2. See below, Vol. III, ch. II.

3. C. O. 31:1 (July 31, 1660), containing the commission; Harlow, *Barbados*, p. 125.

4. *Calendar State Papers, Colonial*, 1661–1668, §§40, 60. Walrond, the bitter enemy of Modyford, became president of the council in January, 1661, and charged Modyford with treachery. In consequence a deadlock ensued between the president and the council on one side and the assembly on the other, which lasted from January 10

their followers, but he was aided by the "grandees" (as Colleton, Middleton, Rendall, and other planters in the colony and the merchants in London were called, who feared for the loss of their influence) and by the lesser planters, who were alarmed lest they be reduced again to the status of tenants at will should the proprietor be restored. The king, acting on the advice of his newly created council for foreign plantations, decided on a compromise. He took over the proprietorship himself, making Willoughby his governor and captain general for as long as the latter's lease lasted, during which time Willoughby was to receive half the profits of the propriety, the other half going to pay off the Carlisle debts and legacies.[1] Thus Modyford and home rule for the Barbadians were definitely discarded and centralization, not decentralization as in the past, became the keynote of England's policy.

But the colonists had no intention of giving up the struggle to retain that position of independence for which they had been so long contending. Instead of the Puritan leaders of the Commonwealth and Protectorate, they now had against them a combination of king, proprietor on lease, and the returned Colonel Walrond, whom Willoughby at once made his acting governor, until he himself could go out to the colony. To gain their end, as far as it was possible to do so, the aroused colonists determined, at whatever cost, to accomplish four things: first, to free themselves entirely from all proprietary payments; secondly, to obtain a clear title to their lands to be held not as copyhold but as estates in free and common socage;[2] thirdly,

to July 10, 1661. The assembly refused to consent to an address to the king promising a tax of ten per cent and a present in addition. After the new elections in July Modyford was chosen speaker of the house and the issue between council and assembly was joined more vigorously than before. *Ibid.*, p. 46, §134.

1. *Ibid.*, §§83, 181, 309, 387, 478, 489. C. O. 31:1 (Journal of Barbados Council, 1660–1686), contains various preliminary documents relating to Willoughby's commission, the commission itself June 12, 1663, and the instructions June 16, 1663. Willoughby arrived in the colony August 10 of that year. For his connection with Barbados and the "case" after 1660 see Clarendon, *Life*, III, 932–945, and the same at somewhat greater length in Clarendon's tract vindicating himself in *A Collection of Several Tracts* (1727), pp. 25–33.

2. They wanted "Tenure in Soccage to bee held of the King &c by paying Such an acknowledgem* as the Governor Counsell 2nd Assembly shall agree unto," C. O. 31:1, 76–77. In Historical Manuscripts Commission, *Portland*, III, 277, is a letter, September 11, 1663, from Sir Robert Harley to his brother Sir Edward Harley (father of the Earl of Oxford) in which he says that the assembly "would not confess the king to be proprietor, and so receive confirmation of their estates from him 'but would have their possessing it dureing these troublesome times to be a good title.'"

to secure the privilege of transporting their sugar to the port of any country in amity with England; and, lastly, to prevent the king, as far as they could, from making appointments from England to positions in the island, in the form of patent offices, which were usually held by deputy.[1] In the third and fourth particulars they failed, but in the first and second they were successful, a success won by the assumption voluntarily of a burden that was to prove one of the greatest, if not the very greatest, of their grievances in the years to come—the four and a half per cent export duty on all "dead" commodities raised in the island.[2] Willoughby, who took over the governorship on August 10, 1663, immediately on arrival demanded the settlement of this issue by the establishment of a permanent fund from the island to be placed at the royal disposal. The issue was one which the English authorities were to raise with nearly all the royal colonies, but successfully only in the case of Jamaica and in part with Virginia. Willoughby was willing to accept a compromise as of mutual advantage, but the assembly opposed the grant of any fund at all and it was only after a stubborn resistance on the part of the representatives of the planters, lasting for three weeks, August–September, 1663, during which both sides reached a state of such exhaustion from the heat as to bring some of them to a state of collapse and the debate to an end. The measure was passed, September 12, and in return for the four and a half per cent duty—reduced from ten per cent—the king promised to confirm all lands as freeholds, to abolish all the proprietary dues, and to use the money received from the duty for the administration and upkeep of the island itself.[3] The last named part of the bargain was never kept by the crown, and as it happened the fund was used for all sorts of purposes, from paying the salaries of other royal governors to furnishing pensions and perquisites for royal dependents in England. This misuse of the fund was a constant cause of complaint, particularly in the eighteenth century.

The last phase of the controversy took the form of a struggle be-

1. C. O. 31:1, pp. 76–77.

2. The history of the four and a half per cent has never been written. The material for such a history is widely scattered and voluminous. Among the Blathwayt Papers, II (Huntington Library), is a group of documents relating to the subject during the period before 1715, one of which is entitled "Concerning the 4½%," an important paper.

3. C. O. 29:1, pp. 47–50. The act is printed in Bryan Edwards, *History of the West Indies* (ed. 1793), I, 343–346.

tween Willoughby as governor, representing the prerogative, and the assembly elected by the freeholders, to save the colony from autocratic and interfering rule. In order to strengthen the power of the executive, Willoughby began his administration in unconciliatory fashion, calling an assembly only when he was obliged to—there was no session from the end of 1663 to 1665—and reducing the number of the courts.[1] When, because of a lack of supplies, he was forced to summon the assembly in 1665, its members in somewhat the same manner as in Bermuda under Sir John Heydon and in New York under Dongan, demanded a redress of grievances before voting an appropriation, taking as their model parliament's action in adopting the petition of right.[2] Willoughby dissolved the body, sending its members home, exiling one of the leaders and imprisoning others.[3] Just how the matter would have ended we may not prophesy. Willoughby by his commission was forbidden to lay any impositions upon the people without their consent, and having no way of raising money he stood with his back to the wall.[4] Probably in the end he would have had to give in. But he was not called upon to face the inevitable. While on an expedition to St. Christopher, to recover the island from the French, he was drowned during a hurricane, which partly destroyed and partly scattered his fleet. He was succeeded by his younger brother, William, who as William Lord Willoughby, fell heir to the barony and the lease, and with more tact, but with equal determination, took up his brother's inheritance and his burdens also.

The war with the Dutch divided the colony into factions, for though the new governor was able to draw many of his brother's opponents to his support, he still faced a strong body of those who wanted a corporate charter, such as the New England colonies had, the abolition of the four and a half per cent, and freedom of trade

1. *Calendar State Papers, Colonial*, 1661–1668, §833.

2. *Ibid.*, 1018, I, June 8, 1665; Historical Manuscripts Commission, *Portland*, III, 292, 293, 295, 296. Farmer was the "framer" of this petition, and it was he whom Willoughby sent to England for trial as "a very dangerous fellow, a great Magna Charta man and petition of right maker," *ibid.*, 1036.

3. Historical Manuscripts Commission, *Portland*, III, 292, 293; *Calendar State Papers, Colonial*, 1661–1668, pp. 419, 542. From July 1, 1663, to February 10, 1665, the colony was governed only by ordinances issued by the governor and council. The precincts of the courts of common pleas were reduced in number. Not until February 10 and April 14 was the passing of acts resumed. On those days two appropriation bills were passed.

4. *Calendar State Papers, Colonial*, 1661–1668, §§1161, 1166, 1167.

in return for a lump sum. When the king's advisers put the amount at £5000 a year and the payment of the colony's debts,[1] the council and assembly balked at the offer and refused to consider it. No settlement had been reached at the time of William Lord Willoughby's death in 1673, when with the expiration of the lease the colony came directly into the hands of the crown. From this time forward Barbados was in all respects a royal colony and Sir Jonathan Atkins, who arrived on November 1, 1674, was the first royal governor, properly so called. For many long years Barbados continued to show the marks of her early experience. It is not too much to say that there, as in Maryland in the seventeenth century, the attempt of the planters to free themselves from the burden of proprietary authority strengthened the determination of the popular assembly to resist the royal prerogative also and to secure for the colony as large a measure as possible of local privilege and self-control.[2]

The early history of Barbados is suggestive and enlightening to any one who wishes to comprehend in their widest connotations the problems of the continental colonies. Starting as a proprietary possession, where were mingled proprietary, mercantile, and popular factors, it passed through a period of economic and political independence, followed by subordination to the authority of the Commonwealth, Protectorate, proprietary, and king, until it emerged as a full-fledged royal colony, but unlike most of the other royal colonies, particularly of the mainland, it emerged burdened with a heavy financial obligation. Without adequate contiguous territory available for expansion, it was thrown back upon its own resources for the strength wherewith to oppose the power of the prerogative and to avert royal interference in its affairs. Its powers of resistance were depleted by emigration and by the gradual exodus of the lesser planters, as the sugar interests became dominant and small estates were consolidated into large ones, until in time it tended to become a sin-

1. C. O. 1:21, nos. 102, 156; 23, nos. 20, 33, 36, 65; C. O. 31:1, pp. 210–212; *Calendar State Papers, Colonial,* 1661–1668, §§1565, 1642, 1801, 1816, 1819, 1857; 1669–1674, §845.

2. Beer, *Old British Colonial System,* I, 162, says that Barbados "was in the forefront of every movement of opposition to England's economic measures." This was true of the seventeenth century but not of the eighteenth, when the Barbadians lent themselves without serious demur, as may be seen in the case of the Molasses Act, to the limitations imposed by British policy and when the Barbados assembly seemed to be less insistent on its privileges and less sensitive to affronts on its dignity than were the assemblies of some of the other British colonies.

gle great sugar plantation controlled by the crown, owned by absentee planters, and worked by negro slaves. It was in large measure subordinate to English authority and adapted itself more or less willingly to the demands of the mercantile system, sending its one staple to the mother country and depending for its prosperity on the place of that staple in the economic world. Barbados was ultimately affected seriously by gluts in the sugar market, as one region after another entered the competition, causing the supply to outstrip the demand and so far to depress the price as to discourage the continuance of the industry.

During the eighteenth century the efforts of the Barbadian planters were mainly directed to the attainment of three objects: first, the preservation of certain constitutional advantages, which it inherited from the days of its early independence; secondly, the warding off of competition in the sugar trade, that was menaced not only by rivalry of the nearby French colonies but also by the addition of new island territories by Great Britain herself; and, lastly, the securing of relief from the burden of the four and a half per cent, which despite all their efforts they were unable to obtain for expenditure within the island itself.

While thus the history of Barbados and the Leeward Islands is essential to any proper understanding of the constitutional and commercial development of the English colonies in America, it must always be remembered that these islands formed a part of the colonial world within which the merchants, agriculturists, and seafaring men of the continental colonies had their being. From New Hampshire to Pennsylvania and in a lesser degree from Maryland to Georgia, ships with provisions and other supplies sought these British West India islands and found there that market which they more and more needed as their cultivable areas expanded, their staple products multiplied, and their population increased. Many an inhabitant of Newport, Boston, and Philadelphia owned plantations in one or other of the islands, and derived a part of his income from thence, while the monetary conditions in the continental colonies would have been much worse, bad though they were, had not trading exchanges brought in hard money whereby commercial business could be carried on. Finally, no adequate grasp of England's colonial policy, which was shaped by that country's experience with all, not a part of, her colonies, can be obtained unless we have an understanding of all the colonies taken together that made up the English colonial world. England's policy toward the colonies that revolted in 1776 was determined by a well conceived and entirely defensible programme of control from the point of view of the mother country, in the formulating of which the British possessions in the West Indies played a prominent and influential part.

NOTE: It is not necessary to enter here upon the confused and bewildering story of the difficulties arising from the attempts to settle all these claims to the lands in the islands and to the enjoyment of their revenues. Williamson in *Caribbee Islands* and Harlow in *Barbados* have dealt with the subject admirably. But as a matter of convenience a brief statement may be made and a few facts added. In 1638 the second earl of Carlisle sued the trustees on the ground that their appointment and powers were invalid. This suit was probably compromised by his appointment as co-trustee. A second suit was begun in the same year by two of the creditors, who carried the case to the House of Lords, whence it was returned to chancery and decided in the creditors' favor. This suit was reopened in 1644, when the creditors attempted to distrain for their money, but probably without result. The lease to Willoughby added a new claim in the Carlisle category, while a third claim was created when in 1660 the second earl died and left by will a share to his cousin, the Earl of Kinnoul.

At the end we have five parties in England interested in these West India lands and revenues (for a slightly different grouping, Williamson, p. 198): (1) the Courteen merchants and planters, who contested the Carlisle patent and demanded recompense for their losses by dispossession; (2) the Carlisle-Willoughby-Kinnoul group, the first of whom had a claim that continued only as long as the proprietorship lasted (though all of the money arising from this claim was probably due the creditors), the second till 1668 only (a new lease was effected in 1661, *Calendar State Papers, Colonial*, 1661-1668, §§309, 489, 994), and the third indefinitely (see below); (3) the Earl of Pembroke, who based his claim on the Montgomery-Pembroke patent, which he sold to the Earl of Warwick, probably in 1638, thus giving Warwick an interest in Tobago (*Calendar State Papers, Colonial*, 1661-1668, §1368) and in Trinidad (above, Vol. I, 498, note 2); (4) the third earl of Marlborough who had a £300 rent charge, which he declared, when he took over his grandfather's claim, was eight years in arrears; (5) the creditors, eighty in number, who demanded £37,000 with litigation costs of £1200, no part of which had been paid up to 1660. These same creditors, apparently despairing of their payment, sought to recoup themselves during the Dutch war, 1665-1666, by fitting out vessels for which letters of marque and reprisal were obtained. The Duke of York, as lord high admiral, checkmated this scheme by issuing orders to Lord Townshend, vice-admiral of Norfolk, "to make stop of all Ships and Vessels which now or shall come in any Ports within your Jurisdiction that are set forth by the Creditors of Sr Will Courteen deceased or their Assignees." This document (in private hands) is dated "St. James: 12th July, 1666."

A settlement was arranged in 1663 (*Acts Privy Council, Colonial*, I, §599; *Calendar State Papers, Colonial*, 1661-1668, §§482, 485), but it is quite certain that its terms were never carried out, except in the case of Kinnoul. The latter persisted longer than any of the others (*Acts Privy Council, Colonial*, I, §882), for his claim was brought before the House of Lords in 1702 (Stock, *Debates*, II, 453) and in 1738 one of his descendants applied to the Duke of Newcastle for the governorship of Barbados, apparently on the ground of his claim (Additional Manuscripts, 32,691, pp. 284–287). He and his heirs received the annuity until it was assigned away to others many years ago. Those into whose hands it came, or their children, may still be enjoying it as far as I know (Davis, *The Cavaliers and Roundheads of Barbados*, pp. 176–177).

There is in the Huntington Library among the Blathwayt Papers ("Barbados-Caribbee Isles") a sheaf of seventeen documents, of date June, 1663, to December, 1670, relating to the Carlisle interests in Barbados, some of which are duplicates of those entered in the *Acts Privy Council, Colonial.*

CHAPTER VIII

PROPRIETARY MARYLAND

IN striking contrast with the circumstances attending the proprietary settlement and early history of Barbados are those of the proprietary colony of Maryland, the second of the colonies of this type to be founded by Englishmen in the New World. The promotion of settlement in the West Indies was, as we have seen, the work of merchant-capitalists of London, searching for opportunities of trading profit and utilizing in the customary manner ships, captains, seamen, and colonists for the purpose of starting agricultural plantations where staples of a tropical or semi-tropical nature might be raised that could be sold in the English or Continental market. To ensure a valid title to the soil of their discovery they sought among the nobility of England for patron-proprietors, who because of their place at court and nearness to the king were able to obtain from the royal chancery charters that conveyed land and rights of government, enabling the patentee to exercise the privileges of proprietary control. These noble patrons were not expected to take any personal part in the actual settlement and development of the territory and, as it happened, no one of them ever went out to the colony itself or interfered in matters of strictly local concern. Though some of them manifested considerable interest in promoting colonization, their main solicitude was for the returns that accrued from the ownership of the soil, which was cultivated by settlers who were legally, though probably never actually, tenants at will of their lords.

The trouble and dissension resulting from the conflicting proprietary claims led to difficulties and litigation at home and to hostilities in the colony that in the early years retarded the prosperity of the planters and brought some of the merchants to the verge of bankruptcy. Though distance, for instance, enabled the Barbadians to obtain after 1640 a considerable measure of domestic peace and political independence, the ensuing struggle between king and parliament and the eventual victory of the Puritan party again divided the islanders; and it was not until after the Restoration, when in 1663 the king took the colony into his own hands, that relative calm came to the troubled land. Even the controversy over proprietary rights and the claims of the merchants in England lasted twenty years longer and traces of it continued to be visible for two centuries.

Nevertheless out of this welter of discordant claims Barbados emerged a powerful colony, singularly influential in determining England's attitude toward her colonies as a whole, and becoming after the turn of the century a wealthy and prosperous West India possession. It was highly valued by the government at home because of its sugar staple, and on the political side was to show itself as sturdily opposed to an undue extension by the crown of the royal prerogative as were any of the colonies on the mainland. As Virginia was "the Old Dominion," so Barbados became known as "Little England," and is so known today, the most English of Britain's colonies. In any study of the rise of the popular assembly and in any estimate of the state of popular feeling in America in the eighteenth century, Barbados offers a fruitful field for comparison and contrast.

The circumstances attending the settlement of Maryland, though equally proprietary in all essential particulars, were entirely different from those narrated above. The founder of Maryland was a single proprietor, acting on his own initiative and responsibility and guided by definite plans already formed. No merchant or promoter influenced him or had any part in his undertaking. George Calvert was no arm-chair colonizer or court favorite seeking largesse at the hands of the crown. He had himself gone twice to America—once to Newfoundland, "on a long journey to a place which," as he wrote Wentworth, "I have had a long desire to visit and have now the opportunity and leave to do it";[1] and once to Virginia, where though not allowed to remain on account of his religious convictions, he was able to inspect the country and plan for a new colony of his own. He would undoubtedly have made a third journey had he not died before final arrangements could be perfected. But two of his sons and others of his family and relatives were to live in Maryland and to take an active part in its affairs.

There was trouble enough to come for the Maryland proprietors, both in England and in the colony, but in neither case was there a disputed proprietorship or rival claims to proprietary revenues. Maryland was a single province, its lands were contiguous and com-

1. *The Earl of Strafford's Letters and Dispatches*, I, 39. Thomas Wentworth, the future earl of Strafford (1640), was Calvert's colleague as one of the representatives from Yorkshire in the parliament of 1621.

pact, its head was one absolute lord and proprietor whose difficulties, differing in nearly all respects from those that confronted the Barbadians in the formative years of their history, were such as arose from the attempt to establish proprietary rule in America.

George Calvert, Sir George after 1617 and Lord Baltimore after 1625, had been for many years deeply interested in colonization and in touch with many of those who were already engaged in colonizing activities. Born some eight or nine years before the defeat of the Spanish Armada, he matriculated at Trinity College, Oxford, in 1594, and was graduated in 1597, receiving his degree February 23 of that year. He became secretary to Sir Robert Cecil, was later a clerk of the Privy Council, and sat in parliament from 1609 to 1624. In 1619 he was raised from his clerkship in the council to be one of the principal secretaries of state, an office much less important then than it was destined to become in the eighteenth century.[1] His family connections and official relations were influential factors in shaping his colonizing ambitions. On one side he was brought into touch with the Wroths and the Riches, for his first wife, Anne Mynne (d. 1622) was the granddaughter of Lady Mary Rich Wroth, the great aunt of the second earl of Warwick, and she was also a cousin of Sir Thomas Wroth who had married the sister of Sir Nathaniel Rich, Warwick's cousin through an illegitimate son of his grandfather. As Warwick and Rich were among the leading gentlemen-adventurers of the day, their influence undoubtedly induced Calvert to become a member of the Virginia Company and to subscribe to its stock, though he probably never attended any of its meetings.

On the other side he was allied with the Roman Catholic family of Arundel—Sir Thomas Arundell of Wardour, whose daughter his son Cecil or Cecilius married and by whom it is said he was converted to the Church of Rome,[2] and Thomas Howard, second earl

---

1. On Calvert, Wilhelm, "Sir George Calvert," *Fund Publications,* no. 20; "George Calvert at Oxford," *Maryland Magazine,* XXVI, 109–130; Historical Manuscripts Commission, *Downshire,* II, index (before 1610); Johnson, *Foundations of Maryland,* appendix B (Arundell); "Calvert Family Pedigree," *Maryland Magazine,* XVI, 50–59 and later numbers. The last named article contains some misleading statements. Calvert was not appointed "to the high office of Principal Secretary of State." He was one of the two secretaries (the other being Sir Robert Naunton and after him Sir Edward Conway) who together made up the office of principal secretary, which was then an important office about the king's person (or "at the court," as the phrase went), but not the influential executive department it later became. Calvert's position in no way represented that of a present day prime minister, as the writer says.

2. Father Russell doubts this, *Maryland, The Land of Sanctuary,* p. 52, note.

of Arundel and Surrey, who by his own marriage and the marriage of his son, Lord Maltravers, was linked with the families of Shrewsbury and Lenox, at the wedding of one of whom the younger Calvert was a witness.[1] He was associated with Arundel and Surrey and Lenox as a member of the Council for New England and received with them the first "dividnet," to be known as "New Albion" lying between the Kennebec and Penobscot rivers. It is not at all unlikely that his alliance with the Arundel family and his friendship for Lord Maltravers, who in 1632 bought the Heath patent to lands south of Virginia and in 1637 obtained from the king the allotment of a county there for plantation purposes, may have had something to do with his first application for a grant in that direction. In his official connections he was familiar with Sir Robert Naunton, Sir Robert Heath, and Sir William Alexander, secretary for Scotland, and he personally knew both Vaughan and Falkland, who had a part, as he had, in the Newfoundland venture. He was acquainted, sometimes intimately, with scores of others, among them Lord Cottington[2] and Lord Dorset, who aided him in obtaining his charter.

In 1620 Calvert was appointed one of a committee, which included Lenox, Pembroke, Arundel and Surrey, and Viscount Falkland, with instructions to report on Guy's plantation in Newfoundland, at this time under the governorship of Captain John Mason, and it may be that one result of this membership was his purchase from Sir William Vaughan of that strip of land which became the seat of his Avalon settlement. While carrying out this experiment, an account of which has already been given,[3] he resigned his secretaryship, on the accession of Charles I,[4] partly no doubt because of his

1. Above, pages 222–223. For the pedigree of the Arundel house see Mary Hervey, *The Life of Thomas Howard, Earl of Arundel* (1921). Cecilius Calvert and Lord Maltravers joined in support of Richard Kemp as secretary of Virginia (*Calendar State Papers, Colonial*, 1574–1660, p. 305) after Harvey's recall in 1639. It was at this time that Maltravers made his application for a county (Norfolk) in Virginia, a request that was granted in 1637 (see Vol. III, index).

2. In 1630 Baltimore in his letter to Wentworth speaks in such a manner of receiving a packet from Lady Cottington, as to show intimacy between the two families. Cottington was a Roman Catholic, at least in sympathy, and, we are told, supported Roman Catholic propaganda in England (*D. N. B.*).

3. Above, Vol. I, 308–312.

4. "The first act of King Charles has been to confirm all the Members of his father's Privy Council in their offices, and on Monday last they took the usual oaths, with the exception of Lord Baltimore, Secretary of State, who remarked to his Majesty that, as every one knew him to be a Catholic, he could not now serve him in the same high office, without exciting jealousy in others, nor was he willing to

conversion to the Roman Catholic faith, and partly because of his desire to give more time to the execution of his colonizing plans. He was raised to the peerage on the Irish establishment in 1625 as Baron Baltimore of Baltimore in the county of Longford,[1] and in the same year removed to Ireland, where and at Kiplin Hall in Yorkshire he continued to reside, except for occasional absences, until his death in 1632. He had also a London house in Bloomsbury and at one time occupied lodgings in Lincoln's Inn Fields. He soon realized that Newfoundland was not a suitable place for a colony, and turned his eyes southward to the more salubrious climate of Virginia, with which he had become familiar during his period of membership in the Virginia Company and from his service on the Mandeville commission of 1624. Thither he voyaged with his wife, children, and goods in 1629, searching for a warmer climate, "where the winters be shorter and less vigorous," with the intention of finding somewhere south of Jamestown, a place where he might plant a second colony. Though well received by the authorities there, who hoped that he might settle among them, he was compelled to withdraw because he could not take the oath of supremacy, which the governor and council, acting under orders from England, were obliged to tender to him.[2] Returning home he set the proper machinery in motion for a separate colony of his own.

Charles I, friendly to Baltimore as was his father and perhaps anxious to increase the number and add to the strength of the English baronets in Ireland, endeavored to dissuade him from his course,

take an oath so wounding to his religious feelings. It is said that his Majesty replied 'that it was much better thus to state his opinions, rather than to retain an office by equivocation as some did.'" From the Florentine ambassador to the Grand Duke of Tuscany, April 11, 1635. Historical Manuscripts Commission, *Skrine*, p. 3.

1. Wilhelm, pp. 115–119. In Sir Francis Bacon's recommendations for planting Ireland, made in 1607–1609, the idea is broached of "raising some nobility" for the purpose of drawing persons of great means and estates into the action. As Calvert in 1622 had received a pension from the king (Historical Manuscripts Commission, *Laing*, I, 192) and an estate in Ireland, it is possible that his elevation to a lesser baronetcy ("an inferior Irish lord," his opponents in Maryland called him, *Maryland Archives*, V, 140) may have been due in part to the hope that he would settle there permanently, despite his devotion to his ancestral home, Kiplin Hall in Yorkshire. A contemporary entry of May 23, 1625, says "Lord Baltimore, with all his family, has gone to Ireland where he has large estates" (Historical Manuscripts Commission, *Skrine*, p. 15), but whether he remained there or returned to Kiplin Hall in the years before 1632, we do not certainly know. The plan of an Irish baronetage was in line with the policy adopted earlier for the settlement of the province of Ulster and with the project of 1624 for creating baronets in Nova Scotia (above, Vol. I, 316–317).

2. *Maryland Archives*, III, 16–17.

expressing the hope that he would not go so far away and calling his plans foolish and impracticable, "because men of his condition and breeding" were better fitted "for other employments than the framing of such plantations."[1] But Baltimore was not to be turned aside. He was under the impelling influence of motives and obligations that were more imperative than those of a mere colonizer— among which was the sacred duty of finding a refuge for his Roman Catholic brethren, an obligation which had been felt by the Arundel group for many years.[2] He made his first application early in February, 1632, with the drafting of a warrant signed by his friends in the Privy Council, Dorset, the lord chamberlain, Wentworth, lord deputy of Ireland, and Cottington, chancellor of the exchequer, which he sent to William Nye, attorney general, asking for "that tract or precinct lying from the Bay of Chesapeack and the River of Pohatan otherwise called James River on the North . . . unto the Passamagnus on the South . . . with the same conditions of honours and advantages as the other patent was granted which he had from the late King his Majestie . . . for a part of Newfoundland." The warrant was followed by the king's bill which reached the privy seal on March 17, 1632. But when the news of the proposed patent came to the ears of the members and friends of the defunct Virginia Company, who were still hoping to obtain a renewal of "their antient charter,"[3] they raised so loud a protest against it that the bill was recalled before it reached the great seal and a new warrant drawn, signed by the Earl of Arundel and Surrey, the Earl of Carlisle, Wentworth, and Cottington.

The new warrant said that "upon further consideration his Maj[tie] conceiveth that that Plantation intended soe neere unto the other will too much restraine the old planters," and hearing that the Dutch were encroaching to the northward thought it fitter, in order to check such encroachment, to locate the colony above rather than below Virginia. To this change of location Baltimore agreed. The territory named in the warrant was "that whole peninsula lying between the ocean on the east and the great Bay of Chesapeack on the west and between Cape Charles on the south and Delaware Bay on the north . . . and it shall be called Mariland in memory and honor of the Queene." Two important comments may be made on

1. *Calendar State Papers, Colonial*, 1574–1660, pp. 95, 100–101, 104.
2. Above, Vol. I, 79.   3. *Virginia Magazine*, VIII, 153.

this warrant: first, that "Mariland," as first conceived, was to cover only what is now known as the Eastern Shore; and, secondly, that had Baltimore asked for the northern "precinct" first he might possibly have seen, before his death, the patent drawn in his own name and not, as was to happen, in the name of his son. Yet even that is doubtful, for no sooner had the new bill started on its way through the seals than again former members of the Virginia Company entered objections and brought the matter to the attention of the Privy Council. The latter referred it to its committee on trade and plantations,[1] which reported to the king, June 5, 1632, that the objections were reasonable as far as the southern end of the Eastern Shore was concerned, and it recommended that a third warrant be drawn placing the southern boundary at Watkins Point instead of Cape Charles.

In the meantime Lord Baltimore had died at the early age of fifty-two and left to his son, Cecilius, his lands, plans, obligations, and hopes.[2] A man, trustworthy and honorable, with a keen sense of justice and a marked instinct of loyalty and affection toward those whom he respected and served, George Calvert nevertheless often allowed his personal devotion and his fine sense of duty toward others to override his better judgments. He was never a great statesman or an effective official, nor was he ever ahead of his time either in thought or in action, except perhaps in religious matters. In this respect he was tolerant and sympathetic, benevolent rather than liberal, for he could write to Wentworth, "Thus your Lordship sees that we Papists want not charity toward you Protestants, whatsoever the less understanding Part of the world thinks of us." How far he was responsible for the final draft of the charter it is impossible to say, for all that may certainly be traced to him is the Avalon patent and the warrant of February, 1632, which asked for a duplicate of the former charter. It is more than likely, however, that the essential parts of the final document are his handiwork, for his son Cecilius was but twenty-six at the time of his father's death, and if he had any part in shaping the instrument must have reproduced very largely his father's wishes. These wishes were, as we shall see, for a type of land-holding and government that England had already in

1. For this committee, Andrews, *British Committees*, pp. 13–14.
2. Calvert's will is printed in *Calvert Papers*, I, 48–50, and in *Maryland Magazine*, XXI, 319–324.

large part outgrown. In his official career George Calvert was only moderately successful; while in his domestic relations he was, as he wrote, "for a long time a man of sorrows." Only in his work as a colonizer was he to stamp his name upon the history of England and the New World.

As a result of the report of the Privy Council, June 5, a new warrant was drawn, instructing the attorney general "to prepare an exception to be inserted in the Lord Baltimore's Bill lately signed by his Majtee and consequently in the signett and Privy Seal already passed, if convenientlie it may be done, or else you are to take the former grant into your Custodie and prepare a new Bill," altering the boundaries as stated in the report. But when it was discovered that altering a bill in the seals was impossible,[1] a fourth warrant was prepared which authorized the making of the proper correction, but seemingly authorizing a wide extension of the territory to the westward of the Chesapeake along the fortieth parallel, for the boundaries in the charter as finally issued carried the northern line from Delaware Bay westward along the fortieth parallel to the "first fountain of the River of Pattomack" and the southern line eastward from that point along the south bank of that river and across the bay to Watkins Point. Who was responsible for this huge enlargement of the grant we do not know. Certainly not the elder Baltimore; possibly his son; there is no evidence. It may have been even the king in council, in order to present a barrier between Virginia and the encroaching Dutch, for a colony limited only to the Eastern Shore would hardly have accomplished this purpose, as the king and his council must have realized when they came to know their geography better. These many warrants and the bills which followed in three cases must have cost the family a great deal of money, for getting a charter through the seals was an expensive business.[2] But the fourth

1. This fact is of importance in view of the belief held in some quarters that the Massachusetts Puritans were able to have the place of residence struck out of their charter while that instrument was passing through the seals (see above, Vol. I, 371, note 2). Similarly, William Penn was unable to get the name of his province changed, after the bill had passed the king's sign manual, even though he offered the undersecretary twenty guineas to effect it (Hazard, *Annals of Pennsylvania*, p. 500).

2. Exact statements regarding the cost of passing a charter through the seals are rare. We are told that in 1663 and 1665 the account of fees for passing a duplicate of the first charter of Carolina came to £106 11s 6d and for passing the second and last patent, 1665, £71, 2s, 4d (*Calendar State Papers, Colonial*, 1661–1668, §§1027, 1192; *North Carolina Colonial Records*, I, 115; *Shaftesbury Papers*, pp. 55–56).

warrant was the last, and with the way thus made clear the final bill passed the seals and the charter was issued June 30, 1632.[1]

The Maryland charter is a remarkable document, holding a place among the proprietary patents similar in its uniqueness to that occupied by the charters of Connecticut and Rhode Island among the patents to trading companies. In its conveyance of governing powers it is, however, almost identical with that of Avalon, and differs only in the form of its tenure, its *hactenus inculta* ("hitherto uncultivated") clause, and, of course in its boundaries. The elder Baltimore was undoubtedly responsible for the change of tenure from *in capite* or knight service (Avalon) to free and common socage (Maryland), a step that he had taken some years before in connection with his Irish estates, for the purpose of relieving himself of the heavy obligations of tenure *in capite*. As one familiar with the intricacies of chancery procedure, he was able to obtain the kind of patent he wanted and to introduce into the original petition the most favorable terms —that is, a maximum of rights with a minimum of obligations, thereby placing the least possible restrictions upon himself as proprietor that were devisable and tangible. The yearly payment of two Indian arrows at the castle of Windsor, for it was "as of our Castle of Windsor" that he held his lands, and the taking of an oath of allegiance can hardly have affected his complete proprietary independence in any material way. The introduction into the charter of the princely bishop of Durham clause (as also into the charter of Avalon) to the effect that he was to hold his lands and exercise his authority as the bishop had held and exercised the same "at any time heretofore," made the lord palatine in Maryland in a sense a king there, for according to an old time maxim "What the king has without the bishop [of Durham] has within."

Baltimore was, of course, not a monarch but he was an absolute lord, with complete control over administration, defense, and the upkeep of his province. All writs were to run in his name and not in that of the king and appeals and the confirmation of laws lay only with the proprietor and his courts. The abrogation of the statute of Quia Emptores made it possible for him to enfeoff any part of his territory as he pleased, to be held of him (and not of the king as

1. These warrants, either the originals or copies, were sold (with other Maryland documents) at Sotheby's, June 25, 1929, and are at present inaccessible in the possession of a private owner in Baltimore. Fortunately the Sotheby catalogue furnishes nearly all the information that is needed.

would have been the case had the statute been enforced) at such services and rents as seemed to him fit and agreeable. And, then, as if these provisions were not sufficiently sweeping, the charter contained a blanket clause to the effect that every interpretation of its terms should always be "beneficial, profitable and favorable" (*benignior, utilior et favorabilior*) to the patentee. From the point of view of English law the palatinate of Maryland was as free from royal intervention and control as ever had been any one of the palatinates in the fourteenth century along the Welsh and Scottish borders. It was a feudal seignory of a medieval type, located in a frontier land three thousand miles away, carved out of the territory granted to the old Virginia Company in 1612, which the king considered himself free to dispose of because the company's charter had been annulled in 1624 and because the region was uninhabited and possessed only by "Barbarians, Heathen and Savages." Its extent, as later determined, amounted to between ten and twelve millions of acres, a noble grant.[1]

When the terms of the charter came to be known they aroused bitter opposition in certain quarters. The planters of Virginia de-

---

1. How much Baltimore knew of the past history of the Palatinate of Durham, particularly of its period of greatest independence, 1300–1400, is of course uncertain. I am inclined to think that he knew a good deal about it, enough to be familiar with the conditions prevailing there before the passage of the parliamentary act of 1536, which greatly reduced the bishop's regalia. How otherwise he could have caused to be written into his charter the same powers that the bishop had in the fourteenth century is difficult to explain. On the palatinate, see Surtees, *History of the County of Durham*, which Bassett used for making up his brief account (Johns Hopkins University *Studies*, XII, 117–123) and Lapsley, *Palatinate of Durham*. which deals chiefly with the earlier period.

The charter was somewhat of the nature of an octroyed constitution, incapable of alteration or amendment except by concession from the grantor, the terms of which the proprietor interpreted strictly and without compromise (for his own ideas on the subject, *Maryland Archives*, I, 263–264). It may fairly be said that the troubles which arose after 1660 were due to the fact that a charter conferring powers representative of the fourteenth century circumscribed the activities of free-born Englishmen of the seventeenth century by making them the "subjects" of an absolute proprietor, whose prerogatives dated from medieval times. This was the more serious in that it hampered the economic and political development of the province and placed the people of Maryland in a position unlike that of other free-born Englishmen either in the colonies or in England, and made them not subjects of the king but tenants of a medieval lord. Baltimore possessed governmental powers which in a majority of cases he delegated not to the people themselves but to members of his family, relatives, and friends. The system was not only an anachronism at the time, but was one which, because based on rigid and unchanging formulae, was certain to breed dissatisfaction and if rigorously adhered to, as the proprietor adhered to it, to end in revolution.

nounced a grant that despoiled them of their territory and restricted their trade, and they asserted that the division of the area of their own original patent into several governments would do them irreparable injury.[1] The king referred the petition to the Privy Council, which obtained an opinion from its legal adviser (or from the legal adviser of the old company) that the provisions of the Maryland charter were far too comprehensive, particularly those that had to do with the enfeoffing of land and the elimination of control by the crown. This opinion said that the king's failure to reserve rights of appeal and his concession of such extensive powers of sovereignty, in a province so near to Virginia which had no such powers, was bound to be inconvenient and dangerous. In general the legal adviser objected to the charter as opposed to the rights of Englishmen, in that it conveyed privileges that were out of accord with the spirit of the time when it was issued.[2] But despite this opinion, the council

1. There seems to have been a number of petitions at this period for grants north and south of Virginia. We have already noticed the Plowden patent of 1632 (*Calendar State Papers, Colonial*, 1574–1660, p. 154 (60); *Strafford's Letters*, I, 73). In a letter from Plowden to Cecilius Calvert, August 30, 1639, mention is made of a petition from Withers, deputy governor of the Bermuda Company in England, with associates from Virginia, including Claiborne and apparently Matthews, for a charter of incorporation (date not given) granting the petitioners a part of Virginia and the southern portion of the Eastern Shore peninsula (Sotheby papers). As we shall see later Sir Robert Heath obtained a patent for Carolana in 1629, which he made over in 1632 to Lord Maltravers, who had married the daughter of the Earl of Lenox and, on the death of his father in 1646, became third earl of Arundel and Surrey and Earl Marshal of England. His eldest son was restored to the dukedom of Norfolk in 1660.

2. The objections raised on behalf of Virginia's claim (C. O. 1:6, no. 58) are important as showing certain trends of thought regarding Virginia's rights. These objections are as follows: (1) As by the charter of 1612 Virginia controlled for fifty miles from its first settlement and as the territory was in part occupied, Baltimore had no right in that region. (2) The charter contained no provision for writs of error or of appeal to the king. (3) The Bishop of Durham clause too general and uncertain, as not specifying which bishop was meant. (4) Baltimore's grants in fee were so phrased that anyone—aliens, savages, or enemies, could become landholders and their children denizens. (5) Power to transport any persons contrary to English law. (6) Wrong for Baltimore to be able to make war as likely to involve other English colonies. (7) No restraint upon furnishing savages with arms. (8) Power to grant honors, lands, privileges, and other franchises such as was likely to draw away people from other colonies. (9) Such royal and imperial rights, granted in sovereignty, elevated Maryland at the expense of the others. (10) Right of possession still vested in the Virginia planters. The last claim was based on orders in council of October 8, 1623 (*Acts Privy Council, Colonial*, I, §109) and October 20 (*ibid.*, §112), on the royal commission of July 24, 1624 (*ibid.*, §122; Hazard, *State Papers*, I, 183–188), on the royal proclamation of May 13, 1625 (Brigham, *Proclamations*, p. 52), and on the letter from the Privy Council, October 29, 1625 (an order not otherwise known).

could do no more than accept a situation which had arisen too late to be remedied, and calling Baltimore and representatives of the old company before it for a hearing, recommended that they get together and settle the controversy the best way they could. It finally decided to leave Baltimore in full possession of his patent and advised the remonstrants to follow any course of law they desired. It urged upon both parties that they "sincerely entertaine all good correspondence and assist each other on all occasions in such manner as became fellow subjects and members of the same state."[1] Thus Cecil Calvert passed safely the first crisis which he had met in carrying out his father's plans. But his troubles in England were not yet over.

The seventeen months that elapsed between the issue of the charter and the date set for the departure of the vessels for America (June 20, 1632—August 20, 1633) resounded with the activities of preparation. Baltimore made no attempt at secrecy, but followed the course familiar to all promoters of colonization in that day. With the Jesuit fathers, who were sponsoring the undertaking and were in charge of publicity, and with Baltimore opening an office in Bloomsbury at the upper end of Holborn for purposes of consultation and registration, the selection of applicants proceeded rapidly. The need of advertisement was especially felt in Baltimore's case because of the religious nature of the enterprise and of the danger lest false rumors get abroad were the facts not known. Therefore clear-cut statements were necessary in order to draw the rank and file to his cause. Even as it was the number of applicants was never large, in addition to the many Roman Catholic gentlemen, with their servants, who were already committed to the undertaking and probably shared in the expense. Just how much the expedition cost is uncertain.[2] It has been variously estimated at from £10,000 to

1. *Acts Privy Council, Colonial*, I, §317; *Calendar State Papers, Colonial, 1574–1660*, pp. 169 (76), 170 (78); *Maryland Archives*, III, 17–23; *Calvert Papers*, I, 223–225; *Maryland Magazine*, II, 161–162. Cecilius's reply to his detractors is convincing, *Strafford's Letters*, I, 178; *Maryland Archives*, III, 23.

2. On the cost *Calvert Papers*, I, 228 ("above ten thousand pounds"); *Maryland Archives*, III, 180 ("the greatest part of his fortune"); Chalmers, *Political Annals*, I, 208 ("upward of forty thousand pounds," which may include the £30,000 spent on Avalon); "Narrative," *Fund-Publications*, no. 7, p. 22; *Maryland Magazine*, II, 162; *Original Narratives, Maryland*, p. 167 ("Lord Baltimore's Case," where the statement is made that the whole cost was £40,000, of which £20,000 was Baltimore's). Lord Arundell gave Cecilius the manor of Semley in Wiltshire for love of that son-in-law who had "weak fortune in that he had sunk himself in a plantation," *Maryland Magazine*, IV, 252.

£40,000 but the actual outgo must have been a continuing one and not limited to the initial disbursement, and later the Maryland assembly made some effort to compensate Cecilius Calvert for his charges by granting him a special subsidy.[1]

Now that he was ready for departure Cecilius had to face further efforts made by members of the old Virginia Company and by merchants interested in Virginia, this time to prevent the sailing of the vessels by renewed appeals to the Privy Council and by attempts to seduce the seamen engaged for the voyage. To meet the latter danger he instructed his brother Leonard, whom he appointed deputy governor, and the two commissioners, Cornwallis and Hawley, to make inquiries and gather proofs on shipboard, and he warned them when reaching the Chesapeake to avoid going to Jamestown and to keep out of range of the guns at Point Comfort lest something untoward happen there.[2] The greater danger, however, came from the Privy Council, which having been informed that one of the vessels had left Gravesend contrary to orders and that there some of those on board had refused to take the oath of allegiance, held up the actual sailing from August 20, the date first set for the departure of the *Ark* from London, and from September 8, the date for the sailing from Portsmouth, to November 22, 1633, when the oath of allegiance, required by the royal proclamation of 1611, was finally taken, license given, and the ships got under way.[3] Baltimore made vigorous protest against these "molestors" of his plans, for the embargo was threatening him with a further depletion of his inheritance, though the payment of captain and crew did not begin until the sailing of the *Dove* from London, October 16.[4]

It is evident that the Roman Catholic priests and laymen in some way, either by concealment or by boarding the vessels secretly farther down the Channel—some perhaps at Portsmouth, others later—avoided taking the oath which required a denial of the papal authority in England. The number swearing allegiance at Tilbury Hope, the fort opposite Gravesend, where the oath was administered, was

1. *Maryland Archives*, I, 118, 120.
2. *Calvert Papers*, I, 132–133; *Strafford's Letters*, II, 257.
3. *Calendar State Papers, Colonial*, 1574–1660, p. 171 (84). *Maryland Magazine*, I, 352–354; IV, 251–254, for further details.
4. In 1648 two merchants of London, who were sending 400 men, women, and children to Virginia, estimated their loss by embargo at £20 a day. Historical Manuscripts Commission, *Seventh Report*, p. 45a.

reported as only one hundred and twenty-eight, which probably covered most of the Church of England gentlemen, artisans, and laborers, so that the remainder of the passengers must have been taken on afterward. The two vessels, the *Ark*, a new ship of about 360 tons, and the *Dove*, a pinnace of 60 tons, set sail from Cowes, Richard Orchard master, on November 22, and though some of the seamen, who according to Father White were plotting against the proprietor, expected further orders from the council postponing the voyage, no such orders came, and the vessels proceeded down the Channel and headed out into the Atlantic. Separated by a storm, the *Dove* returned to the Scillies and the *Ark* went on without her, laying her course southward toward the Canaries, a route that the *Dove*, in the company of a London ship, the *Dragon*, later followed. Tarrying for some time in the West Indies, where at Barbados the *Dove* joined the *Ark*, the voyagers replenished their stock of water and provisions, laid in a supply of seed corn, and recuperated from the effects of the life on board.

Leaving Barbados for St. Kitts, the *Dove* again separated from the *Ark*, stopping at Montserrat and Nevis and narrowly escaping capture, but both arrived within the Capes of Virginia on February 27, 1634, having been on the voyage three months and at sea about seven weeks and a half. Though they expected nothing but "blows" from the Virginians, they were in fact well received, thanks to the friendliness of Governor Harvey,[1] who gave them what provisions they needed, and later his successors responded frequently with offers of help. Though they had brought with them a barge in separate parts, with which to explore the creeks and small rivers, they hired another small boat of the Virginians, which Leonard Calvert used to search out the lesser waterways. On March 3, 1634, they started up the bay, and on the northern side of the Potomac landed on an island which they called St. Clements (now Blakiston). On March 25 they celebrated mass, erected a great cross hewn out of a large tree, and solemnly took possession of the country. Later they moved southward along the coast and took up their location permanently at the Indian town Yoacomaco, later St. Mary's, near the head of St. Inigoes Creek. There they bought land, thirty miles in length, of the friendly Yoacomaco Indians, for a stock of trading hatchets, axes, hoes, and cloths. During the next month they built

1. *Calendar State Papers, Colonial*, 1574–1660, p. 193 (31).

and palisaded a fort, upon which they mounted guns, put up a rough storehouse and chapel, began to erect houses—of hewn logs probably[1]—planted corn and other crops, and for a time lived on the supplies brought with them and on food furnished by the Indians.[2] They were fortunate in finding a part of the land cleared and cultivated in Indian fashion and were able to escape anything comparable with the starving time of some of the other colonies.[3]

There landed on the soil of Maryland between two and three hundred people. Baltimore gives the number as above two hundred in one place and as three hundred laboring people in another.[4] A frequent modern estimate of over three hundred is probably too high. There were two Jesuit priests—Fathers Andrew White and John

1. The first houses are called "cottages," and even as late as 1678 the dwellings at St. Mary's are described as "mean." Cornwallis, who built the first mill, seems to have been the first also to build a house of sawn timber, a story and a half high, with a cellar and a chimney of brick. His venture at milling turned out badly. *Maryland Archives*, I, 174.

2. Calvert sent the *Dove*, June, 1634, to Massachusetts Bay for fish and other commodities and the captain in charge incurred his reprimand for spending four months on the voyage. It was on this trip that trouble arose with Orchard over the wages, which led eventually to the suit before the High Court of Admiralty.

3. There are seven accounts of the circumstances preceding, accompanying, and following the settlement of Maryland. I, *A Declaration of the Lord Baltemore's Plantation in Maryland*, 1633 (reproduced in facsimile, 1929, with a preface by Lawrence C. Wroth, which analyzes the relation of the first four of these documents to each other). II, *An Account of the Colony of the Lord Baron of Baltamore*, 1633, *Fund-Publications*, no. 7, pp. 44–53 (Latin and English texts); Original Narratives, *Maryland*, pp. 3–10 (though stated at the end as compiled by Cecilius, this account was probably written by Father Andrew White, chief of the Jesuit missionaries accompanying the expedition and, after Baltimore himself, the leading promoter of the undertaking). III, *Relatio Itineris in Marylandiam*, April, 1634 (believed to have been composed by Father White and better known in translation, *Narrative of a Voyage to Maryland*. Both versions are printed in *Fund-Publications*, no. 7, pp. 10–43). IV, *A Relation of the successful Beginnings of the Lord Baltimore's Plantation: being an Extract of certain Letters written from thence by some of the Adventurers to their Friends in England. From Saint Mairie's 27 May 1634*. Sabin's *Reprints*, with a prefatory note and appendix by F. L. Hawks (1865); *Historical Magazine*, IX, 293–298. V, *A Brief Relation of the Voyage unto Maryland, by Father Andrew White*, 1634, *Calvert Papers*, no. 3, pp. 26–45; Original Narratives, *Maryland*, pp. 27–45. VI, *A Relation of Maryland. Together with a Map of the Country, The Conditions of Plantation, His Majesties Charter to the Lord Baltemore, translated into English September the 8 Anno Dom. 1635*, Original Narratives, *Maryland*, pp. 65–112 (the first chapter is Father White's narrative altered and abridged; the remainder probably the work of Cecilius). VII, "Short Treatise by R[obert] W[intour] in a Letter written to his worthy friend C[aptain] J[ohn] R[eade], September 12, 1636," Sotheby Papers. (This account I have not seen as the manuscript is now in private hands and the text has never been printed.)

4. *Calendar State Papers, Colonial, 1574–1660*, p. 228; *Strafford's Letters*, I, 179.

Altham (others including Father Copley came later)—with two lay
brothers Gervase and Wood; sixteen gentlemen-adventurers, with
wives, children, and servants, one of the seventeen who started having died on shipboard; and something over two hundred others,
mostly handicraftsmen, laborers, and servants, men and women,
with a few of the yeoman-farmer class and a gentleman or two—a
majority of whom were Protestants of the Church of England. Many
of the servants were not indentured, but were of a menial or domestic status, from the households of the Roman Catholic gentlemen
and presumably were Roman Catholics themselves.[1] It would be a
mistake to assume that all the rank and file were Protestants. Many
of the servants who came afterward were indentured, brought over
with newly arriving planters or bought on landing from the ships,
for Baltimore continued to keep his Bloomsbury office open for all
those who desired "to adventure in this plantation." Lands were
assigned at once and continued to be so assigned for half a century
according to the number of those coming voluntarily or who were
transported at the charge of the free adventurers. The Jesuit fathers
and some of the Roman Catholic gentry obtained their lands under
assumed names, as was not uncommon in England where the laws
against Popish recusants were particularly severe.[2]

Cecilius, Lord Baltimore, was not of the company. He had expected to go with the first contingent, planning to join the ship,
with all his company, at Portsmouth, August 20, 1633.[3] On January
10, 1634, he wrote Wentworth that at last he had sent away his ships,
but was obliged to defer his own going until another time. Almost
every year until 1643 he hoped to get away, but was unable to do so
because of the necessity of being at home to meet any emergency
that might arise in a period of English history unfavorable to proprietors. Though he lived forty years longer, till 1675, he was never
sufficiently free from the cares and responsibilities of his landed

1. Some of the Protestant servants were on five year terms. There were also unin-
dentured servants from the households of some of the gentry, among whom, probably,
were the maids who were upset in landing at St. Clements and were almost drowned
"by the overturning of the shallop, besides the loss of much linen . . . which [says
the writer] is a very main loss in these parts" (*Historical Magazine*, IX, 294). The
loss was Father White's.

2. The English Jesuits and their pupils were known by assumed names at St.
Omer, the Roman Catholic college on the Continent, which itself was always referred
to in correspondence as "Flamsteed."

3. *A Declaration* (no. I, above), pp. 7–8; *Calvert Papers*, I, 136–137.

estates in England and Ireland and of the intrigues of his enemies to leave the country.[1] Therefore he had to govern his colony from afar; to send over men and equipment, commissions and instructions, rules for the distribution of land, laws drafted by his attorneys in England for acceptance by the assembly, and letters to his brother and others to whom he deputed powers vested in him as proprietor. Government at long range, as all found out who were compelled to exercise it two and three centuries ago, has many disadvantages.

Cecilius entrusted the governorship of the colony to his brother Leonard, at this time but twenty-eight years old, who four years before, in 1629, had seen service in Newfoundland as the captain of a ship, the *St. Claude,* taken from the French, which the king had loaned Sir George Calvert for the purpose of carrying provisions to Ferryland.[2] Only a week before the sailing Cecilius had given him and his commissioners a body of instructions, the provisions of which disclose better than any formal document of authority the deep-lying desire of the proprietor to erect a colony free from religious animosity and contention, in which Roman Catholic and Protestant might live together in peace and harmony. The charge which he gave to his fellow religionists was to preserve a good understanding and a friendly attitude in all their relations with their Protestant associates and to be silent upon all occasions of discourse relating to matters of religion. In so stating his policy he set the stamp of his conviction upon the whole adventure, as far as his wishes were concerned. But he could not so easily control the reli-

---

1. He became involved in land disputes with his brother-in-law, William Arundell, in 1642, because of which the latter obtained a writ from the House of Lords *ne exeat regno.* Baltimore petitioned against the issue of the writ, asking that service be deferred until he could be heard by counsel and saying that he had no intention of leaving the country suddenly (Historical Manuscripts Commission, *Fifth Report,* pp. 14ab, 51a; *Lords Journal,* IV, 675. For the chancery suit, *Maryland Magazine,* V, 245-249. Cecilius planned to go over to the colony in January, 1643, *Maryland Archives,* III, 135; Kilty, *Land-Holder's Assistant,* p. 35, but was prevented from doing so because of the threatened issue of the writ). Probably the writ was never actually issued or if issued never served. On November 24, 1646, Cecilius nearly lost his charter at the hands of parliament and petitioned against an order vacating it (March 4, 1647, Historical Manuscripts Commission, *Sixth Report,* p. 142a). Again in 1648 he became involved in a dispute over land with the Earl of Shrewsbury, the details of which are given in *Lords Journal,* X, 43-44, 272. After that date he was forced to remain to save what he could of his plantation, a situation that will be discussed later.

2. Historical Manuscripts Commission, *Southampton Manuscripts,* p. 129; Steiner, *Report,* American Historical Association, 1905, I, 118.

gious ardor of those whom he enjoined. That the proselyting zeal of the Jesuit fathers in the years which followed aroused fears and ill will and brought complaints was inevitable in an age when religious bitterness of feeling was intense and easily awakened and when recusancy in England was the object of hostile legislation. But the significant fact remains that in no other colony of the period was the experiment even tried of Roman Catholics and Protestants actually living side by side on terms of equality, amity, and forbearance.[1] In that respect the settlement of Maryland holds a unique place in the history of English colonization.

At the same time it must be remembered that George Calvert would have had great difficulty in carrying out his plans had he tried to depend for their success on his co-religionists only. As it was "he found very few who were inclyned to goe and seat themselves in those parts" and he must have realized the necessity of offering to those who applied very advantageous terms in order to overcome the reluctance of the humbler classes, who were generally loyal to the Church of England, to join in an enterprise that was reputed to be identified with Roman Catholic gentlemen of rank. As Charles, Lord Baltimore, said in 1675, "Many there were of this sort of People who declared their Wyllingnesse to goe and Plant themselves in this Province soe they might have a Generall Toleraccon settled there by a Lawe by which all of all sorts who professed Christianity in Generall might be at Liberty to worshipp God in such Manner as was most agreeable with their respective Judgm^ts and Consciences without being subject to any penaltyes whatsoever for their soe doeing . . . without the complying with these condicons in all probability. This Province had never beene planted."[2] That the first Lord Baltimore was willing to accept such articles of agreement, even under necessity, is a witness to his consistency of character and desire for peaceful intercourse with his fellow men. That his son should have been willing to carry out his father's promises is a proof of his own integrity and loyalty to his father's memory.

Cecilius wanted peace without as well as harmony within. He was well aware of the opposition his colonists might encounter in their

1. There was nothing "miraculous" about this experiment. It was a very human and at the same time a very noble ideal that failed in the application. Alsop coined the phrase "Miracle of the Age." Original Narratives, *Maryland*, p. 349.

2. *Maryland Archives*, V, 267–268.

relations with their neighbors, particularly in Virginia, and he had already become unpleasantly aware of the enmity of William Claiborne of that colony, located on Kent Island in the Chesapeake, who had gone to England in 1630 in part for the purpose of preventing, if he could, the issue of the Maryland charter. Cecilius gave his brother a letter from the king to Governor Harvey, bidding the latter furnish the newcomers all the help possible and treat them with the respect and courtesy due a person of Baltimore's rank and quality, who was under the king's protection.[1] This Harvey did, at the expense of his own popularity in Virginia.[2] Leonard wrote Claiborne asking for an interview, saying that his brother had had some dealings with his partners in London but would do nothing more until he knew how he stood with Claiborne in the colony.[3] He also wrote Governor Winthrop sending his letter with the *Dove,* which reached Boston August 29, 1634, with corn to exchange for fish and other commodities, and this correspondence was continued for some years.[4] Three or four years later (May, 1638) he wrote to Governor Kiefft at New Amsterdam, expressing a desire for a friendly exchange and inquired about ships for hiring.[5] After the taking of New Netherland by the English, Philip and Charles Calvert corresponded with Governor Nicolls and there is evidence to show a considerable interchange of letters and commodities between 1664 and 1667.[6] In this and other ways Leonard and his successors made every effort to carry out the proprietor's advice that they be conciliatory and friendly toward all.

Having started the settlement with the aid of the friendly Indians, Leonard and his commissioners proceeded step by step to put into operation the proprietor's instructions regarding the distribution of land and the conditions of plantation. Gradually during the next few years the region below the Patapsco was laid out according to a seignorial and manorial plan. Overlaying the Indian towns and

---

1. *Ibid.*, III, 22–23.

2. On the situation in Virginia and the unpopularity and eventual expulsion of Harvey, Wertenbaker, *Virginia under the Stuarts*, ch. III.

3. *Calvert Papers*, I, 134–136.   4. Winthrop, *Journal*, I, 131–132.

5. Sotheby Papers, "I feel some difficulty about the payment which you propose to make in Tobacco which is abundant here and exported to Holland and New England."

6. Huntington Library, Blathwayt Papers. Some of the letters to Nicolls are from Nicholas Utie, a well known Maryland planter and insurgent and a negotiator in the controversy with New York over the Delaware lands.

fields where the colonists first settled, stretching up the northern side of the Potomac, along both sides of the Patuxent, and including Kent Island there came into existence in somewhat shadowy fashion, the forms, tenures, and social relations of a baronial estate, reproducing intentionally but very sketchily proprietary conditions at home. The entire area was a palatinate or great barony, within which, standing in a feudal relationship with the proprietor, were the lords of the manors and the freeholders with their tenements. During the period from 1635 to 1665, the proprietor issued many detailed instructions regarding the way the land should be allotted and seated,[1] and though the conditions were frequently altered in matters of detail, they conformed very closely to a common type and that type one familiar to the proprietary class at home. They set the stamp of a decentralized and rural plantation system upon the colony, organized on a manorial plan and imitating as nearly as possible the features of an English barony. Within his own seignory, particularly within that portion of it which lay south of the Patuxent, he seems to have provided in a vague way for honours and baronies, the purpose and extent of which are not very clear except that they appertained to the proprietor himself.[2] We find mention of the

1. For the many "conditions of plantations" see Kilty, *Land-Holder's Assistant,* chs. III, IV; *Maryland Archives* (as below). The original system underwent many modifications later, some of the conditions being made more liberal, others more restrictive. The peculiarly manorial grants did not outlast the seventeenth century and probably were beginning to disappear before 1660 (though we meet with manorial grants in 1669). The "headright" system ended in 1683. The following references may be given: *Maryland Archives,* I, 201; III, 47–48, 99–100, 223–228, 231–237, 329, 341, 458–459; V, 55, 63–64, 530; XVII, 239–241 (ending of headrights); XX, 434–435; XXII, 481; XXIII, 87, 211. The "Land Grants," "Land Notes," "Land Records," and "Rent Rolls" printed in the *Maryland Magazine* are indispensable. Also Mrs Sioussat, *Old Manors in the Colony of Maryland,* I (Potomac), II (Patuxent), III (Patapsco, planned but never issued); Forman, *Early Manor and Plantation Houses of Maryland* (chiefly architectural); "First Grants on the Patapsco," *Maryland Magazine,* III, 51–60; Bond, "Quit-Rent in Maryland," *ibid.,* V, 350–365; Giddens, "Land Policies and Administration in Colonial Maryland," *ibid.,* XXVIII, 142–171; Gould, "The Land System of Maryland," Johns Hopkins University *Studies,* XXI, no. 1; and *Maryland Archives,* LI, *passim.* On the proprietary manors, Berkley, *Maryland Magazine,* XXIX, 237–245.

2. For a detailed account of such a system as that which Baltimore had in mind and tried to reproduce in Maryland see *The Berkeley Manuscripts,* III, "History of the Hundred of Berkeley," where we find the manor of Berkeley called a "great manor" and a "hundred," with lesser manors within, freeholds and copyholds, and with all tenurial and judicial obligations appertaining thereto. Where the Berkeley conditions are time-honored and complete, those of Maryland are new and very incomplete. But the resemblances are perfectly clear, even to the existence of small

barony of St. Mary's and the honour of West St. Mary's, and once in 1638, when the budding assembly audaciously brought in a bill for baronies, the bill was disallowed by the proprietor, probably because it dealt with a matter that did not concern that body.[1] While Cecilius may have had some idea at the beginning of creating such a feudal jurisdiction as appertained to an honour—because he had a right to do so since he possessed the dignity of a lordship—and to a barony—because he was a baron by patent—he was unable to give vitality to such archaisms, though the name "honour" continued to be used on into the eighteenth century.[2] The barony in Maryland never had that reality which the barony in South Carolina was to have, but in the effort that Baltimore made to transfer the landed institutions of England to his province in America he far outstripped any other founder of a proprietary colony. Sir Ferdinando Gorges was his closest rival, and what Baltimore did in Maryland Gorges would have been glad to do, on even a grander scale though with less absolute authority, in New England.[3]

During the seventeenth century some sixty manors were erected, not including those which the proprietor and his relatives laid out in 6000 acre tracts, each for his own use.[4] There was also the abortive

manors or submanors held of a great manor (*ibid.*, pp. 61, 78, 197; *Maryland Archives*, LI, 139–140).

1. *Maryland Archives*, I, 20.

2. Kilty, *Land-Holder's Assistant*, pp. 101, 102. A good example is Westbury Manor, "To be holden as of our Honour of West St Maries." January 10, 1642 (*Maryland Magazine*, V, 172). The lord of this manor was our old friend of the Pilgrims, Thomas Weston, as is made clear by the designation "Thomas Weston, merchant" at the time of his death (1647) and by the fact that a claim was entered against his estate by one Stone of London, merchant (*Maryland Archives*, I, 230). Weston was "to hold, use, and enjoy within the said Manor Court Leet and Court Baron with all powers, rights, and profits to the said Courts or either of them belonging by the Law and Custom of England." The manor of Evelinton was in the "Baronie of St. Maries" and the manor of Hope was to be held "as of the Honour of St. Mareys." See also, *ibid.*, LI, 27, LIV, 6.

3. We know that the charter which Gorges hoped to obtain from the crown in 1632 for the Council for New England was based on Baltimore's charter of four months before (above, Vol. I, 405, note 1), and that his own charter of 1639 for Maine had the same charter as its model. The powers granted were less absolute than those conferred on Baltimore because the Bishop of Durham clause in it granted only such privileges as the bishop had at the time of issue.

4. Kilty, *Land-Holder's Assistant*, p. 99. On these manors, one-sixth part, lying together in a contiguous place, was to be the lord's demesne, the rest was to be disposed of under instructions (*Maryland Archives*, V, 57, 95–96. Also XV, 30, XVII, 231). As late as 1669 Baltimore ordered that two manors of 6000 acres each should be laid out as proprietary reserves in each county.

Indian manor of Calverton, across the Patuxent from Mattapany, where a form of copyhold tenure was provided for on paper but never given effect in use.[1] Manors held of the lord proprietor might contain anywhere from one to three thousand acres, and if formally created by patent, were endowed with all the rights and privileges belonging to a manor in England. "We have therefore of our Meer grace of and with the advice of &c and according to our Special Letters under hand and Seale, bearing date at Warder Castle 29 August 1636 &c with Wrecks &c Court Leet and Court Baron, according to the forme and usage of England &c will have it called St. Anne's yielding therefore 200 weight of good wheat &c."[2] That the holding of courts leet and baron was practiced on many of the manors at the beginning is likely enough, for the right so to hold was regularly conferred, but the record of only one such court has come down to us.[3] The payment of a rent—"the common mannor rent and conditions"[4]—in corn, tobacco, or other produce of the soil was required by the free and common socage tenure, in which all the lands were held. Required also was the oath of fidelity to the proprietor, the wording of which seems to have been drawn up by Cecilius in 1648,[5] though an earlier form undoubtedly existed. It was proposed in 1639 that a lord of a manor should be tried only by his peers, unless there should not be enough lords in a county to

1. *Maryland Archives*, I, 330. This manor was never actually erected, and in 1662 grants were made to others out of the territory, *Calvert Papers*, I, 230; *Maryland Archives*, LI, 162, 490, 493.

2. *Maryland Magazine*, VI, 197, also 198, 201–202, 264–265; VIII, 268 ("A court Leet & Court Baron, wth all things to the said Courts or eyther of them belonging, by the Law or Custom of England"; for the same right at Snow Hill, XLI, 535. For Leonard Calvert's manors, Trinity, St. Michael's, and St. Gabriel's, IX, 40–41.

3. Johns Hopkins University *Studies*, I, no. 7, pp. 31–38. The manor is St. Clements, St. Mary's County, Thomas Gerrard, lord, John Ryves, steward, 1652–1672. The right to hold courts leet was granted to the lords of manors in New York erected by Governor Dongan. Note especially the grant of the lordship of the Manor of Queens Village, James Lloyd, first lord, New York Historical Society, *Collections*, 1926, pp. 72–77.

4. *Maryland Archives*, XVII, 491.

5. *Ibid.*, III, 196–197. The oath of 1648 contains no reservation of allegiance to the king, which was not added until 1684 (*ibid.*, XIII, 31, 254, 257). In 1656, the Committee of Trade, to whom the Maryland situation had been referred, made some alteration in the oath (below, p. 320), probably inserting the "Engagement" required by the Commonwealth "I do declare and promise that I will be true and faithful to the Commonwealth of England, as it is now established without King or House of Lords (Firth and Rait, *Acts and Ordinances*, II, 325; *Maryland Archives*, III, 342). It is possible that the insertion of this clause had something to do with Fendall's "pigmie rebellion" of 1660 (below, p. 323).

make up a jury, in which case freeholders might be used, but such proposal, though embodied in a bill, never became a law.[1] Later only lords of manors were allowed to sit as members of the governor's council.

Far more numerous than the lords of manors were the freeholders who had tenements, which they had taken up under the conditions laid down by the proprietor.[2] The size of a freehold—a term which of course included the manor also, but is here used to mean a tenancy only—might range from less than a hundred to more than a thousand acres, some freeholds being very small, others as large as a manor. The mere possession of land did not make a man the lord of a manor, for manorial rights could be created only by patent, therefore a freeholder might possess more land than a lord and still be only a freeholder. Many of these tenements lay within the bounds of some manor, outside the lord's demesne, just as did the freeholds of an English estate, and there were many land transactions involved in this location, such as forms of lease, sales, and testamentary dispositions, with which the proprietor had nothing to do, unless the tenements were a part of the proprietary manors. In either case these were strictly intra-manorial matters as were also the obligations to do suit and perform service. All landholders—manorial lords and freeholders—had to pay a quit-rent to the proprietor—a universal charge which made up a large part of the proprietor's revenue from the province. Many of those who received grants of land, even those holding manors or tenements elsewhere, received in addition, during the first few years, allotments in the fields or town of St. Mary's—"town land," it was sometimes called—and there was always the hope, though never realized, of making towns out of the two chief centers in the life of the colony, St. Mary's and Kent Island. At a later time a similar hope was entertained of making towns elsewhere, and a sort of boom was started in real estate transactions in sundry selected places, accom-

1. *Maryland Archives*, I, 54.
2. *Ibid.*, VI, 367; VII, 192. For example: grant of three hundred acres to William Smoote, who had transported himself, wife, and two children into the province, "to be holden of us or our heyres as of the mannor of New Towne, Yelding & paying therefore yearly [to the proprietor] at our usual Receipt at St. Maries six shillings in money sterling or three Bushels of Corn." Sometimes the rent was paid in barrels of Indian corn at five bushels to the barrel. The amount seems to have been always stated in sterling, with its equivalent in tobacco or corn (*Maryland Archives*, LI, 296, 297).

panied by a good deal of rivalry and ill will, but nothing of importance came of the attempt in the seventeenth century. Just as the manors bore a great variety of names, some religious (Trinity, St. Michael's, St. Gabriel's, St. Cuthbert, and the like), others secular (Snow Hill, Westbury, Brook Place, Evelinton), so most of the freehold-plantations bore names, as they usually did in England, both descriptive and jocose, such as Cook's Rest, Peverall, Hog's Neck, Parker's Folly, Owlet's Nest, Gum Neck, and so on in great and ingenious variety.[1] Servants at first, both men and women, and later servants and negroes formed the laboring class, the former under indenture for a term of years, at the expiration of which time their masters were obliged by the custom of the colony to give every one on departure a year's provision of corn, clothes, and planting tools.[2] Many of the plantations were under the immediate direction of overseers, whose compensation was a share of the crop and the sequelae, and whose customs and methods of management followed very closely those of Virginia.[3]

On the social and tenurial sides Maryland stands in a class by itself among the other colonies of the English world. No such form of aristocratic and seignorial life characterized either Barbados or the Leeward Islands and no such transplanting of a manorial system took place in any other of the English continental possessions. At the beginning Maryland was no mere palatinate on paper; it was a land of actual manors, demesne lands, freehold tenements, rent rolls, and quit-rents. The lords of these manors, from the proprietor down, profited from the returns incident to these tenures, while the proprietor himself enjoyed the *jura regalia* of his palatinate, among which were the casual revenues from alienation fees, deodands, waifs and estrays, fines and forfeitures, felons' goods, and even the wild animals (stray cattle included) and wild fowl of the region.[4] The

1. These names appear in the rent rolls and very frequently in the chancery court proceedings (*Maryland Archives,* LI).

2. *Maryland Archives,* V, 16; XIII, 454; LI, index. In 1676 the Fendall party said that "a great many of us came in servants to others, but all adventured our lives for it and got our poore living with hard labour out of the ground in a terrible wilderness" (V, 140). As a corrective of Alsop's unduly flattering account one should read the preface to volume XLIX of the *Archives.* Much new information has come to light since McCormac's essay was written (Johns Hopkins University *Studies,* XXII, nos. 3, 4).

3. *Maryland Archives,* XLIX, 326–329.

4. *Ibid.,* XVII, deodand; II, 89, 90, wild animals. The estates and goods of Claiborne, Fendall, Godfrey, and Talbot were all declared forfeited to the proprietor, but

proprietor never attempted to take heriots or reliefs, but he had his manors, his reserves of vacant land, both cultivated and uncultivated, and his rights of escheat, which many of the colonists believed he exercised unfairly and even illegally. These rights he retained throughout the colonial period. He could hand over his privileges to any local lord he wished and he did this in a few instances, but such concessions were neither frequent nor important. All the manors were divided, as we have seen, more or less unevenly, into demesne and freehold lands, both taking the form of plantations, where was cultivated what Cornwallis called the "stinking weed of America," because the colonists "were uncapable of carrying on any other worke to procure a livelyhood."[1]

Socially there was a great gulf fixed between the upper and lower classes, between the gentility and the mass of the people. Manors and plantations lay remote and widely scattered, with wooded spaces between, chiefly along the rivers and fronting Chesapeake Bay. Family distinctions were clearly marked and the lines which cut through provincial society in England found their counterpart in the smaller world above the Potomac. The proprietary family, relatives, and friends were in the ascendant and were accorded the prominence due their rank and official leadership. Roman Catholicism was the prevailing religious faith among them, and at St. Mary's and on many of the larger manors were to be found priests, chapels, and the regular services of the church. The story of Maryland in the seventeenth century is that of the gradual breaking down of this rigid and inelastic proprietary control and of the hopeless efforts of the proprietary family to maintain its position and its charter rights in the face of a rising tide of popular and religious opposition and of the expansion of England's commercial and colonial policy. The processes of transformation are sometimes imperceptible and sometimes violently manifest, but they led eventually to the elimination and displacement of the most outstanding proprietary features on the governmental side. They were never complete legally or in respect of the proprietary control of the soil, for Maryland, after a few years intermission as a royal colony, continued as a proprietary province throughout the entire period of our colonial history.[2]

the judgments were never actually executed. In the Talbot case the question of forfeiture to the proprietor was in agitation for many years.

1. *Maryland Archives,* I, 271; V, 16; *Calvert Papers,* I, 176.

2. The significance of Maryland's history in the seventeenth century has been in

But the seignorial organization of Maryland was more than social and tenurial, it was political and administrative as well. Even the later division of the territory into hundreds and counties, following English precedent, was rather for judicial than administrative purposes,[1] while the parishes were ecclesiastical units, each in the hands of its vestry. Even these powers, judicial and ecclesiastical, were centralized in the proprietor under the charter and were by him delegated to his deputy in the colony, who directed their distribution. This deputy was Leonard Calvert until his death in 1647. It does not appear that Leonard had any formal commission before 1637. He had earlier instructions, but if an earlier commission was issued it has not survived. The first document of the kind is of date April 17, 1637, and the powers therein delegated are princely in their scope. Leonard was created lieutenant general, admiral, chief captain and commander on land and sea, and all officials in the colony of whatever rank or station were to recognize his authority and submit to his will. They were to aid him to suppress all insolencies and mutinies on pain of punishment for contempt of the proprietor's prerogative. He was also made chancellor, chief justice, and chief magistrate, with authority to appoint all judicial officers for the maintenance of the peace and the execution of justice, and was given full right to regulate the commercial activities of the planters, to keep in his possession the great seal of the province for the issuing of writs, commissions, licenses, and pardons, and to hear all final appeals in criminal and civil actions, except only in capital cases, which were reserved for the proprietor himself. He could appoint the members of the council and in case of his own disability or absence could delegate his powers to whomsoever he pleased. He was the autocrat and dictator of the province, centralizing in himself every branch of the government and the tenure of every official,

some measure obscured by the debatable character of some of its incidents and the disputatious spirit of some of its exponents. The pros and cons of the Claiborne issue, the prolonged and often unfruitful controversy over religious matters and the Act concerning Religion, and the interminable quarrel over the Maryland-Pennsylvania boundary question have often sunk the historian in the partisan and absorbed attention at the expense of an impartial consideration of other phases in the development of the colony that have, historically speaking, more vital consequence.

1. In 1697 there were eleven counties—St. Mary's, Calvert, Prince George, Charles, Ann Arundel, Baltimore, Somerset, Dorchester, Talbot, Kent, and Cecil. These were divided into seventy-one hundreds, while standing between the hundreds and the counties were the parishes to the number of thirty, thus giving six and a half hundreds and three parishes to a county, *Maryland Archives*, XXIII, 17–25.

each of whom held only during his pleasure.¹ Though commissions generally ran in the name of the proprietor, they were often issued from St. Mary's by Leonard himself, and in some instances were sent out in his own name.

By his commission of 1637 Leonard was to assemble the freemen of the province or their deputies on January 25, 1638, and to issue laws only with their advice and consent. But for succeeding years he need summon them only when he wished, and could adjourn and dissolve them at any time he pleased. Furthermore he retained, according to his own interpretation of the charter, all right to initiate legislation, leaving to the assembly the privilege of acceptance or rejection. There had been an assembly of some sort within a year after the arrival of the colonists, in 1635, but how it was called, of whom composed, or what it accomplished is unknown because of the loss of the records. That its proceedings were not to the liking of the proprietor appears from his instruction to Leonard that the latter was to signify to the new body his entire dissent to the laws which it had made "heretofore or at any time" and his decision that these laws were "voyd"; he was willing that it should present a set of new laws to be accepted without alteration or to be rejected if they so preferred. Thus at the very beginning, in the history of the province, the question was raised, of the utmost importance as it happened, as to how far the assembly of freemen had the right to originate laws of their own and how far they could alter those which the proprietor sent over from England, drawn up by himself and his lawyers there. The proprietor denied this right in both particulars and continued to deny it in theory and in part in practice for many years to come.²

The assembly of 1638 was a mixed affair of men of prominence summoned by individual writs and of freemen summoned under a general writ, some of whom appeared in person, others by proxy, while a considerable number did not come at all. Occasionally a freeman revoked his proxy and turned up himself. The result, as far as the make-up of the assembly was concerned, appeared on the fourth day, when a vote being taken on an important issue, the nineteen persons present cast sixty-nine votes, showing how completely the control of affairs lay in the hands of leaders of the colony, most

1. *Ibid.*, III, 49–55.
2. Cornwallis to Lord Baltimore, April 6/16, 1638, *Calvert Papers*, I, 169–181, an illuminating letter throwing much light on the early history of the colony.

of whom were office-holders. The right of the governor to adjourn and prorogue came up early, when Leonard, replying to an objection from the house, declared that in him alone lay the power to adjourn and that he would be accountable to no man for it; and again in March, 1642, when the assembly, influenced perhaps by the conduct of the Long Parliament in England, resolved that it could not be adjourned or prorogued except by its own consent. To this resolution the government paid no attention. From the beginning the assembly took on a parliamentary character, in its organization, rules, and the use of committees and in its decision that the members be allowed the privileges of parliament during the sitting of the house. At all points the proceedings were dominated by the proprietary element, though there is evident throughout a want of sympathy and agreement between Leonard and his quondam commissioner, Thomas Cornwallis, who took the side of the freemen against the governor, demanding for them greater privileges, immunities for the Roman Catholics, and a relaxation of the proprietor's monopoly of trade.

Later assemblies, except that of 1647, which was composed of governor, council, and freemen, were made up, in a more regular manner, of delegates from the local division—hundreds, the island of Kent, and the hundred, manor, or precinct of Mattapany (not from the counties until 1654)—together with councillors (lords of the manors) summoned by writ, though proxies were still given and freemen continued to attend in person. All assembled as a single house, without a speaker, in the fort at St. Mary's or in the secretary's house at St. John's. The members were called together by the beating of a drum and the proceedings were governed by rules similar to those of the parliament at home. A desire expressed in 1642 that the delegates sit as a separate house was negatived by the governor and the separation was not effected until 1650, when it was enacted that all laws passed by a majority vote in each house and ordered by the governor should be as truly binding "as if they were advised and assented unto by all the freemen of the province personally."[1] The laws of that year are an important landmark in the

1. *Maryland Archives,* I, 130, 272–273. Until 1670 the assembly represented the freemen not the freeholders of the colony. The former were men who owed no service and did not necessarily own land. The disfranchisement of the freemen became an important issue later, the more so as indentured servants out of their time increased in number and swelled the ranks of the freeman class. *Maryland Archives,*

history of the province; the Protestants were in the ascendant and a strong undercurrent of opposition to the proprietor's absolute authority is visible in the proceedings. Furthermore in England conditions were endangering Baltimore's hold on his province and in the colony a general expectation that he was soon to lose his charter was quickening the movement which had as its object the curtailment of his privileges. He made no concession to this expectation, but insisted on his full proprietary rights, demanding that the assembly recognize them and that the members renew, in revised form, the oath of fidelity to himself.[1] Only in the matter of the initiative, regarding which he had been wavering for a number of years, was he willing for the moment to throw a sop to Cerberus and to placate the men that were organizing against him. The growth of the assembly during these years when the province was in disorder gave to it a maturity and a self-consciousness that was to stand it in good stead during the struggle that ensued after 1660. The effectiveness of its organization was to no small extent due to its familiarity with English precedent and procedure and its use of the rules of English parliamentary law. Such familiarity was true not only of the assembly but of the chancery court[2] and the county courts also, the latter of which were courts of common law though doing much other business.

From the beginning of their efforts to obtain a charter for Maryland, the Calverts had been confronted with the determined opposition of William Claiborne, a man of energy and persistence, who possessed many admirable qualities, as well as others that were less praiseworthy. He was highly thought of in Virginia, where for half a century (he died about 1677) he held successively the offices of

I, 170 (Weston case); II, 47, VII, 354; XV, 138; Johnson, *Old Maryland Manors*, appendix C; *Maryland Magazine*, V, 171.

1. *Ibid.*, I, 299–300, 304–306, 320, 325. Cecilius apparently conceded the right of initiative in 1642, when he instructed Leonard to call an assembly for the purpose of "consulting, preparing and enacting of wholesome laws and ordinances" (III, 110). It is an interesting commentary on the Englishman's state of mind that the proprietor should have thought it possible for laws to be drawn up by lawyers in England suitable for a distant colony and satisfactory to the colonists there. The assembly of 1650 represents the farthest point up to this time reached in completeness of organization and independence of action. The assembly was passing on its own membership, defying the council in the matter of secrecy, and voting not to pass any law "when they shall find their liberties or consciences infringed by it" (276). The Puritans were clearly running away with the assembly, though their complete control was not attained until 1654.

2. *Ibid.*, LI, 290.

surveyor, secretary, keeper of the seal, and treasurer. He frequently sat on the council there, and was zealous—in fact overzealous—in upholding that colony's interests. He was conscientiously opposed to Roman Catholicism, had been among those who forced the first Lord Baltimore to leave Virginia in 1630, and allowed his religious convictions to influence his later refusal to recognize the authority of Cecilius over him and his plantation on Kent Island. Coming to Virginia in 1621, he had accepted from that colony[1] a commission to explore Chesapeake Bay to its head, and in order to forestall the Dutch, whose aggressive trading activities were troubling both king and colony, he had begun to open up a trade with the Indians for corn, skins, and other commodities. In the course of his voyaging he had come upon Kent Island and neighboring islets half way up the bay and with the aid of freemen and servants from Virginia had established there a frontier trading post at his own expense.

Following Baltimore to England in March or April, 1630, he interviewed several merchants in London and persuaded them, five in number, to form a partnership—a voluntary joint-stock company—for the purpose of furnishing additional equipment and servants, with himself as their agent or factor. He presented an alluring prospect of profitable trading connections with the Indians of the back country from Virginia to the Great Lakes and of the Chesapeake and Delaware bays, the Hudson River, New England and Nova Scotia.[2] The leading partner, William Cloberry, on May 15, 1631, obtained under the royal signet of Scotland a commission or license to trade, signed by Sir William Alexander, the secretary for Scotland, who was himself in the last gasp of his endeavor to settle Nova Scotia. The next day this license was confirmed to Claiborne by Charles I.[3] Undoubtedly this enterprise was bound up closely

1. *Ibid.*, V, 159–164. 2. *Maryland Magazine*, XXXII, 20.

3. Our knowledge of the organization of the Kent Island settlement and of Claiborne's dealings with the merchants has been greatly increased by the discovery of documents among the records of the High Court of Admiralty. I found these documents in the Public Record Office many years ago (*Guide*, II, 308, 312) but the printing of them in the *Maryland Magazine* has made them readily accessible to all. The most important are: Cloberry's libel, XXVI, 112–114; Claiborne's libel, XXVII, 19–28; Cloberry's answer, 99–112; Evelyn's answer, 112–114; Morehead's answer, 191–192; Cloberry's answer, 192–205; Accounts, 1631–1636, XXVIII, 30–43, 172–189; Grinder's deposition, 190–195, 257–259 (Grinder was Claiborne's servant); Turtle's deposition, 260–265 (Turtle was a carpenter and millwright). With these should be examined the papers accompanying Claiborne's petition (*Maryland Archives*, V, 157–239). A supplemental account of Kent Island covering the period from November

with the general activity of the merchants of this period to utilize the American field as a source of trading profit.

The agreement with the merchants was perfected May 24, 1631, and Claiborne sailed immediately for Virginia reaching there on July 20. On August 11 he left for Kent Island, where with the aid of supplies shipped from England he began the first settlement north of the Potomac and south of the Dutch in New Netherland and on the Delaware. During the next five years he established quarters at the lower end of the island, erected there a fort and palisade, storehouses, dwellings, a church, several mills, gathered a considerable body of artisans, laborers, and servants, men and women, provided a pinnace, a shallop, and several small boats, started gardens and orchards, raised tobacco, corn, and vegetables, and prepared pipestaves for shipment. This well developed community was in no sense a Virginia undertaking; it represented the mercantile activities of a group of Londoners, with whom after 1635 and 1636 Claiborne's relations became strained and almost hostile. Unfortunately, on October 18, 1631, soon after his arrival and while he and his servants were absent, a fire consumed much of his equipment, tools, dwellings, and clothes, and his failure to receive supplies from England further sapped the strength of the settlement. Finally he was displaced by a new agent, George Evelyn, with power of attorney to take possession of the place. Claiborne deemed this act, committed without his knowledge or consent, a violation of the agreement with the merchants and an affront to himself after a service of six years, and he realized that his repudiation in England was bound to weaken his position in America in his inevitable contest with Baltimore.

The points at issue may be briefly stated. Baltimore claimed the island as within his propriety and under his governmental authority, and in his negotiations with Claiborne promised the latter full liberty of trade if he would admit that Kent Island was a part of Maryland and would hold his land of the lord of the palatinate. This Claiborne refused to do, partly because he did not wish to be the

6, 1656, to June 7, 1662, is by Steiner in the *Maryland Magazine*, VIII, 1–33. The population was about 500 at that time.

These documents are not of any particular importance for Maryland's history, but they are illuminating as throwing light on the way the London merchants went about the business of pushing trade in America, much as the East India Company was pushing trade in India, but with very different results.

tenant of a Roman Catholic proprietor and partly because he preferred to stand by Virginia in her claim to the island as Virginia
territory. The only argument that had validity was based on the
hactenus inculta clause of Baltimore's charter, for Kent Island was
occupied and cultivated territory, but even if this argument were
allowed the question remained as to whom the island legally belonged. Not to Virginia, whose claim had been rejected in England.[1]
Not to Claiborne, even though he had purchased it from the Indians,
for neither he nor the partners had any grant of it, even from the
governor and council of Virginia and certainly not from the king.
They had a royal license to trade, but were never able to obtain a
patent under the great seal conveying title and rights of government,
though they made many efforts to do so, a point on which Claiborne
laid great stress in his suit before the High Court of Admiralty.[2]
Baltimore was the only one who had a clear patent to the soil. Perhaps the strongest point in Virginia's favor was that Kent Island
had sent burgesses to sit in the Virginia assembly and so was construed as a part of the area of the colony, but even so this act meant
nothing more than that Virginia persisted in her claim. The act had
no legal significance, for Virginia was legally helpless. That colony
had no charter and its claim to have inherited the entire property
and rights of the defunct company was not recognized at home.

1. The letter from the Privy Council, July 24, 1634 (*Acts Privy Council, Colonial*,
I, §336) to the governor and council of Virginia (*Maryland Archives*, III, 167–168)
was read December 6, 1634 (*Virginia Council Minutes*, I, 481). It does not say that
Virginia had a right to all the land named in the charter of 1612, an assertion that
no English authority could possibly have made at this time, when the crown was
disposing as it pleased of lands north of the Potomac. The same is true of the two
orders in council of October, 1623 (*Acts Privy Council, Colonial*, I, §§109, 112),
which concern only the titles of private persons (*Maryland Archives*, V, 178–179).
The arguments on the Virginia side are given above, p. 284, note 2, and in "Virginia and Maryland, or the Lord Baltamore's Printed Case Uncased and Answered,"
1655 (Original Narratives, *Maryland*, pp. 188–197).

2. Claiborne petitioned the crown for "a confirmation under the great seal" (*Maryland Archives*, III, 72) probably at the end of 1637. The petition was referred to the
Laud commission in February, 1638, before which the parties appeared with their
counsel and the case was fully heard. The board, after scrutinizing the earlier decision, which referred Baltimore to the right of his patent and the "molestors" to the
course of the law, reached the same conclusion in the Claiborne case and agreed not
to recommend the grant of a patent to Claiborne but "to leave both sides to the
ordinary course of justice." In June following Claiborne addressed a letter to Secretary Coke, imploring his assistance (*Maryland Archives*, III, 77–78) and the king in
reply bade the proprietor stop interfering with the traders (78–79), but in no way
committed himself as to the ownership of the island. Virginia accepted the situation,
October 4, 1638 (79–80).

Baltimore's title was the only one that substantially expressed the king's will. Even the royal sign manual of October 8, 1634, repeated in 1638, answering Claiborne's petition, merely estopped Baltimore from interfering with Claiborne's trade and said nothing about the title to the soil. When the matter came before the Laud committee on foreign plantations, that body reported, April 4, 1638, that Kent Island "was absolutelye belonginge to the said Lord Baltimore and that no plantation trade ought to be had or made thither without his licence."[1] It is difficult not to accept this decision.

At the same time it is equally difficult to condone the attitude of Baltimore in the case. He was unnecessarily dictatorial and unconciliatory. Perhaps he had to be. At first in his instructions to Leonard he expressed the hope that Claiborne would yield to friendly overtures, but when these were rejected and Claiborne continued to trade in defiance of what the proprietor considered his rights of trade and the rights of those to whom he issued trading licenses in conformity with the terms of his charter—rights for which he had contended from the first as one of the objects of his settlement—his tactics took a more aggressive form. He ordered Claiborne to leave Virginia and take up his residence in Maryland, where he belonged, and he instructed Leonard, if Claiborne refused, to seize him, imprison him at St. Mary's, and take possession of Kent Island. Claiborne did refuse and in this was upheld by the Virginia council.[2] Hearing reports—perhaps originating with Captain Henry Fleet,[3] Claiborne's rival in the fur trade, who had thrown in his lot with Maryland—that Claiborne was stirring up the Indians against the settlement—reports that were certainly not true—he determined to employ force. On April 5, 1635, Fleet seized Claiborne's vessel, the Long Tail, for trading, without permission, in Maryland waters,[4] and two weeks later mimic seafights took place, April 23 and May 10, between Claiborne's vessels and two of Baltimore's pinnaces under Cornwallis. Each side charged the other with being the aggressor, Baltimore[5] raising the cry of murder and piracy and mali-

1. *Maryland Magazine*, XXVI, 18–19, 111. For Claiborne's "breviate," *Maryland Archives*, III, 32, 158. For Virginia's contention, V, 178–180. For the decision of the Laud commission, III, 71–73.

2. *Virginia Council Minutes*, I, 481.

3. *Maryland Archives*, V, 165–167; Original Narratives, *Maryland*, p. 57.

4. *Calvert Papers*, I, 141–149; *Maryland Archives*, V, 214.

5. *Ibid.*, V, 169–170, 224.

cious practice. Claiborne paid no attention to these charges but continued his trading for another year.[1]

What the outcome would have been we may not conjecture, but Claiborne's cause was lost when the merchants sent over Evelyn to take his place in November, 1636. The latter, though at first inclined to be inimical to Baltimore's pretensions, in the end, acting perhaps under instructions from England, turned against Claiborne, seized the island, and persuaded Leonard Calvert to come across the bay at the head of armed men and take possession. Later, December 30, 1637, Leonard appointed Evelyn commander of the island,[2] and the assembly completed the work by passing, March 24, 1638, a bill reciting the "insolencies and seditious acts" of "William Clayborne, Gent" and demanding that he be attainted for the crimes committed against the proprietor and his property—lands and tenements—and that all his goods and chattels be forfeited to the lord proprietor of the province.[3] Thus far had the assembly gone in assuming to itself, within three years from its inception, a judicial function rarely exercised even by the High Court of Parliament itself, an act of supremacy, half judicial and half legislative, that was looked upon even in England with grave doubts as to its legality, in that it condemned a man without giving him a right to be heard. Whether the charges against Claiborne be justified or not there can be no question as to the legal injustice of the bill of attainder.[4]

We have discussed the Claiborne case at some length because of its effect upon Baltimore's tenure of his province. The situation thus created was an inauspicious beginning for the infant colony, insecure at best because of its quarrel with Virginia, because of its form of

1. *Maryland Archives*, V, 168. Claiborne had been greatly encouraged by a royal letter of October 8, 1634, sent to the governor and council of Virginia, in response to complaints from the merchants in London, stating that the trade of Cloberry and his associates was not to be interfered with and demanding that they aid and assist in so laudable an undertaking (III, 27–29). This letter in no way committed the king to a recognition of Cloberry's title to Kent Island.

2. *Ibid.*, III, 59. Evelyn's conduct at Kent Island in the spring of 1637 was made the subject of a series of depositions by Virginia and Kent Island witnesses in 1640. Their evidence, manifestly in reply to set categories, reads as if they had been coached beforehand, and is uniformly in favor of Claiborne (V, 181–229).

3. *Ibid.*, I, 23–24. The Maryland assembly was apparently fond of drawing up bills of attainder (II, 494, 500–501, 503–504, 512–513, case of Major Truman, 1676).

4. McIlwain, *The High Court of Parliament*, pp. 224–229; Claiborne, *William Claiborne of Virginia*, ch. VII, the only helpful chapter in an otherwise mediocre book.

land tenure and government which was peculiarly unsuitable for a frontier settlement, and because of its broad-minded but premature experiment on the religious side. The mingling of Roman Catholics and Protestants in a common colonizing venture, at a time when overzealous religious antipathies were powerful motives governing men's thoughts and actions, and at a time also when conditions in England were singularly unfavorable to such an experiment was a hazardous act of religious knight-errantry. The Long Parliament met in 1640; civil war began in England in 1642; Charles I was beheaded in 1649; and for ten years the kingdom was in the hands of a Puritan minority, hostile to prerogative and at enmity with Roman Catholicism in every part of the English world. Lord Baltimore was involved in family land quarrels during the greater part of the decade from 1642 to 1650, and was forbidden to leave England. He nearly lost his charter at the hands of parliament in 1647 and only succeeded in warding off the blow by dint of considerable dexterity and shrewdness.

In the colony itself conditions went from bad to worse. An Indian war threatened the settlement and as the proprietor could not come over, Leonard crossed the Atlantic to consult with his brother regarding the outlook. He left Maryland at an unfortunate time. Claiborne was burning with a desire for revenge and, returning from England whither he had gone to prosecute his case against his partners, he made an effort to recover Kent Island by force. At about the same time a swashbuckling captain and tobacco trader, Richard Ingle by name, a Londoner posing as an enemy of prerogative and an ardent Protestant, angered at his arrest by Giles Brent, acting governor, for treasonable words against the king, started on a career of incendiarism and robbery. Leonard returning in the autumn of 1644 was obliged to flee into Virginia. Claiborne, now definitely committed to the parliamentary cause, retook Kent Island, Ingle captured St. Mary's, and for two years, known in Maryland history as "the Rebellion" or "the Plundering Time," during which there was no settled government, the colony was in an uproar. Though Leonard, with the aid of Governor Berkeley of Virginia, recovered his province and affairs became once more fairly normal, Ingle followed up his attempt to overthrow Baltimore's authority in America by going to England and charging the proprietor with enmity to the government of the Commonwealth and accusing the Roman

Catholics in the province with being tyrannous recusants. After many delays the council of state gave the case a hearing and found that Ingle was "unprovided [with evidence] to prove" his charges, and on further consideration, acting on advice from Doctors' Commons, finally dismissed Ingle's plea, leaving Baltimore "to pursue his cause according to law."[1]

The effect upon the colony was deplorable. Under the influence of local disturbances and of reports of what was taking place in England the harmonies of 1633–1634 were breaking into discords. Alarming rumors increased the growing antipathies. Few colonies suffered more from innuendo and whispering manoeuvres than did Maryland, not only during the lean years when the proprietor was fighting to save his province but even to a greater extent afterward when he and his successor were employing every agency possible to save their prerogatives. In 1651 a bill was proposed in the assembly to punish such "as published false news" and over and over again after 1660 and even after 1689 complaints were made of "common empty rumour," "vain and giddy headed notion and noise" and "frivolous and idle charges," and bills were passed to punish those who stirred up popular opposition by means of utterances that were construed

1. Ingle also charged Cornwallis with being an agent for the setting up of a popish faction in Maryland. For documents in the case, *Calendar State Papers, Colonial,* 1574–1660, pp. 331–337; *Maryland Archives,* I, 244–255; III, 267. Leonard Calvert had had a commission from Charles I, January 26, 1644, to seize the vessels and property "of any Londoners whatsoever . . . in rebellion against us" (*Maryland Magazine,* I, 211–216). On the whole episode, Edward Ingle, "Captain Richard Ingle," *Fund-Publications,* no. 19; Thompson, "Richard Ingle in Maryland," *Maryland Magazine,* I, 125–140, and Steiner, "Maryland during the English Civil Wars," Johns Hopkins University *Studies,* 1906, 1907, 1911; Historical Manuscripts Commission, *Sixth Report,* pp. 101, 102.

It is curious that at this time (1638) Claiborne should have proposed to the Providence Company that it grant him and his associates the island of Ruatan (Rattan, Roatan), of an area somewhat larger than that of Kent Island, "discovered within the company's patent, to be called Rich Island in honor of the Earl of Holland," brother of the Earl of Warwick and head of the company. This island, one of the Bahia isles, lies off the coast of Honduras. The grant was made, but just what happened we do not know. The island was taken by the Spaniards in 1642, but retaken by the English in 1741–2 and a fort erected there (Andrews, *Guide,* II, index), but in 1748 the fort was abandoned and the island finally surrendered to Spain in 1763. The surrender was not effective, however, as the control of the island got mixed up with the controversy between Spain and England over the right to cut logwood. The island today belongs to Honduras. Why Claiborne wished to go there is something of a puzzle. Had he done so he would have been either carried off or killed by the Spaniards.

as seditious.[1] It was the religious condition in the colony that in large part was responsible for the form these rumors took.

During this period of anxiety and distress, when the second civil war was just ending in England and the fate of Charles I was under solemn consideration by the Rump Parliament; when the sequestration of the lands of papists and royalists was already decided on; and when all Roman Catholics and other delinquents who had adhered to the enemy were placed under bonds of removal and restraint and threatened with imprisonment—then it was that Cecilius prepared the text of a document famous in the history of Maryland, the Act concerning Religion.[2] He had only recently recovered his province from the hands of Claiborne and Ingle and knew that the attacks on him in England had not ceased. Though he knew also that toleration for Roman Catholics was foreign to the purposes of the Long Parliament, he realized that there was a growing interest at large in a new idea—the idea of liberty of conscience, a phrase that had not appeared before and is nowhere to be found in any of Baltimore's utterances of the first fifteen years. This phrase was introduced into the act as "conscience in matters of religion." On Baltimore's part the drafting of the act was no trimming of sails to meet an on-coming storm, for the policy of toleration for all Trinitarians had prevailed in the colony from the beginning. The necessity of such public and statutory declaration must have been borne in upon him in order to meet the charge, which had been brought by those who sought the annulment of the charter, that Maryland was a hot-bed of popery. To be able to say that in Maryland no one professing to believe in Jesus Christ should henceforth in any ways be molested or discountenanced for or in respect of his or her religion or the free exercise thereof, and to provide for the severe punishment of such as disobeyed the law, was not only certain to aid his cause in England but was likely to draw into his colony many who could not find peace elsewhere. The act rejected all outside the Trinitarian fold and it is not pleasant to read the fate which it meted out to those who denied the divinity of Christ. This inhuman clause was no part of Baltimore's original text, for it was an amendment added by the Puritan-Protestant assembly in the colony to accord with the spirit of the act of the Long Parliament of May 2, 1648,

1. *Maryland Archives*, I, 335; XX, 328; XXII, 122.
2. *Ibid.*, I, 244–247; *Maryland Magazine*, IV, 377–379.

punishing heresies and blasphemies.[1] The act did not guarantee full religious liberty, freedom of religious thought, or separation of church and state, for though there were men of the period who envisioned such an ideal, it was not part of the common human consciousness in the middle of the seventeenth century.[2] The act went no farther than to give, as a matter of expedience and necessity, formal expression to that toleration of one religious body by another, which had already found place in the instructions which Cecilius had issued to his brother in 1633 and in the oath required in 1648 of the first Protestant governor, William Stone, when the latter

1. Ordinance of May 2, 1648, Firth and Rait, *Acts and Ordinances,* I, 1133–1134. It is well known to writers on Maryland history that the Act concerning Religion is in two parts, each with its preamble. It is probable that the first part was added after the second, the part framed by Lord Baltimore in England, had been placed before the assembly. Though it has a Puritan ring, yet the later law for the punishment of blasphemy, passed in 1699, for which the Puritans as such were in no way responsible, was equally severe. It imposed for the first offense boring the tongue and a very heavy fine or imprisonment for six months; for the second, branding and a heavier fine or a longer imprisonment; for the third, death. *Maryland Archives,* XXII, 523. These laws should be studied in the light of the history of blasphemy, and an excellent article on the subject can be found, "The Evolution of the Law of Blasphemy," *Cambridge Law Journal,* I, no. 11.

2. The term "liberty of conscience," so frequently used during this period went no further than to cover "all persons professing the faith of our Lord Jesus Christ." Only those who thus believed were to enjoy this liberty. For the term as applied to Jamaica in this sense (equally true of all the royal and proprietary colonies after 1663) see *Calendar State Papers, Colonial,* 1661–1668, §§374, 630; 1669–1674, §§264, 264, iii, 1425; 1675–1676, §799 (p. 342). For the case of the Jew, Dr. Jacob Lombrozo (afterward turned Christian), who might have suffered under the act for remarks derogating Christ's divinity had not Baltimore recovered his province in the nick of time, see *Maryland Archives,* XLI, 203; XLIX, xxv. The depth of Lombrozo's Christianity may be inferred from XLI, 590–591. Jews were not excluded from the colony. Mr. Hartogenesis had discovered at least twenty living in the colony during these years, only one of whom, Lombrozo, abjured the faith of his fathers. It is a fact, however, that Jews avoided Maryland during its colonial period.

For another but quite different case, that of Father Fitzherbert, charged with rebellion and mutiny and public propaganda of the Roman Catholic faith, *ibid.,* XLI, 566–567. In the controversy that followed the decision was reached that the term "Holy Church," mentioned in an act of 1639 and interpreted by the Act concerning Religion, meant any church the members of which professed to believe in the Trinity —a very doubtful decision. In view of the harshness of the penalizing clause in the Act concerning Religion it would seem hardly worth while to ascertain whether Protestants or Roman Catholics were responsible for its passage. Yet Father Spalding ("Colonial Maryland," *Illinois Catholic Historical Review,* XI, 209) finds satisfaction in believing that the measure was passed by Roman Catholic votes. Bozman thinks that the majority was Protestant (*History of Maryland,* II, 354) and Dennis the measure was forced through the assembly, the deputies responding to the proprietor's whip (*Report,* American Historical Association, 1900, I, 123). There is nothing to support the latter contention.

swore, "I will not molest any person in the province professing to believe in Jesus Christ and in particular no Roman Catholic."[1]

Thus the act may have been drafted by Cecilius as a kind of ratification of the original purpose of his father and himself and for the protection of the Roman Catholic church in the province. The Protestants had always been a numerical majority in the colony, but the Catholics, though steadily dwindling in numbers, had been in control of the offices, dominant socially, and better organized, with the proprietor, his governor, and the council on their side. In 1648, however, the Protestant majority was largely increased by the influx of a considerable body of Puritans (part of whom had been in Virginia since 1629), variously estimated at from four to six hundred, who left Nansemond County and the James River region, under the leadership of Richard Bennett, to enjoy religious liberty in Maryland. They accepted the invitation of Governor Stone and took up their location on the Severn River, near the site of the present city of Annapolis, calling their settlement Providence. There they lived as a self-governing community, advancing rapidly in influence and taking full advantage of the political and religious freedom which the act allowed. In 1650 they sent seven burgesses to the assembly, one of whom, Coxe, was elected speaker in April of that year. With the proprietor in England preserving what appeared to be a strict neutrality, though keeping on friendly terms with the Commonwealth government at home, and with the province in Protestant hands, the position of the Roman Catholics, and particularly of the Jesuit fathers, though vigorously defended, was becoming less and less secure. The attack was coming not only from the Protestants, but from Baltimore also, who had no intention of handing over the control of the province to the Jesuits, even though they had been his ardent allies in the promotion of the enterprise. Within five years after the planting of the colony he was obliged to enter into a painful controversy with them over the question of land ownership.[2]

---

1. *Maryland Archives,* III, 210.

2. Dennis, "Lord Baltimore's Struggle with the Jesuits, 1634–1649," *Report,* American Historical Association, 1900, I, 105-126; Johnson, "The Foundation of Maryland and the Origin of the Act concerning Religion," *Fund-Publications,* no. 18, where the secret conditions and other important documents are given, pp. 69–92; Copley's letter to Lord Baltimore, April 3, 1638, *Calvert Papers,* I, 157–169, threatening excommunication under the bull *In coena Domini* of all who sought to restrain ecclesiastical liberties (165); and Baltimore's letter to Leonard Calvert, *ibid.,* 216–221, which discloses the intensity of his feelings against the Jesuits.

The issue was quite definite. Baltimore was determined to check any attempt on the part of the Jesuits to extend to the colony the canon law of Rome or to set up what might easily become a kind of independent spiritual dominion possessing temporal authority within the province and looking to the pope as its ultimate head and superior. As can be readily inferred from the wording of the Act concerning Religion, he had always opposed the idea of making the Roman Catholic Church the established church of the colony, and in 1641 he issued a new set of conditions of settlement, in which he declared that the acquirement of any lands by the Jesuits, either by gift or purchase from the Indians, should be void and that the Statute of Mortmain, which forbade the giving of land to societies or corporations in England, should apply also in Maryland. The Jesuits, led by Father White, chief of the Maryland mission, fought the issue with all the arguments at their command, determined to acquire land as essential to their spiritual independence—a determination similar to that which underlay the arguments defending the temporal power of the papacy. In the end the proprietor won the victory. The question was referred to Father More, father provincial in England, and by him to Rome, where it came before the Sacred Congregation for the Propagation of the Faith, which ordered, through Father More, that the Jesuits abandon their attempt and renounce the rights which they had claimed. The decision, as Bradley Johnson points out, has left its impress upon the Maryland law of today, in that land cannot be acquired for any religious use except by act of legislature, no priest or clergyman can sit in the general assembly, and no marriage is valid without the sanction of the church.[1]

In 1650 the contesting forces were fairly well matched, with the odds in favor of the Protestants. The proprietor was still in possession of his province and his prerogatives were well buttressed by the oath of fidelity acknowledging and defending his authority. The Roman Catholics, though greatly in the minority and though the Jesuits among them had lost their fight for secular and spiritual independence, were assured of complete toleration, not only by statute but also by the oaths taken by the officials in authority over them.[2] They were possessed of as full liberty of action as was any

1. Johnson, as above, pp. 60–61.
2. Thomas Matthews, burgess from St. Inigoes, refused to take the burgess oath,

other person in the province, thus justifying, at this time at least, a remark made later that Maryland was "the only colony where Roman Catholics are entitled to the rights of man."[1] But the Protestants, a majority of whom were probably Puritans, were dominant in the assembly, with a Protestant governor at the helm and with Protestants numbering at least half in the council, where before 1648 all had been Roman Catholics.

In his effort to live up to his principles and perhaps to weaken the Jesuits by admitting Puritans to settle within his province, Baltimore had opened the doors to a powerful body of religious insurgents, who were determined to nullify all his efforts to organize his government on the broad basis of toleration and justice to all. Though successful in his struggle with the Jesuits, he now went down to defeat at the hands of the Puritans. The latter were strengthened in their opposition by the passing in England of the famous prohibitory act, mentioned above in the account of Barbados, which gave to the Council of State of the Commonwealth power and authority to reduce to subjection the colonies of Bermuda, Antigua, Barbados, and Virginia. Presumably Maryland also was to be included, because Greene, temporarily acting as governor in Stone's absence, unwisely and without the knowledge of the proprietor, proclaimed, on No-

because he considered the obligation to secrecy an infringement on the free exercise of his religion, evidently on the ground that he wished to be guided in matters of conscience "by his spirituall councell" which would not be possible if because of his oath he could not consult his father confessor. The house expelled him. *Maryland Archives*, I, 274-275.

1. Historical Manuscripts Commission, *Various*, VI, 292 (undated, but after 1763). It is not easy to reconcile this statement, made after 1763, with the action of the Maryland assembly in 1753, when it passed an act to prevent the growth of popery within the province (*Maryland Archives*, L, 198-205, 514-519). In 1765 the attorney and solicitor general of England said, "We are humbly of the opinion that his Majesty's Roman Catholic subjects residing in the countries ceded . . . by the Treaty of Paris are not subject in those Colonies to the Incapacities, disabilities and penalties to which Roman Catholics in this kingdom are subject by the laws thereof," *idem, Dartmouth*, II, 548. This pronouncement is distinctly an advance on that of Attorney General Edward Northey, October 18, 1705 (*Calendar State Papers, Colonial, 1704-1705*, §378), in reply to a query from the Board of Trade (§1377) "as to whether the Laws of England against Romish Priests are in force in the Plantations." Citing 27 Elizabeth, c. 20, and 11 William III, c. 4, Northey said, "I am of opinion if the Jesuits or Priests be aliens . . . H. M. may by law compell them to depart Maryland; if they be H. M. natural born subjects they cannot be banished . . . but may be proceeded against by law." He believed that the act of 11 William extended to the plantations, because it contained the phrase "within this Realm or the Dominions thereto belonging" (iii). After 1763 there appears to have been, on the part of the English lawyers, less desire to interpret the law so literally.

vember 15, 1649, Charles II "as the undoubted rightfull heire to all his ffathers dominions."[1] Baltimore is supposed to have exercised sufficient influence with the council to prevent the name of Maryland from being inserted in the commission issued soon after for the reduction of the colonies to the authority of Parliament. His reorganization of the province in the years from 1648 to 1650, his Act concerning Religion, and his concessions to the Protestant majority now stood him in good stead and we are told that the council felt it to be only just to strike Maryland out of the document.[2] Nevertheless, despite this fact, in the text of the instructions as finally issued, there appears the equivalent phrase "all the plantations within the bay of Chesapiak," which in the eyes of the commissioners covered Maryland as well as Virginia. The men selected as chief commissioners, were Dennis and Stagg, sea-captains trading with the colonies, Bennett, the Puritan leader at Providence, and Claiborne, Baltimore's old enemy.[3] It has been thought that Claiborne was in some way responsible for the phrase in the instructions, whether interpolated or not, and when Dennis and Stagg were drowned in the wreck of the *John* on the way over, he made use of the opportunity to strike back at his former antagonist. However that may be, on March 29, 1652, after receiving the submission of Virginia, Courtis, who took the place of Dennis and Stagg and probably knew little about the business, as he had had nothing to do with it in its earlier stages, allowed Bennett and Claiborne to carry out the "reducement" of that colony. The latter went to St. Mary's, ejected Stone and his council, appointed another council under themselves as commissioners "to govern and direct the affairs thereof," and demanded that henceforth all writs and processes should run in the name of the keepers of the liberties of England.[4] Thus Baltimore lost control of his province and Claiborne had won, temporarily at least, a revengeful victory.

But the commissioners had reckoned without their host—the people of Maryland. Warned by outspoken expressions of popular

1. *Maryland Archives*, III, 243–244.

2. Langford, "Refutation of Babylon's Fall," Original Narratives, *Maryland*, pp. 256–259; "The Lord Baltemore's Case," the same, pp. 167–169. Langford says that Dennis and Stagg were present at the council board when the name Maryland was struck out of the instructions and he implies that if they had not been lost in the *John*, they would not have allowed Maryland to be subjected, p. 257.

3. *Virginia Magazine*, XI, 38–40; Thurloe, *State Papers*, I, 197–198.

4. *Virginia Magazine*, XI, 34; *Maryland Archives*, III, 271–272.

disapproval they reversed their own decision and claiming that Stone and his secretary Hatton had been "left out upon some misapprehension or misunderstanding,"[1] found themselves obliged to reinstate a part of the former government on the understanding that those in office should issue writs in the name of the Commonwealth, but might save their oaths to the proprietor "until the pleasures of the state of England be further known." There followed a hearing before the Council of State to discover what these "pleasures" were.[2] Bennett and others of his persuasion demanded that Maryland be joined to Virginia and that both be ruled by the Puritans as a single colony. Baltimore, London merchants, and others friendly to the proprietor opposed this demand, sent in petitions, and caused to be issued a pamphlet, *Lord Baltimore's Case*, presenting a summary of their arguments.[3] The matter was referred by the Council of State to its committee of the navy and by the latter, after a hearing, "to the judgment and further directions of the parliament itself." But before action could be taken, if it was ever intended that action should be taken at all, the Rump Parliament came to an end, and Cromwell, though not yet Protector until the following December, 1653, was, with his soldiers, the master of England. The Barebone's or Little Parliament, which met in July, 1653, was in no position to interfere. Baltimore immediately wrote to Stone,[4] telling him that he had not lost his province and instructing him to cancel all his obligations to the commissioners, to issue writs once more in the name of the proprietor, to reconstruct the membership of his council,

1. *Ibid.*, III, 275; "Lord Baltimore's Case," 1653, pp. 169–170.

2. Stock, *Debates*, I, 230–232; *Virginia Magazine*, XVII, 287–288; *Maryland Archives*, III, 280–281; *Maryland Magazine*, III, 181–182; Original Narratives, *Maryland*, pp. 178–179.

3. "The Lord Baltemore's Case" is reprinted in *Maryland Magazine*, IV, 171–182, and in Original Narratives, *Maryland*, pp. 167–180.

4. *Maryland Archives*, III, 311–312; Original Narratives, *Maryland*, p. 225. Langford says that Captain Samuel Tilghman brought word to Stone that Baltimore had not lost his province and handed him "some instructions and certainties" from Cromwell, in which the latter addressed him as "Capt. Stone, Governor of Maryland" (*Maryland Magazine*, IV, 240). It is interesting to note how eager each side was to hear from Cromwell, believing that he was favorable to its cause. Neither Baltimore's instructions, which all writers agree came out of England in 1654, nor Cromwell's alleged letters are in existence, as far as is known. The latter contained favorable recommendations of a Captain or Doctor Luke Barber and a certain Luke Gardner, who had been a domestic servant in Cromwell's household (Original Narratives, *Maryland*, pp. 203–204; *Maryland Magazine*, IV, 248), and were sent to Governor Stone. The Puritans claimed that these letters were forgeries.

and to exact from all a new oath of fidelity. Thus did the proprietor declare war against the commissioners and their Puritan supporters, and in demanding a renewal of the oath of fidelity rendered inevitable a trial of strength between the two parties.[1]

The Puritans had been in Maryland for about five years, and at Providence (Arundelton, 1673, Annapolis, 1696) had attained a position of exceptional strength and independence. Their home on the Severn River was a long way from St. Mary's and the seat of government and being in a hitherto unoccupied quarter they were able to set up a veritable city of God, Puritan like, in the wilderness. There, to use a contemporary Puritan phrase "the wild boar" could not "destroy the Lords vineyard" and "sectaries and prophane persons" could not interfere with "the free passage of the Gospel" or pollute "the waters of the Sanctuary."[2] At first they held aloof from the conflicts of civil life, but reluctantly taking their place in the assembly their leaders began to model their plans after the Commonwealth of England, and after the commonwealth of Massachusetts Bay at that time at the zenith of its success as a quasi-sovereign community. They seem to have dreamed of setting up a Puritan commonwealth in Maryland and even of extending their sway to Virginia also. In no way different from their brethren in New England were the Puritans of Maryland in their determination to extend their jurisdiction and boundaries as widely as aggressive measures would allow. Convinced that Baltimore was on the eve of losing his charter at the hands of parliament, they greeted with resentment and charges of persecution the resumption by Governor Stone in 1653 of the proprietary prerogatives, which threatened the end of what they believed to be their divinely directed ambitions. In January and March, 1654, seventy-eight of them in one petition and sixty-one in another protested against the obligation to take the oath of fidelity, because of its reference to Baltimore as absolute lord and proprietor and as conflicting with their liberty of consciences as Christians and with their obligations as subjects of the Commonwealth of England.[3] In these protests they were upheld by the com-

1. The Fendall party said later that the war which followed originated in the demand that the Puritans take the oath of fidelity, *Maryland Archives*, V, 139. Baltimore was requiring the taking of an oath "such as every lord of a manor required from his tenant," showing that the Maryland war was a conflict of allegiances.

2. *New York Colonial Documents*, III, 140. On the Puritans in Virginia, *Virginia Historical Index, s.v.* "Puritans," and on the migration, 1645–1655, Warfield, *Founders of Anne Arundel* (1905).

3. *Original Narratives, Maryland*, pp. 218–221.

missioners, who advised them to resist "any pretence of power from Lord Baltimore's agents and any other whatsoever to the contrary."[1] That a deep-seated hostility toward the Romish religion and fears lest its followers become dominant in the affairs of the colony underlay these protests is apparent in the wording of the documents.

While these events were taking place, Bennett and Claiborne had been in Virginia, but roused by what Stone was threatening to do and by the protests from the men of the Severn, the Patuxent, and Kent Island—the centers of disaffection at this time and for long afterward—they hurried back to Maryland and reproached Stone for his attempt to revive the proprietor's authority. Receiving from him "onely opprobrious and uncivill language," in reply to their charge of treason to the Commonwealth, they deposed him from office and appointed a Puritan, William Fuller, in his place. Furthermore, as no assembly had met since 1651, they instructed Fuller to call such a body, but to take care that no one who had borne arms against parliament or who professed the Roman Catholic faith should be allowed to vote or to be elected a deputy.[2] When the assembly met on October 20, 1654, it first repudiated the authority of the proprietor, root and branch, recognizing the authority only "of his highness the lord protector," and then proceeded to repeal the Act concerning Religion and to put in its place another that was in part borrowed word for word from the Cromwellian Instrument of Government, which had been adopted in England the December before. The new law declared that "none who profess and exercise the Popish religion . . . can be protected in this province" and that freedom to worship God should not be extended to the adherents of "popery or prelacy."[3] The Puritans in Maryland were reproducing not only the law laid down by the Puritan minority in England but the intolerant spirit of those in Massachusetts Bay who could find no place in that commonwealth for any other form of ecclesiastical discipline than their own. All that can be said for the new law is that it accorded well with the Puritan idea of service to God and with the hopes that the Maryland Puritans entertained of as complete an hegemony in Baltimore's province as those of Massachusetts Bay were obtaining north of the Merrimac at the same time.

The issue was now fairly and clearly joined.[4] Stone, whose anger

---

1. *Ibid.*, p. 222. 2. *Maryland Archives*, III, 312–313.
3. *Ibid.*, I, 340–341; Firth and Rait, *Acts and Ordinances*, II, 822 (sec. xxxvii).
4. The story of the conflict can be followed in: (1) "Virginia and Maryland, or

was easily roused, encouraged by what he considered the support of Cromwell and acting under peremptory orders from Baltimore began to resist, but in none too tactful a manner. He enforced the proprietor's authority in order to resume full control of the government and sent one Hammond to obtain possession of the records from the house of Richard Preston, a Puritan living north of the Patuxent, who had been the speaker of the assembly of 1654. He then set about the more delicate and difficult task of compelling the recalcitrant Puritans and parliamentarians to take the oath of fidelity. Hammond, who tells us of his vexatious experiences in trying to get the records, reports that the southern counties, St. Mary's and Calvert, submitted to Stone's demand without a struggle, but that Ann Arundel and Kent refused to recognize Stone as governor or to take the oath.[1] Thus the resort to arms that followed in the month of March, 1655, took the form of a petty civil war, on one side between the proprietor and his prerogatives, upheld by the southern counties, and the Puritans and Commonwealth men of Ann Arundel and Kent on the other. The contending forces, a few hundred in number, were led by Stone for the proprietor and by Fuller for the insurgents and met on the shores and waters of the Severn River. Aided by the captain of the *Golden Lion,* Roger Heamans, a New England trader and probably a Puritan, but not connected with either party, the Puritans won a complete victory, March 25, 1655, just eleven years from the day when Roman Catholics and Protestants landed on St. Clements isle and began the experiment

the Lord Baltamore's Printed Case Uncased and Answered," 1655 (Original Narratives, *Maryland,* pp. 201–205, 218–228), a reply to "The Lord Baltimore's Case," 1653; (2) "Heamans Brief Narration," 1655 (*Maryland Magazine,* IV, 140–153), a vivid but partisan description by an eye witness on the side of the Puritans; (3) Strong, "Babylon's Fall in Maryland," 1655 (Original Narratives, *Maryland,* pp. 235–246), a very Puritan document; (4) "A Refutation of Babylon's Fall" by John Langford, 1655 (the same, pp. 254–275), defending the proprietor; (5) Hammond, "Leah and Rachel," 1656 (the same, pp. 302–305), containing very little on the subject of the conflict; (6) "Hammond vs. Heamans" (*Maryland Magazine,* IV, 236–251), a reply to Heaman's "Brief Relation," "Lord Baltamore's Case Uncased," and "Babylon's Fall," without date, but written in 1654–1655 and published in 1655. The temper of this pamphlet appears from its characterization of the Puritans as "inhuman, ungrateful, blood-sucking Sectaries."

1. "Leah and Rachel," p. 304. In the Kent County court of 1658 no man was to be present with his hat on or to use uncivil language, the reason assigned being that the "custom of England grounded upon the word of God required that due respect be given to magistrates" (*Maryland Magazine,* VIII, 4). Kent was a Puritan stronghold at this time.

of trying to live together in harmony. The experiment might have succeeded better but for the injection of the Puritan element. The Puritans may or may not have been responsible for the war, but in their day of triumph they wreaked a savage vengeance, in Old Testament fashion, condemning to death ten of the invaders and actually executing four in the spirit of the god of battles. The houses of the Jesuits were plundered and the fathers fled secretly to Virginia, where they lived in misery.[1] The Puritans imposed heavy fines upon their opponents and confiscated much property, though it is doubtful if the sequestrations were ever followed up. From this time forward for three years the Puritans were in full possession of the province.

But even with this success the commissioners were not content, nor would they have been content as long as Baltimore's patent remained intact. A second battle, albeit a verbal one, had to be fought out in England. In January, 1656, Baltimore complained to Cromwell that he had been interrupted in his rights and jurisdictions in Maryland, because of which his province had endured many mischiefs. Soon after, Bennett and Matthews (in place of Claiborne who had been appointed secretary of Virginia), having gone to England to present their side of the case, likewise petitioned the protector, presenting arguments against Baltimore and his patent.[2] The two petitions with the accompanying explanatory papers were referred to Lords Widdrington and Whitelocke, whom Cromwell frequently consulted on foreign business and who had been assigned with nearly seventy others to the Committee of Trade in 1655. They made their report, May 16, 1656, but that report, undoubtedly favorable to Baltimore, is not extant. It was referred by the Council of State to the Committee of Trade, July 31, and the latter made reply, September 16. This reply too is lost and its contents are unknown, except so far as we are informed that the committee reviewed the case, considered the Widdrington-Whitelocke report, heard the parties, made some alterations in the wording of the oath of fidelity, demanded the reënactment of the Act concerning Religion, and then bade the parties present their proposals for settlement. This the parties did and in so doing paved the way for a final agreement, Bennett and Matthews expressing themselves as satisfied with Balti-

1. Jesuit letter, 1656, *Fund-Publications*, no. 7, pp. 91–92.
2. Thurloe, *State Papers*, V, 482–487.

more's proposals.[1] The committee embodied the agreement, with certain amendments of its own, in its report to the Council of State. The latter, for want of leisure to act in the case, sent the report on December 16 to its committee on foreign affairs with instructions to speak with the parties and see what ought to be done.[2] But because of the pressure of more important business, the committee pigeonholed the papers and as it happened never brought the matter to a decision.

Realizing the danger of longer delay, Edward Diggs, governor of Virginia, 1655–1656, and at this time in England, took a hand in the affair and as a friendly intermediary[3] brought the parties together. The final agreement, based on the report of the Committee of Trade, was reached on November 30, 1657; its terms were read in the colony the following February, and in March arrangements were made for their enforcement.[4] Baltimore came through the trial practically unscathed, saving both his patent and his province. He was restored to the full control of his government, and all the inhabitants were ordered to take the oath of fidelity and to give due obedience and submission to his authority in matters of administration and the exercise of justice. He in turn promised to forget the past, to grant land to all applicants without discrimination, as if nothing had happened, and to let anyone who wanted to remove from the province. He promised also to stand firm for the Act concerning Religion, in

1. The preliminary agreement in England is not extant, but it may be represented by the instructions to Fendall of October 23, 1656 (*Maryland Archives,* III, 325–326), together with the appointment of Fendall as governor. The final settlement was made November 30, 1657, and published in the province the February following (332–334).

2. *Ibid.,* 324–325, 330; *Calendar State Papers, Colonial,* 1574–1660, pp. 435, 435–436, 447, 453; Thurloe, *State Papers,* V, 482. The arguments by Bennett and Matthews are contained in four lengthy papers, the contents of which run the gamut of the objections raised during the preceding twenty years and sum up all that could possibly be said by Baltimore's enemies. The documents contain also a very Puritan version of the battle of the Severn. The writers urge the discontinuance of Baltimore's patent and stress the unwisdom of maintaining "a popish monarchical government" in Maryland, as inconsistent with all that the Protectorate stood for and a menace "to the liberty and freedom of English subjects" (Thurloe, *State Papers,* 482–487). From their willingness to compromise it would appear that they saw no hope of carrying through extreme measures. They may have been more subdued at Whitehall than they were on the Potomac. This view of the case is, however, rendered doubtful by the fact that as late as October 16, 1656, they were still hoping to get rid of Baltimore, and by the strongly partisan statements contained in the papers mentioned above, which were enclosed in the letter of that date.

3. Thurloe, *State Papers,* III, 596.   4. *Maryland Archives,* I, 369–370.

order that all those professing to believe in Jesus Christ (so the agreement reads) should have freedom of conscience, and he pledged his word of honor to carry out the terms thus mutually adopted. The articles were signed by Baltimore and Matthews and witnessed by Diggs and four others.[1]

Feeling sure of ultimate victory after the Widdrington-Whitelocke report had been handed in, of which he must have had some knowledge beforehand, Baltimore on July 10, 1656, more than a year before the compromise was finally effected, appointed Josias Fendall governor in place of William Stone. Fendall entered upon his office February 26, 1657. He had taken part in the battle of the Severn on the side of the proprietor and in the October following had been arrested and imprisoned by the Puritan justices of the provincial court for having acted openly, contrary to his oath taken to the Puritan government, "to the disturbance of the public peace and the distraction and damage of the people." He had denied the jurisdiction of the court, but had been compelled to swear that he would keep quiet until the matter of the government had been settled in England by a legal hearing.[2] These events may have seemed to Baltimore a sufficient reason for entrusting Fendall with the governorship, but the choice was not a wise one. Fendall was not successful as a governor and his later career shows that he was at heart lukewarm in the proprietary interest and a declared enemy of the proprietary prerogatives.

Hardly had the new assembly opened on February 28, 1660, and organized for business than the lower house, after marking time and accomplishing little for three weeks, drafted a paper which it sent to the upper house declaring itself to be a lawful assembly without need of governor or council, just as the Rump Parliament had declared in 1649 that it had no need of king or house of lords. Naturally the upper house strongly dissented to this proposal, and the matter would probably have passed without further result had not Fendall, acting in association with such members as Thomas Gerrard and Nicholas Utie, with whom he may have had a previous understanding, surrendered his commission from the proprietor and accepted one from the assembly. This act, which Alsop calls a "kind of pigmie rebellion" and Baltimore characterized as "mutiny and

---

1. *Ibid.*, III, 332–335 (the articles of agreement are given on pages 333–334); I, 369–370.
2. *Ibid.*, X, 427–428, 463.

sedition agt our Governm^t and Jurisdiction," may have been in Fendall's mind a step preliminary to the setting up of a commonwealth of a single house, with himself playing the part of a miniature Cromwell. If so he had chosen an unfortunate time for enacting the rôle. On May 8, less than two months later, Charles II was proclaimed in London King of England and, on petition from Baltimore, wrote a personal letter, July 12, 1660, to the governor of Virginia bidding him assist the proprietor in the restoration of his jurisdiction and the recovery of all his just rights under the charter.[1] Baltimore immediately revoked Fendall's commission and appointed as governor his half brother Philip, the youngest son of the elder Baltimore by his second wife and at that time the secretary of the province. In November, 1660, Fendall came before Governor Calvert and the council and submitted himself to the "Government of the Lord Proprietary." He was ordered to be imprisoned, his goods confiscated, and himself eventually banished, but he was later released under bonds for good behavior, pardoned, and his estate restored. He was, however, forbidden ever to hold office again.[2]

In the history of the early colonies in America there is no more suggestive study than that of comparing the careers of Maryland and Massachusetts Bay from their founding to the year 1689. Whereas the latter colony profited by the course of events in England during these years, the former suffered in corresponding measure. From 1650 to 1660 Massachusetts, which had declared herself a commonwealth in 1652, was on a tidal wave of confidence and prosperity; exactly the reverse was the case with the lord proprietor of Maryland. The Puritan victory in England placed him and his Roman Catholic brethren in a position that was not only embarrassing but dangerous, and while Massachusetts was increasing in wealth, power, and territory, Maryland was torn with internal dissensions and menaced by outside dangers. As we have seen, the colony finally fell into the hands of the Puritans, whose aims were the same as those of their co-religionists of New England, and from 1655 to 1658 Baltimore was deprived of his government, which he was able to recover only through a wise handling of a delicate situation. But in 1660 when Charles II came to the throne the conditions were reversed. For Massachusetts the return of the monarchy marked the begin-

1. *New York Colonial Documents*, II, 118.
2. *Maryland Archives*, III, 391–392, 396–397, 400, 405–409, 445.

ning of the end, so far as the continuance of the colony as an independent commonwealth was concerned; while on the other hand it brought security to the Maryland proprietor and an opportunity for an equally assertive enforcement of his proprietary privileges. How those privileges were finally lost forms one of the most interesting chapters in the long struggle fought out on the soil of America against institutions that were antipathetic to a frontier people, living their own lives and working out their own destiny in a hitherto unoccupied part of the world.

CHAPTER IX

FALL OF THE PROPRIETARY IN MARYLAND

BY the compromise of 1658 Baltimore had been restored to the full control of his province according to the terms of his charter. Distressing and vexatious as had been his experiences during the preceding ten years, these experiences had cost him no loss of prestige either abroad or in the colony. His proprietary authority was in no way impaired, and what that authority meant in the eyes of his opponents was well and accurately expressed, with perhaps some excess of conviction, by Bennett and Matthews, when they sought in England to obtain the annulment of the charter. "The lord Baltimore," they wrote, "exercised an arbitrary and absolute government, undertook a princely jurisdiction, stiles himself absolute lord and proprietor, constituted a privy council, most of Papists, and the rest sworn thereto. This privy council must be the legislative power, that is to put in execution such laws, the laws which the lord Baltimore himself makes and imposeth, and he makes what laws he pleases. The people indeed are called to assemblies, but have neither legislative power nor judicature, that being appropriated to the privy council or upper house, so that what is determined by them admits of no reference or appeal."[1] If this was the nature of the prerogative in 1656, it was no less so in 1658 when the compromise was effected, or in 1660 after the ill-timed attempt of Fendall and his associates had miscarried. Barring certain terms of the agreement, which in no way affected his charter rights, Balti-more had come out of the long ordeal with increased rather than diminished influence, and at the same time his ability to maintain and enforce his proprietary privileges in the colony was enhanced by the return of the king to the throne of England.

Baltimore remained in England and from there as absolute lord and proprietor continued to govern his province. He appointed as temporary governor his younger brother, Philip, and the latter after a year's tenure, with the factional disorders suppressed, peace with

1. Thurloe, *State Papers*, V, 486.

the Indians secured, and the machinery of administration in good working order, was created chancellor, chief and only judge in chancery, according to the law and usage of England, and leading member of the council and head of the provincial court, a position he held until his death in 1682. In 1661 Cecilius appointed in his place as governor his own son Charles, at that time but twenty-four years old and destined after his death in 1675 to become third Lord Baltimore and the proprietor of the province. He invested his son with the entire command of the province, making him chief governor, commander in chief, lieutenant general, chief captain and chief admiral, head of the military forces and of whatever navy the province might possess. Also he granted him power to exercise martial law against all rebellious, mutinous, and seditious persons, to pardon or release all offenders against the law as he saw fit, and to pass under the great seal, to all who applied, such grants of land as were in accord with the conditions laid down. He enjoined him to observe inviolably the Act concerning Religion, as under the terms of the compromise Fendall had been enjoined to do in 1659. He bade him call general assemblies "for the giving of the advice, assent and approbation by the freemen to such laws and acts as shall be by us att any time ordayned made and enacted and under our seale published and under which the advice, assent and approbation of the freemen shall be at any time requisite and necessary."[1] In all that Cecilius did in thus issuing commissions and instructions to his son he was not straining his charter rights or assuming of powers that he did not rightly possess. As Charles Calvert said, after he himself became pro-

---

1. Charles Calvert's commission of February 16, 1666, is printed in *Maryland Archives*, III, 542–545; XV, 306. (Hereafter in this chapter the *Maryland Archives* will be referred to without the title of the volumes, except when necessary to avoid confusion.) The "by us" in the latter text is printed "by &" in the former, a manifest misprint, for the "by &" does not make sense. See also, 107, 189–190; XVII, 428, where the "by us" appears. That Baltimore was still insisting in principle on his full right of initiative is evident, for in his instructions to Charles he speaks of "all such bills Lawes or Acts as you shall hereafter receive from us" (XV, 10). Nevertheless as time went on he accepted many measures that originated in the province, either in the upper house, the lower house, or a joint committee from both houses (I, 403; II, 181; VII, 401). The act for the cessation of tobacco planting, which he disallowed in 1666 (III, 561), grew out of suggestions from the upper house, the leading members of which were the governor and his councillors (II, 35, 49). The lower house in this case said that it did not wish "to act or determine anything which may reflect upon his Lordship's Rights Interest or Prerogative" (II, 36). It is quite clear that during this period the legal right of initiative lay with the proprietor, even if at sundry times it was exercised by the chamber of deputies.

prietor in 1675, he did not propose to give away any of his rights but was resolved always to exercise them for the ease and welfare of the freemen under his care.[1] Both Cecilius and Charles were probably quite right in believing that if they gave way in one direction they would have to give way in others also, and that their only safety lay in an unyielding adherence to the prerogatives they possessed by virtue of the royal grant. The conflict in the colony, therefore, lay between the governor and his council, who with a few others constituted the upper house, and the members of the lower house who represented the voters of the province. This conflict was never noisy or violent, but no compromise could be reached because it was rooted in an irreconcilable difference of claim. When the upper house spoke of its privilege, honor, and dignity it was referring to a charter the terms of which are traceable to the fourteenth century; when the lower house spoke of its privileges, it had in mind the precedents and practices of the House of Commons in the seventeenth century which it used as guides of its own organization and conduct. That the two houses got on fairly well together was due chiefly to the fact that the lower body, though frequently calling for a copy of the charter that it might know certainly what it contained, was always willing to recognize his lordship's rights and privileges as something legally possessed. The upper house, on the other hand, denied vehemently that the lower house was in any sense the equivalent of the House of Commons, so that the deputies had to get what they could by processes of attrition, whereby they gradually wore down the opposition of the prerogative and in one detail or another made good their pretensions. The sensitiveness of the two bodies found expression even in minor points of etiquette, as when the upper house ruled that no deputy should enter the council chamber with his hat on, and the lower insisted that no upper house member should enter the assembly chamber wearing a sword.[2]

The proprietor's interpretation of his own position in the province and of the province's position in its relation to himself appears in the language of his official documents. There is a touch of royalty in the words used. "Our province," "our commissioners," "us and our council," "our city of St. Mary's," "our officers," "our provincial court," "our judge," "our court of chancery," "our militia," and,

1. VII, 355.
2. VII, 356, 379, 409, 414, 492, 572, 578–579, 582, 587–588; XIII, 50, 81.

above all else, "in the —— year of our dominion" or "in the —— year of the Dominion of the Rt. Honble Charles." It appears also in the appointment of two principal secretaries (perhaps Charles Calvert was remembering that his grandfather had been one of the two principal secretaries of state under James I), and in the use of the broad arrow, a symbol of the king's right of possession, employed in Maryland in cases of seizure by the sheriffs to indicate that the articles or commodities detained were in the proprietor's hands and when seized for debt took precedence over all private claims.[1] It appears in the right of the governor to forbid anyone's leaving the province without a pass issued by the secretary and in the occasional grants of perquisites to favorites in the province after the royal fashion of pensions and monopolies.[2] It appears also in the setting up of the proprietary arms in all the court rooms, where were held the provincial and county courts. In matters concerning the distribution of land and the revenues of the soil the province was Baltimore's own private baronial domain, and when in 1684, after the abolition of the headright, he established a land council, he placed upon the board a group of his own councillors, all relatives, to administer the affairs of what was in effect a private land office.[3] In matters of government he was almost equally supreme.

Nothing is said in the charter of the appointment of a council, but following the precedent of the bishopric of Durham, Baltimore in his commission to Leonard Calvert, 1637, appointed three men to act in that capacity, who were to inform him from time to time regarding the needs of the province. But no advisory body anywhere else in the English colonies reached anything like the high level of complete identification on the part of the government with the interests of the proprietary family and the proprietary prerogative as did the councils which Cecilius named in 1666 and later years. In 1666 he called eight men to that office, the chancellor, the secretary, the surveyor general; the muster master general, and four others "to be

1. I, 196; III, 474; XLI, 174; XLIX, xxvi–xxvii, 85, 138.

2. V, 406–407 (1684), where the proprietor by special writ handed over to Henry Darnell and William Diggs (relatives by marriage, councillors, justices of the peace, regents for the young Benedict, and in 1684 joint keepers of the great seal. See Note A at the end of this chapter) the third part of the fines and forfeitures allowed the governor from ships condemned for breaches of the navigation acts.

3. XVII, 142–143. The new land conditions are dated April 5, 1684, and the commission for the Land Council, May 5. The appointees named are H. Darnell, Diggs, N. Sewall, and J. Darnell.

of our private secret and continual council to us and our Leivetenant General and Cheif Governor,"[1] three of whom—the chancellor or the secretary always being one—were to constitute a quorum. Thus a group of three councillors (who not so much at first as later, when family marriages had been suitably arranged, became closely identified with the Calvert clan)[2] was able to exercise almost regal powers. Each bore the title of "Honorable" and all were invested with a dignity and sense of self-importance that was strangely out of keeping with the primitive conditions of life prevailing along the Chesapeake.

By order of the proprietor the eight councillors, mentioned above, who were themselves always lords of manors, were to be supplemented by seven others, each of whom had to be a manorial lord in order to qualify for the position. These fifteen councillors formed an upper house of assembly, which composed as it was of the "ablest planters" came as near as did an upper house in any colony to being a house of lords. Maryland had something like a local peerage, a privileged class, showing that Cecilius, relieved of his troubles of the past and once more basking in the sunshine of the royal favor, was interpreting his charter in terms of high prerogative. He even thought of creating class and caste differences "by the wearing of habbits Meddales or otherwise," in order that "some visible distinction and Distinctions" should be drawn between the administrative and judicial officials of the province (the appointment of whom lay entirely in his own hands) and the rest of the people. Acting on the firm conviction that the "County Pallantine of Durham have had liberty to Coine," he proposed in 1661 to set up a mint and obtained a law from the assembly to that effect on the ground that the want of a coinage was the main hindrance to the advancement of the colony "in Trades Manafactors Towns and other things which conduce to the flourishing and happy State thereof." But nothing was ever done about it, probably because it was doubtful if the English government would have allowed Baltimore a privilege which it positively refused to grant in the case of any of the other colonies. However, immediately after the restoration of the propriety in 1658 Cecilius caused a number of coins to be struck off in England for the

---

1. XV, 7. This council frequently bore the name "Council of State" and "Privy Council," and the councillors were sometimes called "councillors of state" and "privy councillors" (I, 315; V, 42; XVII, 252, and elsewhere).

2. See Note A at the end of this chapter.

use of the colony and some of these coins were shipped and put into local circulation, an act being passed to equate these coins to the foreign coins coming in from outside. But the Protectorate government issued orders for Baltimore's apprehension and the seizure of his instruments for coining, so that it is doubtful if any coining took place in England after 1659. It is quite certain that the coins were but little used and had entirely disappeared long before 1700. The debate which took place from 1681 to 1683 regarding trade, towns, and the need of bringing money into the province would seem to preclude any appreciable use of Baltimore's coins at any time in the colony.[1] In Maryland as elsewhere hard money was always scarce and the English government did nothing to help out the situation.

In order to bind officials and the freemen generally in loyalty and obedience to the proprietor and his prerogatives, Baltimore revived the oath of fidelity and fashioned other oaths to be taken by councillors and those holding administrative, judicial, and financial positions. The official oaths called for true and faithful service and a loyal defense, by every means at command, of the proprietor's rights and prerogatives; the oath of fidelity for entire devotion to the proprietor and a complete abstaining from any words or actions, in public or in private, that would derogate from the lord's authority, provided so doing did not "infringe or prejudice the freeman's liberty of conscience in point of religion." There is some reason to think that in practice the latter oath was "seldome administered butt to those in Civil and Military offices," and we know that later it was dispensed with entirely in the case of the Quakers. This oath had been drawn up, for the first time as far as we know, in 1643 and was renewed in even more stringent form in 1648 and 1650. It was supplemented in the latter year by an "act of recognition," requiring

---

1. On Baltimore's coinage, III, 365, 383, 385; V, 271; Ogilby, *Description of the New World* (1671), p. 188; Blome, *America* (1687), p. 197. Both Ogilby and Blome thought that the coins were in circulation at the time of their writing. The right to coin in the Palatinate had been given up before 1632 (Lapsley, *County Palatine of Durham*, pp. 281–282). On the general subject, I, 399, 400, 414–415, 429, 439, 444; II, 286–287. For the scarcity of hard money in the colonies, Nettels, *The Money Supply of the American Colonies*, ch. VI. In Maryland tobacco was the medium at the ratio of 10 lbs. to six pence, though the rate varied (XVII, 139, 189, 190). In 1678 Baltimore wrote, "wee have not as yett Coine amongst the people here Inhabiting to carry on Trade" (XV, 224). Between 1671 and 1688 rents were legally rated to the proprietor at two pence per pound of tobacco, but the proprietor's receivers had been accustomed to demand sterling, an infringement of the law of 1671 that constituted one of the grievances of the lower house in November, 1688 (XIII, 171).

every freeman in the province to accept Baltimore's title and powers, jurisdiction, and authority and to defend Baltimore and his heirs "until the last dropp of our blood be spent."[1] In 1654 it was declared null and void by the Puritan assembly of that year and in 1657 was "not pressed," when an "engagement" to the Protectorate of a much less coercive character was imposed by order of the committee of trade in England and the act of recognition was retained. In 1661 the oath was revived in all its pristine strength and, literally interpreted, restrained every freeman of the colony from uttering any word or committing any deed that could be construed as having a seditious or rebellious character, on pain of banishment.

As far back as 1649 Lord Baltimore had obtained from the assembly a law punishing all mutinous and seditious speeches and acts by imprisonment during pleasure, fine, banishment, boring of the tongue, slitting the nose, cutting off one ear or both ears, whipping, branding with a red-hot iron in the hand or forehead, according as the provincial court, the justices of which were the chief members of the council, should think fit. Other punishments of the time were losing the right hand, being nailed by the ears to the pillory, and being put to other corporal shame or correction, not extending to loss of life. A counterfeiter condemned for the third time was liable

---

1. I, 300; LI, 145, 313 (persons summoned to appear before the chancery court "under pain of their fidelity," 1674, 1679). For the oath of fidelity, I, 304–306; V, 310–311; LI, 390–391 (1671). For other oaths, I, 315, 320–321; XV, 14, 17–18, 36–37; LI, 222 (coroner), 384, 387, 392, 567, 568, 570 (officials of St. Mary's City, charters of 1668 and 1671). It was reported in London in 1678 that the oath of fidelity to his lordship neutralized the requirement to take the oath of fidelity and allegiance to the king. The council declared such a report to be a foul scandal and said that the freemen of Maryland had ever been "true Leigemen" to the king (XX, 233–234). In 1684 the act for taking the oath was redrawn and a clause added "saving alwayes my Allegiance which I owe to my soveraigne Lord his Majesty the King of England his Heires and Successors" (XIII, 31, 32). There was some objection to this clause in the lower house, possibly because it was designed to be perpetual. The proprietor demanded that the clause be accepted before his departure, but it is not clear that this was done. The debate was prolonged, but apparently in the end the deputies promised to accept the oath (for this debate, 13, 15, 24, 31, 32, 49–50, 59, 61, 65, 77, 80, 82, 91, 92, 109, 153, 154).

The oath of fidelity occupies a place fundamentally important in the history of the province, yet it is not always clear how it operated. Apparently every freeman in the colony was to take it, but if so why in 1676 did the upper house order that every deputy to the lower house should take the oath before the election of the speaker? Did deputies have to take the oath twice? All freeholders had to take it, for this was required of everyone who took out a patent for land (II, 508), but that every freeman actually took it is not so easy to demonstrate.

to perpetual banishment.[1] Did any one deny Baltimore's title to the province or dominion of Maryland or refuse to declare that he was the only true and absolute lord and proprietor, to whose powers, jurisdiction, and authority all men in the province were to subscribe and they and their heirs to maintain with their lives, he was liable to life imprisonment, to banishment, and even to death, with a confiscation of all his goods. While there can be no doubt that some of the more cruel penalties were designed less to be carried into effect than to terrify evil doers, the fact remains that no one could deny or oppose the proprietor's authority without punishment. At the same time few appealed to his clemency without relief and few confessed their offenses without receiving forgiveness and a more or less complete pardon.[2] Both Cecilius and Charles Calvert were naturally possessed of kindly and pacific instincts and each was paternally minded and desired to be the father of his people; but the feudal impulses were strongly intrenched. Neither was arrogant, arbitrary, or wilful, but each was absolute lord, even though his power was exercised for the good of the province and his prerogative was softened by benevolence and a willingness to pardon and condone.

The strength of the proprietor lay to no inconsiderable extent in

1. I, 248, 249, 286; V, 149–152; VII, 332. The articles of war of 1676, drawn up by the council, said that any officer or soldier who blasphemed or presumed to speak against any known article of the Christian faith should have his tongue bored through with a red-hot iron, and if he profaned any place of worship he should suffer death (XV, 80). Though Indians were executed for murder, white women for infanticide, and white men for buggery, there is nothing to show that the more inhuman punishments were ever inflicted. Whipping was common, probably ears were occasionally cropped, and two men in 1664 were branded "in the brawne of their righte handes" (XLIX, 235), but except for imprisonment, fines, lying in irons, and banishment few more severe punishments were ever inflicted. Four witchcraft cases are reported: Elizabeth Bennett, "Returned not presentable (1665) and cleared by proclamation; Mary Lee (1654) executed at sea; John Coman, reprieved on the gallows with the rope around his neck (1675); and Elizabeth Richardson (offense not stated) executed at sea, 1659 (III, 307–308; *Fund-Publications*, 7, p. 91; II, 425, 444, 447; XLI, 328; XLIX, 486, 508), but this execution on board ship was not approved by the provincial government and cannot be charged against the province. In 1681 Fendall was told that for his offense he ought to suffer the extreme penalty of the law, but that the court would refrain, imposing only fine, imprisonment, and banishment (V, 328).

2. The proprietor, or the proprietor and council, almost invariably replied favorably to petitions, that were sometimes backed by the lower house, for remission of sentence (II, 342, 377; XVII, 79, 140, 189, 347, 418; XLIX, 10, 545, for example). Vol. LI (index) contains entries of so many pardons (some of which are not easy to understand as no reasons are given) that the exercise of the right would seem to have been a little overdone.

the fact that members of his family and relatives by blood and marriage were continuously present in the colony and in possession of the most important positions of influence and control.[1] Whenever Charles himself was absent, either as governor or proprietor, there was apt to be some confusion and a measurable loss of prestige. Cecilius wanted his son to return to England in 1664, but the latter could not manage it. However he got away in May, 1669, and was gone for more than a year leaving the government in the hands of deputies. During that time he undoubtedly consulted with his father regarding sundry details of proprietary management and came to definite conclusions as to policies to be followed. Again he went away in June, 1676, intending to be gone only a few months, but he did not return for two years or until the autumn of 1678. He placed the province in the hands of his young son, Benedict Leonard, but nine years old, with Jesse Wharton at first and after his death Thomas Notley as deputy governor in charge. He went to Virginia in 1682, for what reason is not certainly known, possibly to confer on the tobacco cessation and cutting issue, but he was gone only a month. Finally, he went home in May or June, 1684, unwillingly[2] and with every expectation of an early return, but his affairs in England were in such a state as to require his continuous presence there and he never came back to the province. This enforced absence was owing partly to his trouble with the king whose displeasure he had incurred because of his infringement of the navigation acts which had led the Lords of Trade to declare that if he continued so doing they would recommend the issue of a quo warranto against his charter;[3] partly to the necessity of meeting the issue of the boundary line between Maryland and Pennsylvania; and partly to the efforts he was called upon to make in 1686 and 1687 to save his charter and prevent the province from being annexed to the Dominion of New England under Andros.[4] Three times at least, and

1. See Note A at the end of this chapter.
2. "Where the great Exigency of my affaires not my own inclinations, nor love of this place doth now drawe me . . . . It is to preserve my interest [in the controversy with Penn] and to settle my Child in an Undisturbed right afore I die that causeth me to resolve upon this voyage" (XIII, 5, 54).
3. *Calendar State Papers, Colonial*, 1681–1685, §§319, 320, 321; *Maryland Archives*, V, 305, 358.
4. V, 541–542, 545; *Calendar State Papers, Colonial*, 1685–1688, §§632, 645, 1231, 1275; *Acts Privy Council, Colonial*, II, §§64, 193; *New York Colonial Documents*, III, 363.

possibly four, did the Maryland proprietors face the loss of their prerogatives in the field of government and three times did they succeed in staving off the danger and retaining what the king had granted to them and their heirs. There is some reason to think that these absences worked to the proprietor's disadvantage. In 1678 Christopher Rousby called Charles "a Runnaway or words to that effect and [said] that he deserved to be sent home fast or in chains," and in 1681 the lower house in a petition and address called attention to "the Inconveniences that may happen in case of your Lordships Departure at any time out of this Province."[1] The significance of his final departure will appear as the story develops.

After 1660, with a Stuart once more on the throne of England, the relations of the proprietor with his assembly became fairly amicable and harmonious. The Puritan opposition in the colony was reduced to a minimum and with the king supporting the proprietary prerogatives, attempts at resistance were futile. The assembly, though frequently calling for a copy of the charter that the members might know what it contained on certain points (and once or twice it objected to what the upper house sent down and demanded a true copy), was willing to recognize Baltimore's just rights and dignities and to avoid infringing "his Lordships prerogatives."[2] It could hardly do otherwise in the face of the complete control which the proprietor exercised over its activities. Baltimore not only made all executive, administrative, military, and judicial appointments, issued licenses for ordinaries, ferries, and trade with the Indians, and regulated the management of the land and its revenues—as far as they were proprietary, but he had powers also that distinctly cramped the independence of the lower house of assembly. He could personally or through his deputy governor determine the time and place when the assembly should meet and by the right of prorogation,

1. XV, 229–230; VII, 181. Rousby's remark need not be taken seriously, although it may represent the opinion of others also. The address of the lower house was based on a real grievance arising out of the insufficient powers granted the interim governors in matters relating to the confirmation of laws (XIII, 97, 100).

2. II, 36, 99, 159, 241. It was during this period, 1666, that George Alsop, living quite far away in Baltimore County, wrote his highly flattering account of the province. One would suppose that he, being an indentured servant, would have presented accurately the condition of that class in Maryland, but his unreliability in this particular is so evident as to throw doubt on such of his other statements as concern general conditions in the province. Too much dependence has been placed upon Alsop by writers on Maryland history. He is not a trustworthy witness.

which, following the practice of Charles II in England, he exercised very frequently, he could postpone the gathering of the deputies as often as he pleased. In claim at least, and frequently in fact, he originated bills or allowed the upper house to do so, though he sometimes invited the lower house to join in drawing up a measure.[1] Many of these powers he delegated to his deputy governor in the province, when there was one, but the most important of all—the right of confirming or disallowing all acts passed in the colony—he retained absolutely in his own hands. Not even the king himself could have anything to say regarding what laws should or should not be passed in Maryland, provided such laws were not contrary to the laws of England.[2] The exercise of this right by the proprietor, particularly when he withheld his assent for a considerable time, led at times to expressions of protest and dissatisfaction from the deputies, not so much questioning the right as finding fault with the uncertainty of its operation. Furthermore, the proprietor could give permission for the election of a speaker, who disabled himself before the proprietor or governor, as did the speaker of the House of Commons before the king, and who asked that "the Freedom of speach in their house and other their Antient Priviledges may be continued unto them, which his Lordship did Assure them should be allowed them as formerly had been" (1682).[3] His approval was sought also in the election of the clerk, who was expected to know shorthand (as was certainly the case with John Llewellyn, clerk of the upper house).

To a certain extent, as we shall see, the proprietor was able to control the membership of the house and the qualification of both electors and deputies. How far he was accustomed to bring a personal influence to bear upon the decisions of the members of the two houses is problematical, though there is reason to think that his appointees often interfered in the elections. There is no doubt that Cecilius in England often stated his views very freely to his son in America, and it is equally likely that the son, in his turn, by means of entertainments, the cost of which was met by the assembly, or by

1. See above, p. 302, note 1. In 1672 Charles Calvert in one of his letters to his father spoke of his determination to get "those pernitious provisoes" struck out of an Act of Support, drawn up by the lower house, *Calvert Papers,* I, 257.

2. Baltimore reserved the power to dissent even though the deputy governor in the colony had agreed to a law passed during his absence from the colony, and in 1684 refused to confirm any laws that had been passed during his absence from the colony in 1678. VII, 152; V, 406; XVII, 253, 261.

3. VII, 3, 335.

open-house hospitality, either at St. Mary's or at his residence eight miles away at St. John's, was able to swing votes in the upper and perhaps even in the lower body.[1] When one considers the wide range of the proprietor's powers and the extent to which he kept in his own hands the reins of authority, we can understand somewhat the intensity of the opposition and the extravagance of the sentiments expressed, strongly biassed as these sentiments often were. The governor and council of Virginia avowed with some bitterness, that Baltimore in disallowing the act for the cessation of tobacco planting in 1666 played the part and usurped the right of an absolute sovereign;[2] and the Fendall party in 1676 complaining with a measure of reason that the proprietor "assums and attracts more Royall Power to himselfe over his Tennants than owr gratious Kinge over his subjects in England," charged him with assuming that he was "an absolute prince in Maryland, with as absolute prerogative Royall Right and Power," according to which, continues the complaint, they "set their Compass to steere by and governe by."[3] For this the charter, which gave Baltimore fuller powers in Maryland than the king had or at least exercised at home, was largely responsible.

On the other hand, the lower house of assembly, which represented the freemen, circumscribed though it was, possessed a fairly wide field of action within which to operate and as time went on widened this field and established its right to many of the privileges which it claimed. No law could pass without its consent, determined by majority vote with the speaker present; and only after its accept-

1. II, 432, 454, 455; *Calvert Papers*, I, 256–257, 264–265, 292. Baltimore was later charged with obtaining laws "craftily" from the "unwary Representatives" (VIII, 216). Invitations to dinner or supper, as a method of winning the support of deputies or voters, were utilized by the governor of the proprietors in East New Jersey also (*Proceedings*, New Jersey Historical Society, 2d ser., III, 33–34 [1671]); *Calendar State Papers, Colonial*, 1681–1688, §158). For another use of a dinner, *Pennsylvania Magazine*, V, 330; and for the law in West New Jersey forbidding the use of "Meat, Drink, Money, or Money's worth" to influence the voters, see *New Jersey Archives*, I, 263, a clause that is repeated in Penn's "Laws agreed upon in England," §III (Thorpe, *Charters*, V, 3060).

2. II, 5–9, 15–19; *Acts Privy Council, Colonial*, I, §§729, 733. Historical Manuscripts Commission, *Fleming*, p. 53.

3. V, 138. Culpeper of Virginia had some inkling of the situation when he wrote in 1681, at a time when council and assembly were deadlocked and Fendall was making trouble, "Maryland is now in torment and not only troubled with our disease, poverty, but in very great danger of falling in pieces; whether it be that old Lord Baltimore's politic maxims are not pursued or that they are unsuited to this age." *Calendar State Papers, Colonial*, 1681–1685, pp. 155–156.

ance by the upper house, enactment by the governor, and publication under the great seal (affixed in the presence of both houses by chancellor Philip, who was keeper as long as he lived, and after 1682 by joint keepers duly appointed) could it become the law of the province. Even then it had to be approved by the proprietor, but until the proprietor's pleasure was known, the law was binding on the colony.[1] The lower house persisted in calling itself a parliamentary body, and in its rules of procedure and definition of privileges, which were carefully modeled after those of the House of Commons in England, made good its pretensions, speaking of "the Antient rules & Custome of this hous" (1682). However much the proprietor and the upper house might persist in saying that it was nothing but a provincial council and had no right to parliamentary standing, or could assert that certain assumptions "were new to us and unheard of before in this province,"[2] the lower house stood its ground. It insisted also that it alone represented the freemen of the colony and not the two houses taken together, as the upper house said was legally the case, and that in consequence the freemen, that is, the public, should not have to bear the expenses of the members of the upper house, who, appointees of the proprietor as they were, should bear their own expenses. The upper house receded from its position, as it had to do, inasmuch as each county bore the charges of its elected delegates.[3] The lower house regulated its own business, elected its own speaker, clerk, sergeant at arms, and doorkeeper (with the consent of the proprietor in the case of the first two), determined the qualifications of its own members, and sat on its adjournment. It could impeach but not try, a privilege reserved to the upper house only, but it could prosecute the case, the upper house delivering the sentence and imposing the penalty.[4]

1. II, 64, 133. This question of procedure in the making of laws became a subject of discussion in 1681, when the upper house was of opinion that a law made by the consent of both houses and assented to by his lordship could not be repealed but by the consent of both houses. At that time the proprietor promised to give his approval as soon as possible, and until that was done the law was to continue binding. Should he leave the province he would act within eighteen months (VII, 182, 377, 401, 428; XIII, 38, 40, also 97, when the upper house wanted to make it three years and the lower house objected. Also p. 100, when Baltimore refused to bind his heirs to any definite period).

2. V, 329–330; VII, 34, 113, 119, 123, 124, 125, 127, 135, 178–179, and elsewhere. The upper house had its privileges also, VII, 139–140. See note 4.

3. VII, 354, 373, 377, 419.

4. II, 163–173; VII, 363, 383–384, 394, 560, 561, 598. The case in point is that of Jacob Young, charged with conspiring with the Indians to invade the province;

That the proprietary prerogatives did not pass unchallenged is evident from the murmurs of dissatisfaction and doubt, by questioning and the drafting of grievances, and by the attempt of one Charles Nicholett, in a sermon preached to the lower house (1669), "to stir up the Lower House to do their duty," an attempt in which he was egged on by some of the members, preaching on liberties "equal to the people of England." For so doing Nicholett was ordered by the upper house to acknowledge his error in dealing with matters of government which did not concern him, to crave pardon of proprietor, deputy governor, and assembly, and to pay a fine for uttering seditious words.[1] On April 20, 1669, the house brought in a statement "of the real grievances of the province," which covered assent to laws, levy of taxes, privileged attorneys, exactions of the sheriffs, fees, and informers. This statement so provoked the upper house that it sent the chancellor and a committee down stairs to the lower chamber to require the deputies "to raze the mutinous and seditious votes contained in the paper out of their journal," which was agreed to on condition that the upper house obliterate from their journal the words "mutinous and seditious." At the same time the lower house considered the request a breach of its privileges, whereupon the upper house told the lower that they were "not to Conceive that their privileges ran parallel to the Commons in the Parliament of England," for "if no Charter there is no assembly, no Assembly no privileges."[2] For a time the issue hung fire and the

though Young was too sick to travel (XIII, 21), he was convicted and sentenced to fine and banishment, but the sentence was manifestly not executed, as Young appears afterward in the employment of the province as interpreter in negotiations with the Indians (XIII, 234). The impeachment of Morecroft in 1669 was a curious affair (II, 172–173). There were other impeachments also—of Thomas Truman and Charles James, for example.

1. II, 159–163.
2. II, 168–169, 173–184. The upper house added that the lower house was in the same class with "the common council of the City of London, which if they act Contrary or to the overthrow of the Charter of the City run into Sedition and the Person Questionable" (178). A month later "An Act of Gratitude for the Lieutenant General" was dissented to in the lower house, after it had passed the upper. The latter demanded that the deputies come up stairs for a conference and give reasons for dissenting. The latter refused to go, because in doing so they would be yielding on a matter of privilege. They were willing to confer on unfinished business but not on such as was finished (193, 217). In 1681 when the relations between the upper house and the lower house were rather more strained than usual, the latter said regarding its own privileges that the records and authorities of the customs and usage of the House of Commons formed "the only Rule to walk by" (VII, 123). A spirited exchange of opinions followed (123–127), which will be noticed in an-

governor threatened to dissolve the assembly; but finally the lower house grudgingly submitted, said that it did not mean to style the proprietor's rights grievances ("God forbid") and declared its willingness "to have our Journal contradicted, expunged, obliterated, burnt, anything." This was compliance with a vengeance, but the question may easily be asked whether it was sincere. The whole incident had been an ominous ending to nearly a decade of fairly peaceful team-work. Even the "God forbid" could not conceal the fact that the proprietor's prerogatives had been questioned and the independence of the lower house maintained. But the questioning had not gone far, for the lower house had for the moment given in and the prerogatives had emerged from the attack to all appearances undamaged, and, in the eye of the proprietor and his son, the governor, secure. During the period his lordship was more concerned with his estates and revenues than with matters of governmental control. His rights of government rested on the unchangeable text of the charter, whereas the returns from his proprietorship of the soil were always variable and uncertain because they could not be exactly fixed or determined.

In 1669 Charles Calvert went to England and while there must have presented to his father the story of the preceding four years.[1] Whether definite measures were agreed upon whereby the ascendancy of the proprietor might be maintained cannot be said, but something of the kind probably took place, for almost immediately after his return, which was before November 7, 1670, he caused to be issued an order from the proprietor to the sheriffs of the counties, dated December 18, 1670, limiting the suffrage. Thus, by a stroke of the pen Lord Baltimore disfranchised all freemen of the colony who had less than fifty acres of land or a personal estate within the county of less than forty pounds sterling value, cutting off the poorer inhabitants from voting and limiting the right to freeholders only, a questionable interpretation of the charter which uses the

other connection. For the differences over the tobacco planting issue of 1666 see II, 38, 39, 40, 42, 105, 106, 159. Even as early as that date it was found practically impossible to square the privileges claimed by the lower house with what the upper house considered the interests of the proprietor and the needs of the province.

1. The letters of Charles Calvert to his father, 1664–1673, deal with but few other subjects than those which relate to estates, escheats, and revenues (*Calvert Papers*, I, 229–305). Note also the new instructions issued by Lord Baltimore in 1669-1670 (V, 54–58, 63–64), which deal almost entirely with land grants, proprietary reservations, and quit-rents.

term *liberi homines,* not *libere tenentes,* freemen not freeholders. This order may have been modeled after the Virginia law of October, 1670, to the same effect, though the latter was somewhat more liberal in that it included householders as well as freeholders.[1] Inasmuch as freemen were taxed without distinction, except in the case of ministers and priests,[2] a grievance was immediately felt and expressed. The reverberation of the order was to be heard for many years and its issue was to bring into sharper relief than ever before the whole question of proprietary authority in the province. The rising tide of discontent with Baltimore's manipulation of the assembly was carried to the flood, when a few years later in 1676, though authorizing the sheriffs to provide four deputies from each county, Baltimore (Charles Calvert, now proprietor) issued writs for the coming of but two to sit in the assembly meeting in June of that year. The lower house entered a vigorous protest against this reduction in its numbers and made complaint that not only were the inhabitants dissatisfied because "they have not their free vote" but that the house itself had an insufficient number of members wherewith to do business. Just what the proprietor's idea and purpose were in thus altering the conditions of representation it is difficult to say, as no very satisfactory explanation of the change is anywhere given. Cecilius, Lord Baltimore, had put himself on record in 1667 as sympathetic with "the poorer sort of planters (who are the most in number and of whom [he] must have as tender a care as of the sick)";[3] and we know that one of the grievances of the assembly was "the great charges incurr'd to the public" by the frequent and prolonged sessions.[4] Perhaps the proprietor wished "to save their purses," by cutting down expenses, but the same result might have been achieved by reducing the number of deputies without disfranchising the poorer classes. Just how either course would enhance his proprietary prerogative it is not easy to see, except by showing his "absolute command of right" and control over the make-up and meetings of the assembly.[5]

---

1. Hening, *Statutes,* II, 280. The distinction between freeholders and freemen in Maryland is frequently indicated, VIII, 50, for example, where the interesting classification appears of "Gents, Merchants, Planters, Freeholders and Freemen."

2. II, 399.   3. V, 17.

4. VII, 353. In 1676 "The great Clamour is against the greatness of the Taxes," XV, 137.

5. The only explanation given is that of the governor and council in 1676, when they issued "A Remonstrance of the true State of the Province & of the causes and

However that may be, for the next six years the disfranchising of the propertyless class and the reduction in the number of delegates from the counties became subjects of a heated controversy between the two houses which came to a head in 1681, when the proprietor expressed his disapproval of the demand of the lower house, and issuing his ordinance and proclamation for the assembly of 1681, instructed the sheriffs to bring about the election of but two members.[1] For nearly three years the matter was hotly debated, during which each house stood by its guns, the upper sustaining the proprietor and his prerogatives and preparing the text of its own bill for the electing of deputies; and the lower house preparing another bill allowing the counties to elect as many as they chose up to four. The issue was complicated by the further demand that as the numbers in the existing house were not sufficient for doing business the speaker be allowed to issue warrants for the filling of vacancies. According to the practice of the House of Commons, followed afterward in Maryland, the speaker issued his warrant, in case of a vacancy, to the principal secretary or his deputy who in turn issued a writ for the election of another member to fill the vacancy. This demand touched the proprietor's privilege, just as the disfranchising of the freemen was construed as touching the privileges of the assembly.[2] On this issue the houses were deadlocked.

The next year, 1682, the controversy continued.[3] Neither house would accept the other's bill, each charging its antagonist with wasting time and adding daily to the "great charge accruing to the Publick." The proprietor and the upper house took their stand on the charter and to the demand of the lower house replied "non possumus," calling its bill "a needless bill" as his lordship had already

reasons of the publique Taxes" (XV, 137–140). "As to the votes of ffreemen who have neither lands nor visible personall Estate, in the Election of Delegates for the Assembly, wee doe say, that as the Lord Proprietary can call Assemblys by his patent whensoever and in what manner shall seeme most fitt and convenient, Itt is no wonder that he should chuse this as the fittest and most convenient manner, and most agreeable to the Lawe and Custom of England," etc., at great length. The idea seems to be that freemen without estate might outvote the freeholders who had everything at stake. The Remonstrance called attention to the practice in England where "infinite numbers" did not vote and where but two members were sent to parliament from each county.

1. XVII, 16; XV, 378–379.

2. VII, 12, 60–63, 110–111, 120, 123, 125–127. For a claim of privilege by the upper house, II, 512–513.

3. VII, 307, 345–346, 353, 355, 360, 452–453, 488, 575.

settled the matter. The lower house saying that the freemen at large were discussing the situation and were insisting on their four delegates, they prepared another bill as did also the upper house. No progress was made. The situation became the more serious, because the upper house was promoting important measures for the advancement of trade, levying war, and defraying the public charges, with which the lower house would have nothing to do until the election bill was accepted. So at the end of the session the matter stood. Finally, in November, 1683, after nearly three years of wrangling, some sort of a compromise or understanding was reached, because it became evident that in the presence of a threatened invasion by the Indians the two houses were neglecting the needs and defenses of the province. The lower house, which was upholding its claims to what the proprietor called its "Imaginary privileges," and was adopting what the same proprietor called "irregular and unparliamentary ways of proceeding,"[1] was exhibiting a steadfastness that was akin to obstinacy and was finally compelled to yield. When a new assembly was summoned that met in April, 1684, shortly before the proprietor left the province, only two members came up to St. Mary's from each of the ten counties;[2] and during the nearly four weeks of the session (April 1–26) nothing was said about an election bill, the time being spent in a feverish effort to catch up with necessary legislation, by passing a large number of other bills, both public and private. Relations between the houses and with the proprietor were friendly, and measures were taken for the advancement of trade, the planning of towns, the setting up of a public post, the building of a new state house, the granting of the two shillings a hogshead to the proprietor (first made in 1676), the prevention of usury, and the naturalization of many foreigners. This session was as fruitful as those from 1679 to 1683 had been barren. Not a word was said about privileges and there were few

1. XIII, 5; XVII, 41.
2. XIII, 3–126. That but two members appeared from each county is evident from the mention of the fact that the burgesses from Cecil County, who took eight days to reach St. Mary's, were two in number. There is also mention of "the [other] Delegate" from Dorchester (XIII, 56, 106). The assembly usually met at St. Mary's, but in 1683 for greater convenience was moved to John Larkin's house at the Ridge in Ann Arundel County. In 1684 it was called back to St. Mary's that it might be near the proprietor who was soon to leave the province. There it remained until March, 1695, when the sessions were held permanently at Annapolis. The council met at various places in the houses of its members.

disputes and dissents. Lord Baltimore must have left for England
with the thought that all was well with his province.

But all was not well with his province. For nearly twenty years
there had been murmurings among the people, notably in the less
populated districts, and after 1670 much discoursing of such issues
as the suffrage question and the reduction of the number of deputies. There are but few early instances of angry and abusive remarks
and what there are seem born rather of personal grudges or drink-
sodden intellects than of hostility to the proprietary. Governor Nicholson said in 1697 that there was far too much drinking prevalent in
the colony.[1] That outspoken complaints were not more common is
possibly due to the severe laws that were enacted from time to time
against mutinous and seditious speeches, for studying such records
as remain one senses an undercurrent of dissatisfaction beneath even
the smoothest and most placid of surfaces. There were those who
slandered the officials, called the governor and members of the assembly "Rogues, Papists and puppies," and invited the lower house, as
did Charles Nicholett, to realize how heavy taxation was and urged
it, as a house of commons, to demand its liberties and to make laws
in accord with their status as free-born Englishmen. Despite the
harsh legislation the results in these cases were either acquittal or
such moderate punishments as whipping, demand for an apology,
or remand to the provincial court, the sentences of which are only
in one instance disclosed.[2]

But with the decision of the proprietor to disfranchise the poorer
freemen and to reduce the representation from the counties a situation arose which needed only the stimulus of leadership to take on
the form of a deliberate act of resistance. On Sunday, September 3,
1676, at the plantation of Thomas Barbary upon Patuxent River in
Calvert County, some sixty persons met insistent on a redress of
grievances. In a paper, deemed seditious by the government, they
demanded certain concessions, immunities, and freedoms which the
proprietor did not think it within his power to grant without the
consent of the assembly. The paper complained of excessive taxa-

1. XXIII, 81.

2. I, 532; III, 445 (Jenkins, 1661), 494-495 (Fuller's wife, 1664); XLI, 530-534,
542-550 (William Bretton, 1664); XLIX, 260, 279 (Marmaduke Snow, 1664); II,
55-56 (Erberry, 1666), 159-160 (Nicholett, 1667); V, 60 (James Clifton of Virginia,
1669); XV, 20 (James Lewes, 1671). Clifton's offense was affronting the king of
England.

tion, the cost of the frequent meetings of the assemblies, the depriving of the freemen of their vote, the taxing of the poor equally with the rich, as in the poll tax, and the obligation of all to take the oath of fidelity as if they had no higher rights and duties as subjects of the king of England. The movement was headed by William Davyes, ensign in the militia and gentleman, Giles Hasleham, and John Pate, who may have been connected with the Pate of Gloucester County, Virginia, the participant in Bacon's rebellion there. The council sent messengers to the insurgents demanding that they lay down their arms and disperse, promising all but the leaders a free pardon. But the insurgents refused to obey, and all marched away with drums beating and colors flying. The council then proclaimed them mutinous and seditious and liable to the death penalty. But in reality they were protestants rather than rebels, men who found something wrong in the whole proprietary arrangement, made the more unbearable it may be by the low price of tobacco and by poverty in general. They thought that their condition might be bettered if they were allowed to make an appeal to the king and parliament and so to obtain redress in a legal way. But the proprietor and council thought otherwise, expressed surprise at the ingratitude displayed and the concern expressed for the poorer freemen "who have nothing to entitle themselves to a being in this province," and pursued the leaders in their flight into the Delaware region.[1] Davyes and Pate were taken at New Castle, brought back by force to the place of the uprising, and hanged at The Cliffs overlooking the Chesapeake.[2] Many of their accomplices who submitted were pardoned while others, more obdurate, were heavily fined.

Much more serious and widespread was the movement which found its seat of origin in Charles County, a forest and frontier land lying west of St. Mary's at the bend of the Potomac, adjacent to Stafford County in Virginia, the latter a frontier land lying farthest from Jamestown, where Indian raids had started the movement

1. The insurgents of 1689 considered the Davyes-Pate uprising as "occasioned by his Lordspps Writts of Elleccon commanding Four Representatives for each County to be elected as an Assembly out of which Four, his Lordspp afterward called only two that he thought most fitt for his interest to be an Assembly who laid the greatest Levy upon the People that ever was laid in that Province. Which they refused to pay as not being laid by their legall Representatives." VIII, 225.

2. The Cliffs or "Clifts," as they were often called, ran from just north of the Patuxent to the "town of Herrington" on Herring Creek in Ann Arundel County, about half way to Annapolis.

known as Bacon's Rebellion. That there was a more or less close connection between Maryland and Virginia and the Albemarle section to the southward can easily be demonstrated and that the impact of Bacon's uprising in 1676 upon the men living in Charles County started the new agitation is capable of proof. The two men, who by popular repute were mixed up in the affair at large, though by no means necessarily in collusion, were Josias Fendall and John Coode, and Baltimore not unnaturally looked upon them as "two Rank Baconists," the chief contrivers among "the evil disposed spirits" who had "been tampering to stirr up the Inhabitants of Maryland and those of the north part of Virginia to mutiny."[1] For his faithlessness to the proprietor in 1660 Fendall had been debarred from public office, and the fine and penalty imposed upon him had galled him ever since. To get into office he now set all his wits at work inciting to resistance the people of Charles County and even tampering with the justices at St. Mary's.[2] He was influential in Charles County, where lay his plantation, and where he was a leading planter and man of business. From there in 1677 he had been returned by the voters to the assembly. The chancellor would not accept him, but Fendall said that if elected again he would sit. Furthermore, he added, he would on word from England, with the aid of thirty or forty men, send his lordship packing home, and having suffered much heretofore he knew the time was soon coming when he could right himself.[3] These and other remarks were construed as "Divers false and malitious scandalous Reports" against the proprietor and Fendall was ordered to appear before the council; but he refused and fled.

The years from 1679 to 1682 were a time of great agitation in England and the events of that period were known in America in the form of garbled reports, brought chiefly by the ships' captains who came to the commercial ports of New England and in considerable numbers frequented the Chesapeake and its rivers. Though St. Mary's was the official center of the colony, the Patuxent was

1. Baltimore distinctly says this in his letter to the Earl of Anglesey, V, 281. See also XV, 127–132, 137–138, 344; VII, 110; V, 143, 144, 147. It was to prevent this "broaching of Lyes and false Stories" that several acts were passed at this time and at other times against "Divulgers of false news," XV, 391–392.

2. Letter from Philip Calvert to Colonel Henry Meese, December 29, 1681. This letter is not in the Bodleian, as stated in the preface to volume XX of the *Maryland Archives,* where it is printed, but in the Public Record Office, C. O. 1: 47, no. 120.

3. XV, 192, 246–248.

scarcely less commercially important, and ships loading tobacco went from place to place, wherever the scattered plantations could supply a cargo. Information about England spread broadcast was unreliable enough, but that which drifted through to the colonies must have taken on many strange forms and exaggerated colorings as it was bandied loosely from mouth to mouth. News from home was eagerly welcomed in Maryland, discoursed upon in ships' cabins, in private houses, and wherever people gathered together,[1] and one can easily imagine that men, and women too, listened with rapt attention, mingled with fear and foreboding, to the tales of plots and plottings, troubles between king and parliament, rumored activities of Papists and Frenchmen, party manoeuvers for and against the Duke of York, and the beginnings of the Monmouth uprising.[2] It was an age when change and progress were foreign to men's thoughts, when chartered rights were considered safe from all except the king who granted them, and when no one of conservative sympathies could realize the anachronism of a medieval institution, such as that of Baltimore, continuing to operate in the seventeenth century. A grant from the king, whether of land and government in a royal letters patent or of an administrative office under the great seal or one of the lesser seals, became a vested interest, a franchise or liberty, a family property or benefice, from which was to be derived a continuous and permanent revenue. After making full allowance for the personal elements involved, we must conclude that the struggle in Maryland was in largest part a protest against the continuance of a proprietary system that in its particular form had long since outlived its usefulness and that advanced the interests of a few private individuals only (and those at the summit of the social and

1. V, 278; XV, 245–246; XVII, 55.
2. Ogg, *England in the Reign of Charles II*, II, pp. 559–613. Mr. Ogg says, "Plotting was one of the spare-time occupations of the seventeenth century . . . [in] an age of oaths, perjurers, and informers . . . when the Scarlet woman was more prominent than the Economic Man . . . [and when opinion widely prevailed] that pope Innocent XI had deputed to the Jesuits supreme control of the Roman Catholic interest in England for the purpose of overthrowing king and government." In addition to all this many men believed that there was to be "a massacre of Protestants and a French invasion of Ireland." Between February, 1679, and January 18, 1681, Charles II summoned and dissolved two parliaments, the second because of its persistent efforts, which failed, to exclude the Duke of York from the throne. "There seemed no limit to the insanity through which the nation was passing," as seen in the "pope burnings," the "papist plottings," the exhibitions of personal fears of the French, and the prevailing dread, panic, and prejudice that were at work in men's minds.

political pyramid) who, however kindly disposed they may have been, represented in all essentials a "benevolent despotism." It is a mistake to read into such a protest anything democratic or anything anticipatory of the American Revolution, for the agitation was for those rights enjoyed by Englishmen of the seventeenth century and nothing more. Such a system, absolute and paternal and demanding from all within its jurisdiction unqualified submission and obedience, provoked resistance, because it did not guarantee to the people of Maryland the rights of free-born Englishmen, such as the subjects of the king were then enjoying at home.

Fendall continued to be the mouthpiece of this growing discontent. He told the people of the lower counties that they were fools to pay taxes, even if levied by act of assembly; that because there was warfare in England between king and parliament nothing was treason and a man might say what he pleased; and that it would be easy to overthrow the government by seizing the proprietor, the chancellor, the secretary, and of the councillors Colonel Henry Darnell, who was suspected of preparing a troop of Catholic horse to go against the Protestants. No one else, he said, mattered.[1] In a manifesto, couched in the form of a complaint, undoubtedly written by Fendall or by one or more of his party, the grievances against the proprietary government were outlined at length. These grievances were very real and though the authors of the complaint expressed themselves crudely and in a laboriously exaggerated manner, catching at every possible defect in the way things were managed, without much regard to the facts in the case, they wrote with great intensity of feeling, and what they said represents without doubt the emotions at work in many minds in many parts of the province. Men were coming to believe that they were unjustifiably taxed to fill the pockets of the proprietor's family and friends, that they were inadequately protected from Indian attacks, that fees and charges were excessive, that the poorer freemen were disfranchised in order to make it easier for the proprietor to rule the assembly, "mealy mouthed, affraighted," as that assembly was and "cringing" before the "frowns and breathings" of the upper house which scared its members into compliance. They found the roots of evil to be the proprietary prerogatives and the influence of the Roman Catholic members of the council, provincial court, and upper house, and

1. XV, 269; XX, xiii.

imagined that the Roman Catholics would join with the French and the Indians to drive out or destroy the Protestants. In the frequency of Indian murders they saw the hand of the Papist, working to injure the poor frontier folk, and assumed that the weakness of the Anglican church in the colony was due to the proselyting activities of the Jesuits and of Roman Catholic priests—pope's messengers, as they called them, in secret correspondence with their brethren, the French priests in Canada.[1]

Above all they objected to the proprietor's charter and particularly to the palatine clause in it, because the charter shut them out from the enjoyment of their rightful heritage as subjects of the king of England. They believed they were despoiled of many things that were legally theirs—right of appeal to the king and parliament, duty of allegiance which was denied by the proprietor's oath of fidelity, and the privileges of free-born subjects, with the franchises and immunities belonging thereto. They saw the king barred from all interference with the affairs of the province, without right of disallowance of the laws or the prosecution of justice in his name, and they were resentful that the proprietor should be able to stand in their way and play the part of king, assuming more power over his tenants (for so the Fendall group classified the Maryland people) than the king had over his subjects in England. They wanted the king to take the Maryland government into his own hands, appointing Protestant governors and ministers, swearing and ruling the people

1. The fears expressed were of the partiality and favor shown the Roman Catholics on all occasions, regarding which the Privy Council in England wrote the proprietor, warning him to be careful; of a combination of Papists, French, Irish, and Indians against the Protestants; and constantly of Indian attacks, particularly of the Sinniquos at the head of the bay, who were believed to have been persuaded by the proprietor to come down and murder the Protestants (V, 152, 300–301; VII, 486–487; XV, 348, 359–360, 387, 393, 406, 408, 420, and elsewhere). As showing the hysteria of the time, the case of Dr. Edward Husbands may be cited, who in 1678 was charged with menacing and cursing the members of the assembly and of trying to endanger their lives by putting poison in a "duck py." He was ordered whipped (twenty lashes), forbidden to practice, and forced out of the province (VII, 49–50, 105, 160). In May, 1679, Captain Nickley of the ship *Francis and Mary* of Bristol brought the news that it was common talk along the docks there that Lord Baltimore was a traitor and that Monmouth was the true proprietor of the country (XV, 250). In February, 1680, Dr. James Baree was charged with sedition in saying that the Roman Catholics under Darnell and Coursey in three days' time would cut off the Protestants and that the fact was well known in England (XV, 269–273). In July, 1681, James Tyrling was brought to book for declaring that the proprietor had furnished the Indians with powder and shot for the purpose of killing off the English (XV, 386–387; V, 300–301).

according to the custom of England, and regulating taxation and the export dues not in the interests of a few but for the benefit of all. Clumsy and overwrought as is the language of the complaint, one will not find it difficult to analyze the emotions that gave it birth or to understand why the writers, in the name of the rest, should cry out to the king "are wee rebells?"[1]

Stirred by the news from England, Fendall at various times in the years 1680 and 1681, in coöperation with others, raised the standard of revolt in Charles County uttering, according to the charges brought against him, "false scandalous mutinous and seditious English words" of and concerning the lord proprietor, and attempting with others in April, 1681, "with force and armes" to secure and imprison the lord proprietor and several of the council—the chancellor, secretary, and Colonel Darnell. He was seized and tried in November at the provincial court, sitting at the proprietor's residence at St. John's, before a jury a majority of the members of which were Protestants. He was found guilty and sentenced to a fine of 40,000 pounds of tobacco, imprisonment until paid, and then banishment. The sentence was considered moderate, the secretary, who was one of the justices, telling him that under the law he might have had his tongue bored through and his ears cropped and have suffered other corporal indignities. Fendall went to Virginia, where he was carefully watched. Baltimore was afraid he might start another revolt, for during the trial the report was spread abroad that the people of Charles County, seemingly sympathetic, were planning to rescue him. In 1684 it was noised abroad that he had returned, but he could not be found; and in 1688 he died.[2]

The man charged with being the ringleader in the proposed attempt to rescue Fendall was George Godfrey, a justice of the peace, lieutenant of horse under Captain Randolph Brandt in Charles County, who when he heard of Fendall's arrest and noted that the

1. "Complaint from Heaven with a Huy and Crye and a petition out of Virginia and Maryland," submitted to the king and parliament and to the lord mayor and aldermen and the citizens and merchants of London (V, 134–152). This document, very inadequately calendared, is twice entered in the *Calendar of State Papers, Colonial*, 1661–1668, §404; 1675–1676, §937. The date is nowhere exactly given, but from internal evidence the complaint must have been written sometime between the first of December, 1676, and the last of January, 1677.

2. V, 281, 311–334; XV, 244–249, 388–390, 400; XVII, 272–274; *Maryland Magazine*, I, 76; *Calendar State Papers, Colonial*, 1661–1685, p. 92, §§195, 275, 313, 397, 448.

planters and farmers of the county murmured against it, conceived the plan of unhorsing and disarming Brandt and using the troop on Fendall's behalf. All but two of the troop were Protestants and the plan seemed feasible. They planned to gather at the head of Portobacco Creek, July 17, 1681, and after rescuing Fendall to persuade him to lead them against the proprietor. But the whole miscarried. Godfrey, charged with sedition, was seized by Brandt and Chanler, the high sheriff, tried before a jury at the provincial court, and condemned to death, August, 1681, a sentence that the proprietor commuted to one of life imprisonment.[1]

The general situation was alarming and Baltimore in a proclamation and message to the assembly called attention to the "busy malicious fellows" who had been engaged in "the late rebellion" and demanded of the deputies an act more severe than before punishing sedition. He wanted heavy penalties in order to check "the great licence and liberty several wicked malicious persons give themselves in broaching lyes and false stories,"[2] and to put a stop to the tale bearing and false witnessing by those who, as Fendall said of one of them, were infamous persons and thieves.[3] Among the disturbers of the peace was one John Coode, commonly called "colonel," of whom we shall hear again and often. Though legally a resident of St. Mary's City, he had a house and plantation on Wicocomoco river or creek, up the Potomac in Charles County, which seems to have been something of a resort where gathered at times the disaffected of the neighborhood. There as elsewhere men met and engaged in loose and wild talk about the government, among them Fendall, though Coode does not appear to have had any part in his activities or in those of Godfrey. Coode had a reputation for swearing and cursing and was undoubtedly hot tempered and belligerent. He got into trouble in 1681 and, indicted as a blasphemer and a man of flagitious life and conversation, was haled before the county court. There he behaved "debauchedly and profanely" and was put under

---

1. V, 332–334; XV, 400–411; XVII, 29, 31, 47, 66, 67, 69, 79.

2. Such a law had been first passed in 1649, repealed in 1654, when a Puritan substitute was adopted (I, 343), and renewed in 1671 (II, 258, 260, 265). The proprietor now wanted something with more teeth in it (VII, 147, 156, 158; XV, 391–392, 410). It is suggestive of the situation in Maryland that there should have been need of a similar law as late as 1692, and for another at the same time for the punishment of persons suborning witnesses or committing wilful and corrupt perjury (XIII, 399, 439, 458).

3. XV, 391.

bond to keep the peace, but tore up the order and refused to obey. Remanded to the provincial court for trial, he was put out of his position as a justice of the peace, and in revenge (as was charged) spread more scandalous reports and uttered more mutinous and seditious speeches. As he was a member of the lower house, the upper house demanded that he be disqualified as a member because under indictment. At first the lower house refused on the ground of privilege, but on further consideration finally agreed to expel him, not because of the indictment but because he was a clergyman. Coode was tried at the provincial court and acquitted of all charges against him.[1] We have no knowledge of the evidence in the case, but if it was as unconvincing as was that presented in the steno-graphic report of Fendall's trial it must have been flimsy indeed. As in England so in Maryland one senses the hysteria of the time, the intensity of feeling on both sides, and the ease with which the wild-est rumors of disaffection among the people found credence among the governing classes.

How far such disaffection actually extended in Maryland it is impossible to say. The frontier inhabitants battered by the Indian attacks which had begun as early as 1674 and suffering loss of lives and damage to homes and stock, were ready to believe that the gov-ernment was not doing its utmost to protect them. For fifteen years in Charles County, in the north, and on the eastern shore Indian assaults and murders had involved the province in expensive wars and prolonged negotiations,[2] and had resulted in diversion of energy and heavy economic loss. Adventurers of the type of Fendall and Coode had fished in these troubled waters. In 1682, the proprietor, complaining of aspersions on his administration "from the Malicious evill Reports of some Disaffected Persons," which he knew "to be most Notoriously false," had felt obliged "to draw up a Declaration in Vindication of himself and his honour and Governm^t in the Eyes of the World." In this declaration he was probably referring to noth-ing more recent than the aspersions of those who had already taken part in Fendall's rebellion or in Godfrey's attempt at rescue. Of these there were many, mostly unknown but in a few instances pre-served by name for posterity: Marshall, Humphrey, Fendall's brother

1. See Note B at the end of this chapter.
2. For example, among scores of references, II, 384; XVII, 19 ff., 193, 197, 216, 220–230.

Samuel, and Edward Abbot, the first of whom was a millwright of Charles County, who had threatened the life of both proprietor and chancellor, and the last, occupation unspecified, had abused his lordship "in a very gross manner." Even after 1682 there were others who made speeches reflecting on the Baltimore family or on the king, as was the case with Francis Malden, carpenter of the Cliffs in Calvert County—another center of commotion associated with the outbreak of Davyes and Pate—who in 1684 gave vent to certain caustic remarks, for which he afterward expressed contrition. Another, George Butler, on his dismissal as clerk of the provincial court, abused the proprietor as responsible for his loss of office, and he too confessing his fault was pardoned.[1] Nearly all of these offenders were from the artisan and poorer planter classes.

The substantial planters appear to have been fairly well content with the situation, as they well might be. The colony was making progress, despite the popular unrest, and a measure of prosperity was attained which benefited those with manors and freehold tenements large enough in area to be the scenes of a busy plantation life. Though there is no doubt that the assembly was often cramped in its efforts to legislate for the good of all, as the deputies saw it, by the frequent quarrels over privilege on the part of the lower house and prerogative on the part of the upper, nevertheless something was accomplished. Roads were made, ferries provided and ordinaries improved, a state house was built and county court houses were set up, prisons and jails were constructed here and there after 1674 to relieve the sheriffs from the burdensome necessity of caring for prisoners in their own homes, and a few bridges were thrown across creeks and swamps to meet the needs of travellers, sheriffs, and other persons who were hindered by the freshets and great rains from prosecuting their business. Other building projects were contemplated but were held up by the scarcity of provisions, want of workmen,

1. XVII, 45–47, 53, 69, 70, 80, 135, 265, 412, 459. There was Mary Mallory in 1686, who was charged with lying and uttering scandalous words against Vincent Lowe; Robert Cooper, 1687, one of Claiborne's former servants who was proved guilty of speaking slanderous words against the king; a group of "turbalent spiritts" who said in 1687 that some of Baltimore's office holders had commissions for their lives; and another group, 1686, who said "[the Duke of] York had been a bloody rogue, had poisoned his brother King Charles, and had contrived the plan of setting fire to London in 1666" (V, 507–512, 513, 532–533, 534–535, 546). Unfortunately the records of the provincial court, to which many of these were remanded for trial, have not been printed for this period, but the evidence, as far as available, demonstrates in some instances at least the worthlessness of the testimony.

and the dearth of materials for construction. Coroners were appointed, special commissioners of the peace were named to perfect justice in the counties, and in a few instances, as in the case of the mayor's court at St. Mary's, provision was made for the judicial needs of the merchants. We read much of the methods employed to extend the frontiers to the north and northeast, of the frequent naturalization of foreigners of other than British and Irish descent, of the encouraging the admission of negroes and the keeping out of convicts, and the unsuccessful attempts, many times repeated, to prevent servants from running away. Acts were passed to raise the standards of the legal profession, to check the abuses of those practicing in the courts as "attorneys, councillors and sollicitors at law," whereby causes were delayed, unnecessary suits started, and excessive fees demanded, and to shorten "the long and tedious proceedings" of the court of chancery, regarding which Charles Calvert had consulted with his father when in England in 1670. English law and practice were accepted as of force in the colony, under two conditions: the law of the colony must be silent on the subject, and due regard must be had for local conditions in court, assembly, and province. English law, practice, and custom were followed in matters of outlawry, wills, intestacy, writs of error, weights and measures, and the keeping of ordinaries, and were frequently appealed to in argument, particularly in the matter of representation and privilege in assembly. The exclusion of Coode was justified on the ground that no one in holy orders could sit in the House of Commons. In 1674 a committee was appointed to draw up a list of the laws of England, and at least one conviction was obtained under a statute of James I. Magna Carta was cited several times in debate and Coke at least once.[1]

The most important measure that came before the assembly was that which concerned the erection of towns and the advancement of

---

1. The following reference to English precedents may be given but they do not pretend to be complete even for the years before 1689. II, 106, 135, 379, 346, 347, 349, 350, 368, 374, 425; V, 558, 560; VII, 47, 114, 135, 224–225, 572; XIII, 39, 99, 357; XIX, 397, 437, 451, 479. XIII, 357, question of venue in Maryland, should be compared with XVII, 478–479, the same in Virginia. The delays and costs of lawsuits were frequently a cause of complaint, II, 350; VII, 317; XVII, 191. Two acts of the first assembly have been preserved in abstract: that of February 20, 1635, all offenders in murder and felonies should suffer such pains, losses, and forfeitures as they should or ought to have suffered "in the like crimes in England" (I, 23), and one other guaranteeing to "Holy Church" all her rights and liberties (XLI, 567).

trade. Acting on the recommendation of the select council for plantations in England and under the right granted him in his charter, Baltimore had instructed his son as far back as 1668 to create seaports in the province where goods could be laden and unladen and merchants do their business.[1] The underlying purpose was a dual one, to improve and expand the tobacco trade and to make it easier for the province to collect the proprietor's share of the export dues, the two shillings for every hogshead of tobacco shipped which had been allotted by act in 1671.[2] Though some success was met in the matter of regulating the size of tobacco casks and improving the quality of tobacco no progress was made in the selection of places of trade, until in 1682 the issue was taken up in earnest and for two years led to a deadlock between the two houses. The upper house demanded that the proprietor have the right to name the towns, the lower house wished the right to be exercised by the two houses. Furthermore the lower house refused to advance the measure until the upper house had agreed to the demand of the lower for a restoration of the four delegates, which the proprietor had reduced to two. There the matter stood until in 1683 the lower house finally gave in and passed the trade bill, which was followed by the proprietor's proclamation of February 27, 1684, urging that it be put immediately into execution.[3] The English authorities in their recommendation had set before Maryland and Virginia the example of Massachusetts Bay, where the people had "in a few years raised that colony to breed wealth, reputation and security," but neither of the plantation colonies was able to emulate its northern neighbor. Their "towns" were merely ports or markets of trade, where tobacco was shipped, goods and merchandise received, vessels entered and cleared, customs collected, wharves, ordinaries, and stores built, and men met to talk, drink, and plan. None of these ports was a town in the New England sense and before many years had passed most of them were in decay.[4] The trade of the colony was almost entirely

---

1. V, 31–32 (declaration, June 5, 1668), 35, 47–58 (ordinance, April 20, 1669), 92–99 (second declaration, June 30, 1671).

2. II, 264, 284, 381, 384; V, 113.

3. V, 495–498, 500–503, 527, 564; VII, 350, 352, 368, 378, 520, 609; XVII, 219–220.

4. VIII, 558; X, 495; XVII, 92; XXV, 234. There is mention of "the Jewes store" as early as 1653 (X, 495), of the store of "one John Pryor merchant of London" in 1682, to whom the Indians sold their skins (XVII, 92), of a "roome called the Store" in a private house (XVII, 292, 1684), and of the "store of Mr. Jacob More-

in tobacco shipped and manufactured goods received, for after 1700 there was very little traffic in furs and efforts to produce naval stores and to raise flax and hemp and other staple varieties were never successful. English vessels came to the Chesapeake and departed for home at set times under convoy, and Maryland vessels did a coastwise and West Indian business.[1] New England merchants picked up Maryland tobacco in exchange for food stuffs for purposes of export and in so doing were not always as scrupulous as they might have been in obeying the acts of trade. In 1680 the proprietor could say that the prosperity of the province depended wholly on trade and because there was not enough hard money in the hands of the people to prosecute it successfully, both planters and merchants were forced into debt and far too often into the law courts.[2]

The deliberate and cautious policy of the founder in throwing open the province to all settlers of the Christian faith and the incorporation of that policy in acts of 1635 and 1649 made Maryland beyond any other English colony of the time the home of many different religious groups: Roman Catholics, Anglicans, Congregationalists, Presbyterians, Quakers and Labadists. Roman Catholic and Protestant gentry and planters shared offices under government and mingled in social intercourse, and before the revolution of 1689 there was a large measure of religious amity and good understanding. The Roman Catholics though fewer in number than the Protestants[3] were influential politically and socially because of their rank

land in Calvert County" in 1693, but these need not necessarily have been at the ports of trade. For the decay of these "towns," see Berkley, "Extinct River Towns of the Chesapeake Bay Region," *Maryland Magazine*, XIX, 125–141.

1. For an illustration, XLIX, 61–71. For the shipping, Morriss, "Colonial Trade of Maryland, 1689–1715," *Johns Hopkins University Studies*, XXXII, 87, 114–115. Miss Morriss estimates the number of ships and sloops built in England or Maryland but owned in the province, at a yearly average of from 70 to 75. Governor Hart said in 1720 that "The Inhabitants are not much inclined to navigation but depend on British bottoms," *Maryland Magazine*, XXIX, 253.

2. Commission to the Justices, December 13, 1680, XV, 323–324.

3. In 1708 there were, according to one estimate, 33,833 people, whites and blacks, in the province, of which but 2974 were Roman Catholics (XVI, 362; XXV, 258). Culpeper of Virginia said in 1681 that he believed there were thirty Protestants to one Papist in Maryland (*Calendar State Papers, Colonial*, 1661–1685, §275). In Maryland negroes could be baptized. In 1697 Governor Nicholson said that there were more Quakers than Roman Catholics in the province (XXIII, 81). On the Quakers, *Maryland Magazine*, XXIX, 101–115). Quakers were not allowed to substitute affirmation for swearing until 1688 and then only for service as administrators and executors (VIII, 57–58). Hart reported from 1719 55,000 whites and 25,000 blacks, figures that do not comport well with those given above. The census figures

and nearness to the proprietor, but the proselyting activities of the
Jesuits and Roman Catholic priests gave rise to many complaints.
As early as 1658 the Rev. Francis Fitzherbert was haled before the
provincial court for endeavoring "to seduce and draw from their
religion" certain of the inhabitants of the upper parts of the Patuxent River, gathered "at a general meeting in armes" for the purpose
of mustering. Then it was that "Holy Church" was defined as any
church believing in the Trinity, and Fitzherbert, though charged
with interfering with another man's religious conduct, was acquitted
because under the law he had a right to preach and teach as much
as he liked, for preaching could not be construed as either rebellion
or mutiny.[1] After 1689, under the influence in Maryland of the
Jacobite movement in England, where in 1700 parliament passed an
act for the restraint of popery,[2] the proselyting by "popish priests"
became an issue and was agitated for several years. It was tied up in
Maryland with the rumors of the return of the government to the
proprietor, in the interests of whom both Roman Catholics and
Quakers were believed to be working, and it led to the introduction
of the oath of abjuration and to proclamations by the governor forbidding priests to attend the sick unless invited. The Anglican
Church was made the established church in the colony in 1702 and
from this time forward Roman Catholics suffered many disabilities,
the most serious of which was their disfranchisement in 1718.[3]

In May, 1684, Lord Baltimore returned to England, "in order to
answer any charges against me and defend my right against William
Penn." Expecting to be away but a few months he never returned
to his province. Many interests demanded his attention and the
English authorities had many questions to ask and demands to
make. Baltimore in his turn was confronted also with the imperative necessity of defending his charter against the threatened issue
of a quo warranto, first in 1681 and again in 1686, and for him the
first two or three years in England must have been a time of anxiety
and indeed of embarrassment if not mortification. The matters at
issue were these. First, the favor and partiality shown on all occa-

are not reliable. The method of taking the census does not give one confidence in
the results (XXIII, 104; XXIV, 12-13. "Constables and others appointed to take
such lists are ignorant and illiterate," XXV, 255-259).

1. XLI, 144-146, 566-567.   2. 11-12 William III, c. 4.

3. XIX, 426-430 (1696). This act was disallowed, but a later act, 1702 (XXIX,
265-273), was confirmed. The oath of abjuration is given, 418-419.

sions to the Papists to the discouragement of the Protestants in the province. Second, the insufficient attention paid to the Church of England and the low state of religion which made possible the success of the Roman Catholic propaganda. Third, the interference with the royal custom service in the colony, and the discouragement offered to the royal customs collectors in the execution of their duty. Fourth, the troublesome boundary disputes with Virginia, William Penn, and the Duke of York, covering the southern, eastern, and northern areas. And lastly, the murder of the royal collector, Christopher Rousby, at the hand of Baltimore's nephew, George Talbot, which took place October 31, 1684, after Baltimore had left the province.

The first of these charges and incidents Baltimore was able successfully to refute, (1) by furnishing lists of the principal officers in Maryland, which showed that for 1681 there were in the council four Roman Catholics and four Protestants, though he had to agree that his Roman Catholic relatives held the most important positions; (2) that in the militia there were but two Roman Catholic colonels of foot to six Protestants and of horse two Protestants to one Roman Catholic. Twenty-five Protestants in the colony testified to the same effect and added corroborative evidence.[1] In the face of such strong testimony the charge was not pressed. In regard to the Church of England in the colony Baltimore could easily show that he did nothing to hinder its development and that its low ebb was due to the neglect of the Bishop of London, to whose see all the colonies were attached.

The other issues were not so easily disposed of. The details of the customs situation are too involved for discussion here and cannot adequately be explained from the Maryland end. Suffice it to say that Baltimore, right as to the facts in the case but wrong as to the law, was penalized for his ignorance.[2] He was sharply reprimanded

1. *Calendar State Papers, Colonial,* 1681–1685, §§349, 350. Rousby furnished a list of the council, adding one more Roman Catholic. A "Declaration" signed by twenty-five leading Protestants and sent to England in 1682 avouched that this charge against Baltimore was false, adding to the statement made in the text the further fact that the major part of the commissioners or justices of the peace in each county were Protestant (V, 354).

2. The circumstances and the law will be discussed in the fourth volume of this work. In the meantime reference may be made to a brief statement of the case in the writer's chapter on "The Acts of Trade," *The Cambridge History of the British Empire,* I, 280–282, and to a fuller account in Beer, *Old Colonial System,* I, 95–100;

by the king, fined £2500, the estimated loss to the customs through his negligence, and told that he would lose his charter if he should repeat the offense. There can be little doubt but that Baltimore paid his fine when in England, though there is no record of his having done so. The situation was highly aggravated by the murder, "in the height of passion," of Christopher Rousby, the king's collector, in the autumn of 1684, by Baltimore's hot-headed nephew, George Talbot, in the cabin of the royal ketch, *Quaker,* lying about two miles above the mouth of the Patuxent River.[1] This event made a great stir among the authorities in England and no less a stir in Maryland, where Rousby was thoroughly disliked. Talbot's relationship with the proprietor and his conspicuous position as first councillor and therefore acting governor of the province only made matters worse. When Darnell and Sewall, two of the deputy governors, with Llewellyn and Robert Carvile went on board the ketch to demand Talbot, Captain Allen said that he did not recognize Baltimore's government, that if they had come in the king's name he would give Talbot up, not otherwise, and that the Patuxent River was the king's river not Baltimore's. Evidently Allen was angry at Baltimore's claim to the whole of the Potomac and would take orders only from the governor of Virginia and the royal collector (Rousby himself) in Maryland. He also took offense at Talbot's having set up a fort near Pennsylvania at the head of the Bay and another on Christina Creek, both against Penn, and said they would injure his lordship's case at home. Allen said that those who paid Baltimore the two shillings a hogshead were "fooles and puppyes." Both in its causes and its effects the Rousby murder had many ramifications. Presumably Rousby and Allen were in accord in regard to Baltimore's government and as Talbot dared not attack Allen, he took it out on Rousby. There may well have been many in the colony who felt as these two did. The Privy Council and Lord Baltimore both wanted Talbot sent to England for trial, but the captain of the ketch had already taken him in irons to Virginia, where a quarrel over jurisdiction was averted by his conviction before the council there acting as a court of oyer and terminer with a jury at

the evidence, printed in the *Calendar State Papers, Colonial,* and the *Maryland Archives,* is very extensive.

1. V, 428-430, 336-442; XVII, 299-310, 322-324, 328-338, 347-348, 475-483; *Calendar State Papers, Colonial,* 1681-1685, §1963, i-vi. A biography of Rousby is given in *Maryland Magazine,* XV, 292-296.

Jamestown and sentence to death, April 24, 1686. With the aid of his wife Talbot escaped from the sheriff of Gloucester County, to whom he had been committed, and returned to Maryland. Eventually, September 9, 1686, he was pardoned by the king, on condition of a five year banishment from his dominions.[1]

The Lords of Trade saw in all these Maryland troubles a menace to the authority and revenue of the crown, "it being of very great and growing prejudice to your Majesty's Affairs in the Plantations and to your Customs here that such independent Governments be kept up and maintained without a nearer and more immediate dependence on your Majesty."[2] They therefore recommended, despite all that Baltimore after his arrival in England had tried to do to the contrary, the prosecution of the writs of quo warranto, which had already been issued against the remaining private proprietary colonies.[3] The plan was to vacate Baltimore's charter with the others and to join Maryland to New York as a part of the newly erected Dominion of New England. Culpeper of Virginia had already proposed a grouping of the colonies for purposes of mutual defense and Edward Randolph had done the same in the interest of the revenues. The Lords of Trade acted on these suggestions and the Dominion of New England was brought into existence in 1686, but as events were to show it never extended beyond the Delaware River. Probably the impracticability of administering and maintaining such a widely scattered group of colonies had more influence in estopping the serving of the writ than had Baltimore's arguments, for in the eyes of the Lords of Trade Maryland had a bad record.

The boundary situation in Maryland was not unlike similar boundary situations among other of the continental colonies, arising from doubtful and conflicting claims based on royal concessions and grants. With Virginia two difficulties were encountered early: first the location of the southern line of the eastern shore, which in 1668 and 1671 was run east from the extremity of Watkins Point, the southernmost point of Somerset County, at the mouth of the Poco-

---

1. V, 453; XVII, 355–357, 369–375, 377–378, 410–412, 425–426, 451–452, 475, 481–483; *Acts Privy Council, Colonial*, II, §173.

2. V, 445; *Calendar State Papers, Colonial*, 1685–1688, §283.

3. V, 456–457; *New York Colonial Documents*, III, 363; *Acts Privy Council, Colonial*, II, §§193, 194, 195, 209; Barnes, *Dominion of New England*, p. 29 and footnotes. These quo warrantos were directed against rights of government not against titles to the soil. The dispute between Baltimore and Penn on the other hand concerned titles to land as well as claims to authority and jurisdiction.

moke River, to Swansecut Creek on the seaside; and secondly Baltimore's claim to the whole of the Potomac River as far as high-water
mark on the Virginia side, and his insistence that merchant ships
going up that river enter at a Maryland port, thus, as Virginia said,
abridging the king's jurisdiction, rights, and revenues in that dominion. This claim was based on the words of the charter "unto the
farther banke of the for-said River [of Pattowmeck]." Though the
matter was brought to the attention of the Lords of Trade and referred to the attorney general for report, it seems to have been lost
somehow in the greater issue between Penn and Baltimore over the
northern and eastern boundaries, for no decision by the English
authorities is apparently anywhere to be found.[1]

The conflict between Baltimore and Penn over their boundaries
was the outstanding event that forced the two proprietors to take
the long voyage to England in 1684 in order to defend their respective claims before the Privy Council and the Lords of Trade. Charles
II had notified Baltimore of the grant to Penn in 1681[2] and had
urged upon him the necessity of coming to an understanding with
his northern neighbor as to where the boundary line should be
drawn. Efforts had been made to do this, and prolonged interviews
had taken place in that year between Lord Baltimore and Penn's
deputy governor, William Markham; in 1682 and 1683 between
Baltimore and Penn; and in 1684 between George Talbot and Penn,
no one of which interviews had any other result than to stir up
unpleasant feelings on both sides. Penn had made the tactical mis-

---

1. V, 44, 45 (see Herrman's map, reproduced in Matthews, *Report on the Resurvey*, between pp. 150–151, and on a larger scale in *Calvert Papers*, II, opposite
p. 136). The exact line was not determined until 1877 and the agreement then
reached was ratified in 1878 (Original Narratives, *Maryland*, p. 102, note 2). For the
Potomac issue, with which Baltimore had to cope after his arrival in England, V,
419–420; *Calendar State Papers, Colonial*, 1681–1685, §1750. In February, 1684,
Captain Thomas Smith of the ship *Constant*, who had been trading with Virginia
for years, regularly entering his ship at some Virginia port, was taken into custody
and confined by Maryland officers until he gave bond to enter his ship in the right
of Lord Baltimore and to pay the port-dues to him (*Calendar State Papers, Colonial*,
1681–1685, §§1749, 1750, 1768). Virginia at once entered a protest which was read
by the Lords of Trade, and Baltimore wrote a letter in reply (V, 420) but, as far as
I know, this letter is not extant. It is possible that the first Lord Baltimore, in defining the southern boundary as the further shore of the Potomac, was but following
an accepted tenurial rule in England. Hale, in *De Jure Maris* (p. 35), says that the
barons of Berkeley claimed the whole of the river Severn as time out of mind "par-
cell of that manor" of Berkeley and in so claiming were upheld by the courts.

2. *Calendar State Papers, Colonial*, 1681–1685, §§62, 659.

take of demanding from certain leading inhabitants of the northern counties of Maryland the payment to him of their taxes, for the reason, advanced before the boundaries had been ascertained, that they were residents of his province and therefore within his jurisdiction. This ill-advised demand upon men who were Baltimore's tenants and had taken the oath of fidelity to him so angered the Maryland proprietor that when Penn, disclosing at the very outset the one thing nearest to his heart, offered to buy enough land to ensure him a commercial outlet on the Chesapeake, Baltimore, standing rigidly on a liberal interpretation of his charter, refused to part with an inch of his territory. Things were made more tense by the building of two forts on Penn's border, both under the authority of George Talbot, one at Christina bridge and the other at the mouth of the Susquehanna. By 1683 the differences had become so irreconcilable and the recriminations so pronounced that there was nothing else to do than to lay the whole matter before the authorities in England and ask them for a decision. The Privy Council, which had already received voluminous reports on the case, notified the proprietors that before coming to any conclusion it would await their arrival and the results of a hearing, at which each party could present personally his arguments in the case.[1]

Though the main subject of dispute was the location of the fortieth parallel and the reconciliation of charter statements that could not be reconciled, scarcely less troublesome was the question as to the extent of Baltimore's territory to the eastward, covering what is now the state of Delaware, or as known in colonial times "The Three Lower Counties" or "The Territories." As early as 1670 Baltimore had begun to make grants in the region called the Whorekill —from Bombay Hook to Cape Henlopen—and it has been estimated that he caused to be laid out there, or in its neighborhood, in the years from 1670 to 1682, some forty-seven allotments to forty-five

1. The subject of the Baltimore-Penn controversy over the boundary line has been treated so fairly and fully by Professor Matthews in Part III of *Report on the Resurvey of the Maryland-Pennsylvania Boundary part of the Mason and Dixon Line* (1908), pp. 105–209, with a somewhat overelaborated and uncritical appendix of "Source Material," as to render unnecessary any references here to documentary evidence. The citation of English material in this appendix, however, should have been to the *Calendar State Papers, Colonial*, as well as to the originals in the Public Record Office, where the Colonial Office Papers have been so thoroughly rearranged and reclassified as to render these references to the original documents of very little value.

persons, constituting about 19,000 acres in all, the whole to be erected in time into the county of Durham.[1] But the region to the northward had been occupied after 1638 by Swedes and after 1655 by the Dutch, who made many grants along the west bank of the Delaware,[2] and after the fall of New Amsterdam in 1664, the New York governors, Nicolls, Lovelace, and Andros, issued patents for lands there as well, claiming the territory for the Duke of York as part of the Dutch conquest. In 1682 the duke had deeded the land of the Three Lower Counties to William Penn and in consequence the hearing before the Privy Council was widened to include the eastern boundaries of Baltimore's grant as well as the northern.

These were the various matters that had to be thrashed out in England before Baltimore could return to his province. The first two went by default. The matter of the quo warranto became unimportant after 1687. Of the boundary questions the one which concerned Virginia was never very troublesome, and the one which had to do with the Delaware region was ended for the time being when the Lords of Trade sent in its report to the Privy Council, November 7, 1685, which the council approved on the 13th. This report recommended that the territory lying between the Delaware and the Chesapeake, above the latitude of Fenwick's Island (Old Cape Henlopen) should be divided into two equal parts, the one adjudged to belong to his Majesty, the other to Lord Baltimore. Thus the Durham County of Maryland became the Sussex County of Delaware.[3] But the most formidable of all the problems, that which re-

1. For Baltimore's grants on the Delaware, *Maryland Magazine*, XXV, 157–167; for a review of the situation in 1704, *Maryland Archives*, XXIV, 373–376, 377; and for the rioting along the border in 1721, XXV, 370–417, 488. No attempt is made here to cite references to individual grants, of which there are many in the *Archives*, or to analyze the conditions of plantation (XVII, 222–224, 232, 233–235, 267–268, 275). Nor are we here concerned with the eventual outcome in either case. Supplementing Professor Matthews's admirable treatment in the report of the Maryland Geological Survey, is a paper, *Maryland Magazine*, XXIX, 83–101, "The fight between the Penns and the Calverts," which is useful but very poorly written. For the letter to Frisbie regarding the payment of taxes to Maryland, *Pennsylvania Archives*, I, 39–40. Further evidence may be found in *New York Colonial Documents*, II, 64, 67, 73–76, 80–100, 116–121, 124–125; III, 186, 247, 339–340, 342–346, and a brief but useful summary, by Walter Lefferts, in *Bulletin*, Geographical Society of Philadelphia, October, 1920.

2. *New York Colonial Documents*, XII, 177–183.

3. C. O. 5:723, pp. 107–109; *Maryland Archives*, XXV, 399; *Calendar State Papers, Colonial*, 1685–1688, §§456 (November 13, 1685), 685. There is no doubt that the lords were influenced in their decision by the claim of James II, when Duke of

lated to the line between Maryland and Pennsylvania, was only beginning its long career. It was hardly more than stated in 1689, when Baltimore's return was blocked by the uprising in his province; it was not surveyed as the Mason and Dixon line until the years from 1763 to 1768; and some of the disputed points were not finally settled until very recent times.[1]

The absence of the proprietor left the province somewhat at loose ends, a condition intensified by the conduct of the head councillor and acting governor George Talbot, whose murder of Rousby caused him to become a fugitive from justice. This was a body blow for the proprietor, coming as it did at the very time when he was facing the charges against him before the Lords of Trade and was trying by the best means at his command to mollify the commissioners of the customs for the way the customs situation had been mismanaged in Maryland. The third Lord Baltimore may not have possessed the prudence of his father or the broadminded and conscientious integrity of his grandfather, but he was a good administrator who was genuinely interested in the welfare of his people and the maintenance of peace in his dominion. But he was uncompromising in his adherence to his prerogative rights as defined in the charter and would admit of no modification of the powers which that charter conferred. His period of rule, first as governor and then as proprietor, coincided almost exactly with the reigns of Charles II and James II in England and no such series of events marred its continuance as had shaken his father's proprietary control during the years of the Puritan revolution in England. Despite Indian wars and insurgent uprisings the province had not been badly governed, though its material and spiritual development had been hampered by poverty, by the physical characteristics of the province—divided

York, to the Delaware half of the territory. They dared not decide against the king, though they stated that they found the land in dispute was settled by Christians before Lord Baltimore's patent was issued. They recommend that the tract be divided into two equal parts. This recommendation was approved by the Privy Council, November 18, 1685, and reaffirmed June 22, 1709.

1. The last part of the line to be determined was that which separated Pennsylvania and Delaware, where the tangent met the curvature of the arc, as determined in 1701, twelve miles northwest of New Castle. This tiny "flat iron" area or "horn shaped strip," as it was called, was finally transferred from Delaware to Pennsylvania in the year 1921. The center of the circle or twelve mile radius, selected in 1892, when a shortened circle was established, was the spire of the New Castle court house. Powell, *History of Delaware* (1928), pp. 356–358, where a plan is given showing "The Delaware Curve."

as it was by a wide bay and broken by many creeks and rivers—by the thin and scattered population, and by an inadequate and heterogeneous grouping of religious bodies and an almost complete absence of educational and intellectual facilities.[1] Its economic prosperity was more or less at the mercy of a fluctuating tobacco market and an unreliable currency and its people were dependent very largely on outside merchants and traders, chiefly from England and New England, for the disposal of their products. Financial transactions of every kind were rendered slow and difficult by the use of tobacco as a medium of exchange. The control of government by a very small office-holding class and the accumulation of offices and estates in the hands of the proprietor, members of his family, and others of the wealthy planters made for landed and class distinctions and brought it about that there was present in the colony a disproportionate number of small freeholders, landless freemen, artisans, and servants, many of whom were disfranchised and had no part in government. From among the members of this class agitators such as Fendall and Coode gathered the largest number of their recruits.

Baltimore's absence and Talbot's disgrace left the province without a head. The councillors in charge, well meaning but inferior men, lacked the ability of the proprietor or the prestige that had accompanied his name in the conduct of the affairs of the province. As government by the many is never as efficient as government by a single person, possessed of the authority which the charter conferred, the deputies were never as prompt to act or as steadfast in execution as would have been one man in an emergency. While on the surface discontent was not as conspicuous as in the days of Fendall, it is evident that there was continued dissatisfaction in many directions. Complaints against some of the sheriffs had been heard for a number of years and as these officials were the appointees of the proprietor and came into close and personal contact with the people of their shrievalties (often called "sheriffwicks" in the records), their

---

1. There is mention of a bequest made in 1660 by one John Price of St. Mary's county, to his daughter Ann, who was to receive at the age of eighteen half of his estate and stock, which at her death was "to be Imployed in the Setting fforward a ffree school." The other half, left to a son-in-law, Joseph Bullit, was at the latter's death to be "wholly and Solely disposed and employed about the ffree schole aforesaid." Ann married at the age of sixteen and petitioned that maintenance be allowed her. The chancery court handed over to her her entire share. Nothing further seems to have been done about a "ffree school." LI, 450–455.

conduct in a few specific instances had disastrous effects. They were charged with behaving "proudly and malitiously," "imperiously and insolently," "seeking the utter ruine of the poor man," exhibiting "huff and hector" and abusing their trust. The local justices came in for their share of the obloquy. An attorney practicing in one of the county courts called the justices "fooles and ignorant fooles" and another behaved contemptuously before them, sitting with his hat on and swearing volubly.[1] Robert Carvile, member of the assembly and attorney in the provincial court, on an occasion called the secretaries of the province "fooles," and charged the proprietor with "wyerdrawing" the assembly, that is, making fair promises that he could not perform, and putting no one in office but knaves and fools. Carvile was an important man in the province and though he afterward expressed contrition for his abuse of the proprietor, he must have meant what he said when he declared that "he was as good a Mann as my Lord, what are the Calverts? My family is as antient as the Calverts."[2] There was a good deal of feeling in many quarters against the proprietary government, both within and without the

<hr/>

1. XVII, 42, 43, 57–58, 60, 62–64, 93, 279–281, 283. In the act of 1678 "For the Election of Sheriffe," the statements are made that: "there have lately been great Complaints Generally made from all parts of this Province of the great absurdities and abuses Committed by severall Sheriffs"; and "itt hath Evidently appeared by the Continuall and frequent Clammours of Poore Indigent people that the long Continuance of the severall Sherriffes in their Respective offices hath prompted and imboldned them to abuse Terrify and trample upon the poore Inhabitants." The act speaks also of "their Insolent and haughty behaviour" and to check the evil limited the tenure of office to one year (VII, 68–69; V, 3–4). The "Huy and Crye" of 1676 complains of the sheriffs, "which my Lord puts in and out, whence whom and how long him pleased," 138. At least one sheriff was impeached and many others were brought to book.

2. XVII, 181–184. Robert Carvile was for five years clerk of the lower house, 1669–1674. He was also deputy for the city of St. Mary's and recorder until 1684 and as such administered the oath of office to the mayor. He was in frequent service on lower house business, messenger to the upper house (with Kenelm Cheseldyne, attorney general, 1678), attorney in the provincial court, chairman of the house committee of trade, 1682, member of committees, joint committees, and conferences, and commissioner from St. Mary's for executing the act for advancement of trade, and it was in this connection that he made his remarks (1683). In 1684 he had raised the question whether, in his lordship's absence, appeal should be allowed from the provincial court to the council, as the two were composed of the same men (XIII, 45). He was a witness, after the murder, in the Rousby case, when he gave his age as forty-eight (1684; he was born therefore in 1636). After the revolution he continued to live in St. Mary's as a practicing attorney and was often called upon (with others) for his opinion on difficult legal questions. In 1694 he went on Dinah Nuthead's bond regarding her printing only official documents. He was a freeman of the city of St. Mary's. He probably died soon after 1694.

colony, and many may well have sensed the anachronism of a charter, issued fifty years before, continuing to exist in full force, after the English world had passed through the upheaval of the years from 1642 to 1660, or the absurdity of any one possessing and exercising powers that in many ways were greater, within the smaller field, than those exercised by the king in his dominions. By 1684 many new colonies had come into being and it was inevitable that the men of Maryland should make comparisons to the disadvantage of their own status as subjects of the common king. It could hardly have been otherwise.

Then there is another aspect of the case. Since the issue of the charter of 1632, England's commercial and colonial policy had been gradually undergoing an exact definition and efforts had been in the making for nearly forty years to put the acts of trade into execution. Hence the troubles that arose between Baltimore and the officers of the customs. One cannot but feel that Baltimore in standing on his prerogative either misunderstood or took far too lightly the growing importance to English officials and merchants of the foreign and plantation trade. He had been warned in 1682 in the Badcock and Rousby cases that he must walk warily or he would lose his charter and in 1685 was actually threatened with the serving of a writ of quo warranto.[1] The immediate cause of this threat of the Privy Council was the information received of the obstructions which the royal collector, Nehemiah Blakiston, had met with from the deputy governors in his efforts to execute the orders of his superiors in England. Blakiston said that Darnell and Diggs had disowned his commission, torn and burnt his orders, and allowed many evasions of the acts, without his knowledge or privity, to the great loss of revenue to his Majesty. Whatever may be the truth of Blakiston's charges—and they constitute a long indictment of the government of Baltimore's deputies—it is clear that they were believed in England, where the king's revenue was a subject of lively concern, just as other complaints later, of Basse, Quary, Larkin, and Randolph, were accepted at their face value. Baltimore, writing three thousand miles away from his province and depending on infrequent letters and the reports of sea-captains and merchants, tried to refute the charges, but that his statements were not convincing to the Lords of Trade appears from the fact that when on August 10,

[1]. *Acts Privy Council, Colonial,* II, §§64, 193.

1685, the king issued instructions to his collectors in America, which were drafted in course by the commissioners of customs, he inserted a special clause intended for Maryland only. By this clause Baltimore was informed that he must stop allowing his own locally appointed collectors to receive the duties imposed by parliamentary statute, must render a strict accounting of all moneys received and seizures made by any of them in the past, and must aid and assist the royal collectors, named by the commissioners of customs under authorization from the Treasury, in the performance of their duties.[1] This instruction was a serious blow to Baltimore's prestige and to the prestige of his deputy governors in the province, for by just so much it cut into Baltimore's complete control of his own administration.

Until the autumn of 1688, the council, including among its ten or eleven members the eight deputy governors appointed by Baltimore when he found he could not return in 1685—all of whom were also justices of the provincial court—was in charge of the government, acting in Baltimore's name and on behalf of Benedict Leonard Calvert, a lad of nine years old, the titular governor.[2] The entire board was rarely present at any one time and its numbers were sometimes reduced to four or five. Just how well the two houses got on together, after the departure of the proprietor in May, 1684, we do not know, as the record of proceedings of meetings that were held in 1685, 1686, and 1687 (if such were held other than in 1686, of which the laws remain) are lost, but we do know that some important laws were passed, particularly those for the advancement of trade and the

---

1. V, 436–444, 451 (9), 484; XVII, 449–457, 461.
2. The deputy governors were Tailler, Lowe, N. Sewall, H. Darnell, Diggs, Stevens, Burges, and Clement Hill, any three or more of whom, always including either Darnell, Diggs, or Sewall, being competent to act (XVII, 426–429). Clement Hill, called to the council for the first time, had been deputy to the lower house from St. Mary's City, was justice of the quorum for St. Mary's county, and had just been commissioned deputy surveyor general. He had been appointed by the proprietor on important missions in the past connected with the Pennsylvania boundary dispute and the demand for the return of Talbot by Virginia. Thomas Trueman was likewise honored as councillor, but he appears to have had very little to do with affairs (430). On the provincial court were Coursey, chief justice, Tailler, Lowe, Darnell, Diggs, Stevens, Burges, Sewall, Pye, Trueman, and Hill justices (431–432). Thus of the eleven justices, Coursey was the only one at this time not of the council, and though not a Jacobite was also not a revolutionist. Diggs and Sewall were the secretaries, Darnell and Hill, judges of probate, Diggs and Sewall, keepers of the great seal, Lowe, surveyor general. Thus the members of the council after 1685, led by Sewall, Diggs, and Darnell, to an extent even greater than before, held the chief offices and ruled the province.

increase of hard money in the province. The fact that Baltimore, as his last word of advice to the lower house before his departure, had felt obliged to insist that at the next meeting of the assembly all the members should take the oath of fidelity; to rebuke those who had presumed "to come before his lordship in the upper house with their hatts on"; and to express the hope that the whole house would show "more modesty and better manners thereafter," may mean much or nothing.[1]

When in 1688 Baltimore realized that he would not be able to leave England, he sent over as president of the council, and therefore chief deputy governor, one William Joseph, of whom we know nothing beyond the deductions to be drawn from his own words and conduct. Where Baltimore got him and why he appointed him are alike matters of conjecture, but that he was distinctly the wrong person to send to Maryland at this time does not admit of doubt.[2] Among the laymen of that day he belonged to the group which advocated strenuously and conscientiously high prerogative. He was in entire sympathy with the divine-right school, represented pre-eminently by the high churchmen, who condemned the doctrine that civil authority was derived from the people and that government was based either on a social compact, such as was advocated by Hobbes, or on a contractual relationship between rulers and ruled, such as was already accepted by the Whigs and was soon to be presented by Locke in two famous essays. He believed in the ecumenical and sacrosanct principles of government that were expounded in the extreme royalist programme put forth by Filmer in his *Patriarcha* (1680), and he was temperamentally ready to enforce his ideas about kingship in the office to which he was now called.[3]

The proprietor's selection of Joseph as his representative in the province throws a flood of light upon the working of his own mind and upon the attitude up to this time of all the Maryland proprietors toward their charter rights. That Baltimore should have dared to send over such a man, in view of the unrest already prevailing in the colony, can only be explained by a study of the circumstances

---

1. XIII, 49–50, 81. 2. See Baltimore's letter, VIII, 42–43.

3. Joseph followed the current views, held by the prerogative lawyers and high churchmen, regarding the divinity of kings, expressed as follows: "The King hath his Right from God, and as supreme is accountable to none, his person is sacred, and by our Laws he can do no wrong." Debate in the House of Commons on the Disabling of the Duke of York, 1680. *Debates in the House of Commons, 1680, p. 97.*

surrounding him in England during the years of his residence there. He followed his king in construing as sedition and mutiny any opposition to divinely appointed authority and could not understand the manifestations of discontent in Maryland any better than could Charles II and his ministers understand similar manifestations on a larger scale that were evident in England toward the end of the Stuart period. England after 1680 became the scene of a popular agitation and revolt greater than at any time in its history, unless we except (as we probably should not) the period of the Puritan Revolution. Baltimore may have taken his cue from the coercive methods of the English government of his time and have made up his mind to suppress, as the royal authority was endeavoring to do, the disorders and disquietudes disclosing the determination of the mass of the people to preserve what they considered their liberties, that is, to check and control what the conservative elements were calling "the malice and insolence of the restless spirits." Baltimore and his forbears were conservatives in that they were opposed by tradition and conviction to experiments in political and social life and could find no other course to follow than a strict and uncompromising adherence to the letter of the written text which defined the powers the king had granted to them.

On November 14, 1688, Joseph met his first assembly. He began his address with the following general statement, which defined succinctly and consistently his patriarchal doctrine. "There is no power but of God," he said, "and the Power by which we are Assembled here is undoubtedly Derived from God, to the King, and from the King to his Excellency the Lord Proprietary and from his said Lordship to Us." With this as his text he divided his discourse, sermonlike, into four parts and elaborated each, with expositions of duty along lines of moral conduct specially referring to the sins of drunkenness, adultery, swearing, and breaking the Sabbath. Declaring that kings were the Lord's annointed and their commands binding upon their subjects, he referred to certain royal orders that were to be obeyed, threatening the members of the assembly with the wrath of the king should they prove disobedient to his will. He bade them pass an act of general thanksgiving to God for the recent birth of a prince and to keep holy the day of birth during the prince's lifetime. He ordered them to pay without complaint whatever was or ought to be the proprietor's dues, to suppress all public sin and scandal, and to consider only such measures as would secure the good of the people in general, sinking all private and self-interest in their concern for the proprietor and inhabitants of the province. He demanded that every one present take the oath of fidelity, and closed his address with a warning to the deputies that they were not to begin breaking the old laws before turning their attention to the making of new ones. Later in the session he found occasion to supplement what he had said with additional remarks of a similar character.[1]

What the deputies thought of the message as a whole is not recorded, but from statements made by the upper house in their report to the lord proprietor it is clear that the address, however much it may have irritated and displeased them for its rather harmless sanctification of the proprietary head, contained one order that they did not like and would not obey. They would not take again the oath of fidelity. They declared that they had already done so and, while more than willing to affirm their loyalty to the proprietor, taxed the president and the upper house with trespassing on their rights and privileges.[2] Joseph called their behavior rebellious, said that no business would be done until they submitted, and ended his chiding with the pious wish, "So God in his mercy direct you." Thoroughly resentful of this charge of rebellion, the deputies took up the challenge, drafted a series of resolutions, and refused in their turn to do business until the upper house recognized their privileges and atoned for its own unparliamentary conduct. The debates became "hot and high" and the air was filled with "heates" and recriminations, until the upper house could report that "the more they refused the more reason we had to mistrust 'em." The situation was similar to that of 1681 but much more serious. "All mild perswasions failing," Joseph sent for them to attend the upper house. Twice they refused to go, on the ground that his lordship was not there in person, but the third time they went and were duly informed that his lordship's rights and laws must be maintained, for as the upper house afterward said, "wee were not Ignorant of the fatall Consequences hereof if denial of fidelity were thus permitted Rebellion might be the next step." To give the lower house time to meditate and cool off Joseph

1. XIII, 147–153, 159, 162–163, 163–164, 189. Cf. VIII, 65.
2. XIII, 153–164.

prorogued the assembly for two days. In the end the deputies gave in and all took the oath, but the dispute had left its mark.

For a time the two houses worked amicably together, but soon arose new causes of disagreement. The lower house, more sensitive than ever regarding its privileges, accused the upper house of inter-fering to prevent the attendance of one of its own members and with assuming to itself certain rights as to the appointment of clerks of committees, a privilege that the lower house had always claimed for itself. The upper house in reply talked about "groundless heates" and the "Lord Proprietaries Prerogative" and called the attention of the lower house to certain unparliamentary forms of procedure of which it had been guilty. The latter drafted an elaborate body of "grievances," eight in number, "burthens that we now feele and Lye under," relating to various matters of proprietary management,[1] and made the further inquiry as to how soon, now that the proprie-tor was far away in England, laws would be confirmed or disal-lowed. Some of these matters were debated in conference, others postponed for a hearing with the president, while the question of assent or dissent was put up to the proprietor himself. The assembly was prorogued on December 8, 1688, to meet the April following. Then on the ground that "noe occassion relateing to the state or welfare of this province at present offers that requires the sitting" in April the assembly was further prorogued until the last Tuesday in October. But before that day arrived the control of the province had passed out of his lordship's hands. The "heates" of 1688 gave no warning to those in authority of the rebellion of 1689.

Important events were taking place in England. The accession of James II, February 5, 1685, his marriage to the duchess, Mary of Modena, and the birth of an heir to the throne, June 10, 1688, seemed to forbode the fastening of a Roman Catholic régime upon England. The victories of Louis XIV in Holland and the growing strength of absolute kingship in France portended a possible alliance of Louis XIV and James II against the Protestant states of England and the Netherlands. Should such an alliance become effective then its field of operation might well be extended overseas where the activities of the Jesuit missionaries in conjunction with the French of the Dominion of Canada and in combination with the Indians were

1. *Ibid.*, 171–172, 196, 203.

arousing in New England, New York, and Maryland fears of aggression toward the Protestant settlements and settlers there. Rumors
to that effect which had been widely current in Maryland at the
time of the Fendall uprising, due to the reports of the Popish Plot
and other plots of 1679–1681, brought over by sea-captains and merchants, and narrated in letters from the other side, were even more
loosely bruited in 1688 and 1689. The fact that a majority of the
deputy governors were Roman Catholics and the further fact that
all the members of the council, Roman Catholic and Protestant,
were in sympathy with the cause of James II and the proprietor led
to the formation of what may be called a Jacobite group in the colony, which viewed with alarm and with almost fanatical disapproval
the course of events in England. These men execrated the advent
of William of Orange, vehemently denied his right to the throne of
England, and even after his elevation to the throne continued to
pray for the happy restoration of the deposed sovereign. The apparent failure of Lord Baltimore to send over orders for the proclamation of the new king and queen or of the council to publish them if
sent and received, added to the popular unrest and seemed to confirm the current belief that Maryland was to be given over to Roman
Catholicism.[1]

1. VIII, 109, 112–114. Baltimore apparently sent the order on or about February
26, 1689, but according to his own statement the messenger died at Plymouth (67–
68, 114). He sent a duplicate, dated February 27. Spencer of Virginia, writing in
June, said that the people believed the order to have come, and Coode, writing in
August, charged the deputy governors with "stiffling and concealing" it (109, 112).
As late as August 30, 1689, and again on January 7, 1690, the Lords of Trade were
informed that no proclamation had ever been made in the colony until after the
revolution had been brought about there. The dates are perplexing. William and
Mary became king and queen of England on February 13, 1689; the Lords of Trade
sent Baltimore the form to be used in proclaiming the sovereigns on February 26.
If Baltimore sent off his messenger at once, how could he have learned that the order
had miscarried in time to despatch a duplicate the next day? There is nothing to
show that the duplicate was actually sent, or if sent was ever received, or if received
was ever acted on. As the order required the taking of the oath of abjuration (69),
we can well believe that the Roman Catholic deputy governors would balk at it and
probably refuse to obey. Here is a situation that has never been adequately explained,
for it has been assumed, perhaps too readily, that the proprietor's order for the proclamation never reached the colony at all. This is far from certain. The inhabitants of
Maryland believed that the order had been received and suppressed. On the other
hand, as late as November 1, 1689, Deputy Governor Blackwell of Pennsylvania could
say that he had received no orders to proclaim the new sovereigns, and he did not
know what to do about it (*Pennsylvania Colonial Records,* I, 303–305). What he did
do, with the advice of the provincial council, was to proclaim William and Mary
without orders. The Privy Council's order of February 19, 1689, was sent by Penn

Despite the repeated statement of members of the council, first made toward the end of March, 1689, that the rumors were false—the work of designing men to affright the people and then to plunder them—and that everything was once more quiet and peaceful, the popular discontent was not allayed. The fear of Indian attacks was hardly lessened and the distrust of such of the governors as Darnell, Sewall, and Pye was as great as ever. Though Diggs being a Protestant was looked upon as "the onely person left wee can trust" and though the hope was expressed that if he would espouse the Protestant cause the whole country would faithfully stand by him,[1] he remained firm in his loyalty to the proprietor. Judicial business was laxly conducted, the provincial court was hardly meeting at all, and the county court of Somerset, for example, was in abeyance for nearly five months. When April came and the freeholders learned that the meeting of the assembly was put off till October, they and the people generally were still further alarmed as they saw themselves unprotected by their representatives, with a small Jacobite group in full and unrestrained control.

Emotions that had been so powerful as to create "all over the Country . . . a greate uproar and tumult . . . as will not be easily pacified" (for so Colonel Jowles wrote to Colonel Diggs in March of that year) could not be quieted at will. The Indians had been a menace for more than a quarter of a century and reports of plots based often on uncorroborated evidence gathered strength as they spread and the men who believed them were not always the ignorant and illiterate. Two general statements have been made that are of doubtful validity or at least are open to considerable qualification: first, that if Baltimore had been personally present in the colony, he could easily have surmounted the difficulties of the crisis; and, secondly, that the revolution which followed was the work of a small cabal of ambitious men working on the incredulities of a frightened people. The problem is not as simple as all that. There were many shades of opinion in the colony, and these opinions, ranging from conservative to radical, were not those of unthinking men. Some of the conservatives, generally Roman Catholics, had strong Jacobite leanings; others, among whom were Protestants as well as Roman

Oct. 30 but not received in the province till July 15, 1690. It was not published (*ibid.*, 340–341).

1. VIII, 71. Cf. 85.

Catholics, favored the proprietor though not necessarily the Stuarts. A few were Monmouth men. On the other hand, there were large numbers of Protestant supporters of the revolution in England, who wanted a Protestant on the throne as well as a Protestant leadership in Maryland. They were opponents of the proprietor, partly because he was a Roman Catholic, partly because they thought him in alliance with the French, and partly because they believed that his charter rights were opposed to the liberties of Englishmen. Among them were two groups, characteristic of all the insurrections of the period, made up, first of those who, thoroughly disliking the use of force and hating Coode and his associates, wished for the sake of the advantages to be reaped that the colony be taken into the king's hand in order to profit both politically and commercially from the closer association with the mother country;[1] and secondly of those who were connected with the customs service and saw only harm to the king's revenue as long as the proprietor retained his governmental powers.[2] One may not call such men as Jowles, Cheseldyne, and Blakiston mere demagogues fishing in troubled waters for the sake of personal ambitions. They were representative of the same sentiment as that which directed the policy of the Lords of Trade in the latter's determination to reduce the private colonies to a closer dependence on the crown, and it is worthy of note that it was in 1690 that the Privy Council made a final but unsuccessful effort to vacate Baltimore's charter by writ of scire facias, the same writ that had been used against the Massachusetts Bay charter six years before.[3]

We know little or nothing of what happened in Maryland between April and July, 1689, for there are almost no records in existence. In England William III, "the champion of Protestantism and

1. VIII, 128–147.

2. No attempt is made here to analyze the reasons given by the insurrectionists to justify their conduct. These reasons are such a hopeless mixture of truth and untruth as to render them as a whole unworthy of credence. They do, however, disclose the motives governing the uprising, and so have historical value (Original Narratives Series, *Narratives of the Insurrections*, "Declaration of Protestant Subjects," pp. 305–314; *Maryland Archives*, VIII, 101–107, 215–220, a series of fifty-two charges, more deserving of consideration than is the "Declaration" of 1689).

3. VIII, 200. As early as April 20, 1689, the Lords of Trade recommended the policy that the Board of Trade adopted after 1696, that the proprieties be brought into a nearer dependence on the crown (100–101). One of the frequent mistakes of writers on the period is to call this a Stuart policy, and to tie it up with the attack by James II on the borough charters of England. In 1689 William III was on the throne and the policy thus adopted represented a necessary part of England's colonial and commercial programme. It was not Stuart even in origin.

the liberties of Europe against French ascendancy" was on the throne and in May had joined the League of Augsburg and declared war upon France. The news came to Maryland and must have greatly increased the excitement there. As the deputy governors made no effort to proclaim the new sovereign or to call an assembly which they probably did not dare do, news came that they were fortifying the state house at St. Mary's and the Sewall residence at Mattapany and raising men to keep the same.[1] John Coode had been busy since the beginning of July gathering recruits in Charles County[2] and he was now joined by Jowles, Cheseldyne, Blakiston, and others. With two hundred and fifty men, poorly armed, they advanced on St. Mary's where Diggs was obliged to surrender because his men would not fight, and then upon Mattapany, whence Joseph (who, sick at the time, had become a mere puppet in the hands of the others), Sewall, Darnell, and two priests surrendered the fort and fled to Virginia. The terms of surrender[3] were signed on August 1, 1689, by Joseph, Darnell, Sewall, Pye, and Hill, and the revolution was over. Certain outlying counties, Ann Arundel and Somerset, had to be brought into line, but to all intents and purposes Maryland was in the hands of the insurgents, calling themselves the Protestant Association. An assembly was called, August 22, to which all but ten of the forty-two members came (and some of these came later), which set up a committee with Blakiston as president for the government of the province and adopted an address to the king, asking that Maryland be made a royal province. The Lords of Trade had been considering the disposition of Baltimore's province since April, 1689, and had come to the decision that it would have to be united to the crown. Baltimore made an effort to hold on the government of his province and drafted a commis-

1. There are several accounts of the revolution, none of them very satisfactory (VIII, 115–118, 225–228). Coode's own account, in a letter to Leisler, is in *Documentary History of New York*, IV, 42–44.

2. XX, 143–145. Coode was given the epithet "Masaniello" as were also Bacon in Virginia and Leisler in New York. Tomaso Aniello was the fisherman who led a revolt in Naples in 1647 and attained to a great notoriety in his day. Midon, *Masaniello* (1729); Schipa, *Masaniello*, from the Italian; *Massinello, or a Satyr against the Associations and the Guild-hall Riot* (London, 1683); Clarke, *A Mirrour or Looking Glasse both for Saints and Sinners* (1657), pp. 518–538. Clarke drew his information from "a book, published by the Lord Girassi, and translated by J. H. Esqr." D. C. Knowlton, "The Rising of 1647–1648 in Naples," *American Historical Review*, VIII, 290–293, gives references to Italian literature on the subject.

3. XIII, 231–232, 239–240.

sion for Colonel Lionel Copley to be governor, but the attorney general rejected it and after a hearing, at which Baltimore, Coode, and Cheseldyne were present, came to the opinion that in a time of extraordinary emergency, such as this was, the king could commission the governor, even though the proprietor's charter remained intact. Despite Baltimore's vigorous opposition, after long delay, the commission passed the seals, June 27, 1691, and Maryland became a royal province.[1] Baltimore lost his government but retained his rights to the soil, and from 1692, when Copley finally arrived, until 1716, when the proprietor's son, turned Protestant, was restored to his full governmental rights, had nothing to do with the province except to receive his revenues. The absolute lordship had ceased to exist, never to be revived, for when the proprietorship was restored, the actual head was no longer the proprietor but his governor, and with a few survivals of proprietary privileges Maryland became to all intents and purposes a royal province.

NOTE A: The following list will show the relationships and connections of the proprietary family.

Philip Calvert. Uncle of Charles Calvert, Lord Baltimore after 1675. He married (1) Ann, a first cousin of Jane Lowe Sewall, and (2) Jane Lowe Sewall's daughter, a stepdaughter of Charles Calvert. Philip was chancellor and a Roman Catholic, with whom Charles was not on the best of terms (*Calvert Papers,* I, 151) and who was not popular in the province (II, 350; XV, 245). He was born in 1626 and in 1681 made his second marriage at the age of 55, to a young girl (Jane Sewall) probably less than twenty years old, as she was born shortly before Henry Sewall went to England in 1664.

Henry Sewall, secretary, an intimate friend of the governor, who returned to England in 1664 and died soon after. He had married Jane Lowe, daughter of Vincent Lowe, Senior, and sister of Vincent Lowe, mentioned below. She had one son and four daughters, so that when Charles married her in 1666 he acquired a stepson and four stepdaughters, each of the latter of whom he provided with husbands and the husbands with offices in the colony. Henry Sewall was a Roman Catholic, as was each of his children. According to a statement by John Coode he was of humble ancestry.

Baker Brooke came over with many Brooke relatives in 1650. He became councillor and surveyor general, and married a sister of William Brent, a nephew of the proprietor. He was a Roman Catholic.

Jesse Wharton married Elizabeth Sewall, who afterward married William Diggs. Wharton was a Roman Catholic, a doctor, colonel, member of the upper house, and for a time secretary. He acted as guardian of Charles Calvert's nine year old son when the proprietor left the province in 1676.

William Diggs was a Protestant, who married Elizabeth Sewall, widow of Jesse Wharton, the proprietor's stepdaughter. He held many important positions—chancellor,

1. VIII, 100–101, 207, 229, 230–231, 232, 240, 263–280.

justice of the peace, captain of militia, and customs collector. After 1685 he was one of the chief deputy governors and at the time of the revolution was in command at St. Mary's, while Darnell was in command at Mattapany. He was a native of Virginia and a former inhabitant there. It was at his house in Virginia that Joseph and others took refuge. He belonged to the Jacobite group.

Benjamin Rozer was a Protestant, a colonel of militia, who married Ann Sewall, one of the proprietor's stepdaughters. He came to the province in 1661 and died in 1681.

Edward Pye married Ann Sewall after Rozer's death. He was a councillor and a colonel of militia in Charles County (1686). He was probably a Roman Catholic.

William Calvert was the proprietor's cousin and the secretary of the council. He was a Roman Catholic.

Nicholas Lowe was a Roman Catholic and Lady Baltimore's brother. He served as clerk of St. Mary's County and in 1687 as coroner. He was frequently absent in England in the capacity of merchant and agent.

Vincent Lowe was a Roman Catholic and Lady Baltimore's brother. He was councillor, surveyor general, and colonel of foot in Talbot County.

Henry Lowe was his son and Lady Baltimore's nephew. He was at one time collector of customs.

Henry Darnell was a Roman Catholic and a cousin of the proprietor's first wife, —— Darnell, maiden name unknown. He was a lawyer, of the Temple, and acted as one of the deputy governors for the young Benedict Leonard Calvert. He was treasurer in 1688 and naval officer. He returned to England in September, 1669, but was back the following year as Baltimore's agent in the colony. He was rated with Coursey, Diggs, and others as one of "the grand leaders of the Jacobite party" (VIII, 343).

Thomas Notley was speaker of the lower house, was commissioned deputy governor in 1676, and governor in 1678. He was a professed Roman Catholic, but to Father Fitzherbert not a satisfactory one, and is rated a Protestant in the Declaration of 1682. He was not related to the proprietor, but was a prerogative man and the proprietor's ardent supporter. He lived at St. Mary's and served at one time as lieutenant of militia.

Henry Coursey was a Protestant, clerk and speaker of the lower house, chief justice of the provincial court, councillor, colonel of foot in Cecil and Kent counties, and frequent negotiator with the Indians. He was not related to the proprietor, but was a prerogative man and opposed the revolution both in England and in Maryland. A Jacobite.

Thomas Tailler (Taylor) was a Protestant, a justice of the peace and colonel of militia. He was a councillor and one of those in charge of the province after 1684–1685. He went to England in February, 1689, but returned and opposed the revolution.

William Stevens was a Protestant, coroner, colonel of horse in Dorchester and Somerset counties, a councillor, and deputy governor (1685). He was often engaged in Indian negotiations.

George Talbot was a Roman Catholic, the proprietor's nephew, son of Grace, youngest child of George Lord Baltimore, who married Sir Robert Talbot.

Sir William Talbot, Bart., was a Roman Catholic and a nephew of the proprietor. In 1670 he was made principal secretary and keeper of the records.

Nicholas Sewall was a Roman Catholic, who married the daughter of William Burgess. He was the proprietor's stepson, was secretary of the province in 1686, was a deputy governor after 1685, and one of the "confederates" in the murder of Payne. He fled to Virginia, but was allowed to return and the case against him was eventually dropped. He was one of those who, with Joseph, H. Darnell, Pye, and

Clement Hill, surrendered at Mattapany, August 1, 1689. He remained in Maryland, living at St. Mary's.

John Darnell was a brother of Henry's and a Roman Catholic, who was named one of the principal secretaries in 1683.

William Burgess was a Protestant, colonel of foot, Ann Arundel County, and the father-in-law of Nicholas Sewall.

William Chandler was a Protestant, sheriff of Charles County, and colonel of foot. He married Mary Sewall, the proprietor's stepdaughter, who afterward married George Brent (1687).

Thomas Burford was attorney general, 1681–1686, and the leading lawyer in the province. He was a Protestant, a burgess from Charles County, and a justice of the quorum.

NOTE B: John Coode was a strange and unsavory character. In 1678 he had been commissioned captain of the proprietor's yacht, the *Loyal Charles,* for the defense of the proprietor against the pirates. Later he became an officer in the militia, served against the Indians, was a justice of the peace and of the quorum, and a deputy from St. Mary's City as far back as 1676, in which capacity he played an important rôle on committees and in conferences. The lower house refused to disqualify him when he was indicted in 1681, until he had first been proved guilty, because it deemed the attempt of the upper house to persuade it to do so as an interference with its privileges. Later when Coode was proved to have been a clergyman of the Church of England it did deprive him of his seat. After the revolution of 1689 Coode and Blakiston (XIII, 407, 408) went to England to present the case of the Protestant Association and to beg William III to take the province into his own hands, which William did. As a return for his services Coode was appointed sheriff for St. Mary's, lieutenant colonel in the militia (when it was proposed that the military forces should be remodeled "as near as may be" according to the manner of England, XIX, 451), his Majesty's receiver of the one shilling a hogshead collected in Potomac River, and a vestryman in the Anglican Church at St. Mary's. But in 1696 he was again indicted, this time for shortage in his accounts as receiver and as custodian of certain moneys received at the time of the revolution. The offense was greatly aggravated by certain blasphemous speeches that he was reported to have made and that brought down upon his head the wrath of Governor Nicholson who was a high churchman. To embezzlement therefore was added the crime of blasphemy (the speeches are given in XX, 492, 493, 514). As a result he was deprived of all his offices and when the governor demanded that the lower house expel him, he was disqualified by the house as having once been a clergyman, a fact that he now acknowledged ("Yes, I am both Deacon and Priest in the Church of England"). Proceedings were started against him and others, chiefly his stepson, Gerrard Sly, Philip Clarke (XXIII, 412–416, 504–506), and Robert Mason, formerly sheriff of St. Mary's. These men were charged with abetting the Roman Catholics as against the governor and the Anglicans generally (XXIII, 448–449), just as the Jacobites in England opposed William III. They were accused of acting in conjunction with a Romish priest, Rev. William Hunter, who had been charged with endeavoring to seduce her Majesty's good subjects in Maryland from the Protestant faith (XXV, 75). Hunter was not a Jesuit. All of these men had brought charges against the government of a defamatory and incendiary character. Coode fled to Virginia, Sly and Clarke were seized, convicted, and sentenced to imprisonment, but on making apologies were pardoned. Orders were issued for Coode's apprehension, but he eluded capture. Finally he returned voluntarily, was tried, fined £20 sterling, and condemned to be whipped, but the corporal punishment was remitted because of his past services. He applied for pardon, which was granted, and was again elected deputy to the assembly, but again, on Nicholson's demand in 1708, was disqualified as a deputy, though he was allowed to practice as an attorney in the provincial courts. He died in 1709 (II, 481, 483, 484; V, 329–330; VII, 112, 113, 115, 116, 135–136, 137, 138, 139; XVII, 30, 44, 216; XIX, 265, 438–440, 469, 475–487; XX, xiii, 126, 130, 152, 250, 453, 487, 498, 490, 491, 493–494, 511, 515, 560, 561–565, 582; XXIII, 448–449, 504–506, *passim;* XXIV, 212; XXV, 5–7, 75, 80, 236; XXVII, 270–271, 410, 411 [deceased]).

was granted, and was again elected deputy to the assembly, but again, on Nicholson's demand in 1708, was disqualified as a deputy, though he was allowed to practice as an attorney in the provincial courts. He died in 1709 (II, 481, 483, 484; V, 329–330; VII, 112, 113, 115, 116, 135–136, 137, 138, 139; XVII, 30, 44, 216; XIX, 265, 438–440, 469, 475–487; XX, xiii, 126, 130, 152, 250, 453, 487, 498, 490, 491, 493–494, 511, 515, 560, 561–565, 582; XXIII, 448–449, 504–506, *passim;* XXIV, 212; XXV, 5–7, 75, 80, 236; XXVII, 270–271, 410, 411 [deceased]).

INDEX

ABBOT, Edward, discontented Marylander, 352

Abbot, George, Archbishop of Canterbury, 146n, 148

Abbot, Maurice, London merchant, 146n, 148

Abigail, ship, 76

Account of the Colony of the Lord Baron of Baltamore, An, 288n

Act concerning Religion, Maryland, 298n, 310–312, 312n, 313, 315, 321–322; provisions of, 311n; repeal of, 318; reënactment of, 320

Act of Uniformity, English, 46

Administration of Estates Act, English, 207n

Admiralty, High Court of, 288n, 303n, 305

"Admitted inhabitants," Connecticut, 104–106, 108, 111, 115, 117, 137, 138n

Adventure, ship, 176n

Agawam. *See* Springfield

Agriculture, 144, 177, 180, 215, 216, 251, 252

See also Sugar, Tobacco

Albany, 98

Alcock, John, Connecticut, 82n

Aldersey, Samuel, London merchant, 146n, 147

Aldredge (Plymouth widow), 13n

Alexander, James, New York, 232

Alexander, Sir William, 222, 224, 277, 303

Allen, Captain, Maryland, 358

Allerton, Isaac, 154n, 174n, 175

Allyn, Lt. John, Connecticut, 137

Alsop, George, Maryland, 291n, 334n

Altham, Father John, Maryland, 288–289

Amazon Company, 223

Amsterdam, 149, 149n

Andrews, William, New Haven, 157

Andros, Sir Edmund, 66, 130, 362

Angell, Thomas, Rhode Island, 4n; goes to Narragansett, 4–5

Anglican Church. *See* Church of England

Annapolis, Maryland, 312, 317, 342n

See also Arundelton, Providence

Ann Arundel County, Maryland, 299n, 319, 342n, 375

Anne, Duchess of Hamilton, 225n

Antigua, 59, 314; settlement of, 245; allegiance of, to exiled king, 255, 259; condition of, 258, 259; government of, 261

Antinomianism, 8, 12, 39, 84, 151

Apothecaries' Company, 216

Apprentices, in Connecticut, 105n, 115, 117, 178

Aptucxet, Plymouth trading post, 71n

Aquidneck Island, 155; settlement of, 8–10; Coddington makes separate colony of, 10, 11, 17, 23, 24, 25, 31–34, 40, 54, 84

Archdale, Gov. John, of South Carolina, on liberty of conscience, 49n

Architecture, early New Haven, 182

Ark, ship, 286, 287

A Relation of Maryland, 288n

A Relation of the successful Beginnings of the Lord Baltimore's Plantation, etc., 288n

Arlington, Earl of. *See* Bennett

Arnold, Benedict, Rhode Island, 14, 36, 62

See also Arnolds

Arnold, William, Rhode Island, 5, 22n, 36, 243n

See also Arnolds

Arnolds (of Pawtuxet, Rhode Island) 13n, 14, 15n, 22, 24, 34, 54

Arundel and Surrey, earl of. *See* Howard, Thomas; Maltravers, Lord

Arundell, Sir Thomas (of Wardour), 276, 285n

Arundell, William, 290n

Arundelton, 317

See also Annapolis, Providence

Ashford. *See* Setauket

Ashton, Col. Henry, Antigua, 259, 259n

Aspinwall, William, Massachusetts, 8; on Gorton, 12n

Atherton, Maj. Humphrey, 15n, 37

KAYNELL, Col. Christopher, Antigua, 259

Kellond, Thomas, royal agent, 185

Kemp, Richard, Virginia, 277n

Kennebec River, 277; Winslow's journey to, 68

Kent, England, 161n

Kent County, Maryland, 319, 319n

Kent Island, 292, 293, 296, 301, 307n, 309n, 318; settlement on, 303n, 304; struggle over, 304–307, 308

Keswick, copper mines of, 213, 213n

Ketelby, Abel, landgrave, 226

Kew, England, 163

Kiefft, William, Governor of New Netherland, 292

Killingworth, Connecticut, 120

King Philip's War, 64

King's Province, Rhode Island, 15n, 52

Kinnoul, Earl of, 250, 272n

Kirke, David, 202n, 223

Kirke, Thomas, royal agent, 185

Knapp, Goody, witch, 116n

Knight service, 202, 202n, 282

LABADISTS, in Maryland, 355

Laconia, grant, 224

Lake Saltonstall, 172n

Lamberton, Capt. George, 153, 154n, 170n; deserts Rogers group, 153n; activities on Delaware, 169; goes down on "phantom ship," 175, 176, 176n

Land, in Rhode Island, 6, 8, 10, 10n, 24; distribution of, in New Haven, 154; New Haven purchases, from Indians, 154–155; tenure of, in England, 201–209; desire for, in New World, 221–240

Larkin, John, Maryland, house of, 342n

Laud, William, 86, 145, 149; influence of, on Davenport's life, 148; elevated to See of London, 148; becomes Archbishop of Canterbury, 148; on departure of Davenport, 149n

See also Laud Commission

Laud Commission, 145; on Baltimore–Claiborne controversy, 305n, 306, 306n

Laurence, Edward, his Duty of a Steward to his Lord, 209n

Law, English, regard for, in Rhode Island, 9, 9n; Gorton's devotion to, 12–13, 16–17; embodied in acts and orders of 1647 in Rhode Island, 26, 29–30, 42n; reproduced in colonies, 105n; as basis for Massachusetts law, 156; admission of, desired in New Haven colony, 183; position of Maryland under, 283; and Roman Catholics in colonies, 314n

Law-making power, in Rhode Island, 48

Laws, appeal and recall of, 27, 28n; review of colonial, in England, 48; vigorous enforcement of, in New Haven, 181; in Maryland, 301–302

See also Codes of laws

League of Augsburg, 375

Leeds, manor of, erected by Lord Fairfax, 238

Leete, Gov. William, New Haven colony, 161n, 187; warned about regicides, 185; seeks aid of Connecticut, 186; as spokesman against Connecticut, 188–189; replies to Connecticut, 190n

Leeward Islands, 125–126, 245, 250, 256, 258, 261, 271, 297

Leigh, Charles, 243

Lenox, 2d duke of, 222, 277, 284n

Lenthal, Rev. Robert, Newport, Rhode Island, 31

Ley, James. See Marlborough, Earl of

Liberty, individual, 112–113; of speech, 108

Liberty of conscience, denied in Massachusetts, 4; denied in Virginia, 4; in Rhode Island, 7–8, 7n, 8n, 9, 10, 11, 42n, 46, 47, 49, 61; Williams and, 7–8, 18, 19–20, 19n, 24–25, 45, 49, 61; Gorton and, 15–16; in proprietary colonies, 46; denied in England, 46, 49; in Jamaica, 46, 311n; in South Carolina, 49n; and Lord Baltimore, 310, 317

Library, first public, in New Haven, 182

Ligon, Richard, History of Barbados, 251, 252, 253

Lincoln's Inn Fields, 209n, 278

Liquor, 179, 180, 181

See also Wine

Little Baddow, England, 90n

Little Compton, Rhode Island, 51

"Little England." See Barbados

Livestock, 124–125, 180

See also Cattle, Hogs, Horses, Sheep

Llewellyn, John, Maryland, 335, 358